METHODISTS IN DIALOGUE

METHODISTS IN DIALOGUE

Geoffrey Wainwright

KINGSWOOD BOOKS
An Imprint of Abingdon Press
Nashville, Tennessee

Library of Congress Cataloging-in-Publication Data

Wainwright, Geoffrey, 1939–
    Methodists in dialogue / Geoffrey Wainwright.
      p.   cm.
    Includes bibliographic references.
    ISBN 0-687-01133-7 (alk. paper)
    1. Methodist Church—Relations.   2. Methodist Church—Doctrines.
    3. Christian union.   4. Christian union—Methodist Church.
    I. Title.
    BX8328.A1W35   1995
    187—dc20   95-6911

Dedicated to

Joe Hale

Church diplomatist and
Christian gentleman

Contents

Preface

Apart from the introduction and the conclusion, all the chapters in this book spring from occasional pieces I have written in the past decade as a Methodist participant in ecumenical dialogues. The introduction is intended to show how a Wesleyan and a Methodist imbibes ecumenism with his mother's milk: our eighteenth-century founder laid out the spirit and themes of a dialogue that is to serve Christian unity, and it is therefore quite natural that Methodists should have played a prominent part in the twentieth-century ecumenical movement. A little recent history, sometimes with a personal touch, helps to provide the various settings for the substantive papers that then constitute the body of the present work. Thus introduced, the central chapters show a particular Methodist, officially or unofficially on behalf of other Methodists, in dialogues both bilateral (with Roman Catholics in chapters 1–4, Lutherans in chapters 5–7, Reformed in chapter 8, and Orthodox in chapters 9–10) and multilateral (especially in the framework of Faith and Order, in chapters 11–13); and the attempt is then made to state more thematically, and to illustrate, some Methodist principles of ecumenism that have (one hopes) guided the previous chapters as well as these more deliberate treatments: doctrinal responsibility (chapter 14), spiritual engagement (chapter 15), missionary orientation (chapter 16), and trinitarian doxology (chapter 17). The conclusion asks how a Wesleyan and Methodist voice may continue to be heard in ecumenical theological conversations into the future.

In reviewing these writings for publication in the present book, I have sought to avoid the gift of hindsight. The odd fact has been corrected, an occasional bibliographical reference added, a stylistic improvement introduced here and there. But I have deliberately allowed the pieces to retain the flavor accruing to them from the circumstances of their original composition. Their dialogical character thus remains evident. The repetitions that persist across the chapters point to themes I consider of greatest significance.

My thanks are due to all the people who appointed me to the various positions, assigned me the writing tasks, and invited me to give the lectures that have now issued in this book; the original appearances of these chapters are documented at the back. My colleague Karen Westerfield Tucker encouraged me to put this collection together and has kept my nose to the electronic grindstone while the book was being given its present shape; her substantive suggestions contributed to the original composition of some of the chapters, and her critical acumen has improved the final form of them all. Rex Matthews of Abingdon Press has been a most careful and helpful editor.

The book is dedicated to Dr. Joe Hale, General Secretary of the World Methodist Council since 1976, and whose deep commitment to the making visible of Christian unity has become increasingly apparent to me since I assumed the chair of the WMC standing committee on dialogues and ecumenism in 1986. I treasure my own relationship with this truly Wesleyan "friend of all and enemy of none."

Geoffrey Wainwright
Duke University
Advent 1994

INTRODUCTION

Methodists in Dialogue

I. Wesley, Methodists, and Ecumenism

"Come, my brother," wrote John Wesley in his open *Letter to a Roman Catholic* of 1749, "and let us reason together. . . . And let us resolve in all our conversation, either with or concerning each other, to use only the language of love; to speak with all softness and tenderness, with the most endearing expression which is consistent with truth and sincerity."[1] And then, in his more generally addressed sermon of the following year on a "Catholic Spirit," Wesley indicates that with "all who believe in the Lord Jesus Christ, who love God and man," he is prepared, once the vital hand of fellowship has been exchanged, to "talk, if need be, at a more convenient season" of such matters as theological "opinions," "modes of worship," and "forms of church government."[2] In the twentieth century, opportunities have arisen—such as Wesley could scarcely have imagined—for the Churches to move towards what he called "external union" and what we call "visible unity." In the modern ecumenical movement, the aim has been to discern, and then to achieve, whatever is necessary and sufficient for unity among Christians and among the Churches. An indispensable instrument has been dialogue, and its spirit and agenda are those adumbrated above by Wesley: to "speak the truth in love" (Ephesians 4:15), for what have sometimes been called "the dialogue of truth" and "the dialogue of love" should in fact be mutually informative;[3] and to treat issues of faith and order, as the need is recognized, for the sake now of a glimpsed possibility and task that exceed what Wesley envisaged.

Ecumenical opportunities have not simply arisen; they have been created and grasped. And people and institutions in the Wesleyan tradition have played important parts in the shaping of the modern movement. In any account of its history, an early and prominent place is accorded to the lay member of the Methodist Episcopal Church, John R. Mott (1865–1955).[4] General Secretary of the World's Student Christian Federation from its inception in 1895, and then chairman from 1920 to 1928, Mott served the WSCF under the mottos of "that they all may be one (*ut omnes unum sint*)" and "the evangelization of the world in this generation." As chairman of the first World Missionary Conference at Edinburgh in 1910, "Dr. Mott presided," says the official account in a description that allows one to recall the significance which "Christian conference" has always borne as a means of grace in the Methodist tradition, "with promptitude and precision, with instinctive perception of the guidance required, and with a perfect union of firmness and Christian courtesy, of earnest purpose and timely humor, which won for him alike the deference and the gratitude of the members."[5] Permanently associated with the resultant International Missionary Council, Mott was also active in the rising movements of Faith and Order and of Life and Work; and it was entirely fitting that, at the age of eighty-three, he should preach during the opening service at the inauguration of the World Council of Churches (Amsterdam 1948), the institutional form then taken by the movements which Mott had served in the causes of Christian unity, and of peace and social justice, as well as evangelism and mission.

While few people could match the breadth of concerns characteristic of the first generation of pioneers, other Methodists have made notable contributions to the modern ecumenical movement, and particularly to the activity of theological dialogue in its intervening stages. Robert Newton Flew (1886–1962), Principal of Wesley House, Cambridge, and a President of the British Methodist Conference, chaired for Faith and Order, between the World Conferences of Edinburgh 1937 and Lund 1952, the Theological Commission on the Church, not only contributing insights gained in his work of leading the British Methodists in their Conference Statement on *The Nature of the Christian Church according to the Teaching of the Methodists* (1937) and his authorship of *Jesus and His Church: A Study of the Idea of the Ecclesia in the New Testament* (1938), but even writing (as appeared necessary in face of the official reticence of the Roman Catholic Church towards the ecumenical movement at the time) the exposition of Catholic ecclesiology in the Faith and Order Commission's volume on *The Nature of the Church*.[6] As a leader among British Methodists in the multilateral dialogues concerning matters of faith and order, both national and international, Flew was succeeded in the next generation by Harold Roberts, Rupert Davies, Gordon Rupp, and Raymond George. The last-mentioned served with an Anglican and a Lutheran as active consultants in the wide-ranging work of liturgical revision undertaken by an ecumenically awakened Roman Catholic Church after the Second Vatican Council.

The outstanding American Methodist contributor to the broad doctrinal dialogue at international level has been Albert C. Outler (1908–

1989), long-time professor at Southern Methodist University.[7] Outler chaired the North American section of the Theological Commission on Tradition and Traditions (which included such luminaries as Georges Florovsky and Jaroslav Pelikan), in preparation for the Fourth World Conference on Faith and Order at Montreal in 1963; and at Montreal itself he helped to shape the document on "Scripture, Tradition, and traditions" that was to set the methodological outlines for future Faith and Order work in such significant projects as "Baptism, Eucharist and Ministry" and "Towards the Common Expression of the Apostolic Faith Today."[8] Outler served as a Protestant observer at all four sessions of the Second Vatican Council and inspired a successful "resolution of intent" at the General Conference of the United Methodist Church in 1970 that, under a reconsideration and reassessment of the Reformation-period anti-Roman polemic in the Articles of Religion, all the denomination's standards of doctrine should be interpreted "in consonance with our best ecumenical insights and judgment." As part of its 1968 constitution, the United Methodist Church, believing that "the Lord of the Church is calling Christians everywhere to strive toward unity," is in fact committed to "seek, and work for, unity at all levels of church life"—through "world relationships with other Methodist Churches," "through councils of churches," and "through plans of union with churches of Methodist or other denominational traditions." Besides Albert Outler, other important American Methodist contributors to ecumenical theological dialogue at the WCC level have been J. Robert Nelson, John Deschner, and Jeanne Audrey Powers.

The missionary thrust of the modern ecumenical movement matched Wesley's passion for evangelism and the intervening history of Methodist engagement in home and, above all, overseas missions. Methodist leaders in ecumenical missiological reflection have included Daniel Niles from Sri Lanka, Philip Potter from the Caribbean, and Emilio Castro from Uruguay. Prominent already at the Tambaram International Missionary Conference of 1938, D. T. Niles (1908–1970) argued powerfully in *Upon the Earth: The Mission of God and the Missionary Enterprise of the Church* (1962)[9] for the continuing significance of crossing geographical and cultural boundaries as testimony to the saving gospel of Jesus Christ and his universal lordship. Philip Potter (b. 1921) and Emilio Castro (b. 1927) both served as general secretary of the World Council of Churches, the former from 1972–1984, the latter from 1985–1992. A favorite part of the work of all three of these Methodist missiologists was their Bible studies, where each showed himself to stand in the tradition of Wesley as "a man of one book."

II. Methodists and Multilateral Dialogues

My own engagement in international multilateral ecumenical dialogue has taken place largely through WCC Faith and Order. Beginning from my attendance as a youth delegate at the meeting of the Faith and Order Commission in Aarhus, Denmark, in 1964, I have had a continuous association with the work in various capacities, including fifteen years as a member of the plenary commission. Chapters eleven and twelve in the present book stem from that context and reflect the two principal projects of Faith and Order during that time, *Baptism, Eucharist and Ministry* and *Confessing the One Faith*.

Chronologically, *BEM* comes first. On and off, the themes of baptism, eucharist and ministry have occupied Faith and Order since the First World Conference at Lausanne, Switzerland in 1927, since these are areas in which the commonalities and differences among divided Christians come to focal expression as the Churches seek to end separation and to manifest the unity of Christ's Body. The 1960s saw a renewed concentration on these three topics and a growing awareness of their interconnectedness. A draft document entitled *One Baptism, One Eucharist, and a Mutually Recognized Ministry* was put out by the Faith and Order Commission from its Accra, Ghana, meeting in 1974. In light of numerous comments from a wide variety of sources, we then worked at what would become *Baptism, Eucharist and Ministry*, often called not simply *BEM* but "the Lima text," after the meeting place in Peru at which the document was given its final form by the Faith and Order Commission in 1982. The Commission was persuaded that it had discerned and recorded "a remarkable degree of agreement" in the three areas under consideration.[10]

The "meaning of baptism" was displayed as "participation in Christ's death and resurrection," "conversion, pardoning and cleansing," "the gift of the Spirit," "incorporation into the body of Christ," and "the sign of the kingdom." On the tangled problems regarding the relation of faith, water baptism, and the Spirit, the Lima text affirmed that "baptism is both God's gift and our human response to that gift. . . . The necessity of faith for the reception of the salvation embodied and set forth in baptism is acknowledged by all Churches"; it stressed that "both the baptism of believers and the baptism of infants take place in the Church as the community of faith"; and, while observing that "Christians differ in their understanding as to where the sign of the gift of the Spirit is to be found," it claimed general agreement that "Christian baptism is in water and the Holy Spirit."

The eucharist is called by *BEM* "a gift from the Lord," and it is said that every Christian receives "the gift of salvation through communion in the body and blood of Christ." The "meaning of the eucharist" is displayed according to a trinitarian pattern and the fivefold sequence of the ancient creeds as "thanksgiving to the Father," "memorial of Christ," "invocation of the Spirit," "communion of the faithful," and "meal of the kingdom." Touching the historically controversial questions concerning presence and sacrifice, the Lima text speaks of "Christ's real, living and active presence in the eucharist," which is "the living and effective sign of Christ's sacrifice, accomplished once and for all on the cross and still operative on behalf of all humankind."

The final section of *BEM* opens with "the calling of the whole people of God" and places the ordained ministry within that framework. The ordained ministry is regarded as a reminder "of the dependence of the Church on Jesus Christ, who is the source of its mission and the foundation of its unity." As one factor within the broader reality of an "apostolic Tradition" that is transmitted in several ways, the "episcopal succession" is proposed as "a sign, though not a guarantee, of the continuity and unity of the Church"; and it is claimed that "the threefold ministry of bishop, presbyter and deacon may serve today as an expression of the unity we seek and also as a means for achieving it."

Having contributed in various ways to the theological dialogues that issued in the *BEM* text, Methodist Churches accepted with some vigor the request of Faith and Order for official responses; and a constructive analysis of the Methodists responses is made in chapter twelve of the present book.[11] Beyond what Msgr. John Radano of the Pontifical Council for Promoting Christian Unity called "the decade of *BEM*," the stimulus of the Lima text continues to be felt in the Churches and in the dialogues among them. Even before *BEM* itself was completed, however, it had become evident within Faith and Order that convergences on baptism, eucharist and ministry belonged in a wider dogmatic and ecclesiological context: they themselves—and certainly their effective contribution to the cause of greater visible unity—depended on their being part of more extensive agreements that would stretch across the entire range of the Christian faith concerning God, the gospel, the Church, and the final hope. Chapter eleven of the present book looks from a Methodist angle at the "Apostolic Faith" study which WCC Faith and Order had begun preparing in the 1970s and whose continuing importance was urged on the Churches by the Fifth World Conference on Faith and Order at Santiago de Compostela in 1993.[12]

Already the classic ecumenical vision of Christian and churchly unity formulated by the Third Assembly of the WCC at New Delhi in 1961 included "holding the one apostolic faith." The Fifth Assembly at Nairobi in 1975 called on the Churches to "undertake a common effort to receive, reappropriate, and confess together, as contemporary occasion requires, the Christian truth and faith, delivered through the apostles and handed down through the centuries." Faith and Order moved in that direction with its studies on "Giving Account of the Hope that is in us" and "How Does the Church Teach Authoritatively Today?" The Joint Working Group between the Roman Catholic Church and the WCC gave its blessing with a text entitled "Towards a Confession of the Common Faith." The sixteen-hundreth anniversary of the Council of Constantinople 381 then focussed attention on the Creed of Nicea-Constantinople. Finally, the Faith and Order Commission at Lima in 1982, endorsed by the Sixth Assembly of the WCC at Vancouver 1983, resolved on a major study "Towards the Common Expression of the Apostolic Faith Today."[13]

The Nicene-Constantinopolitan Creed was adopted by the plenary Commission of Faith and Order as "the theological basis and methodological tool for the explication of the apostolic faith." This decision came only after serious wrestling with the difficulties it posed both for so-called non-creedal Churches, which are suspicious of fixed formularies of faith, especially those imposed at times past by political authorities, and also for Churches in cultures where the phrases used in the Creed to exclude Arianism are felt to depend on an alien metaphysic. The decision to go with the Creed provided, nevertheless, an interesting opportunity for Methodists, for it was by way of an expansion upon the Nicene-Constantinopolitan Creed that John Wesley expounded "the faith of a true Protestant" (and Christian!) in his *Letter to a Roman Catholic*. The Faith and Order text of some 100 pages was produced over the years 1983–1990 and, under the title *Confessing the One Faith*, is circulating in the Churches for study and use.[14]

The Apostolic Faith study, and with it the entire concern for authentic Christian unity in the truth of the gospel, is well located by Günther Gassmann in its contemporary context:

> [There is among the Churches a widespread] desire to reaffirm the foundations of Christian identity and communion in a world of increasing pluralism and religious choice. And with this goes the felt need to provide a deeper theological and spiritual basis for the faith and life of individual Christians and their churches. This is felt because they are more than ever before challenged to render their witness in words, deeds, and suffering by facing the complexities of our world, a world which has all the potentials of God's good creation which at the same time are being distorted in a way which threatens even the survival of humanity.[15]

So far, we have been concerned with Methodist participation in multilateral theological dialogues. Most of the international multilateral dialogues have taken place in the context of Faith and Order. Faith and Order also facilitated a series of forums (1978, 1979, 1980, 1985, 1990, 1994) in which representatives of the world Christian communions came together to compare notes on the several bilateral dialogues in which each was engaged, in an effort to ensure consistency among the positions adopted and reached by each in relation to the variety of partners. We shall come in a moment to the various bilateral dialogues in which the World Methodist Council has been a partner. Meantime we note a multilateral project that was sponsored by a single world Christian communion, namely the Lutheran World Federation.

The Strasbourg research institute of the LWF, under the direction of Harding Meyer and André Birmelé, has pursued the notions of "fundamental agreement" and "basic difference." Which goes deeper, and (in particular) how are remaining "basic differences" between Christian confessions to be detected and overcome? For Lutherans, the crucial question is that of the difference between Lutheran and Roman Catholic, which is sometimes formulated as that between Protestant and Catholic. Chapter thirteen in the present book springs from that project (and particularly from its most comprehensive study session, at Nice, France, in 1989), while implicitly criticizing the attempt to find a single "basic difference" as mistaken, or at least overly simple. Each confessional type, following a hint in John Henry Newman, may rather be seen as a complex organic entity, even if its profile be specially characterized by a particular prominent feature.[16]

III. Methodists and Roman Catholics

While bilateral dialogues have been practiced from earlier days in the modern ecumenical movement (e.g. between Anglicans and Old Catholics, and between Lutherans and Reformed), it was above all the official entry of the Roman Catholic Church into the movement, with Vatican II, that occasioned their more recent flourishing. Although a modest number of Roman Catholic theologians now figure among the official membership of the WCC Faith and Order Commission, the Roman Catholic Church itself is not a member of the WCC. As by far the largest communion in Christendom, Rome would, if present even in rough proportion to its numerical strength, inevitably threaten to dominate the WCC as an institution. It has seemed wiser that Rome should engage in a variegated series of relationships with other world Christian communions as best fits the particular histories and traditions. Hence there have developed since

19

the late 1960s a very considerable number of bilateral dialogues in which the Roman Catholic Church is one of the partners. In turn, several of the other world Christian communions have, at various rhythms and according to various needs and opportunities, developed bilateral dialogues among themselves. The bilateral dialogue partners of the World Methodist Council comprise respectively the Roman Catholic Church, the Lutheran World Federation, the World Alliance of Reformed Churches, the Anglican Communion, and (incipiently) the Orthodox Churches under the aegis of the Ecumenical Patriarchate of Constantinople.

The dialogue with the Roman Catholic Church was the first to begin (in 1967); and its story is told below in chapter one, which was written to mark the silver jubilee of the dialogue and to honor an early participant, Fr. Michael Hurley, S.J., who has been a tireless and imaginative worker for Christian unity in Ireland. My own participation in the dialogue between the World Methodist Council and the Roman Catholic Church dates from 1983, and I have chaired it on the Methodist side since 1986. Chapter two in this book springs from the preparation of the 1986 Nairobi Report, *Towards a Statement on the Church*. The discussion turned on pastoral and teaching authority, and my paper attempted to approach a notion familiar to Catholics but problematic for Methodists, namely infallibility, by way of a notion familiar to Methodists but problematic for Catholics, namely assurance. Stress was placed on the soteriological value in each case: the Catholic teaching serves to give the believer an assurance concerning the Church's proclamation of the gospel, while the Methodist believer's gift—which is not ultimately grounded in our own spirit but in the Holy Spirit—points to what the British *Methodist Hymn Book* of 1933 called the "privileges and security of Christ's Church," which is well captured in Charles Wesley's words:

> See the Gospel Church secure,
> And founded on a rock;
> All her promises are sure;
> Her bulwarks who can shock?
> Count her every precious shrine;
> Tell, to after ages tell,
> Fortified by power divine,
> The Church can never fail.[17]

Although the move back and forth between the individual believer and the Church needs to be carefully made (and ecclesiologies are at stake in this also), the Joint Commission was willing to explore the proposed approach as an attempt towards a commonly understood or agreed account of how to meet a commonly recognized "need for an authoritative way of being sure, beyond doubt, concerning God's action insofar as it is crucial for our salvation":

> It is the typical Methodist teaching that believers can receive from the Holy Spirit an assurance of their redemption through the atoning death of Christ and can be guided by the Spirit who enables them to cry "Abba, Father" in the way of holiness to future glory. Starting from Wesley's claim that the evidence for what God has done and is doing for our salvation, as decribed above, can be "heightened to exclude all doubt," Methodists might ask whether the Church, like individuals, might by the working of the Holy Spirit receive as a gift from God in its living, preaching and mission, an assurance concerning its grasp of the fundamental doctrines of the faith such as to exclude all doubt, and whether the teaching ministry of the Church has a special and divinely guided part to play in this.[18]

By the following quinquennium (1986–1991), it had become clear that, rather than a speedy move from the early Church to contemporary questions (as had been undertaken in the Nairobi Report), more attention needed to be given, historically but above all theologically, to the nature of tradition, and particularly the maintenance of the Church in the apostolic faith. The eventuating Singapore Report of 1991 was entitled *The Apostolic Tradition*. The Tradition was seen to entail a pattern of Christian faith, a pattern of Christian life, and a pattern of Christian community. The historically contentious questions of ministry were set within this more comprehensive context: ministry and ministries are to be regarded as "serving within the Apostolic Tradition." The third chapter in the present book was a contribution to that discussion. To speak, with Wesley, of "the end of all ecclesiastical order" is not to advocate anarchy but rather to indicate the purpose of ministerial structures and functions within the Church; and these are, once again, soteriological in intention, to "bring souls from the power of Satan to God, and to build them up in His fear and love." It is in the context of evangelization and of the edification of the Church that Methodists and Catholics should be negotiating their historical differences over ministry.

Chapter four of this book examines a particular set of relations between Catholics and Methodists from the angle of two other primary Christian activities, namely prayer and work. The occasion was not this time the official dialogue but a conference on sanctification in the Benedictine and Wesleyan traditions. Following up, among other things, a hint from Albert Outler that Methodism's true character is as "an evangelical order" within "a catholic Church,"[19] the Joint Commission between the Roman Catholic Church and the World Methodist Council, in looking for "ways of being one Church," had indeed noted that "the history of John Wesley has suggested an analogy between his movement and the religious orders within the one Church. Figures such as Benedict of Nursia and Francis of Assisi, whose divine calling was similarly to a spiritual reform, gave rise to religious orders, characterized by special forms of life and prayer, work, evangelization, and their own internal organization. . . . Such relative autonomy has a recognized place within the unity of the [Roman Catholic] Church."[20] And, following up another hint from Outler, James Udy, a minister of Methodist background in the Uniting Church in Australia, then propogated the idea of a conference between Methodists and Benedictines, which came to fruition for some 130 international participants at Rocca di Papa, near Rome, in July 1994. Full engagement throughout the week came from the Abbot Primate of the entire Benedictine Order, Fr. Jerome Theisen, and the Abbot General of the Sylvestrine Congregation of Benedictines, Fr. Antonio Iacovone, as well as from such Methodist bishops as Ole Borgen and Walter Klaiber. Participants sensed an astonishing convergence of hearts and minds, which would perhaps have been less surprising had we each already known the other's and our own traditions of *ora et labora*, or "the works of piety" and "the works of mercy." The convergence augurs well for an ecumenism of spiritual engagement between Benedictines and Methodists.

IV. Methodists and Lutherans

The next oldest bilateral dialogue in which the World Methodist Council has been engaged was that with the Lutheran World Federation, which lasted from 1977 until 1984. While recognizing that some topics merited further exploration (providence, the two kingdoms, some aspects of theological anthropology, and forms of unity), the Joint Commission concluded that there was sufficient agreement on the authority of the Scriptures, salvation by grace through faith, the Church, means of grace (Word and sacraments), and mission (evangelization and ethics), for it to be able to recommend the sponsoring Churches not only to engage in "common efforts of witness and service in the world" but also to "take steps to declare and establish full fellowship of Word and sacrament." This has now occurred in West Germany (1987), East Germany (1990), Austria (1991), and Sweden (1993). Discussions are current (1993–1995) concerning a suitable form of relationship between the Methodist Churches in Europe and those Lutheran and Reformed Churches that are signatories of the Leuenberg Agreement of 1973 on table and pulpit fellowship.

The LWF/WMC report of 1984 was entitled *The Church: Community of Grace*. While not arising in the immediate context of the official dialogue (and being indeed written before the final report was published), chapter five in the present book compares ecclesiological tendencies in Luther and Wesley. Our two families each depend in a striking way on a single founding father; and, as the LWF/WMC report noted, the differences between the Methodist and Lutheran communions cannot simply be identified by reference to a series of specific doctrinal points without the recognition that differences "in expressions of faith, life, ethos and order . . . are often the result of the specific origins and subsequent developments of both Churches."[21] The chapter suggests that real theological differences remain and looks to a eucharistic ecclesiology as the best place to accommodate them.

In the United States, Methodist and Lutheran Churches have existed side by side in relatively equal strength and mutual ignorance. Chapter six brings a paper, written upon Lutheran invitation, to consider possible steps towards "uniting what was never divided." The argument is that closer relations between American Methodists and Lutherans would be mutually beneficial if Lutherans could draw sufficiently on their Reformation tradition to help Methodists mitigate their only-too-successful adaptation to American culture which is the reverse side of the flexibility that aided their spread, and if Methodists could draw sufficiently on the Anglican side of their heritage to help compensate for the theological unilateralisms that understandably characterize Lutheranism since its sharp initial reaction to medieval Catholicism. How, on the broader scene of Western intellectual and cultural history, both Methodists and Lutherans might be helped to cope with persistent modernity is then the theme of chapter seven. In a paper written for a scholarly conference on "Grundtvig and the English-speaking World," an analogy is drawn between John Wesley and the nineteenth-century Dane N. F. S. Grundtvig, comparing and contrasting the ways in which the two of them drew on Scripture and Tradition in their engagement with an Enlightenment that was in part a product of Christianity yet also had other and conflicting sources.

V. *Methodists and Reformed*

Quite remarkably, the dialogue between the World Methodist Council and the World Alliance of Reformed Churches has so far required, or generated, only two sessions. After a first meeting in 1985, an enlarged dialogue team was able to produce in 1987 at Cambridge, England, a report entitled *Together in God's Grace*.[22]

The peculiarity of the relationship between Methodists and Reformed

23

resides in the fact that denominational unions have already taken place which include them both, as in the United Church of Canada (1925), the United Church of Zambia (1965), the United Protestant Church of Belgium (1969, 1978), and the Uniting Church in Australia (1977);[23] and yet the two families remain apart in other areas of the world. Has it, then, been doctrinally wrong for Methodists to unite, where such unions have occurred, with Presbyterians, Congregationalists, and the Reformed of continental European origin (or vice versa)? Are the historic controversies between Calvinists and Wesleyans, theologically speaking, properly church-dividing? Or have existing unions between Methodists and Reformed in practice had deleterious doctrinal effects? Is there perhaps in some places an overcommitment to visible unity or in other places an undercommitment?

Such questions demanded a fundamental reexamination of the theological, even doctrinal, differences between Reformed in the Calvinist tradition and Methodists in the "evangelical Arminian" tradition of Wesley. Participants in the dialogue could recognize that "grace has been a principal emphasis in both our traditions. From first to last our salvation depends on the comprehensiveness of God's grace as prevenient, as justifying, as sanctifying, as sustaining, as glorifying. Nevertheless, in seeking to preserve this primary truth, our traditions have tended to give different accounts of the appropriation of saving grace, emphasizing on the one hand God's sovereignty in election, and on the other, the freedom of response."

It could nevertheless be recalled that, at the Annual Conference of 1745, John Wesley declared that Methodists might properly "come to the very edge of Calvinism: 1. In ascribing all good to the free grace of God; 2. in denying all natural free-will and all power antecedent to grace; and 3. in excluding all merit from man, even for what he has or does by the grace of God." The 1987 dialogue then went on to consider the remaining area of dispute in this central matter. Since the resultant text, of great density and high quality, is little known, it will be worth quoting it extensively, remembering also the decisive part played in its formulation by Dr. Norman Young on the basis of his experience in the discussions preceeding the coming together of Methodists, Presbyterians and Congregationalists in the Uniting Church of Australia:

> It was only when, from the basis of this fundamental agreement [that Wesley states with Calvinism], the question "who are the saved?" was approached, that the conflicting stances identified as Calvinist and Wesleyan were adopted. In each case the stance taken leaves questions that demand answers consistent with the three accepted tenets just mentioned. Methodists who follow Wesley must

face two objections in particular from Calvinists. First, Calvinists object that the necessary freedom to choose salvation was lost in the fall, and that to claim otherwise is Pelagian. Wesley in response agreed that all are dead in sin by nature, but maintained that none is now in a mere state of nature. Prevenient grace, which he saw as the universal inheritance of Christ's atoning work, restores this lost freedom of choice, while not guaranteeing salvation. Calvinists then object that this dishonours God by denying his sovereignty, since it claims that human freedom to deny is greater than God's will to save. Wesley's reply was that in creating people with free will, God chose to limit his power at this point. Therefore the human capacity to say no to saving grace is, according to Wesley, just as compatible with God's sovereignty as is the human capacity to sin.

In their turn, the Reformed who follow Calvin must face two questions in particular from Wesleyans. First, Wesleyans ask how the predestinarian approach avoids understanding God's freedom as anything more than arbitrariness, and human freedom as anything other than illusion, if the eternal destiny of every creature is already determined. The Calvinist answer is that since God as creator is the author of justice and his ways are not our ways, it is a fundamental category mistake for us to judge him at the bar of our human and limited reason. The second Wesleyan question is, how can the missionary and evangelical imperative be maintained if, no matter what, the saved will be saved and the lost lost? Calvinists affirm in reply that obedience to the sovereign God commits the church to the proclamation of the Gospel so that people may hear and believe, and thus God's will to save be fulfilled. Consequently, impetus for, and result of, missionary and evangelistic outreach are evident no less in the Reformed than in the Methodist tradition, although the motivation may be understood and expressed somewhat differently.

These questions that we put to each other lie in the realm of theological problems, and answers can be given which in each case are consistent with the basic agreed affirmations and find scriptural support. But for both Methodists and Calvinists there is a question which cannot be answered, not because it is difficult, but because to propose an answer would be to destroy the very terms of the problem. Those who claim that prevenient grace gives to all the freedom to come to faith cannot answer the question "why do these choose salvation, and not those?" without denying the very human freedom they wish to affirm. Those who contend that only the elect may come to faith, and thus be saved by grace, cannot answer the question "why does God choose these and not those?" without limiting God's sovereign freedom which above all they wish to maintain. That these questions, which are unanswerable in principle, exist at all, points to the fundamental mystery underlying both the theological problem and the answers. Both traditions have gone wrong when they have claimed to know too much about this mystery of God's electing grace and of human response.

Therefore, that Wesley and Calvin advocated conflicting ways of holding together what they affirm in common should not constitute a barrier between our traditions. Even if Wesley and Calvin are followed without modification (which gives their approaches greater authority than they themselves allowed any human interpretation), what they both affirmed is not only the fundamental mystery of God's saving grace witnessed to in Scripture. It is also the underlying theology of grace that was stated in three points at the beginning of this section [again, where Wesley agrees with Calvin] and that provides the context with[in] which that mystery is to be recognized, received and celebrated.

The central issue of election and freedom gets prolonged in historic controversies between Wesleyans and Calvinists over perseverance and perfection. Chapter eight of the present book brings a contribution—prepared for the Reformed-Methodist dialogue—on that entire nexus of "quaestiones disputatae" concerning salvation.[24] On the matter of "perfect salvation" the 1987 report concluded thus:

Both Reformed and Methodist traditions affirm the real change which God by the Spirit works in the minds and hearts and lives of believers. By the sanctifying grace of God, penitent believers are being restored to God's image and renewed in God's likeness. To imitate God, says Wesley, is the best worship we can offer. What God is in heaven, says Calvin, he bids us to be in this world: the loving kindness of God is to be reflected in the love Christians bear toward their neighbours. Our traditions agree that, on the human side, salvation consists in the perfect love of God and neighbour, which is to have the mind of Christ and fulfill his law. We are to love God with singleness of heart, and to seek God's glory with a single eye. We are to love without reserve the sisters and brothers for whom Christ died.

The work which God has begun in us, says Calvin, he will surely complete. What God has promised, says Wesley, he is ready and willing to realize now. In the two traditions we are taught to strive and pray for entire sanctification. The Reformed stress on election and perseverance gives believers the confidence that God will keep them to the end. The Methodist preaching of perfection affirms that we may set no limit to the present power of God to make sinners into saints.

Methodists and Reformed agree that "man's chief end is to glorify God and to enjoy him for ever." The heavenly fellowship of praise and bliss is, by God's grace, to be anticipated now, as we "with one heart and one voice glorify the God and Father of our Lord Jesus Christ" and together share his benefits. We are saved into community; and, as Jesus prayed that his disciples might be "perfected into one," so the closer sharing of life between Christians in the Reformed and Methodist traditions will be evidence of growing participation in the communion of the Triune God.

One further matter treated by the Reformed-Methodist dialogue was the understanding of covenant. Historic differences come to expression here, too; but our common contemporary context provides an incentive to take up the theme together:

> Both traditions have found the concept of covenant to be a central way of understanding the Church. Nevertheless, there has been diversity of understanding even within the traditions, and our conversations have sought clarification and common ground. The Reformed tradition began as an attempt to reform and restore the Western Church on the basis of the newly perceived Word of God and in obedience to that Word. The Reformed family understands the Church as a covenant community called together by God's grace. Election and covenant find their expression in the existence of the Church. The Church is grounded in the eternal purpose of God to send Jesus Christ into the world as the head and saviour of all things. The Methodist movement began as a mission to the unevangelized, and saw itself at first as a society within the established Church. In different places and at different times, it came to understand itself as a distinct Church. John Wesley thought of Christian community as a means by which members build each other up in faith and life. Within Methodism, covenanted life has been realized through societies, conferences and Christian fellowship, and is reaffirmed in annual covenant services.
>
> Both traditions confess that we have allowed individualism to undercut our sense and practice of corporate churchly life. Often our religion, under the influence of contemporary culture, has retreated into a merely private realm. The recovery of the centrality of covenant is therefore urgent. Through a conversion of the heart, one appropriates the covenant relationship with God and with other people. Thus, the sacraments are to be understood as signs and seals of faithful participation in the covenant community, and not individualistically. Accordingly, baptism is the sacrament of adoption into the family of God, incorporation into the Body of Christ, and reception into the koinonia of the Spirit. Likewise, our communion with the Lord and with one another in him is expressed and sustained at his Table. We acknowledge that our life together in our present

27

church structures is in constant need of re-evaluation and reformation as we look forward to the consummation of the covenant when Christ will be all in all. Our acting as if we could exclude others from the covenant, and our failure to exercise our stewardship of the world and its resources, are both a denial of the covenant which God has established with humankind and all creation.

That last paragraph provides an ecclesiological framework within which the traditional tensions between Wesleyans and Calvinists may, and must, continue to be debated and lived. If any of the Churches uniting the Reformed and Methodist traditions have drifted into doctrinal indifferentism, that will be a cause, effect, or symptom of a failure to take the classically controversial issues seriously; and it will then be theologically responsible, even necessary, to revive consideration of the issues. On the other hand, the international dialogue judged that such issues "ought not to be seen as obstacles to unity between Methodists and Reformed"; and the development of closer relations between Methodists and Reformed, where these do not yet exist, will therefore provide a gracious opportunity for faithful common reflection on these doctrinally and theologically vital matters within a deepening ecclesial fellowship.[25]

VI. Methodists and Orthodox

At Dublin in 1976 the World Methodist Council voted to seek a dialogue with the Eastern Orthodox Churches. Initial contacts bore no apparent fruit, until a delegation of World Methodist Council leaders, in the course of a pilgrimage in 1990 to the sites of the ancient Church, was received by the Ecumenical Patriarch, Demetrios I. As chairman of the WMC committee on dialogues and ecumenism, I drew analogies between the golden tongue of an earlier Archbishop of Constantinople, St. John Chrysostom, and the importance of preaching in the Methodist movement, and between the Byzantine tradition of hymnography and the significance of Wesleyan hymnody; and I pointed to the fact that Methodists and Orthodox were living side by side in various parts of the world. His All-Holiness agreed that the time was ripe to begin exploratory conversations towards an official dialogue. A small group met twice for this purpose, in Oxford, England, in 1992, and in Constantinople in 1993.

My own acquaintance with Orthodoxy began in 1963, when I attended a week's intensive study of Orthodox theology and liturgy at the Ecumenical Institute of Bossey, Switzerland, followed by sharing in the services of Holy Week at the St. Sergius' Institute in Paris. My doctoral advisor at the University of Geneva was Nikos A. Nissiotis, the Greek

Orthodox lay theologian. The writings of Fr. Alexander Schmemann, of St. Vladimir's Theological Seminary, were a formative influence on the thinking represented in my book, *Doxology: The Praise of God in Worship, Doctrine and Life*.[26] Chapter nine in the present book is dedicated to the memory of Fr. John Meyendorff, also of St. Vladimir's, and a former moderator of the Faith and Order Commission of the World Council of Churches. It was written for the Orthodox-Methodist meeting at Constantinople in 1993 and was part of an attempt to address the Orthodox suspicion that Methodists have little sense of the deeper Tradition of the Church and the Methodist suspicion that the personal experience of faith may be underestimated in Orthodoxy.

Clearly, conversations between Methodists and Orthodox are at an early stage;[27] but it is hoped that the recommendation of a fuller dialogue will be brought to the present Ecumenical Patriarch, Bartholomew I, and to the World Methodist Council in 1996. The significance of the Orthodox participation in the modern ecumenical movement is assessed, from a Protestant viewpoint, in chapter ten of this book, written for the celebration of the thirty years of Archbishop Jakovos as Archbishop of the Americas and the Oceans in the Easter season of 1990. From a Methodist angle, a dialogue with Eastern Orthodoxy acquires particular importance from the reemergence of Methodist work in parts of the former communist world where the Church had been oppressed and even suppressed.

VII. *Methodists and Anglicans*

Bishop William Cannon and I attended the 1988 Lambeth Conference as official observers on behalf of the World Methodist Council. The worldwide assembly of Anglican bishops noted "with regret"—and apparent surprise—"that there is no international theological dialogue between the Anglican communion and the World Methodist Council" and requested "the Anglican Consultative Council to initiate conversations with the WMC with a view to the beginning of such a dialogue." The WMC responded favorably, and an official dialogue began with a meeting in Jerusalem in 1992. By the second meeting, in Dublin in 1993, it was already possible to produce an interim report, with a request to the constituent churches of each body for comments that would aid the completion of a text for presentation to the World Methodist Council in 1996 and the next Lambeth Conference (probably in 1998).

The interim report of the Anglican-Methodist International Commission is entitled *Sharing in the Apostolic Communion*.[28] At this stage, the Commission is suggesting that sufficient doctrinal agreement exists between the two families in their official standards for the establishment of "full communion in faith, mission, and sacramental life." The most delicate point remains that of forms of ordained ministry. It is recognized that *episcopé* has been exercised in different ways within the Anglican Communion and among the various Methodist Churches, whether by personal bishops (throughout Anglicanism and in American Methodism, although in the latter case without "any claim to historic succession in the way that many Anglicans have understood it") or (also) in "corporate or conciliar" forms (conferences and synods function in historically and geographically variable ways in the two communions); in all these cases, the Commission is prepared to "recognize in each other's Churches, within the Anglican and Methodist families, the intention being faithfully carried out" to provide "faithful *episcopé* for the congregations of Christ's people" and to "guarantee the faithful witness to the Gospel, of which Jesus Christ is the foundation and to which prophets and apostles bore the same witness in their day." The Commission looks forward "to the historic episcopate becoming again, for all of us, one element in the way by which the ordained ministry is transmitted with due order," while being "quite clear that this must be done in such a way as not to call into question the ordination or apostolicity of any of those ordained as Methodist or Anglican ministers according to the due order of their churches."

The relationships between Anglicans and Methodists are particularly sensitive on account of the origins of Methodism within the Church of England, whether the separation be seen as due to schismatic impatience or to a failure to seize evangelistic opportunities and meet pastoral needs. British Methodism in particular, in recent generations, has experienced hurt at the slowness of the Anglican Communion as a whole to recognize the union that brought Anglicans and Methodists of British and Australasian origin into the Church of South India (1947) and by the failure of the deliberative bodies of the Church of England to achieve a sufficient majority for the plan of union with the Methodist Church of Great Britain (1969 and 1972) and for entry into a covenant for unity with the British Methodists, the Moravians, and the United Reformed Church in 1982. On the worldwide scene, Anglicans and Methodists have shared so much together in the broader ecumenical and liturgical movements, and face so many common challenges to evangelism and service, that the healing of their historic breach could appropriately become part of that "all-round ecumenism" which Archbishop Robert Runcie called for at the 1988 Lambeth Conference.[29]

VIII. The Nature of the Dialogues

So far, the word dialogue has been used in ways that have become customary over the past couple of generations; but before inviting the reader to tackle a series of contributions to various ecumenical theological dialogues, it may be useful to make explicit some of the features of such dialogues.[30]

First, the partners must perceive from the start that a certain common ground exists between them in faith and practice. That perception may contract or expand or otherwise shift during the course of the dialogue; but it is always necessary to have a conceptual and a real meeting area. Part of the ecumenical exercise is to map such territories, with a view to developing mutual recognition and joint action.

Second, dialogue presupposes that there are interesting and important differences between the parties that require definition and resolution. The dialogue may reveal that some differences are due to misunderstandings, that others are genuinely matters of indifference (adiaphora), that others again can be taken as complementary emphases within a larger framework, and that others yet again are substantively conflictual and need settlement before closer relationships become possible. Incompatible with dialogue is a pure unbounded pluralism that assumes the various positions to be either incommensurable or all without epistemic significance or salutary importance.[31]

Third, if the dialogue is not to be pointless, the partners must have a goal in view. The very basis for membership in the World Council of Churches declares that the churches "seek to fulfill together their common calling to the glory of the one God, Father, Son, and Holy Spirit." A little more precisely, the constitutional aim of Faith and Order is to aid the churches toward "the goal of visible unity in one faith and one eucharistic fellowship, expressed in worship and in common life in Christ, in order that the world may believe." The stated aim of the Methodist-Roman Catholic international dialogue, taken up also by the Anglican-Methodist international dialogue, is "full communion in faith, mission, and sacramental life." Only as the dialogue progresses can the contours of the goal become sharpened, for the very definition is part of the substance of the conversation, as are the means to achieve the end.

Fourth, bilateral and multilateral dialogues operate with somewhat different types of dynamics; and indeed within each category, each dialogue will display some peculiarities. Bilateral dialogues have the great advantage of allowing the two parties to concentrate on the particular issues that have divided them, the precise agreements that still or already join them, or the special common opportunities that lie ahead of them.

But each bilateral dialogue takes place within the broader ecumenical movement, whose complexity is ensured by the fissiparous history of Christendom that it seeks to mend. Partners engaged respectively in several bilateral dialogues have discovered that they need a forum in which to compare and contrast progress and results. And most churches are in any case engaged, simultaneously with their bilateral commitments, in the broader ecumenical dialogue that has been multilateral from the start, as instantiated in the Faith and Order movement.

In comparison with the bilateral dialogues, multilateral dialogue in the modern ecumenical movement bears the following characteristics.[32] First, multilateral dialogue displays the intricacy and multidimensionality of interchurch relationships. As the issues under discussion shift, it is not always easy to say who stands to one's "right" or to one's "left," who holds the "higher" or the "lower" churchmanship. Having confronted the subtle diplomacy of seating arrangements at the First Assembly of the World Council of Churches at Amsterdam in 1948, the Russian-American Orthodox theologian Alexander Schmemann liked ever after to say that he belonged with the Quakers on some matters rather than his ostensibly nearer neighbours among the Old Catholics or the Anglicans.[33] Most churches have in fact discovered in and through multilateral dialogue that there are worthwhile relationships to be cultivated in all directions.

Then multilateral dialogues require skill in pacing, as the attempt is made to clarify the manifold positions of the Churches, to develop a convergence from many different starting points, and to keep the greatest possible number of the participants in a state of positive engagement for the furthest possible advance. The patience of the process may be rewarded by the maturity of the results, as was the case with "Baptism, Eucharist and Ministry."

Next, multilateral dialogue helps to keep the Churches honest in what they affirm with various particular partners in their respective bilateral dialogues. Less suspiciously put, it encourages the Churches to develop positions that are both internally consistent and simultaneously mindful of their effect on all interlocutors. Positive signs are the borrowings of material which take place between multilateral dialogues and the various bilaterals.

Finally, multilateral dialogues are able to draw directly on the broadest range of resources in scholarship, expertise, and experience. In turn, they offer the widest scope of opportunities for results and action.

In both the multilateral and the bilateral exercises, authentic Methodist participation will be Wesleyan in both spirit and substance.

IX. *Wesleyan Spirit and Substance*

"To speak the truth in love" would be a Pauline and a Wesleyan motto for dialogue. Both elements are important: to speak the truth *in love*, and to speak *the truth* in love. Wesley's sermon on "Catholic Spirit" not only breathes a generous spirit but also affirms catholic substance. At their best, Methodist contributions to ecumenical dialogue will accordingly be marked by the following four Wesleyan qualities.

First, Methodist participation will be characterized by doctrinal responsibility. Wesley's magnanimity regarding theological "opinions" was limited to those that did not "strike at the root of Christianity"; he would not compromise on "the main branches of Christian doctrine" (God, the divinity and redemptive work of Christ, original sin, justification, sanctification). That is the burden of chapter fourteen of the present book, which arose in the context of a 1987 Puerto Rico conference sponsored by the Lutheran World Federation as part of its study on "fundamental agreement/basic difference," but which is applicable to Methodist participation in all ecumenical dialogues. The classic modern ecumenical movement has always been concerned for unity in the truth of the gospel and the content of the faith as they come to expression in the Scriptures and in authentic Tradition.

Second, Methodist participation in ecumenical dialogue will be marked by a spiritual engagement. Faith, hope and charity are profound realities that exceed their visible expression, and a purely institutional unity would never be sufficient. On the other hand, Christians involved in the ecumenical movement have already found it possible to discern sanctity also beyond one's own ecclesial institution. If, then, according to the Russian Orthodox dictum, "the walls of separation do not reach up to heaven," the recognition of graced lives in other Christian communities should encourage the divided Churches to make unity in Christ more manifest on earth. Chapter fifteen in the present book examines John Wesley's teaching on the communion of the saints and rejoices in the growing reception of his person and work into the calendars and practice of other parts of Christendom. The deliberate integration of the prayers and examples of the saints into the ecumenical movement should strengthen its effectiveness in helping the visible Church better to become that community of love toward God and neighbor in which, according to Wesley, true religion consists.

Third, Methodist participation in ecumenical dialogue will bear a missionary orientation. The soteriological interest which lies at the heart of concern for assurance in the faith (chapter two) and governed Wesley's views on church order (chapter three) has a universal scope. Having

33

received the gospel, the Church is—in the words of the Wesleyan hymn which set the theme of chapter sixteen in the present book—"sent to disciple all mankind." For the sake of evangelistic proclamation, Wesley could "look upon all the world as [his] parish."[34] When Jesus prayed for his disciples "that they all may be one," it was "in order that the world may believe" in the divine mission of the Son for the world's salvation (John 17:20-21). The cause of unity which ecumenical dialogue subserves has, at the very least, the purpose of removing those divisions among Christians that are a counter-testimony to the gospel of reconciliation. Positively put, Church unity itself belongs to the witness concerning the summing up of all things in Christ which is God's saving design.

Finally, Methodist participation in ecumenical dialogue will aim at the glorification of the Triune God, in communion with whom human bliss consists. According to the Apostle Paul in Romans 15:5-6, Christians are to "live in such harmony with one another, in accord with Christ Jesus," that they "may with one mind and one voice glorify the God and Father of our Lord Jesus Christ." As chapter seventeen of the present book demonstrates, John Wesley held firmly to the trinitarian gospel and faith of the Church, whereby every work of God towards the world begins with the Father, is mediated by the Son and comes to completion in the Holy Spirit, and in turn we have access in the Holy Spirit through the Son to the Father. What the Westminster Catechism defined as the "chief end" of humankind, namely "to glorify God and enjoy him for ever," Wesley describes thus in his sermon on "The New Creation": "There will be a deep, an intimate, an uninterrupted union with God; a constant communion with the Father and his Son Jesus Christ, through the Spirit; a continual enjoyment of the Three-One God, and of all creatures in him."[35] That is the final vision held out also by the classic ecumenical movement, and it remains vital to authentic Christianity in our time.[36]

METHODISTS AND ROMAN CATHOLICS

CHAPTER ONE

Roman Catholic-Methodist Dialogue: A Silver Jubilee

I. *From John Wesley to the Joint Commission*

It is tempting to date the beginnings of dialogue between Methodists and Roman Catholics, not from the start of conversations after the Second Vatican Council, but rather from John Wesley's *Letter to a Roman Catholic*. Then we should be celebrating, not the mere 25 years since the first meeting of the Joint Commission between the Roman Catholic Church and the World Methodist Council at Ariccia in 1967, but rather the almost 250 years that have elapsed since Wesley penned his irenic open epistle at Dublin on 18 July 1749. In all honesty, however, we should then have to admit that those two and a half centuries contained long periods of silence on account of mutual ignorance as well as some sharp bursts of express mutual dismissal and polemics. A word about Wesley's generous letter may nevertheless not be out of place at the outset of these reflections on the contemporary dialogue.

Albert C. Outler, a Methodist observer at Vatican II and then a member of the first three series of the Joint Commission, took the initiative of including what he called Wesley's "olive branch to the Romans" in his widely used anthology of *John Wesley* in the Library of Protestant Thought published by Oxford University Press, New York (1964). It was left to Michael Hurley, a member on the Catholic side for the first ten years of the Joint Commission, to republish *John Wesley's Letter to a Roman Catholic* in monographic form. After recruiting prefaces from Bishop Odd Hagen, the current President of the World Methodist Council, and Augustin Cardinal Bea, Hurley's fellow Jesuit and at that time President of the Vatican Secretariat for Christian Unity, Hurley himself furnished an informative and perceptive introduction to the volume.[1]

Calling for an end to mutual bitterness and barbarities, Wesley in his *Letter* grounded an appropriate mutual regard between Catholics and Protestants in the fact that both were created by the same God and

37

redeemed by his Son. Even more, they shared to a large degree a common faith and a common ethic. Wesley sets out the belief of "a true Protestant" in terms of an expansion upon the Nicene Creed[2] and describes how a true Protestant serves God and loves his neighbor in ways that Wesley is convinced must meet with a good Catholic's approval. This is sufficient, Wesley judges, for Catholic and Protestant "to provoke one another to love and to good works," loving one another and endeavoring "to help each other on in whatever we are agreed leads to the Kingdom."

This was not all that Wesley had to say to or about Roman Catholics. At the doctrinal level, he could be polemical as well as irenical, as is shown in the fiercely critical "A Roman Catechism faithfully drawn out of the allowed writings of the Church of Rome, with a Reply thereto."[3] At times, Wesley could view the Roman Catholic Church as at least "a part" of "the Church"[4]—and this notwithstanding the presence in it of "unscriptural doctrines" and "superstitious modes of worship."[5] Yet at other times it seems rather that he valued individual Roman Catholics as Christians practically *in spite of* their institutional allegiance.[6]

As late as the World Methodist Council's agreement in 1966 to enter upon a dialogue with the Roman Catholic Church, Michael Hurley could note an admission by Arthur Worrall that many Methodists "still believe that the Roman Catholic Church is not part of the Christian body but is an insidious conspiracy of the devil."[7] By its most recent report in 1991, the Joint Commission found it possible and necessary to acknowledge that "while Wesley and the early Methodists could recognize the presence of Christian faith in the lives of individual Roman Catholics, it is only more recently that Methodists have become more willing to recognize the Roman Catholic Church as an institution for the divine good of its members."[8] Not dissimilarly, the Roman Catholic Church has in modern times moved from an exclusivist understanding of "no salvation outside the Church" through a more affectionate recognition of "separated brothers and sisters" to an as yet inchoate attribution of some ecclesial status to Protestant communities. Thus again the Joint Commission in 1991: "For its part, the Roman Catholic Church since Vatican II certainly includes Methodists among those who, by baptism and faith in Christ, enjoy 'a certain though imperfect communion with the Catholic Church'; and it envisages Methodism among those ecclesial communities which are 'not devoid of meaning and importance in the mystery of salvation' (*Unitatis redintegratio*, 3)."[9] At stake is what the chairmen's preface to the 1991 report calls "the ecclesiological self-understanding" of Catholics and Methodists respectively and the place which each can recognize to the other. It is thus a matter of the concrete location of the Church which both Catholics and Methodists confess. That is the fundamental issue whose opening first made the contemporary dialogue possible, and to whose exploration the contemporary dialogue in turn has in one way or another devoted itself.

Let us then retrace the work of the Joint Commission over the past twenty-five years and celebrate the measure of its achievement on the occasion of its silver jubilee.[10] Five rounds of dialogue have been spread over five years each, with a report being prepared each time for presentation to the Vatican and to the World Methodist Council at the latter's quinquennial gathering. The reports have become popularly known by the place and date of the WMC meeting to which they were presented: Denver 1971, Dublin 1976, Honolulu 1981, Nairobi 1986, and Singapore 1991.[11] While the chronological sequence will set the framework of this essay, threads will be allowed to crisscross where the substantial discussion demands it.[12]

II. The Denver and Dublin Reports, 1971 and 1976

The work of the Joint Commission was marked in its first ten years by three features: first, it sought to identify certain traits of ethos and style that were characteristic of Catholicism and Methodism respectively and would undoubtedly affect any bilateral dialogue between them; second, it treated certain general themes that were of common interest at the time to the broad body of Christians, such as "Christianity and the Contemporary World" (showing the same obsession with "secularization" as marked the 1968 Uppsala assembly of the World Council of Churches), "Common Witness and Salvation Today" (again in tandem with the WCC conference on mission and evangelism at Bangkok 1973), and "Spirituality"; third, the Joint Commission tackled a number of subjects—eucharist, ministry, authority—that were occupying also other international bilateral dialogues in which the Roman Catholic Church was engaged, notably with the Anglicans and with the Lutherans.[13]

1. Kindred and Affinities

The most far-sighted work was that which attempted to pinpoint the characteristic relationship between Catholics and Methodists, for these considerations have arisen time and time again in the subsequent labors of the Commission. Thus Denver noted, first, that this dialogue had "a singular advantage: there is no history of formal separating between the two Churches, none of the historical, emotional problems consequent on a history of schism" (6). Informally put, the relationship may sometimes be easier between a grandmother and her grandchildren than between a child and its parent (as would be the case between Anglicans and Rome, or between Methodists and Canterbury). At this point, it may also be remarked that even those (American) Methodist Churches which have episcopal government are "not claiming apostolic succession in the sense of the Roman Catholic Church" (Nairobi 1986, 33). Happily, the trauma focused on Rome's condemnation of Anglican orders in *Apostolicae Curae* does not directly affect relationships between Methodists and Roman Catholics. Singapore 1991 declared that "the mutual recognition of ministry will be achieved not only by Methodists and Catholics having reached doctrinal consensus but it will also depend upon a fresh creative act of reconciliation which acknowledges the manifold yet unified activity of the Holy Spirit throughout the ages. It will involve a joint act of obedience to the sovereign Word of God" (94).

Next Denver noted a number of positive affinities between Catholics and Methodists. At the head stood "the central place held in both traditions by the ideal of personal sanctification, growth in holiness through daily life in Christ" (7). If Methodists have seen "the cultivation of 'scriptural holiness' and its spread as a common task, making the Church a fellowship rather than a hierarchy," they can now welcome "the universal call to holiness" found in Vatican II's *Lumen Gentium;* and throughout the dialogue, the Catholic members have endeavored to make clear that the "hierarchy" that attracts Methodist suspicion is in fact at the service of the whole body for its sanctification (as recognized by Singapore 1991 in its entire second half, "Ministry and Ministries: Serving within the Apostolic Tradition"). The concern for Christian holiness was taken up by the statements of Honolulu 1981 on the work of the Holy Spirit in justification, regeneration, sanctification, and the making of moral decisions; and the theme of sanctified discipleship persisted into the important section of Singapore 1991 on "The Pattern of Christian Life" (39–48).

Denver noted, too, that "the disciplined life of the early Methodists, aimed at renewing a lax Church, set standards for the whole of Methodism which have found Roman Catholic parallels more often in the early life of religious foundations such as the Jesuits" (8). Here emerges, at least obliquely, a way of viewing Methodism that may have some ecclesiological significance. In exploring "ways of being one Church," Nairobi 1986 offered the following among elements for a model of organic unity:

> From one perspective the history of John Wesley has suggested an analogy between his movement and the religious orders within the one Church. Figures such as Benedict of Norcia and Francis of Assisi, whose divine calling was similarly to a spiritual reform, gave rise to religious orders, characterized by special forms of life and prayer, work, evangelization, and their own internal organization. The

40

different religious orders in the Roman Catholic Church, while fully in communion with the Pope and the bishops, relate in different ways to the authority of Pope and bishops. Such relative autonomy has a recognized place within the unity of the Church. (24)[14]

Denver implied a doxological affinity between Methodism and Catholicism when it spoke of "a theology that can be sung" (9). It was noted that the hymns of Charles Wesley, and particularly the eucharistic hymns, find echoes and recognition among Catholics. Yet this was a point at which Methodists needed to face the more general question of "how far the Wesleys remain a decisive influence in contemporary Methodism." Interestingly, the Catholic theologian Francis Frost, who was later to become a member of the Joint Commission, observed in a major article written about this time that Methodism retained a fundamental unity in the spiritual heritage upon which Wesley so firmly placed his stamp;[15] but Wesleyan theologians know what a struggle it is to keep Wesleyan impulses to the fore. Thereby is raised a basic methodological principle in all ecumenical dialogue: is a particular ecclesial tradition to be represented in its "ideal," its "classical," or its "empirical" form?[16]

Finally, Denver registered a shared concern between Roman Catholics and Methodists for a "common mission" (10). Evangelization has remained a recurrent theme in the dialogue. Thus Nairobi 1986 included "mission" in its concise formulation of what "full communion" would entail (20) and gave a soteriological grounding to the need and provision for "authoritative teaching": "Because God wills the salvation of all men and women, he enables the Church, by the Holy Spirit, so to declare the truth of the divine Revelation in Jesus Christ that his people may know the way of salvation" (63). And in a statement which Singapore 1991 took up from Nairobi as its own epigraph: "Because God so loved the world, he sent his Son and the Holy Spirit to draw us into communion with himself. This sharing in God's life, which resulted from the mission of the Son and the Holy Spirit, found expression in a visible *koinonia* [communion, community] of Christ's disciples, the Church."

But from the outset, Denver was not blind to the kinds of issues that made dialogue between Roman Catholics and Methodists not only possible but necessary. In regard to three issues in particular (paragraphs 12–13), the first Joint Commission presaged its own work and the themes that would continue in Dublin 1976 and even beyond. First, Catholics who spoke warmly of the Wesleys' eucharistic hymns nevertheless observed that "few Methodists would hold the doctrine of the Real Presence in any sense akin to the Catholic meaning." Second, interest was shown in "recent Roman Catholic writings on ministry, in which reflection on

41

ordinary and extraordinary ministries seems to have many points of contact with the original Methodist situation." Third, it was noted that "Methodists found unacceptable" the "dogmas concerning the papacy." Thus were set as themes for dialogue the eucharist, ministry, and authority.

2. Eucharist

As to the eucharist, Denver set out a concise list of "points of agreement" (83) and "points of disagreement" (84), concentrating on the presence of Christ, the sacrificial dimension of the rite, and conditions of admission to communion. These were then developed—with the help of the English Roman Catholic/Methodist Commission and in light of the Anglican/Roman Catholic International Commission or ARCIC's Windsor Statement on the Eucharist of 1971—in the second round of the dialogue that led to Dublin 1976 (paras. 47–74). According to Denver, both Methodists and Roman Catholics "affirm as the primary fact the presence of Christ in the Eucharist, the Mass, or the Lord's Supper," "a reality that does not depend on the experience of the communicant," although "it is only by faith that we become aware of the presence of Christ in the eucharist." This is "a distinctive mode or manifestation of the presence of Christ," although "the presence in the Eucharist for the Methodists is not fundamentally different from the presence of Christ in other means of grace, e.g. preaching" (Denver, 83–84). Dublin clarifies the last point by saying that "we both affirm that wherever Christ is present he is present in his fullness" (56), and that "Roman Catholics, like Methodists, affirm the presence of Christ in the proclamation of the gospel and the other sacraments" (57). Both Denver (83) and Dublin (54) record agreement between Methodists and Catholics that the eucharistic bread and wine are "efficacious signs of the body and blood of Christ," although the two parties differ over the "transformation" of the elements, which is for Catholic teaching a change in their "inner reality" whereas Methodist understanding goes in terms of their acquiring "an additional significance" (Dublin, 59–60).

While both sides agree that the sacrificial language of the eucharistic celebration refers to "the sacrifice of Christ once-for-all," to "our pleading of that sacrifice here and now," to "our offering of the sacrifice of praise and thanksgiving," and to "our sacrifice of ourselves in union with Christ who offered himself to the Father," Catholics "are also accustomed to speak of the sacrifice of the Mass as something which the Church offers in all ages of her history" (Dublin, 65–66). Catholics explain that this does not "add to" or "repeat" Christ's sacrifice but "makes present in a sacramental way the same sacrifice" (66). "For some Methodists," however, "such language would imply that Christ is still being sacrificed. Methodists prefer to say that Christ has offered one sacrifice for sins and now lives to make intercession for us, so that we in union with him can offer ourselves to the Father, making his sacrificial death our only plea" (ibid.). All agree that the eucharistic memorial (*anamnesis*) is "not a mere calling to mind of a past event or of its significance, but the Church's effectual proclamation of God's mighty acts" (Dublin, 63). While Denver had specified, in an ostensibly agreed way, that the eucharistic memorial "is a re-enactment of Christ's triumphant sacrifice and makes available for us its benefits" (83), Dublin more chastely declares that "some" (and probably not only, we may surmise, among the Methodists) "would wish to link this dynamic view not with 'a re-enactment of Christ's triumphant sacrifice,' but with Christ's being present and bringing with him all the benefits of his once-for-all sacrifice for us" (63).

Liturgically speaking, Dublin notes among Roman Catholics "a renewal in the theology and practice of the ministry of the word" and among Methodists, at least "in many places" (71), "a notable recovery of eucharistic faith and practice"—"a remarkable convergence, so that at no other time has the worshipping life of Methodists and Roman Catholics had so much in common" (51). Canonically, the Roman Catholic Church admits other Christians to eucharistic communion only in cases of urgent pastoral necessity and with firm doctrinal safeguards; Catholics in similar circumstances are expected not to ask for the sacrament "except from a minister who has been validly ordained in the eyes of the Roman Catholic Church" (Dublin, 69–70). Methodists in some places often issue a generous—or lax, depending on one's point of view—"open invitation" to the Lord's Table; but the prevalent historic practice has been to offer, in a more disciplined way, hospitality to "baptized communicant members of other communions who desire to come," while not thinking it fitting for Christians "to receive communion in any denomination at random, for communion with Christ is linked with membership of a local church" (Dublin, 68). Here arises very concretely the basic ecclesiological question of the identification of the Church.

3. Ministry

Denver recorded a fundamental agreement on "Jesus Christ as the One through whom the ministry, whether sacramental or otherwise, is both identified and ultimately authorized. The minister participates"—"by the power of the Holy Spirit" (92)—"in Christ's ministry, acts in Christ's name" (89). Methodists asked Catholics (a) how to understand the "difference in kind and not merely in degree" (Vatican II) between the

43

ordained ministry and the laity, (b) what stood in the way of Roman Catholic recognition of Methodist ministry as "authentic," and (c) what were the "guiding principles for understanding the meaning of orders" as well as the "pragmatic factors" in their development.

In its "joint statement" on ministry, Dublin 1976 was again helped by the English Roman Catholic/Methodist Commission, working this time in light of ARCIC's Canterbury Statement on "Ministry and Ordination" (1973). Christ's earthly and continuing ministry is reaffirmed as "the fundamental ministry," in which those who are called and ordained to "special ministry" within the whole people of God are given a share by the Spirit so that they may "represent" Christ (77–81). It is agreed that "the church's apostolicity involves continuous faithfulness in doctrine, ministry, sacrament and life to the teaching of the New Testament," and that "in considering the ordained ministry of another church we use this faithfulness as our criterion" (84). Yet Catholics and Methodists "differ in the account we give of apostolic succession" (ibid.). For Roman Catholics, "the graded threefold ministry is derived from the teaching of the New Testament through the living tradition of the church. True succession in ministry is guaranteed only by episcopal laying-on of hands in historical succession and authentic transmission of the faith within the apostolic college" (85). Methodists hold that "the New Testament does not lay down any one form of ministry as binding for all times and places" (86), but they "can regard a succession of ordination from the earliest times as a valuable *symbol* of the church's continuity with the church of the New Testament, though they would not use it as a *criterion*" (87). The question of apostolicity will recur in Nairobi 1986 and, above all, in Singapore 1991.

According to Dublin 1976, both Catholics and Methodists "see the central act of the ordained ministry as presiding at the eucharist in which the ministry of word, sacrament and pastoral care is perfected" (97). That vision doubtless illuminates a rather remarkable "agreement" concerning the "difference" and "interrelationship" between the ordained ministry and the "common priesthood of the faithful":

> Roman Catholics and Methodists agree that by ordination a new and permanent relationship with Christ and his church is established. The ordained minister is called and enabled by the Holy Spirit to be the representative person who focuses in his ministry the manifold ministries of the whole church. He is a sign of the gospel and of the oneness of Christ's church, both to the church and to the world; an ambassador of Christ who bids men to be reconciled to God and declares to them the forgiveness of sins; a priest who embodies the priesthood of all believers in which he shares, and by his ministry serves and sustains it. (98)

44

It is a pity that that paragraph has not attracted wider ecumenical attention as a candidate for expressing necessary and sufficient agreement on this matter.

4. Authority

Denver 1971 noted that problems of authority had cropped up throughout discussions of explicitly treated themes and were "implicit in some of the deep 'crevasses' between us," namely "the Mariological dogmas and the doctrines of the Infallibility or Indefectibility of the Church" on the one hand, and on the other "the whole question of the origin and development of Methodism as a work of the Spirit, of an extraordinary and prophetic character, [which] has at some point to be related to the Catholic view of Church order and of its understanding of the authority of Christ in his Church" (100). There followed a discursive mini-essay that bears all the marks of Albert Outler's hand, proposing a concrete survey of the instances of authority in each Church and forecasting that they would differ chiefly in their relative importance and sequence of operation (101–118). Questions of authority came to be more formally addressed by Honolulu 1981, Nairobi 1986, and (in an interesting reversion to Outler's "traditionary" approach) Singapore 1991.

III. *Honolulu 1981*

The third round of the dialogue was marked by a change in method and aim that would continue up to the present. The attempts to cover whole waterfronts are now given up, and the work of each quinquennium is concentrated much more on a specific theme. Each quinquennial report now moves "towards"—with due modesty—"an agreed statement" on the chosen topic, so that common and differentiated declarations no longer have to be dug out from a mass of reportage on mere discussions within the Joint Commission.

Honolulu 1981 is entitled *Towards an Agreed Statement on the Holy Spirit*. The subject was chosen because "Methodists and Catholics repeatedly discover a notable rapport when they speak of spirituality," which is of course properly a pneumatological reality, "the life of the Spirit" (7). Moreover, the Commission wagered that "the doctrine of the Holy Spirit underlies much of the 'ecumenical agenda' still to be considered by our Churches" (ibid.).

Since "the doctrine of the Person of the Holy Spirit has never been a point of doctrine between us," Honolulu found it sufficient to begin with a brief, orthodox statement on "the Holy Spirit in the Godhead" (8–11).

Then the work of the Spirit is seen to begin with creation and the disclosure of its meaning, always in relation to the Word (12). The Holy Spirit operated at every stage of the Word's incarnation in Jesus, at his conception, at his baptism, and during his entire public ministry (13). After Christ's death and resurrection, his work came to consummation in the gift of the Holy Spirit, by which the Church was founded and created as the community of the New Covenant (13; 19). Endowed with a variety of spiritual gifts (20), this community is guided by the Paraclete, who recalls the words of Jesus and enables the Church's missionary witness (17; 21), thus working towards the final glorious transformation of all who love God (21–22).

Close agreement is found between Catholics and Methodists on justification, regeneration, and sanctification, matters on which many Protestants have historically been at odds with Rome: "The Holy Spirit is present and active within us throughout the entire experience of conversion which begins with an awareness of God's goodness and an experience of shame and guilt, proceeds to sorrow and repentance, and ends in gratitude for the possession of a new life given us through God's mercy in Jesus Christ. Justification is not an isolated forensic episode, but is part of a process which finds its consummation in regeneration and sanctification, the participation of human life in the divine" (13). John Wesley and the Council of Trent concur in their emphasis on the prevenience of grace: "Always it is the Spirit's special office to maintain the divine initiative that precedes all human action and reaction. . . . In the restoration [of the sinner to a right relationship with God through the atoning work of Christ], both the initiative, the agency and the consummation is the ministry of the Holy Spirit as he brings Christ to us and leads us to him. When a sinner is led to Christ and receives him, he is re-born and given the power to turn away from a life curved back upon itself towards a 'new life,' opened out to love of God and neighbour" (14–15; cf. 18).

Still under the rubric of the Holy Spirit, further attention is given by Honolulu to the "Christian experience" of believers and to "authority in the Church." By "the Spirit of adoption" the children of God are able to call with confidence on the merciful Father (16), and by the same Spirit the faithful are guided to a knowledge of the truth and to an obedience in which the fruit of the Spirit is manifested (24). "Holiness in heart and life" represents a convergence between John Wesley and "the mainstream of Catholic spirituality" which could have significant implications "for the future of the cause of Christian unity" (26; cf. 30, 32).

To those gathered in Christ as the Church, "Christ's authority is mediated through the Spirit, who is Love, and hence all authority that flows from this source is part of God's good gift. Whether it be the personal authority of holiness or the charism of *episcopé* conferred by the Spirit on the ordained ministry, whether it be teaching or disciplinary, authority implies that what is propounded, commanded or recommended ought to be accepted on the ground that it comes from this source" (33). Boldly, Honolulu goes on to declare that "the papal authority, no less than any other within the Church, is a manifestation of the continuing presence of the Spirit of Love in the Church or it is nothing. Indeed it should in its exercise be pre-eminently such a manifestation. It was declared at Vatican I to be 'for the building up and not the casting down of the Church'— whether of the local Church or the communion of local Churches" (35). That is the pneumatological perspective set by Honolulu for the emotional and theological clarification of the delicate issues of authority in the Church, and particularly the contentious matter of the papacy.

Ecclesiology, in fact, came to the fore in the fourth and fifth rounds of the Roman Catholic-Methodist dialogue, as it did in other bilateral dialogues in the 1980s[17] and as tended to happen on the multilateral scene also when the churches looked for the assumptions and implications contained in the convergences regarding "baptism, eucharist and ministry" in the Lima text of the WCC Faith and Order Commission.[18]

IV. Nairobi 1986

The Nairobi report was entitled *Towards an Agreed Statement on the Church*. For half its length it dealt rather broadly with a general vision of the Church and its unity, with a gentle narrowing of focus to "structures of ministry." The second half of the report then concentrated quite sharply on "the Petrine office," as had become the favored ecumenical term for matters relating to the papacy.

The Church is seen as a community and communion resulting from God's mission of the Son and the Spirit (1–3) and participating already in the life of the Triune God as "sign, sacrament and harbinger of the Kingdom of God in the time between the times" (8). While there is some avowed reticence among Methodists about the direct application of the term "sacrament" to the Church, yet the origination of the Church in the "Mystery of the Word made flesh" as well as the presence of the dominical sacraments in the Church allow the Church to be spoken of at least in a "sacramental perspective" (9–16).

Nairobi notes that the word "church" is used in the New Testament for "Christians meeting together in a house or living in the same city" as well as "in a more universal way for the body of Christ, . . . the communion of the saints on earth and in heaven" (18). Later application of the term also recognized "diversities of language or rite, such as Syrian Church, Coptic Church or Latin Church" (19). But when the usage results from "fundamental differences in doctrine, faith or ecclesial policy, such as Lutheran Church, Methodist Church, or Roman Catholic Church," then "Methodists and Roman Catholics . . . recognize that the divisions underlying this last usage are contrary to the unity Christ wills for his Church" (20). "Obedience to Him who will bring about this unity" entails, says the Joint Commission, commitment to "a vision that includes the goal of full communion in faith, mission and sacramental life" (ibid.). The full communion at which Methodists and Catholics aim must be expressed visibly, without thereby suppressing the gifts with which God has graced the separate communities (21).

Recognizing that an ecclesiology shaped in a time of division cannot be expected to be entirely satisfactory, the Joint Commission then sets about exploring "ways of being one Church" as a means of helping Methodists and Catholics to give proper recognition to each other's ecclesial character and to overcome the present state of division between them (22). Various ecumenically current visions or realities are said to offer "elements for a model of organic unity in the *koinonia* of the one Body of Christ" (24): (a) the notion of *typoi* (associated with the name of Cardinal Willebrands), whereby "within one Church in which there is basic agreement in faith, doctrine and structure essential for mission, there is room for various 'ecclesial traditions,' each characterized by a particular style of theology, worship, spirituality and discipline"; (b) the analogy of "religious orders" within a single Church, already mentioned above; (c) the idea of "sister churches," which might perhaps be broadened from its predominantly geographical sense so as to "envisage reunion among divided traditions as a family reconciliation"; (d) the example of the relations between "Churches of the Roman (Latin) rite and those of various oriental rites in communion with the Bishop of Rome." The Joint Commission broached the question, whether the pastoral care of such traditions would require separate, possibly overlapping jurisdictions, or whether it could be provided by a single exercise of *episcopé* in each place (27).

Attention is then turned more precisely to "structures of ministry." A historical concomitance is recognized between the establishment of the scriptural canon, the formation of the classical creeds, and the clear emergence of a threefold ministry of bishop, presbyter and deacon; but the Joint Commission notes that Methodists and Catholics "are not agreed on how far this development of the ministry is now unchangeable and how far loyalty to the Holy Spirit requires us to recognize other forms of oversight and leadership that have developed, often at times of crisis or new opportunity in Christian history" (29). The question is sharpened by Catholic belief in the primacy of the Bishop of Rome, which Vatican II rests on the affirmation that "to ensure the indivisible unity of the episcopate, [Jesus Christ] set St. Peter over the other apostles (*Lumen Gentium*, 18)" (36). Since Catholics judge this to be "a fundamental principle of unity of faith and communion," Methodists and Catholics are bound to consider questions of the Petrine office and the primacy of the Bishop of Rome in their search for "full unity in faith, mission and sacramental life."

Paragraphs 39–75 do indeed begin a treatment of these matters. Under the exegetical guidance of Raymond E. Brown, then a member of the Joint Commission, an agreed picture of "Peter in the New Testament" is provided (41–47). This is followed by a historical account (51–54) of the early centuries in which the see of Rome, claiming Peter as its first bishop and finding that other churches also "applied" Petrine texts to the apostle's successor in that see, exercised an outstanding role in testimony to the apostolic tradition, so that eventually the bishops assembled at Chalcedon in 451 could declare "Peter has spoken through Leo." This "primacy of love," however, from the fourth and fifth centuries onwards took a "more juridical turn," so that "increasingly developed formulation and applica-tion of the Roman claims and more vigorous resistance to them alike contributed to the origin and continuations of divisions in Christianity, first in the East and eventually in the West" (54).

The historical role and claims of the Roman see may also be set in the sociological context of the "desirability" or "need" in the whole Church for "a leader to exercise . . . a unifying role in service to the worldwide *koinonia*" (48–50). That more pragmatic approach might prove more acceptable to Methodists, who "accept that whatever is properly required for the unity of the whole of Christ's Church must by that very fact be God's will for his Church. A universal primacy might well serve as focus of and ministry for the unity of the whole Church" (58). Thus it is "not inconceivable," says the Joint Commission in adopting the curial style of the double negative, "that at some future date in a restored unity, Roman Catholic and Methodist bishops might be linked in one episcopal college and that the whole body would recognize some kind of effective leadership and primacy in the bishop of Rome. In that case Methodists might justify such an acceptance on different grounds from those that now prevail in the Roman Catholic Church" (62). In the matter of jurisdiction, Roman Catholics in any case "recognize that theological exploration of the relation between the authority of the Pope and that of the local bishop remains unfinished" (61).

Nairobi finally turns to the question of papal infallibility in the larger context of "authoritative teaching" (63–75). It is agreed that "God . . . enables the Church, by the Holy Spirit, so to declare the truth of the divine Revelation that his people may know the way of salvation" (63); that "the Scriptures bear permanent witness to the divine revelation in Christ and are normative for all subsequent tradition" (64); that "properly understood, the decisions of the ecumenical councils which met in the first centuries command assent throughout the whole Church, and there is no reason to think that at the end of the patristic era God stopped enabling his Church to speak in such a way" (65). The difficulty arises when Catholics claim that "in carefully defined and limited circumstances, the Pope exercises the capacity [of the Church to formulate the faith in a manner that is beyond doubt] in and for the whole Church" (69). Indeed, in the concrete cases of Mary's immaculate conception and assumption, Methodists hold that these papally proclaimed dogmas "lack assent and reception by all Christian people," which is "the final judge" of what is in clear "agreement with the Scriptures" (72–73).[19] Clearly, "further study" is needed, and the Joint Commission suggested that Methodists might approach the question of infallibility from the perspective of their own doctrine of "assurance":

> Starting from Wesley's claim that the evidence for what God has done and is doing for our salvation can be 'heightened to exclude all doubt', Methodists might ask whether the Church, like individuals, might by the working of the Holy Spirit receive as a gift from God in its living, teaching, preaching and mission, an assurance concerning its grasp of the fundamental doctrines of the faith such as to exclude all doubt, and whether the teaching ministry of the Church has a special and divinely guided part to play in this. In any case Catholics and Methodists are agreed on the need for an authoritative way of being sure, beyond doubt, concerning God's action insofar as it is crucial for our salvation. (75)[20]

The Vatican's publication of the Nairobi report was accompanied by an invited commentary from the veteran Ottawa ecumenist, J. M. R. Tillard.[21] Recognizing that the report "issues from honest and lucid research together into the points of convergence and points of divergence that emerged in each group's conception of the profound nature and of the structure of the Church of God," Tillard esteems it "a significant document" that will be of interest beyond its immediate Catholic-Methodist context, for it allows one both to take stock of "the emergence of a shared 'given'" and to "identify the major obstacles." He places "among the most beautiful definitions of the Church" the opening description of the Church as a visible *koinonia* resulting from the missions of the Son and the Spirit and embodying participation in the life of the Triune God. According to Tillard, the Joint Commission was right in its judgment, as he reformulates it, that "*koinonia* must not be considered as one model of unity. Rather it is the fundamental reality which any model must make possible and actualise" (cf. 23f.). Proposing to develop further the "sacramentality" of the Church as not only the "manifestation of God's grace" but an "effective help" in God's hand, Tillard calls the Church "the reality which, evangelised by God, evangelises for God, and reconciled with God, reconciles with God, and drawn together by God, draws together for God." Some movement in this direction was in fact to be made in the ensuing Singapore report of 1991. That was the case also with Tillard's complaint that in admitting that "there was no shared understanding of the nature and meaning of apostolic succession," the report did not go beyond diagnosis.

V. *Singapore 1991*

With hindsight, the Joint Commission itself recognized that a gap existed in the Nairobi report between the agreed historical description of the Church in the New Testament period and the early centuries, on the one hand, and the theological discussion, on the other, of issues such as ministerial structures, authoritative teaching, and above all "the Petrine office" which must be settled if contemporary endeavors towards church unity are to succeed. The filling of that gap required, the Joint Commission saw, a historico-theological treatment of the theme and reality of "The Apostolic Tradition." George Tavard, when the Commission met at Lisbon in 1988, provided the working motto for this fifth series of the dialogue: the continuance of the apostolic tradition was to be viewed as *"koinonia* in time."[22]

The aim, as the chairmen's preface to the Singapore 1991 report states it, was to develop historical and theological "perspectives"—"consistent with the doctrinal positions of both churches"—in which it would become possible to start reconsidering controversial matters in ways that allowed convergences to be discerned and then further developed. In particular, it was hoped, as the report itself puts it, that an approach by way of "the teaching, transmission and reception of the apostolic faith" might "set the difficult problem of ministry in a new light, since this topic has hitherto been predominantly considered in its relationship to the administrative and sacramental life of the Church rather than in relation to its teaching" (4). This did not mean that the sacraments and ecclesial structures themselves would be neglected in the report, but rather that they would be treated in relation to the apostolic tradition which they and their ministers respectively embody, enable and serve.

In broad perspective, "Tradition" is defined by Singapore as "the living transmission of the Gospel of Christ, by manifold means, for the constant renewal of every generation" (5). The Church itself is first the *result* of the Gospel: it was born and lives from the gracious purpose of the Father as carried out by the Son and the Spirit, the Son founding the Church by his act of redemption and the Spirit sustaining the Church as its principle of sanctification (7). Then the Church is "the *place* where the Word of God is spoken, heard, responded to, and confessed" (15) and where "the Spirit abides" (29). Finally, the Church is the *instrument* "through" which the mission of the Triune God "continues" as the Church proclaims the Gospel to the world (1).

The "manifold means" by which the apostolic Gospel is transmitted in and through the Church are all governed by the Word and enlivened by the Spirit. Analogously to the coinherence of person, speech and deed in the Word incarnate (9; 17), "every possible human resource is employed: linguistic, ritual, artistic, social and constitutional" (16). Thereby "the risen Christ speaks to us today," provided preachers and hearers have learned "his language" (6); since "Christ was content to speak with other audiences and with later generations through those who became his first disciples" (15), "the written word of Scripture" that contains the apostolic testimony remains the "permanent norm" of the "unbroken process of communication between God and human beings" (16). Since Christ "sends the Spirit to us to open our understanding and to guide our words and actions" (6), each generation is enabled to hear, speak and act for itself (18). To be assured of the "continued hearing and assimilation of the Word of God," "we maintain communion with those who have heard and obeyed the Word before us" (ibid.).

In light of this belief in a communion of the saints, the Joint Commission next proposes as common a reading as it can between Methodists and Catholics of the historical and theological constants in the confession of Christ, Christian experience, and ecclesial identity. In "the pattern of Christian faith" (33–38), a special place is given to the Nicene Creed as the work of "those theologians who provided the earliest elucidations of the faith" and "a comprehensive and authoritative statement" that is "common" to Catholics and Methodists and a factor in "the degree of communion that Catholics and Methodists already share." In "the pattern of Christian life" (39–48), a strongly Pauline account of faithful existence confirms the agreement on justification, regeneration, sanctification and spirituality that earlier rounds in the dialogue had registered. In "the pattern of Christian community" (49–52), it is argued from the New

Testament that a true hearing of the Word of God always entails an obedient shaping of the Church's life (50), and that "the actions that allow the Church to grow in strength and ordered life—the setting-apart of new ministers, or corporate decisions and teaching, for example—are always accompanied by the action of the Holy Spirit, who makes it possible for us to live in communion and harmony with one another (Acts 13:2; 15:28; 16:6–7; 2 Tim. 1:14)" (52). It is precisely here, however, that a common reading of subsequent Christian history becomes difficult for Catholics and Methodists, divided as they are in matters of ordination, decision-making and teaching authority where the differences are both cause and effect of the divisions between them.

That is why the Singapore report, in its second half, must then turn from "the apostolic faith: its teaching, transmission and reception" to the more specific question of "ministry and ministries: serving within the apostolic tradition." In principle, it is agreed that ministry stands in "service of the Word" (54–57) and is made possible by "gifts of the Spirit" (58–61). For the sake of the ministry of all Christians, there is a "specific charism received by those who are called to the ordained ministry" and which is "directed toward the ordering and harmony which must prevail in the exercise of all the gifts" (60). The ordained ministry is "a gift to the Church for leadership in its corporate and worshipping life, for the maintenance and deepening of its order and structure, for the organization of its missionary witness, and for discernment in understanding and applying the Gospel" (61).[23]

According to the Joint Commission, "Catholics and Methodists are at one in seeing in a divinely empowered ministry the guidance of the Holy Spirit and are moving in the direction of greater shared understanding of the nature of ordination and of the structure of the ministry in regard to the responsibility to teach and to formulate the faith" (77). Subsequent paragraphs indeed show a large measure of agreement on the call and commission to ministry, on the rite of ordination as the laying on of hands with prayer, and on the regular duties of the ordained. Nor is the gap a wide one between the "sacramentality" of Catholic ordination and the Methodist view of ordination as "an effective sign by which the grace of God is given to the recipient for the ministry of word and sacrament" (88). The crunch comes with regard to the existence and role of bishops in the matters of both "succession and oversight" (94).

It is part of "the Catholic understanding and practice of apostolic succession" that "bishops," in the historic line, "through the act of ordination share ministerially the high priesthood of Christ, in one degree or another, with other ministers (bishops, presbyters and deacons), who are their fellow workers in carrying out the apostolic duties entrusted to them (cf. Vatican II, *Presbyterorum ordinis*, 2)" (81; cf. Dublin, 85; Nairobi, 31). On the Methodist side, even those (American) Methodist churches which are episcopally ordered do not claim such a succession, even while holding to the orderly transmission of ministry (cf. Dublin, 87; Nairobi, 31, 33); Methodist churches on the British model have no order superior to presbyter (cf. Dublin, 91; Nairobi, 33), though they have in several cases shown themselves willing to accept the episcopal office for the sake of unity with Anglicans who have an episcopacy which, to boot, claims the historic succession (cf. Dublin, 86; Nairobi, 29, 33, 35). Again, on the Catholic side, oversight clearly resides with the bishops (cf. Dublin, 89; Nairobi, 32). On the Methodist side, supreme oversight on the British model clearly resides with the Conference (cf. Dublin, 91; Nairobi, 33), which for over a century has included laypersons, while the American model involves a delicate "separation of powers" between the bishops and variously composed Conferences (cf. Dublin, 90). Catholics and Methodists can agree that "central to the exercise of *episcopé* is the task of maintaining unity in the truth" and that "teaching is," therefore, "the principal part of the exercise of *episcopé*" (93). For Catholics, the form of this is quite precise: "The teaching of a common faith by the college of bishops in union with the successor of Peter ensures unity in the Truth. The succession of bishops through the generations serves the continued unity of the Church in the faith handed on from the apostles" (93). Some Methodist responses to the WCC Faith and Order text on *Baptism, Eucharist and Ministry* allow us to surmise that Methodist churches might accept a historic episcopal succession as, in the Lima phrase, "a sign, though not a guarantee, of the continuity and unity of the Church"; but the Roman Catholic response to *BEM* judges this to be inadequate.[24]

VI. *Retrospect and Prospect*

In the conclusion to Singapore 1991, the Joint Commission offers its own brief retrospect and prospect. Retrospectively, the dialogue since its inception a quarter-century ago "has contributed to the degree of mutual recognition which now exists. It has done so by the clarification of Methodist and Catholic positions and traditions, especially as these impinge on each other. A large measure of common faith has been brought to light, so that the increase in shared life that has begun may confidently be expected to continue" (101). Frankly it should be admitted that "measuring" the current achievement remains difficult because much depends on the "reception" of the Commission's work at the various levels of ecclesial life in Roman Catholicism and Methodism.[25]

Prospectively, "the need now is to consolidate the measure of agreement so far attained and to press forward with work on those areas in which agreement is still lacking. Continuing doctrinal progress should both encourage and reflect the growth in mutual recognition and in sharing in the life of the Triune God" (101).

In March 1992, conversations took place in Rome between the current chairman of the World Methodist Council's executive committee (Donald English), the general secretary of the WMC and co-secretary of the Joint Commission (Joe Hale), the Methodist co-chairman of the Commission (Geoffrey Wainwright), the cardinal president of the Pontifical Council for Christian Unity (Edward Cassidy), the Council's episcopal secretary (Pierre Duprey), the Joint Commission's Catholic co-secretary (Kevin McDonald), and Jared Wicks of the Gregorian University and the author of the Vatican's invited commentary on Singapore 1991.[26] It was generally agreed that the mission of the Triune God in the history of revelation and redemption provided a satisfactory theological perspective. Consolidation and development of existing achievements could take place by their explicit integration into that perspective. That was the perspective, too, in which Bishop Duprey urged that the Joint Commission should return to the difficult question of episcopacy, both diachronically as "succession" and synchronically as "oversight," and its role (from the Catholic side) in the establishment of communion.[27] My own bet is that the Joint Commission will sooner or later need also to grasp more firmly the nettle of baptism and its relation to faith and ecclesial belonging.[28]

The greatest need of all, perhaps, is that local churches become aware of the work of the international Joint Commission and, by their joint study and practical cooperation in the spirit of John Wesley's *Letter to a Roman Catholic*, both benefit from and contribute to its labours. If that task is performed faithfully and effectively over the next twenty-five years, it may not take quite 250 years before Methodists and Roman Catholics enter a "full communion in faith, mission and sacramental life" such as Wesley could scarcely have envisaged.

VII. Postscript

In taking up its work for the next period (1992–1996), the renewed Commission placed its work under the biblical text of 1 John 1:1-3:

That which was from the beginning, which we have heard, which we have seen with our eyes, which we have looked upon and touched with our hands, concerning the word of life—the life was made manifest, and we saw it, and testify to it, and proclaim to you the eternal life which was with the Father and was made manifest to us—that which we have seen and heard we proclaim also to you, so that you may have fellowship with us; and our fellowship is with the Father and with his Son Jesus Christ.

The trinitarian self-revelation of God, which comes by speech and act and is attested by word and sacrament, is to be taken as the theme and context for discussion and progress towards the declared goal of "full communion in faith, mission, and sacramental life" between Roman Catholics and Methodists. According to the initial reflections of the Commission, faith is the product of, and response to, God's self-giving and self-disclosure. Given the dynamism of revelation, the "faith which believes" brings "the faith which is believed" to expression in ways that respect the canonicity of the original witness in Scripture, acknowledge the fecundity of Tradition (where treatment is required of the Catholic doctrine of development, of the place of Methodism in Christian history, and of the significance of the ecumenical movement), and recognize that safeguards are needed against distortion (which is where the vigilance of an apostolic ministry of teaching and discernment comes in). Unity in the positive mission of proclaiming the gospel will require that Methodists and Catholics have an understanding and agreement on the content of the message, its modes of proclamation, the persons of its witnesses, and the scope of its offer. The communal character of the Christian witness and its results finds embodiment in sacramental celebration and life, and so the Commission will take up earlier work on baptism, eucharist, and ministry—now with the benefit of participation on both sides in the *BEM* process of Faith and Order—and examine the nature of sacrament in relation to God's entire work of creation, redemption, and consummation. Given the trinitarian nature and activity of God, and given the character of God's ultimate purposes for humankind, mutual communion is the relationship to be aimed at among Christians and their communities, if, at this stage in God's history with his people, they are properly to reflect their origin and anticipate their destiny.

How all this may be worked out among Methodists and Catholics will be the subject of the next report of the Joint Commission, expected in time for simultaneous presentation to the Vatican and to the next meeting of the World Methodist Council at Rio de Janeiro in 1996.

CHAPTER TWO

The Assurance of Faith: Methodists and Infallibility

I. *Mutual Suspicion and a Real Question*

When a Roman Catholic speaks of papal infallibility, the first reaction of a Methodist is likely to be one of suspicion, if not downright opposition. This response is aroused on several counts:

- First, hamartiologically. Wesleyan teaching on the persistent effects of original sin leads us to doubt whether any individual or institution may in principle be exempt from falling into error. Seeing "how great a distance lies between the message the Church offers and the human failings of those to whom the Gospel is entrusted" (Vatican II, *Gaudium et spes*, 43), we wonder whether sin may not vitiate even the believing discernment, interpretation and proclamation of God's truth.[1]

- Second, historically. Methodists will question the claim, made in the definition of 1870, that it is "a tradition received from the beginning of the Christian faith" that the Roman pontiff possesses infallibility in the sense defined. The doctrine of papal infallibility appears rather to have had a later origin and a longer evolution, scarcely derivable in a direct historical sense from the promises made to "blessed Peter."

- Third, ecumenically. We note that the Roman claim is not allowed even by other ancient Churches, such as those of the Orthodox East, which also confess that the Church is in some sense infallible.

- Fourth, controversially. Methodists find themselves differing from the Roman Catholic Church on some important matters of doctrine. Since we, in the nature of the case, believe ourselves to be on the side of truth at these points, we must with due modesty hold that the teaching of the Roman pontiff is at these points in fact mistaken. *Ipso facto* it is not infallible.[2]

Yet Methodists must upon reflection admit that, both scripturally and systematically, certain issues arise inescapably with regard to the infallibility of the Church, and at least plausibly with regard to a Petrine office in that context:

- First, biblically. Christ promised that he would be with his disciples to the close of the age (Matthew 28:20), and that the Holy Spirit would guide them into all truth (John 16:13). The gates of hell would not prevail against the Church (Matthew 16:18), which as "the Church of the living God" is the "pillar and bulwark of the truth" (I Timothy 3: 15). The promise of Matthew 16:18 was spoken to Peter who had just confessed Jesus as the Christ, the Son of the living God, and been told that "on this rock" (the referent is exegetically controversial) Christ would build his Church. And even at his denial Peter was promised that his faith would not (ultimately) fail, so that when he had "turned again" he might strengthen his brethren (Luke 22:32).

- Then, theologically. The real question of maintenance in the truth arises in a religion according to which God reveals himself in history, so that salvation resides in knowledge of the true God and of Jesus Christ whom he has sent (cf. John 17:3), and the recipients of this saving knowledge are commissioned to transmit the gospel message further. The manifoldness of personal experience on the part of the beneficiaries of salvation, together with the varying cultural circumstances in which the message must continue to be preached, alike make the question of an official, authoritative proclamation unavoidable. Who, in the course of history, is to bear the human responsibility for the identity of the faith?

It is these issues of saving knowledge which are at stake, not only in the whole constitution *Pastor aeternus*, but also in the other dogmatic constitution of Vatican I on the catholic faith, namely *Dei Filius*. And they are issues which Methodists, in common with all other Christians, must face. At the present juncture, we are invited to match our reflections with the solutions proposed by the Roman Catholic Church.

In its Honolulu Report (1981),[3] the Joint Commission between the Roman Catholic Church and the World Methodist Council declared its belief that "emotions surrounding such relatively modern terms as infallibility and irreformability can be diminished if they are looked at in the light of our shared doctrine concerning the Holy Spirit" (35). By way of experiment I want to take up pneumatology at its anthropological end and inquire whether any help is to be found for our problem in the characteristically Wesleyan doctrine of the "assurance of faith" and the consequent call to "entire sanctification" or "Christian perfection."

These very terms may initially arouse suspicion in Roman Catholics. In its decree and canons on justification, the Council of Trent rejected and anathematized the "vana fiducia et certitudo" of the Protestant heretics. Moreover, Roman Catholics have preferred to reserve "sinlessness" for the Church, the Body of Christ and conceived to be hypostatically distinct from its members. There may in fact be difficulties from both the Catholic and the Methodist sides about transferring the categories of assurance and entire sanctification, which for Wesley belong to the "ordo salutis" of the individual Christian, into the corporate realm of ecclesiology. All these problems will eventually be tackled.

Meanwhile I request the patience particularly of Catholics, since the experiment may help at least Methodists to face from a more familiar perspective the very real question to which the doctrine of ecclesial and even papal infallibility points. In the best of outcomes, our procedure might also make a modest contribution to Catholic understanding. A convergence in this matter, however slight, would be ecumenically significant, and the experiment is worth trying.

II. *Assurance and Entire Sanctification*

Let us, then, examine the Wesleyan teaching on assurance and entire sanctification with an eye to the contribution it may make to the question of maintenance in the truth.

1. Assurance

(A) In his study of *The Doctrine of Assurance, With Special Reference to John Wesley*, A. S. Yates concludes about the Aldersgate event that "24th May 1738 was the first occasion on which John Wesley gained an assurance of personal salvation centred in a crucified Christ."[4] The account from Wesley's *Journal* must be examined with precisely our kind of question in mind: "I felt I did trust in Christ, Christ alone for salvation; and an assurance was given me, that he had taken away *my* sins, even *mine*, and saved *me* from the law of sin and death."

(B) Now this represents neither "justification by feeling," as the anti-Pietist among the Lutherans suspect, nor "justification by faith *itself*," which the ninth chapter of the Tridentine decree on justification seems to think all Protestants guilty of holding. Catholics, Lutherans and Wesleyans alike hold faith to be grounded "outside ourselves" in Christ and his work. The "faith which is believed (*fides quae creditur*)" calls for "the faith which believes (*fides quâ creditur*)," and the *fides quâ creditur* is directed to the *fides quae creditur*; the act of faith and the object of faith are reciprocally related. The *assurance* of which Wesley speaks—and we shall see in a moment how far he came to think this normal for Christians—is also objective, in the twofold sense that it is assurance of *a fact* (Christ's saving death and its availance "for me"), and that it is *given* (by the Holy Spirit, and therefore not internally generated by my own imagination). Yet the assurance, like faith itself, is given *to me*, so that by God's grace it becomes also the word for my subjective attitude toward God and, *mutatis mutandis*, the world.

(C) What does Wesley mean when he calls assurance "the common privilege" of Christians?[5] Wesley allows that there are "degrees of faith."[6] In the most general way,[7] "faith is an evidence or conviction of things not seen, of God, and of the things of God" (cf. Hebrews 11:1, where the Revised Standard Version translates *hypostasis* as "assurance"). "More particularly," says Wesley, faith "is a divine evidence or conviction that Christ loved me and gave himself for me." And finally, continuing from the letter of 1760: "When this evidence is heightened to exclude all doubt, it is the plerophory or full assurance of faith" (the expression *plêrophoria pisteôs* occurs at Hebrews 10:22). Whatever may have been the case in the earliest years after 1738, by the later 1740s Wesley held—as the mention of "exempt cases" in the Minutes of the first Methodist Conferences also shows—that a believer might be justified even though not all doubts and fears were yet removed.[8] In 1768 he writes that he has "not for many years thought a consciousness of acceptance to be essential to justifying faith."[9] In later years, Wesley admitted that the early Methodist preachers had not clearly enough understood that "even one 'who feareth God, and worketh righteousness, is accepted of Him'"; so that it might be said—though that "is all that can be said with propriety"—that such a one was already a *servant* of God, even if not yet a *child* of God.[10]

(D) By the (full) *assurance* of faith—and Wesley sometimes omits the adjective even when he has *plêrophoria pisteôs* in mind—Wesley means "an assurance of being *now* in the favour of God."[11] He distinguishes this sharply from the "assurance of hope" (the *plêrophoria tês elpidos* of Hebrews 6:11). Thus in the *Notes on the New Testament*:[12] "The full assurance of faith relates to present pardon; the full measure of hope, to future glory. The former is the highest degree of divine evidence, that God is reconciled to me in the Son of his love; the latter is the same degree of divine evidence (wrought in the soul by the same immediate inspiration of the Holy Ghost) of persevering grace, and of eternal glory." And in a letter of 1781:[13] "The plerophory (or full assurance) of faith is such a clear conviction that *I am now* in the favour of God as excludes all doubt and fear concerning it. The full assurance of hope is such clear confidence that *I shall enjoy* the glory of God as excludes all doubt and fear concerning this."

Of the "full assurance of hope" Wesley knows in 1751 that some claim it;[14] yet in 1768 he remains hesitant about the number who have it: "I believe a few, but very few, Christians have an assurance from God of everlasting salvation."[15] And such "full assurance of hope" he also distinguishes, in the letter of 1781, from the (Calvinist) *doctrine*—which Wesley demotes to an "opinion"—of final perseverance: "This confidence is totally different from an opinion that 'no saint shall fall from grace.' It has no relation to it . . . The giving way to anything unholy . . . clouds the full assurance of hope, which cannot subsist any longer than the heart cleaves steadfastly to God."[16] Here re-emerges in Wesley that same fear of antinomianism which motivated also the Council of Trent to condemn "a rash presumptuousness in the matter of predestination" and a consequent "absolute certainty" about perseverance as the Reformers seemed to teach (Decree on Justification, chs. 12–13, canons 15–16). To this we shall return soon. Suffice it for the moment to say, with the Roman Catholic/Methodist Dublin Report of 1976, that Methodists do not see the assurance of faith as "a form of certainty which removes the need for hope" (12, n.6).[17]

(E) The last point to be made in connection with the assurance of faith is to underline that such assurance is, both directly and indirectly, a work of the Holy Spirit. On the basis of Romans 8:15f. and Galatians 4:6, Wesley taught an inward witness of the Spirit to the human spirit, assuring justified believers that they are "children of God." It gives them the confidence to cry "Abba, Father." In Charles Wesley's words:

> My God is reconciled,
> His pardoning voice I hear;
> He owns me for His child,
> I can no longer fear;
> With confidence I now draw nigh,
> And Father, Abba, Father! cry.[18]

This confidence before God spills over into the proclamation before men of a gospel of forgiveness which, as the allusion to I John 1:1-3 shows, is grounded in the incarnation:

> What we have felt and seen
> With confidence we tell,
> And publish to the sons of men
> The signs infallible.[19]

61

With assurance goes apostolic boldness, *parrhêsia* (Acts 4:31, etc.).[20] According to I Thessalonians 1:5, Paul and his companions preached the gospel "not only in word, but also in power and in the Holy Spirit and with full assurance (*plêrophoriai pollêi*)."

The inward and direct witness of the Spirit is accompanied by an indirect witness, whereby our spirit concludes to our being children of God from the fruit of the Spirit in our lives. Charles Wesley switches from the indwelling Spirit of I John 4:13 and 5:10 to the visible evidences of Galatians 5:22f.:

> His Spirit to us He gave,
> And dwells in us, we know;
> The witness in ourselves we have.
> And all its fruits we show.[21]

Or in the words of John Wesley's second sermon on "The Witness of the Spirit" (1767): "If the Spirit of God does really testify that we are the children of God, the immediate consequence will be the fruit of the Spirit, even 'love, joy, peace, long-suffering, gentleness, goodness, fidelity, meekness, temperance.'"[22]

In the First Letter of John, the ethical test comes in the shape of "keeping the commandments" (2:29; 3:10; 5:18 etc.). The Wesleys join both Paul and John in combining an inward witness which may be "strong and permanent and clear"—

> Holy Ghost, no more delay;
> Come, and in Thy temple stay;
> Now Thine inward witness bear,
> Strong, and permanent, and clear[23]—

with an outward demonstration of the Spirit's work:

> Thus may I show thy Spirit within
> . . . .
> The truth of my religion prove
> By perfect purity and love.[24]

(F) To summarize up to this point. In so far as it may be possible to move from the individual Christian's assurance of faith to the Church's assurance of faith, we would expect the latter to have the following characteristics:

(i) It would be a gift of God by the Holy Spirit.

(ii) It would express a lived and living experience of the redeeming work of God in Christ.

(iii) It would result in a confession of faith in which the *fides quâ creditur* corresponded to the *fides quae creditur*, and vice versa.[25]

(iv) It would focus on truths "of the last importance," entering "into the very heart of Christianity."[26]

(v) It would be the "common privilege" of the Church in its everyday living, teaching, preaching and mission.

(vi) It would concern the rightness of the Church's present faith and proclamation at a given time. There would be no guarantee in face of a loss of living relationship to God, whether past or future.

(vii) The more visible are the fruits of the Spirit in the life of the Church, the greater will be the persuasiveness of the claim that its preaching and teaching rests upon an inward witness of the Holy Spirit. In the words of the Honolulu Report:[27] "The papal authority, no less than any other within the Church, is a manifestation of the continuing presence of the Spirit of Love in the Church or it is nothing" (35).

With that remark, the bridge is made from assurance to entire sanctification. Does this teaching of the Wesleys contain any further hints towards answering our principal question of maintenance in the truth?

2. Entire Sanctification

(A) John Wesley preached, and Charles Wesley sang, entire sanctification as a divine gift to be prayed and striven for by believers.[28] Positively formulated, entire sanctification consists in perfect love toward God and neighbor, in line with the dual great commandment of Mark 12:29-31. Jesus exhorted his hearers to "be perfect, as your heavenly Father is perfect" (Matthew 5:48), and God does not command the impossible. The preaching and teaching of the Church should subserve holiness: for holiness is "religion itself."[29]

(B) Apart from the fact that absolute perfection belonged to God alone, Wesley also recognized, however, that even Christian perfection was in this life limited by the persistent effects of the Fall. While the Christian person was fundamentally oriented toward God in its will and was having its nature renewed in knowledge after the image of its Creator (cf. Colossians 3:10), yet it was not altogether exempt from the frailty and ignorance inherited from Adam. Error thereby remained possible, even to the perfect—though not (and here the correspondence between the *fides quâ creditur* and the *fides quae creditur* comes importantly into play) in "matters essential to salvation."[30] Both the gift of perfection and its limits will be significant considerations, if we try to pass from the "ordo salutis" of the individual to a characterization of the Church.

(C) It would be a pity to waste the positive dynamic of Wesley's

63

teaching on sanctification and perfection. For its thrust is not only emotive and ethical but also epistemological and ecumenical. The high-priestly prayer of Jesus in John 17 is illuminating here. Jesus prayed for his disciples that the Father would "sanctify them in the truth," adding "Thy word is truth" (v. 17). He also prayed that they might "be perfected into one" (v. 23: *hina ôsin teteleiômenoi eis hen*). Since, in God, truth and love are one, it may be assumed that true teaching is best conducive to love, while love will give insight into the truth of God. Loving reconciliation among divided Christians is itself an attempt at conformity to truth, and the process may be expected to bring us closer not only to one another but to God. Striving for perfection in this realm will undergird our effort towards a common proclamation of the one gospel according to the truth of God. It is in this context that the question of communion with the see of Rome must be faced.[31]

It is now time to ask more directly whether the Wesleyan notion of the "assurance of faith" and the consequent call to "entire sanctification" may in fact be helpful to Methodists and Catholics in connection with maintenance in the truth. The difficulty of principle resides in the applicability to the Church of categories originally elaborated with reference to the individual believer.

III. *The Believer and the Church*

(A) The Honolulu Report[32] encourages us to think that it may be acceptable to use the same language of both the Church and the Christian in the area of our inquiry.

Under the heading "The Holy Spirit at Work in Justification and Regeneration," the following statements are made:

> 16. "The Spirit himself is bearing witness with our spirit that we are children of God" (Rom. 8:16). We receive the Spirit of adoption, who dwells in Christians, pouring God's love into our hearts, enabling us to say "Abba" . . .
>
> 17. According to the Fourth Gospel, the ultimate purpose of the mission of Jesus was to give the gift of the Holy Spirit to his disciples (Jn. 20:22f.) . . . It is his role to teach us, the disciples of Jesus, all things necessary for our salvation and bring to our remembrance all that Jesus said (Jn. 14:26). Because he is the Spirit of Truth, he bears witness to Jesus and enables us to be witnesses in our turn (15:26f.). He guides us into all the truth, declares the things that are to come, and so glorifies Jesus (16:13f.).
>
> 18. The Holy Spirit sanctifies the regenerate Christian. Sanctification is a process that leads to perfect love. Life in the Spirit is human

life, lived out in faith, hope and love, to its utmost in consonance with God's gracious purposes in and for his children. As Wesley put it, the end of human existence is the recovery and the surpassing of the perfection in which that existence was first conceived and created. . . .

And then, ecclesiologically, under the heading "The Holy Spirit and the Christian Community" it is said:

> 19. The chief mark of the post-Easter Church is that God gives to it the Spirit and thus creates the community of the New Covenant. . . .
> 21. The Spirit guides the development of the Church. In every age, as the Paraclete, he reminds us of all that Jesus said, leads us into all truth, and enables us to bear witness to salvation in Christ. The Holy Spirit inspires Christians as they seek to obey Christ's commission to make disciples of all nations. At the last God will triumph over sin and death and, in fulfillment of his pledge of the Spirit, bring all who love him to unending glory.

When, in a further section, the Honolulu Report comes to consider "Christian Experience," it "sees it as the Spirit's guiding and ordering work in the Church" and declares:

> 24. Christian religious experience includes the assurance of God's unmerited mercy in Christ, the inner witness of the Spirit that we are indeed children of God, pardoned and reconciled to the Father (Rom. 8:12-17). The same Spirit also guides the faithful to a knowledge of all the truth as it is in Christ Jesus . . . Despite our inability to manifest it properly, the fruit of the Spirit (Gal. 5:22f.) is ever a potent factor in drawing others into Christian fellowship.

(B) Gratifying though they are, it is possible that these agreed statements hide a deep difference as to the relation between the Christian and the Church. This difference may come to light in the way Catholics and Methodists are likely to come from diametrically opposed approaches to our question of the common applicability to Christians and to the Church of categories connected with maintenance in the truth. While Methodists make, within limits, positive claims for assurance and the possibility of entire sanctification in the case of the individual believer, they incline to doubt whether those categories can be applied to the Church as an institution. For they know, in the negative, that many lacking in faith and love remain within the institutional Church and affect its life. Does this not impair the Church's capacity to discern and proclaim God's truth? The question is bound to arise: Who is to be reckoned within the Church?

In the other direction, Catholics following the Council of Trent show the gravest suspicion towards individual believers claiming either the assurance of faith or the assurance of hope, and yet Roman Catholics affirm—in all form since Vatican I—the infallibility and indefectibility of "the Church." According to Vatican I, it is precisely the function of "the Church" to "raise the fallen, to support those who are falling, to embrace those who return, to confirm the good and to carry them on to better things. Hence it can never forbear from witnessing to and proclaiming the truth of God" (*Dei Filius* intro., with appeal to Isaiah 59:21: "My Spirit that is in thee, and my words that I have put in thy mouth, shall not depart out of thy mouth, from henceforth and forever.") And again: "And, that we may be able to satisfy the obligation of embracing the true faith, and of constantly persevering in it, God has instituted the Church through his only-begotten Son, and has bestowed on it manifest notes of that institution, that it may be recognized by all as the guardian and teacher of the revealed Word" (*Dei Filius*, 3).

The question again becomes: Where is "the Church" located? How is it composed? Who are members of it?

(C) The same question can be raised specifically from the angle of authority. Again, the Honolulu Report presents a fine agreed statement:

33. To men and women sealed by the Spirit in baptism, gathered in the Church, in the communion of Christ's gift of himself, Christ's authority is mediated through the Spirit, who is Love, and hence all authority that flows from this source is part of God's good gift . . .

34. There is no disagreement that the Church has authority to teach. In the Church, the revelation of God in Christ comes to us through Scripture, and to maintain God's people in the truth is the loving work of the Spirit in the Church . . . This maintenance is not a matter of mere repetition of formulae. The Spirit moves the Church to constant reflection on the Scriptures which he himself inspired and on their traditional interpretation, so that she may speak with undiminished authority to men in different times and places, in different social and cultural settings, facing new and difficult problems. This is not of course to question the abiding importance of credal statements and such conciliar pronouncements as the Chalcedonian definition. The enduring validity of these does not restrict the power of the Spirit to speak in new ways to the Church, whose living voice never speaks in isolation from its living past. It stands under the living word of God. The old oppositions of Scripture and Tradition have given way to an understanding which we share, that Scripture in witness to the living tradition from which it arose has a normative role for the total tradition of the Church as it lives and is guided still by the Spirit of truth.

66

Yet a later reiteration of these principles in fact leads into a crucial, and willy nilly *ecclesiological*, difference between Methodists and Catholics:

> 46. . . . We are in agreement that the Church must always be subject to the headship of the Incarnate Lord and that the Holy Spirit makes Christ present to us, so mediating his authority to us in love through Word and Sacraments; these in turn are witnessed to by the worshipping community and by Creeds and Confessions. Only then do we come to the point of divergence, which must not be allowed to obscure this agreement. Within this context, *what persons or bodies in the Church can give guidance on moral* [the question could equally have included "doctrinal"] *issues and with what authority?*

The question concerning the location and composition of the Church and that concerning authority in the Church are obviously linked: Who decides on the location and composition of the Church? Who determines its membership? And that leads us back once more to the discernment and proclamation of God's truth, whether the question be put in terms of assurance or in terms of infallibility/indefectibility.

(D) Let us try to come again at the matter of the Church and of Christians, with our principal question concerning maintenance in the truth in view. Hans Küng holds that "the message of Jesus continually produces faith, so that Jesus remains in the community of believers and his Spirit constantly guides them afresh into the whole truth."[33] Thus truth is maintained in "the believing community"—despite the errors attributed to "authorities" and "institutions." This is rather an invisibilist conception of the Church. It approximates the idea that the Church consists simply, at any given time, of the sum of "true believers." That is a position towards which Wesley sometimes tended.[34] It is a permanent inclination, as long as the assurance of faith remains at the individual level. It leaves entirely open the question of how conflicts concerning God's truth are to be regulated. Where is one to look for an authoritative discernment and proclamation of the gospel?

The communal nature of the Church in fact requires institutional bonds in time and space. An official authority, lodged in persons capable of decision, is necessary to discern whether any particular "congregation of believers" is one "in which the pure Word of God is preached, and the Sacraments be duly administered according to Christ's institution"—as Wesley also recognizes, following Article XIX of the Church of England, to belong to a definition of "the visible Church."[35] The various Methodist denominations characteristically lodge this authority in their respective Conferences, though we may admit that this has not been without problems in the practical exercise. The very fact that the need for an official authority is recognized means that the Roman Catholic solution cannot be excluded from consideration if it might help in the solution of problems that arise from the tendency to start viewing the Christian faith from the angle of the individual believer.

Enough hints have now been dropped that Catholics and Methodists might have things to learn from one another in the matter of maintenance in the truth. In conclusion we can tentatively formulate the learning that might take place.

IV. Mutual Learning and the Move Toward an Answer

Methodists might learn from Catholics, first, the valuable part played by the Christian community in bringing the individual believer to an assured faith and keeping the believer in it.[36] It is the larger Church which proclaims the gospel and teaches the faith, supports the waverer and corrects the wayward. It would be an unconscionable let-down if what was ostensibly "the Church" were in fact to be seriously misleading individual seekers, and indeed adherents, in the knowledge of salvation.

Second, Methodists might learn from Catholics to recognize better the diachronic character of the Christian community. The "faith once delivered to the saints" (Jude 3) has found its witnesses in every age. Its sense of "depth in history" constitutes one of the great strengths of Catholicism.[37] The substantive content and spiritual example of the witness of our predecessors in the faith contribute to the assurance of the Church, both in the *fides quae creditur* and in the *fides quâ creditur*. For all the changing circumstances of time and space, the Christian faith does not have to be invented anew in each generation.

The third lesson from Catholics to Methodists brings together the first two by confirming the need for an institutional embodiment of the Church, with a willingness to set substantive conditions of faith and practice for its own membership and a procedure for taking authoritative decisions on doctrine. The 1972 Statement of the United Methodist Church[38] allows that the pioneers of Methodism were "confident that there is a 'marrow' of Christian truth that can be identified and that must be conserved. This living core, as they believed, stands revealed in Scripture, illumined by tradition, vivified in personal experience, and confirmed by reason." But when it came to "our theological task" or "doctrinal guidelines in the United Methodist Church"—the 1972 statement unfortunately confused doctrine and theology, two activities which, though they exist on a continuum, nevertheless need some distinction—the best that could be proposed was a permanent and rather formal interplay among Scripture, tradition, experience and reason. "Rigidity" and "enforcement" are abjured. The question remains: *Who* identifies and conserves the marrow of Christian truth?

In summarizing what Methodists might learn from Catholics, the English Methodist/Roman Catholic Statement on Authority (1978)[39] concluded thus:

> 34. Methodists might be guided by Catholics to a greater trust in God's unfailing promises for the Church of Christ. The victory of the truth to which the Church is called to bear witness is not entirely withheld till the end, for already on the way God preserves the Church from any failure so serious as to make it impossible to hear the gospel. A personal sign of that continuity of the Church in the truth is the succession of local bishops from the early years of Christian history. The historically central see of Rome can be seen to constitute an institutional focus of episcopal and churchly unity. . . .

The same Statement in turn summarizes the possible contribution of Methodists to Catholics:

> 35. Catholics might be led by Methodists to a greater awareness of the fallibility of the human response to the divine promise and guidance. Reforming and prophetic figures have at times been needed to recall the Church to the Christ who is both the way and the goal, and to whom the Scriptures bear permanent witness. . . .

My own further reflection would lead to the following formulation of what a Methodist might hope the Catholic Church would receive from Methodism.

First, the notions of infallibility and indefectibility could take on more warmth and personal character if the language of assurance were used to make clear the concern for the salvation of individual human beings that underlies the Church's claimed need of certitude in its preaching and teaching (*Dei Filius*, 3; *Pastor aeternus*, 4).

Second, a certain modesty is in order, given the entire dependence of the Church on God and the room for error which even entire sanctification leaves on earth.

Third, Methodism has a continuous history of conciliarity and internal consultation. The United Methodist Statement of 1972 said that the early Methodists "turned to a unique version of the ancient 'conciliar principle,' in which the collective wisdom of living Christian pastors, teachers and people was relied upon to guard and guide their ongoing communal life. Wesley's agency for this collegial process he called the Conference. . . ." This is not to claim perfection, even carefully limited, for the way in which the principles of Conference and Connexion have operated in Methodism. But the Methodist pattern offers to a community of love a means by which the faith and gifts of all may be appreciated. In a conciliar and consultative pattern, there is no simple distinction between the teachers and the taught (*Ecclesia docens* and *Ecclesia discens*), even though the particular teaching office of some in the service of all is respected. There could even be room for what the English Methodists and Catholics in 1978 jointly envisaged as the "special and ongoing responsibility of the bishop of Rome" in his "calling of, and active presidency within, a universal council of the Church, whenever the situation demanded decision and action by the whole Church" (36).

The matter of the appropriate relations between the universal, the regional and the local Church is one on which Methodists and Catholics could work together, starting from different ends. Methodists throughout the world trust that they hold a recognizably similar faith, but this sense might not withstand closer investigation. Methodist Conferences in fact rarely treat doctrinal issues in much depth,[40] and there is no structure whereby the *various* Methodist Churches consult one another on doctrine. It is conceivable that the World Methodist Council might be developed in this direction; but ultimately the question is a fully ecumenical one. Roman Catholics, on the other hand, are beginning to explore the relative independence which the principle of subsidiarity allows to the diocese and also, perhaps, to the new institution of national or regional episcopal conferences. This may even, in some geographical areas, allow closer relations with other Churches than are yet possible everywhere. Yet Roman Catholics will not want to forfeit the advantage of a universal communion whose touchstone is Rome.

Conclusion

As between the Roman Catholic Church and the Methodist Churches the crucial questions remain: of how each relates the Church as institution to the Church as community of faith; of whether and in what sense each recognizes the other as Church; and of what more is needed, on both sides and in common, before Methodists and Catholics can recognize each other as Church in the same sense as they recognize themselves as Church and so reach "the goal of full communion in faith, mission and sacramental life."[41] On the latter question, a Methodist may wonder: would the "meta-dogma" of papal infallibility—or, for that matter, scriptural inerrancy—be required belief if the Churches *otherwise* substantially shared the same faith in all things essential?[42] A Catholic might shift the register from law to grace by proposing that the papacy is God's provision to the institutional Church of a living voice to determine and declare the faith by sharing in which all may be saved.

It is certain that there is ultimately only One "who is able to keep you from falling and to present you without blemish before the presence of his glory": and so to this "only God, our Saviour, through Jesus Christ our Lord, be glory, majesty, dominion and authority, before all time and now and for ever" (Jude 24f.).

CHAPTER THREE

The End of All Ecclesiastical Order

"What," asked John Wesley, "is the end of all ecclesiastical order?"
And he immediately supplied his own answer:

> Is it not to bring souls from the power of Satan to God, and to build
> them up in His fear and love? Order, then, is so far valuable as it
> answers these ends; and if it answers them not, it is nothing worth.

In this letter of June 25, 1746, to "John Smith,"[1] Wesley was responding
to charges of "breaking or setting aside order—that is, the rules of our
own Church, both by preaching in the fields and by using extempory
prayer." Note that in locating himself in relation to "order" or "a plan of
Church discipline," Wesley is here treating matters that belong only at the
level of local canonical regulations in the contemporary Church of England. When, in other contexts, Wesley discussed "order" in the profounder
and more permanent sense of the "sacramental" structures of ministry in
space and time, he found the Church of England to match up quite well
to "the scriptural, the primitive."[2] That Wesley was concerned for a
differentiated ministry and for the transmission of ministerial office is
shown by the care he took—however controversially and problemati-
cally—to supply such for the American Church; and we shall return to
those questions later. But it must be clear from the outset that Wesley's
attitude towards "*all* ecclesiastical order" was soteriologically governed
and rather pragmatic in its criteria. That attitude has remained characteristic of Methodism, and it is well for our ecumenical partners to be
aware of the position from which we enter into dialogue.

So let us first of all emphasize the dual ends of evangelism and
edification that Wesley sees Church order as serving: "to bring souls from
the power of Satan to God, and to build them up in His fear and love."

I. Mission in the World

Already in a letter of 1739 to James Hervey, his former Oxford pupil,[3] Wesley justified his itinerant preaching against accusations of "intermeddling" in "other men's parishes":

I look upon all the world as my parish . . . I mean, that in whatever part of it I am I judge it meet, right, and my bounden duty to declare, unto all that are willing to hear, the glad tidings of salvation. This is the work which I know God has called me to; and sure I am that His blessing attends it.

Wesley claims scriptural authority for this: "God in Scripture commands me, according to my power, to instruct the ignorant, reform the wicked, confirm the virtuous [Wesley here appears to be summarizing the charge given to Timothy in the Pastoral Epistles] . . . A dispensation of the gospel is committed to me; and woe is me if I preach not the gospel [Wesley is here aligning himself with the apostle Paul himself]." And in the letter to "John Smith" already cited he makes implicit appeal to the results of his preaching "among the tinners in Cornwall, the keelmen at Newcastle, the colliers in Kingswood or Staffordshire, . . . the drunkards, swearers, sabbath-breakers of Moorfields, or the harlots of Drury Lane."

The *itinerancy at home* and the *sending of missionaries abroad* have been among the most characteristic features in Methodist ministerial practice. If, for various reasons, both these features have recently receded, the theological rationale for whatever replaces them will usually be proposed—however self-deceptively—in terms of evangelism. The "spread of" what is perceived to be "the gospel" is a constant motive in the discussion and exercise of ministry by Methodists.

II. Upbuilding in Fellowship

An internal purpose of the Church is, in Wesley's words, "to build [souls] up in [God's] fear and love." And to "John Smith" Wesley boldly claimed: "Wherever the knowledge and love of God are, true order will not be wanting." The relationship between growth in grace and order in the Church is in fact—or at least in principle—reciprocal. Wesley created a highly structured fellowship in which converts were gathered into "societies," "classes" and "bands" for purposes of pastoral care and mutual support. Communion with God was enjoyed in and through communion with fellow believers.

Charles Wesley's hymns bring out the order of the common body:

Let us join—'tis God commands—
Let us join our hearts and hands;
Help to gain our calling's hope,
Build we each the other up. . . .

Sweetly each, with each combined,
In the bonds of duty joined,
Feels the cleansing blood applied,
Daily feels that Christ hath died. . . .

Hence may all our actions flow,
Love the proof that Christ we know;
Mutual love the token be,
Lord, that we belong to Thee.[4]

Or, in another hymn that recognizes diversity of gift and function for the common good of the "mystic body" in its "one spirit" ("Christ, from whom all blessings flow"):

Move, and actuate, and guide;
Divers gifts to each divide;
Placed according to Thy will,
Let us all our work fulfil.

Sweetly may we all agree,
Touched with loving sympathy:
Kindly for each other care;
Every member feel its share.[5]

Moreover, the local societies into which converts were gathered were linked together in a "connexion" under the oversight of itinerant preachers, the Conference, and Wesley himself. Nor was fellowship lost with

. . . our friends above,
That have obtained the prize.[6]

It remains characteristic of Methodism that all Church structures, including the ordering of the ministry, will be tested by their contribution to communion with God and among Christians.

Evangelism and edification: having thus posed the original Wesleyan—and continuing Methodist—bases, we may now once again examine, from a Methodist standpoint, the questions that arise between Methodists and Roman Catholics concerning ecclesiastical order: the diachronic question of succession in office; the synchronic question of the diversity and range of functions; the magisterial question of a teaching authority; the pastoral question of a ministry of unity. Methodists will be

75

helped insofar as Catholics can show that their understanding and practice in these matters derive from a common concern for evangelism and edification. Catholics may be helped if Methodists can show that their overriding concerns for evangelism and edification have not caused them to neglect what may broadly be called the "sacramental" expressions of ecclesial life, but rather that their very same concerns keep Methodists open to consider (and even adopt, if this would further the causes of evangelism and edification) the institutional forms which the "sacramental" expressions have taken precisely in the Roman Church.

III. Succession in Office

The widest form and context of the question of succession in office is the question of Tradition. Let us begin with a thumbnail sketch of Church history from a familiar author:

> In the fifth century, the non-Chalcedonians split from the hitherto undivided Church. Then the Byzantine East broke away in 1054. The unreformed Roman Catholics were left behind in the sixteenth century, while the continental Protestants had the misfortune of being foreigners. In the eighteenth century, even the Church of England refused Wesley's mission, so that finally only Methodists remained in the body of Christ.[7]

When I first wrote that tongue-in-cheek account, I was of course putting a brave face on things. In point of fact, Methodists do tend to think that they originated in the eighteenth century only. In common with many Protestants who emphasize their sixteenth-century beginnings, Methodists have a rather weak view of the (pre-Reformation) Tradition of the Church. While the Reformers and Wesley held a high view of the patristic Church (though Wesley at least subscribed in some measure to the theory of a "Constantinian fall"),[8] Protestants incline to an episodic view of Christian history, lending some credibility to Newman's dictum that "to be deep in history is to cease to be Protestant."[9] They look on present occurrences that evidently enjoy divine blessing as fresh instantiations of scriptural and apostolic events and structures, or at least of what God was doing in and through those events and structures. Note how Wesley, in a passage already cited, appropriated to his own case the words of Scripture and the commission of St. Paul. Listen now to Wesley's account of the origins and early development of ministerial order in the Church, where it is quite obvious that he is *also* telling—with a view to justifying it—the story of the rise of Methodism under his own itinerant preaching and continuing oversight:

76

The plain origin of church-government seems to be this. Christ sends forth a preacher of the gospel. Some who hear him repent and believe the gospel. They then desire him to watch over them, to build them up in the faith and to guide their souls in the paths of righteousness. Here then is an independent congregation, subject to no pastor but their own, neither liable to be controlled in things spiritual by any other man or body of men whatsoever. But soon after, some from other parts, who are occasionally present while he speaks in the name of him that sent him, beseech him to come over and help them, also. Knowing it to be the will of God, he complies, yet not till he has conferred with the wisest and holiest of his congregation and, with their advice, appointed one who has gifts and grace to watch over the flock till his return.

If it please God to raise another flock in the new place, before he leaves them he does the same thing, appointing one whom God has fitted for the work to watch over these souls also. In like manner, in every place where it pleases God to gather a little flock by his Word, he appoints one in his absence to take the oversight of the rest and to assist them of the ability which God giveth. These are deacons, or servants of the church, and look on their first pastor as their common father. And all these congregations regard him in the same light and esteem him still as the shepherd of their souls.

These congregations are not strictly independent. They depend on one pastor, though not on each other.

As these congregations increase, and as the deacons grow in years and grace, they need other subordinate deacons or helpers, in respect of whom they may be called "Presbyters," or elders, as their father in the Lord may be called the "Bishop" or Overseer of them all.[10]

This understanding of present order as instantiation of the original is not unrespectable. Faith and Order's Lima text on *Baptism, Eucharist and Ministry*[11] designates it the Ignatian view:

> Ignatius of Antioch . . . regards the Christian community assembled around the bishop in the midst of presbyters and deacons as the *actual* manifestation in the Spirit of the apostolic community. (Ministry, 36 comm. "Actual" is to be taken in the French sense of *actuel*, "present.")

Something very similar is to be found in the Roman Catholic notion, common since Vatican II, of the present college of bishops, with the pope in their midst, as the repristination of the apostolic college gathered around Peter (remembering that a common title of the bishop of Rome in the earlier middle ages was "vicar of Peter").

Yet there is also another way of envisaging the connection of present ministry with the original apostolate. The Lima text associates it with Clement of Rome:

> Clement of Rome linked the mission of the bishop with the sending of Christ by the Father and the sending of the apostles by Christ. This made the bishop a successor of the apostles, ensuring the permanence of the apostolic mission in the Church. Clement is primarily interested in the means whereby the *historical* continuity of Christ's presence is ensured in the Church thanks to the apostolic succession. (ibid.)

That view has perhaps predominated in the Church of Rome and still prevails in the Roman Catholic Church today, even if it is now complemented by the "Ignatian" view. Its difficulty for Methodists resides in its insistence on *continuity*. John Wesley wrote to his brother Charles on August 19, 1785: "The uninterrupted succession I know to be a fable, which no man ever did or can prove."[12] At a deeper level (I do not claim Wesley for my authority here), interruptions of the succession would be a kind of negative sacrament of the failures of the Church in fidelty to the gospel, while resumptions in the orderly transmission of ministry would be signs of the renewing grace of God at work in the Church. It was by a Methodist hand (my own) that the Lima document included the following recognition:

> At some points of crisis in the history of the Church, the continuing functions of ministry were in some places and communities distributed according to structures other than the predominant threefold pattern. Sometimes appeal was made to the New Testament in justification of other patterns. In other cases, the restructuring of ministry was held to lie within the competence of the Church as it adapted to changed circumstances. (Ministry, 19)

This point will be further discussed in the next section, when it is a question of the distribution of functions and the range of their exercise; but it needed to be mentioned already here, since such changes have often been interpreted by those who claim an episcopal succession as its loss (and—sometimes no doubt correctly—its deliberate rejection) by the others.

Wesley, in fact, was not so radical. His ordinations for America show that he believed *some kind* of succession worth preserving, or at least an orderly transmission of ministry; and he sought to justify his actions by reference to the early Church.[13] Since reading Peter King's *Account of the Primitive Church* in 1746, Wesley had held that "bishops and presbyters are (essentially) of one order."[14] That would account for his "sacramental power" in ordaining presbyters and deacons. But what of Thomas Coke, who was already a presbyter of the Church of England, and whom Wesley now "ordained" (the term in his private *Diary*), or "set apart" (the term in the public documents), to be "Superintendent" of the Methodist people and work in America? Most likely, Wesley considered that in the "extraordinary" (a word he was fond of using in this connection) circumstances of his (successful!) evangelistic mission, he had become a kind of "apostolic man" (the word is E. W. Thompson's,[15] but see the passage already quoted from the *Minutes* of 1745 for the reality!), who had in point of fact a duty of "oversight" towards his people (that, rather than the basic "sacramental" equation of bishop and presbyter, might be the point of his remark in 1785 that "I know myself to be as real a Christian bishop as the Archbishop of Canterbury"[16]). Coke was now being given a similar "oversight" for America. He was, in fact, to be "Joint Superintendent" with Francis Asbury, who accepted ordination as deacon, elder and superintendent only when his brethren in the Conference had approved of the "appointment" made by Wesley. Even after they started to use the title "bishop," American Methodists appear always to have held that the episcopate is not a "sacramentally" higher order than the eldership but rather an office of wider jurisdiction (though the reversion to the term of "consecration" as in the Book of Common Prayer hardly "proves" this, since the technical terms have rather a fluid history).

Both Wesley himself and the American Methodists, and perhaps even the British Methodists (who have a superintendency to which already ordained presbyters may simply be appointed), appear to share a view of the presbyterate and the episcopate and the relation between them that is quite compatible with a view that was present, and perhaps predominated, in the Latin Church from before Jerome and continued well beyond high scholasticism: presbyters and bishops are "sacramentally" of the same order, though bishops have a wider jurisdiction than presbyters. In the Roman Catholic Church since Vatican II greater favor is shown towards the more "Eastern" idea that bishops have the "fulness" of the sacrament of order (or, to put it colloquially, it is presbyters who are watered-down bishops, rather than bishops who are jumped-up presbyters). But this can scarcely be intended to "invalidate" the succession of ministers who were ordained earlier and on another understanding.

This, of course, does not settle the question of a "valid succession" for Methodists in Roman Catholic eyes. The Nairobi Report states that even American Methodists have "not claim[ed] apostolic succession in the sense of the Roman Catholic Church";[17] while in Britain the matter is perhaps even further complicated by that fact until 1836 entry into the ministry of Wesleyan Methodism was by way of "admission into full connexion with the Conference" rather than invariably by ordination through the laying on of hands.[18] And in any case, Methodist succession in the "pipeline" sense would depend on Anglican orders, which, as is well known, were declared null and void by Pope Leo XIII in 1896. No: when the time comes that Methodists and Roman Catholics declare their *readiness* for that "full unity in faith, mission and sacramental life" which we are working towards, the mutual recognition of ministries will have to be achieved by some creative and constitutive act whose precise nature will depend on the dogmatic agreements to which we have not yet already attained. Meanwhile it may be sufficient for Roman Catholics to note that neither Wesley nor later Methodists have been indifferent to a need for ritual and institutional forms in the matter of establishing and maintaining a ministry in the service of evangelism and edification.

There is, moreover, a third view—beside those of an Ignatian "manifestation" and a Clementine "continuity"—of succession in apostolic office. It has to do with the identity of the message. It can be argued that there is a mutually conditioning, and even dialectical, relationship between the message proclaimed and the authority to proclaim it. If this can be seen as at least a *component* in the doctrine of succession, then the way may be open for a convergence between Methodists and Catholics in which questions of "validity" and tactile transmission can be viewed in a different light. We will reserve that discussion for the next section but one.

IV. *Distribution in Functions*

The development of ministry in the Latin Church has to be seen against the background of the Roman Empire, where the *ordines* were distinguished from the *plebs* and where a graded civil service had its *cursus honorum*. Distinguished from the laity, the clergy acquired its own ladder of promotions through the minor orders to the subdiaconate and diaconate and finally the presbyterate and episcopate. While the notion of a "hierarchy" remains in force in the Roman Catholic Church, there have more recently been hints that a more "horizontal" model is needed to complement, if not supplant, the "vertical" one of superior and inferior ranks. This comes to liturgical expression, for example, in the eucharistic assembly normatively described in paragraph 41 of the Vatican II constitution *Sacrosanctum Concilium*:

> All should hold in great esteem the liturgical life of the diocese centered around the bishop, especially in his cathedral church; they must be convinced that the preeminent manifestation of the Church is present in the full, active participation of all God's people in these liturgical celebrations, especially in the same eucharist, in a single

prayer, at one altar at which the bishop presides, surrounded by his college of presbyters and by his ministers.

The picture is not dissimilar in the Lima text on *Baptism, Eucharist and Ministry*. The ordained ministry is needed by the Church as "a focus of its unity" (Ministry, 8). From the earliest references to a threefold ministry, "the bishop was the leader of the community. He was ordained and installed to proclaim the Word and preside over the celebration of the eucharist. He was surrounded by a college of presbyters and by deacons who assisted in his tasks. In this context the bishop's ministry was a focus of unity within the whole community" (20). Among the "diversity of gifts," "a ministry of *episkopé* is necessary to express and safeguard the unity of the body" (23). Bishops "have pastoral oversight of the area to which they are called" (29). While both the Vatican II and the Faith and Order texts retain the notions of *pre*sidency and *over*sight, the notions of "centre," "focus" and range of responsibility help to spread the functioning of the ordained ministry along a horizontal axis or plane in ways that will be more congenial to Methodists and perhaps even more in conformity with the gospel.

As we have already seen, Wesley willed for American Methodism an ordained ministry of superintendents, elders and deacons. Along with the Anglican Ordinal itself, he believed the form of ministry obtaining in the Church of England—of bishops, presbyters and deacons—to be scriptural and apostolic. However, he did not "find it asserted in Holy Writ" that "God designed the same plan should obtain in all churches throughout all ages." With the case of "the foreign Reformed Churches" in mind, he allows for "numberless accidental variations in the government of various churches," matching the fact that "God variously dispenses his gifts of nature, providence and grace."[19] If Wesley desired to replicate the Anglican pattern in America, it was doubtless because he considered the Church of England to be "the best constituted national Church in the world."[20]

Historians now recognize that it took a while beyond New Testament times for the threefold pattern of ordained ministry to develop and spread. The Lima text puts it with delicate ecclesiastical diplomacy: "During the second and third centuries, a threefold pattern of bishop, presbyter and deacon became established as the pattern of ordained ministry throughout the Church" (Ministry, 19). The Nairobi Report carefully states that "Roman Catholics and *some* Methodists . . . see a similarity . . . under the guidance of the Holy Spirit" between this development and the establishment of the canon of the Scriptures and the formation of the classical creeds (paragraph 29). Even if, however, it is necessary to raise the question of "divine law" and "human law" (*jus divinum* and *jus humanum*) in the matter of ministerial structures, there is perhaps no need to tackle it in "chronological" terms, or even in terms of the relation between Scripture and Tradition (where, in any case, there is an increasing ecumenical repugnance to playing them off one against the other). Methodists would, I think, be truer to themselves if they faced the question in *teleological* terms: "What is the *end* of all ecclesiastical order?"

In the current ecumenical context, one "end" of the threefold ministry is clearly the unity of Christians and among their communities. The Lima text proposes that "the threefold ministry of bishop, presbyter and deacon"—while standing "in need of reform" (Ministry, 24)—"may serve today as an expression of the unity we seek and also as a means for achieving it" (ibid. 22). (We may, I think, legitimately clarify this by locating the needed reform at the "practical" level, while seeing the threefold pattern itself as belonging to a "sacramental" order, broadly understood; paragraph 43 speaks of ordination in terms of God's entering "sacramentally" into historical forms.)

It is, of course, the *episcopal* component that is crucial in moves towards unity. The Nairobi Report notes that "the majority of Methodists already accept the office of bishop, and some Methodist Churches that do not have expressed their willingness to accept this for the sake of unity" (29). More precisely, "Methodist Churches which have an ordained ministry but do not have bishops, believing them not to be essential to a Church, have considered adopting them as an enrichment of their own life and to promote the unity of Christians; such bishops would be a focus of unity and a sign of the historic continuity of the Church" (ibid., 35). In point of fact, Methodists of British origin helped to constitute, and entered into, the Churches of South India (1947) and North India (1970), which are episcopally ordered and whose bishops derived their succession from the Anglican participants; and in Britain, the Methodist Church twice voted its willingness to "take episcopacy into our system" (as the phrase went) in the ultimately unsuccesful plans for reunion with the Church of England (1969) and for a "covenant among the churches" (1982).

Both American and British Methodists appear to regard episcopacy as belonging, at least in certain circumstances, to the "well being" (*bene esse*) of the Church (American Methodists cannot assign it to the "essence" [*esse*], otherwise they would be both unfaithful to Wesley and also out of communion with the British.) The "well being" that is envisaged ecumenically in the acquisition or recognition of an episcopate is the restoration, achievement or maintenance of unity. On neither side should the willingness of a church to become episcopal or have its episcopacy confirmed "for the sake of unity" be minimistically interpreted as a "sop to the Anglicans" or, *mutatis mutandis*, "to the Romans." Rather both sides, even if from different starting points, are setting a high value on episcopacy as (to use again the words of Lima) "an expression of the unity we seek" and "a means for achieving it." The episcopacy is being neither debased nor glorified: it is being properly subordinated to one of its ends, namely ecclesial unity. And communion among Christians—vital to the upbuilding of the Church—is itself soteriologically related to the doxological and missiological ends of communion with God and witness before the world:

> May the God of steadfastness and encouragement grant you to live in such harmony with one another, in accord with Christ Jesus, that together you may with one voice glorify the God and Father of our Lord Jesus Christ. (Rom. 15:5f.)

> I . . . pray . . . that they may all be one; even as thou, Father, art in me, and I in thee, that they also may be in us, so that the world may believe that thou hast sent me. (John 17:20f.)

Before leaving the question of distribution of functions, there is another matter that must at least be broached between Methodists and Catholics, and that is the matter of special priesthood. It is Roman Catholic teaching that bishops and presbyters exercise—particularly in the eucharist—a priesthood that differs in essence, and not merely in degree, from the general priesthood of the Church. Wesley held to his life's end, as the "Korah sermon" of May 4, 1789 shows,[21] that presidency at the Lord's Supper was properly restricted to the ordained as a priestly office. But Methodism has not followed him in this. Indeed British Methodism is constitutionally bound by the Deed of Union of 1932 to the view that ordained ministers "hold no priesthood differing in kind from that which is common to all the Lord's people"; and in both British and American Methodism, presidency at the Lord's Supper is, in carefully regulated circumstances of pastoral need, committed to lay people. Nevertheless the 1932 Deed recognizes the principle of "representative selection" in connection with ordination; and the notion of "representation" has more recently been much invoked in both British and American thinking on the matter, and indeed in wider ecumenical circles, including the Roman Catholic Church.[22] If I may quote what I myself wrote in connection with the Lima text's statement that ordained ministers "serve to build up the community in Christ and strengthen its witness" (Ministry, 12), and that "these tasks are not exercised by the ordained ministry in an exclusive" but rather "in a representative way" (ibid., 13, commentary):

> The notion of an ordained ministry as focalizing and enabling "representation" is good, and helps to break through the badly-formulated alternative of a difference in *kind* or in *degree* between the

83

ordained and the rest. Precisely as *representatives* of Christ and his church the ordained ministers are *distinct*, but *what* they represent is not *other* than the character and mission of the whole church, and this itself is nothing other than participation, by the grace of the Holy Spirit, in the ministry of Christ the Saviour and Head of the church.[23]

This may be applied particularly to priesthood at the eucharist. The eucharist is the preeminent liturgical form of our spiritual oblation; it is the sacrifice of praise *par excellence*. As such, it is made by the whole people in Christ. The eucharistic prayer is offered, from first to last, by the entire company: "Let us give thanks to the Lord our God. . . . through Jesus Christ our Lord. . . . Amen." To call "priests" those who preside in the liturgical assembly and voice its prayers may therefore be regarded as "appropriate," in rather a strong sense of the term, as the Lima text does (Ministry, 17). As a matter of historical fact, it is likely that, from the earliest days of the Church, regular presidency of the worshipping assembly helped to reinforce the leading role of the minister in the whole life of the congregation, just as leadership in the general life of the congregation will have made such persons the "natural" presidents of the worshipping assembly. The function of "the priest," in the ministerial sense, is not to deny the priesthood of the whole people in Christ but rather to help it to expression.

V. Maintenance in Truth

Now we come to the third model or component of a doctrine of succession in office, as promised in section III, namely identity in the apostolic message. Here we shall concentrate on the evangelistic purpose of ecclesial order, the proclamation of the true gospel.

The Lima text valuably locates ministerial succession within a notion of "Apostolic Tradition" that includes also other components: "witness to the apostolic faith, proclamation and fresh interpretation of the gospel, celebration of baptism and the eucharist, the transmission of ministerial responsibilities, communion in prayer, love, joy and suffering, service to the sick and needy, unity among the local churches and sharing the gifts which the Lord has given to each" (Ministry, 34). (One could wish that the Scriptures had been explicitly mentioned among these vehicles of the apostolic tradition.) The ordained ministry, and specifically the bishops, have "a particular task of preserving and actualizing the apostolic faith" (ibid. 35, cf. 36).

Such a location of episcopal succession within the broader apostolic tradition opens the door to an internal dialectical relationship between the episcopate and the apostolic faith. The bishops become the *servants* of that faith; but because there are other manifestations and vehicles of that faith (the Scriptures, the sacraments, the whole Christian life of believers . . .), there are also *criteria for discerning* when bishops are satisfactorily serving the preservation and proclamation of the faith and when they are failing in their responsibilities. This is why Lima can—quite properly, it seems to me—speak of "the episcopal succession as a sign, though not a guarantee, of the continuity and unity of the Church" (Ministry, 38).

That formulation has met with objections in the official responses to *Baptism, Eucharist and Ministry* on the part of the Orthodox and Roman Catholic Churches. They wish to maintain the language of "guarantee." But that depends logically on a Cyprianic ecclesiology, in which only the bishops of one's own community afford the guarantee, while bishops in schismatic bodies are at best dubious. In so far as the Orthodox and Roman Catholic Churches have, in other respects, abandoned a (by the way, mutually exclusive) Cyprianic ecclesiology, the way is surely open for a second, and more positive, look at the formulation "sign, though not a guarantee."

As between Catholics and Methodists, the Nairobi Report stated Roman Catholic teaching in this way: "The sucession in ministry is guaranteed by *episcopal laying-on of hands in historical succession* and *authentic transmission of the whole faith within the apostolic college and the communion of the whole Church*" (31, italics added). Methodists would, I think, like to see more of a dialectical relationship recognized between the two elements I have italicized. Quoting the earlier Dublin Report, the Nairobi Report represents the Methodist view as follows: "Methodists . . . preserve a form of ministerial succesion in practice and can regard a succession of ordinations from the earliest times as a valuable *symbol* of the church's continuity with the church of the New Testament, though they would not use it as a criterion" (31, italics in the original). I myself might prefer to say "as an independent criterion," either necessary or sufficient.

As a way forward, let me suggest two considerations, one of Methodist provenance, the other more of Catholic. In his confrontation with Calvinist doctrines of predestination and perseverance, Wesley held that the divine promises are firm but not unconditional: their benefits hold good *as long as believers continue in the faith*. Similarly, one might suggest that bishops (and their succession) serve the proclamation of the true gospel *as long as they remain faithful to it*. That is saved from being a vain tautology by the fact that bishops are subordinated to the gospel itself, to which there are also other witnesses that, in an admittedly complex way,

85

hold the bishops to account (the Scriptures, the dominical sacraments, earlier testimonies that have been recognized as authentic, the whole Christian life of believers . . .). A more Catholic approach to the unblocking of our problem might draw on sacramental theology: episcopal succession might be viewed as a kind of sacrament which does not always produce its full fruits but is nevertheless not thereby rendered quite ineffective; its efficacy depends on the degree to which it is celebrated and received in (the true) faith. This is prevented from being a vain tautology by the productive power of grace, which nevertheless respects the liberty of human beings to "pose obstacles."[24]

Whether or not these particular perspectives prove helpful (and I am proposing them as ways that allow for a proper recognition of both the divine and the human, the objective and the subjective, the active and the passive aspects of "the assurance of faith"[25]), all future discussion on maintenance in the truth should rest upon the agreement formulated in the Nairobi Report concerning the *soteriological* end of a teaching office in the Church:

> Because God wills the salvation of all men and women, he enables the Church, by the Holy Spirit, so to declare the truth of divine Revelation in Jesus Christ that his people may know the way of salvation. . . . (63)

> Catholics and Methodists are agreed on the need for an authoritative way of being sure, beyond doubt, concerning God's action insofar as it is crucial for our salvation. (75)

There *is* by dominical promise an "infallible" Church, against which "the gates of hell will not prevail" (and its members *are* "the communion of the saints"). As between Catholics and Methodists, the issue is whether one must, or may, (have) be(en) in communion with (a bishop who is in communion with) the bishop of Rome in order to be part of it.

VI. Ministry in Unity

According to the Nairobi Report of the Joint Commission, "the Roman Catholic members are agreed that being in communion with the see of Rome has served as the touchstone of belonging to the Church *in the fullest sense*. . . . Methodist members are agreed that Catholic acceptance of the Roman primacy is *not an impediment* to churchly character" (56, italics added). Obviously, there is still a long way to go: "For Roman Catholics reconciliation with the see of Rome is a *necessary* step towards the restoration of Christian unity. Others see the claim of the Bishop of

Rome as an *obstacle* to Christian unity" (57, italics added). What may be a way forward?

Again, according to the Nairobi Report: "Methodists accept that whatever is properly required for the unity of the whole of Christ's Church must by that very fact be God's will for his Church" (58). Catholics testify that "in collegial communion with fellow bishops and with the Bishop of Rome, [the (Catholic) bishops] cement and express the bond of the universal fellowship" (32), Roman Catholic teaching being that "to ensure the visible unity of the episcopate, [Jesus Christ] set St. Peter over the other apostles" as a "fundamental principle of unity of faith and communion" (36, quoting *Lumen Gentium*, 18).

At this stage, my only suggestion is a renunciation of the language of "necessity" and "guarantee." There is hope in the Roman Catholic willingness to speak of the papal office as "an *effective symbol* of the unity of the Church in faith and life" (Nairobi Report, 61, italics added). As in our previous discussion of the episcopal succession, the papacy could then be seen in a perspective of divine *grace*, the fruits of which do not come independently of *faith* in the gospel. A Petrine ministry is properly and winsomely exercised when it "strengthens the brethren" (cf. Luke 22:32) and so, as good ecclesiastical order, builds up the Church in fellowship among the members and with God.

CHAPTER FOUR

Ora et Labora:
Benedictines and Wesleyans
at Prayer and at Work

I. Strange Company?

Pray and work: the supposedly ancient Benedictine motto of *ora et labora* has lately been shown to date not from the origins of Benedictinism but rather—with a near miss in the fifteenth-century Augustinian Thomas à Kempis—to be the invention of Abbot Maur Wolter of Beuron in the late nineteenth century.[1] Nevertheless, the same historical investigation has demonstrated that, even in the absence of the Latin play on words, the nature and purpose of prayer and work, and particularly the relationship between them, have been concerns of monasticism since its earliest days. These are questions, indeed, not simply for those devoted to the religious life in the technical sense of monks and nuns, but for every Christian and for the whole Church. Recent though it may be as a Benedictine motto, *ora et labora* may therefore appropriately be taken as a rubric under which to explore a theme of holiness as it occurs in the Methodist tradition in comparison with its manifestation among Benedictines.

At first blush, it may seem odd to bring Methodism and Benedictinism together in this way. While declaring it necessary for Christians to "retreat" from the evil in the world, nevertheless Charles Wesley (1707–1788), the hymn-writer of Methodism's two founding brothers, immediately made a polemical point:

> Not in the tombs we pine to dwell,
> Not in the dark monastic cell,
> By vows and grates confined;
> Freely to all ourselves we give,
> Constrained by Jesu's love to live
> The servants of mankind.[2]

89

This corresponded to the statements of his elder brother John Wesley (1703–1791) that "Christianity is essentially a social religion,"[3] and that "there is no holiness but social holiness."[4] Given their time and place in eighteenth-century England, the Wesleys would not have known any living examples of monasticism. And Benedictinism is not necessarily, or properly, struck by their strictures. The vocation of a hermit is reckoned to be exceptional, and the regular form of Benedictinism is cenobitic or communitarian, with ample opportunity for the service, in one form or another, of humankind. Benedictinism may therefore be considered, with no obstacle on the Methodist side, as a possible expression of that love of God and love of neighbor in which the Wesleys judged holiness to consist.

Let us then cheerfully take *ora et labora* as a binome under which to treat a Methodist understanding and practice of sanctification as well as a Benedictine, comparing and contrasting the two traditions where necessary and useful. The relationship between prayer and work is usually seen as a matter of personal spirituality (the contemplative versus the active, "Mary" versus "Martha"), or of ecclesial ethos (the liturgical versus the diaconal). A first solution to the relationship, whether in the case of the individual or in the case of the community, resides in the alternance or the equilibrium between prayer and work, while a more subtle solution lies in the compenetration between prayer and work. Behind these somewhat stylistic questions of personal spirituality and ecclesial ethos, however, stand deeper theological (soteriological) matters concerning the way in which salvation itself is appropriated and the role of the Church in its mediation; and it will, therefore, also be necessary to face issues concerning the relationship of prayer and works to grace and faith, and the status of the Church as the place and instrument of the gospel. All of this, moreover, occurs within the framework of God's salutary purpose for humankind and the history of redemption; and with that the present chapter will begin, taking prayer and work, done within the Christian community, as manifestations of our incipient restoration to the image of God in which we were made and as anticipations of our full and final attainment to God's likeness.

On the Benedictine side, the main resources will be early monasticism, the *Rule for Monks* of St. Benedict,[5] and (very selectively) the history of Benedictinism.[6] On the Methodist side, the chief theological texts will be John Wesley's brief portrait of "The Character of a Methodist" (1742)[7] and his Sermon 85, "On Working Out Our Own Salvation With Fear And Trembling" (1785),[8] with supporting material from the hymns of Charles Wesley (so important in the *lex orandi* of classic Methodism) and illustrations from the life and practice of the Wesleys and of other early and later Methodists. Wesleyanism will be used eponymously for Methodism, although Methodism has broadened somewhat from its origins and has been variously faithful to its founders.

II. *Renewal in the Image of God*

Recognizing the beneficent purpose of the Triune Creator, the fallenness of humankind, and the redemptive work of God in Christ, John Wesley views our salvation—and it is arguably the governing category in Wesley's soteriology—as our renewal in the image of God.[9] This renewal is appropriately attributed to the Holy Spirit. Among the truths of Revelation, Wesley refers in Sermon 85 to "two grand heads of doctrine": "those which relate to the eternal Son of God, and the Spirit of God—to the Son, giving himself to be 'a propitiation for the sins of the world' [1 John 2:2], and to the Spirit of God, renewing men in that image of God wherein they were created [cf. Colossians 3:10]."[10] And, according to "The Character of a Methodist," "the marks of a true Methodist," which "are only the common fundamental principles of Christianity, . . . the plain old Christianity that I teach," include this: "His soul is 'renewed after the image of God' [cf. Colossians 3:10], 'in righteousness and in all true holiness' [cf. Ephesians 4:24]."[11]

While his terminology is not always consistent, for Wesley the *imago Dei* has a spiritual, a political, and a moral aspect. In his Sermon 39, "The New Birth," Wesley gives this threefold meaning to God's creation of humankind in the divine image at Genesis 1:27-28:

> Not barely in his *natural image*, a picture of his own immortality, a spiritual being, endued with understanding, freedom of will, and various affections; nor merely in his *political image*, the governor of this lower world, having "dominion over the fishes of the sea, and over all the earth"; but chiefly in his *moral image*, which, according to the Apostle, is "righteousness and true holiness" [Ephesians 4:24]. In this image of God was man made. "God is love" [1 John 4:8, 16]: accordingly man at his creation was full of love, which was the sole principle of all his tempers, thoughts, words, and actions. God is full of justice, mercy, and truth: so was man as he came from the hands of his Creator . . . [12]

This corresponds neatly to the three main strands in the traditional Christian interpretation of the *imago Dei*: the human creature is ontologically capable of communion with God (our spiritual nature); is cosmologically located to "till the ground" (Genesis 2:5) or administer the earth on God's behalf; is constitutionally a society of neighbors with the opportunity for a life of mutual love. Fallen humankind needs redemption and restoration if it is to fulfill its divinely set ends.[13]

Here, then, Wesley is rejoining a common theme of evangelical, catholic, orthodox Christianity. Eastern Orthodox theologians, reaching back at least as far as St. Irenaeus, have viewed humankind as a royal priesthood, called to be the steward of the earthly creation and the voice of its divine praise, offering the eucharistic sacrifice to God; and this human vocation is essentially a corporate one.[14]

All this fits nicely with the themes of prayer and work which have characterized the Benedictine tradition. Prayer is our communion with God. Work is our stewardship of the earthly creation on God's behalf. To the motto of *ora et labora*, the later moderns have added a communal dimension. According to Fr. A. Watelet, president of the Congregation of the Annunciation, *ora et labora* truly defines Benedictine life only if one adds "in communione fraterna." Fr. Frédéric Debuyst entitled his booklet of 1980 "Prie et travaille au milieu de tes frères."[15]

III. Alternance or Balance of Prayer and Work

The Benedictine and Wesleyan traditions are here examined in turn.

1. Benedictine

Sometimes monastic writers simply juxtapose prayer and work without explicit reflection on their intrinsic relationship to one another. Each is valued, and they are to be practiced alternately, and a balance struck between them.[16] Thus it is possible, in a first move, to consider prayer and work separately, as they each figure in monasticism, and more particularly in the Benedictine tradition.

A. Benedictines at Prayer

In the *Rule* of St. Benedict, the communal office (*opus Dei*) figures most prominently (chapters 8–19), though spiritual reading is also enjoined (chapter 48) and private prayer envisaged (chapters 20, 49, and 52). The original simplicity of prayer according to the divine office gave way to greater complexity and elaborateness in the ninth century under the influence of Abbot Benedict of Aniane and the "liturgical enthusiasm of the Carolingian epoch" more generally;[17] and again in the tenth century, the Cluniac model made of the monastic office "only the basis on which were erected another edifice of prayers. Thus votive offices and processions and repeated celebrations of Masses with many *preces* (intercessory prayers) were added. The simplicity of the celebration was abandoned also, and its place taken by a rich ceremonial."[18] In the twelfth century, the Cisterician movement sought a return to older and simpler forms of the choir office and to more intense meditation on the Scriptures, including the *sermo* or conference from the abbot.[19]

Skipping over the ups and downs in the intervening centuries of Benedictine history, it may simply be noted that the Liturgical Movement in the nineteenth and twentieth centuries has found radiant centers in the abbeys of Solesmes, Beuron, Maria Laach, and Collegeville; and that the rosters of modern liturgical scholarship are graced by such names as Lambert Beauduin, Fernand Cabrol, Odo Casel, Bernard Botte, L. C. Mohlberg, Burkhard Neunheuser, Ambrosius Verheul, Anscar Chupungco, and the Anglican Benedictine Gregory Dix.

B. Benedictines at Work

Like the desert fathers before him, St. Benedict saw work as having the disciplinary or ascetical role of warding off idleness, or even accidie, the characteristic vice of the monastic profession: "Idleness is the enemy of the soul" (*Rule* 48, 1). More positively, Benedict declared in the same chapter on work that "they will be true monks if they live from the work of their hands, as our Fathers and the Apostles did" (*Rule* 48, 8).[20] This points to the recovery of that aspect of the *imago Dei* that consists in the proper use of the material creation or stewardship of the earth. Such work need not be limited to providing for the life of the monastic community. There are indications from the early days of monasticism that the produce of labor may go towards helping the needy neighbor.[21] A further monastic duty has consisted in hospitality towards the visitor, the traveler, and the stranger (as in St. Benedict's *Rule*, 53). Such charitable actions extend beyond the bounds of the monastic community the fulfillment of a further aspect of the *imago Dei*, namely the constitution of social existence, and indeed a fellowship of love.[22]

It appears that manual labor figured prominently in early monasticism and in the early years of Benedictinism. Among Benedictines, however, the monasteries came to employ serfs, renters and secular servants for agricultural and domestic work,[23] and somewhat later there spread from the abbey of Hirsau in the Black Forest (founded in 1050) the institution of lay brothers, "who made the vow of obedience and stability to the monastery, lived outside the cloister and took part in the divine services of the monks only on Sundays. They took care of the manual work and left the monks free for the contemplative life."[24] Again, the Cistercian reform reintroduced the monks to domestic service and to manual labor in the fields.[25]

What work had the Benedictines then fallen to? They had devoted themselves above all to intellectual work; and it is probably still to achievements of learning and scholarship—typified by the Congregation of Saint Maur—that the proverbial "travail de bénédictin" most commonly applies. This work naturally led Benedictines into the educational realm, and gave them an important place in the transmission of the higher culture.[26] The needs of the Church at large also summoned Benedictines into pastoral and missionary work, as indeed St. Benedict himself had been directed from Subiaco to Cassino in order to convert the pagans.[27]

2. Wesleyans at Prayer and at Work

One rough equivalent to the monastic pair of prayer and work may be found in a binome contained in John Wesley's Sermon 85, "On Working Out Our Own Salvation." There he preaches that our "zeal for good works" [Titus 2:14] must include both "works of piety" and "works of mercy," thus moving the emphasis in the latter case from labor to charity. At this point, Wesley does not offer any closer specification of the relationship between duty to God and duty to neighbor. In either case, John Wesley was concerned that the time should be "redeemed," not a moment spent "triflingly": his own diaries show that he typically accounted for every quarter-hour of the day, whether in prayer (corporate or private), reading (often during travel), preaching, good works, or serious company.[28]

A. *Works of Piety*

Here is how Wesley lists the "works of piety" in his Sermon 85, "On Working Out Our Own Salvation":

> Use family prayer, and cry to God in secret. Fast in secret, and "your Father which seeth in secret, he will reward you openly" [cf. Matthew 6:4, 6, 18]. "Search the Scriptures" [John 5:39]; hear them in public, read them in private, and meditate therein. At every opportunity be a partaker of the Lord's Supper. "Do this in remembrance of him" [cf. Luke 22:19; 1 Corinthians 11:26], and he will meet you at his own table. Let your conversation be with the children of God, and see that it "be in grace, seasoned with salt" [cf. Colossians 4:6].[29]

A few comments may elaborate the Wesleyan practice of each of those "means of grace," as Wesley more usually calls them (thus emphasizing their character as divine gift).[30]

Family and private prayer: For personal devotion, John Wesley compiled, with heavy indebtedness to an earlier collection by Nathan Spinkes, a *Collection of Forms of Prayer for Every Day in the Week*. First published in 1733, it went through at least fifteen editions in Wesley's lifetime. He also provided *A Collection of Prayers for Families* (1744, with at least ten editions) and *Prayers for Children* (1772). It should further be noted that the early Methodists occupied themselves in prayer when they met in the small groups known as "classes" and "bands."

Fasting: Wesley's fullest teaching on fasting is contained in Sermon 27, "Upon Our Lord's Sermon on the Mount, VII" (1748).[31] The early Methodist societies practiced Quarterly Fast Days. John Wesley himself practiced and encouraged a modest individual discipline in regular fasting and abstinence.

The Scriptures: Wesley's language in the passage quoted from Sermon 85 echoes the collect for the Second Sunday in Advent in the Book of Common Prayer: "Blessed Lord, who hast caused all holy Scriptures to be written for our learning: Grant that we may in such wise hear them, read, mark, learn, and inwardly digest them, that by patience, and comfort of thy holy Word, we may embrace, and ever hold fast the blessed hope of everlasting life, which thou hast given us in our Saviour Jesus Christ." Wesley's use of the Scriptures will be presented in a little more detail later.

The Lord's Supper: At a time when the Lord's Supper was celebrated as rarely as four times a year in the parishes of the Church of England, John Wesley's diaries show him to have received communion on an average of once every four or five days.[32] He encouraged the Methodist people to request communion more frequently at their parish churches (indeed he spoke more precisely of "*constant* communion"[33]), and he and those of his preachers who were Anglican priests celebrated the sacrament at Methodist gatherings. When, in 1784, he sent ministers and a liturgy for "The Sunday Service" to the Methodist people in the newly independent United States of America, Wesley "advise[d] the elders to administer the Supper of the Lord on every Lord's Day."[34]

Conversation: "Conference," among the preachers in particular, was a vital part of the early Methodist discipline; and the members of the Methodist societies, when they gathered in classes and bands, joined in mutual examination and exhortation.

B. Works of Mercy

Of the "works of mercy," Wesley says in Sermon 85 simply: "As ye have time, do good unto all men [cf. Galatians 6:10], to their souls and to their bodies."[35] This had been further spelled out in "The Character of a Methodist":

> As he has time, he "does good unto all men" [cf. Galatians 6:10]; unto neighbours and strangers, friends and enemies: And that in every possible kind; not only to their bodies, by "feeding the hungry, clothing the naked, visiting those that are sick or in prison" [cf. Matthew 25:35-36]; but much more does he labour to do good to their souls, as of the ability which God giveth [cf. 1 Peter 4:11]; to awaken those that sleep in death; to bring those who are awakened to the atoning blood, that, "being justified by faith, they may have peace with God" [cf. Romans 5:1]; and to provoke those who have peace with God to abound more in love and in good works. And he is willing to "spend and to be spent herein" [cf. 2 Corinthians 12:15], even to "be offered upon the sacrifice and service of their faith" [cf. Philippians 2:17], so they may "all come unto the measure of the stature of the fullness of Christ" [cf. Ephesians 4:13].[36]

Wesley himself visited the imprisoned and worked for prison reform, set up dispensaries for the sick, and established schools for children. Most notably, however, he traveled 250,000 miles on eighteenth-century roads and seaways in the direct pursuit of evangelization to save souls by preaching.

IV. Compenetration of Prayer and Work

Prayer and work (whether, in the latter case, labor or charity) are both necessary to the Christian life. They are, moreover, closely intertwined, and even essentially related. The Benedictine and the Wesleyan understandings and practice of this compenetration will be reviewed in turn and convergences noted.

1. The Monastic Pattern

In the words of St. Isidore of Seville, stimulated by Psalm 28: "To pray without working is to lift up one's heart without lifting up one's hands; to work without praying is to lift up one's hands without lifting up one's heart; therefore it is necessary both to pray and to work."[37] But how to do both without interruption—for did not the Apostle Paul both give order to "pray without ceasing" (1 Thessalonians 5:17) and himself claim to "work night and day" (2 Thessalonians 3:8)?[38]

Rather simply, Aurelian of Arles, a younger contemporary of St. Benedict, developed a counsel of his predecessor Caesarius: "At vigils, while a lesson is being read, work with your hands by plaiting reeds or twisting hemp or something similar, to avoid falling asleep";[39] and conversely: "While doing manual work all day long, do not cease to recite the sacred texts that you know by heart, on account of the Apostle's instruction, 'Sing psalms and hymns and spiritual songs to God in your hearts' [Colossians 3:16]."[40]

With greater theological depth, St. Basil, whom Benedict called his "holy father," had already written in the *Great Rule*, which Benedict doubtless knew in the translation by Rufinus: "While our hands are occupied in work, we can praise God with psalms and hymns and spiritual songs, with the tongue if it is possible, but if not, then in the heart. In this way we thank Him who has given both strength of hand to work and wisdom of brain to know how to work, and also bestowed means by which to work both in the tools we use and the arts we practice, whatever the work may be. We pray moreover that the works of our hands may be directed towards the mark of pleasing God."[41]

St. Benedict mentions nothing of "mixing" work and prayer. Although he may have known the *Rule* of Caesarius,[42] he says nothing about his monks doing handwork during the divine office nor about reciting psalms from memory during worktime. At least implicitly, he shares the deeper theological insight of St. Basil concerning the compenetration of prayer and work. Benedict considers the *prayer of the divine office* to be the supreme *work* of God: "Let nothing be preferred to the *Opus Dei*" (*Rule* 43, 3). (The desert fathers had already treated prayer as "hard work," a *kopos*.[43]) And all the monk's life, every activity, including work, is to be accomplished under God's regard, with attention to God's will and sensitivity to God's presence—"in order that God may be glorified in all things (*ut in omnibus glorificetur Deus*)."[44]

2. The Wesleyan Pattern

In describing "The Character of a Methodist," John Wesley declares that such a one "prays without ceasing." Wesley affirms both public and private worship and teaches that its spirit should extend to all times and places; echoing the eucharistic preface, he states that the raising of the heart to God is always and everywhere right and fitting (*Sursum corda . . . Dignum et iustum est, semper et ubique. . . .*):

It is given him "always to pray, and not to faint" [Luke 18:1] Not that he is always in the house of prayer—though he neglects no opportunity of being there. Neither is he always on his knees, although he often is, or on his face, before the Lord his God. Nor yet is he always crying aloud to God, or calling upon him in words: for many times "the Spirit maketh intercession for him with groans that

97

cannot be uttered" [cf. Romans 8:26]. But at all times the language of his heart is this: "Thou brightness of the eternal glory, unto thee is my heart, though without a voice, and my silence speaketh unto thee." And this is true prayer, and this alone. But his heart is ever lifted up to God, at all times and in all places. In this he is never hindered, much less interrupted, by any person or thing. In retirement or company, in leisure, business, or conversation, his heart is ever with the Lord. Whether he lie down or rise up, "God is in all his thoughts" [cf. Psalm 10:4]; he "walks with God" [cf. Genesis 6:9] continually, having the loving eye of his mind still fixed upon Him, and everywhere "seeing Him that is invisible" [Hebrews 11:27].[45]

This love towards God is constantly accompanied by love towards neighbor: "And while he thus always exercises his love to God, by praying without ceasing, rejoicing evermore, and in everything giving thanks, this commandment is written in his heart, that 'he who loveth God, love his brother also' [1 John 4:21]. And he accordingly 'loves his neighbor as himself' [cf. Mark 12;33]; he loves every man as his own soul. His heart is full of love to all mankind, to every child of 'the Father of the spirits of all flesh' [Hebrews 12:9]."[46]

Such a person's "one intention at all times and in all things is, not to please himself, but Him whom his soul loveth":[47] "And therefore, loving God with all his heart, he serves him with all his strength. He continually presents his soul and body a living sacrifice, holy, acceptable to God."[48] Thus all his works are done to God's glory:

By consequence, whatsoever he doeth, it is all to the glory of God. In all his employments of every kind, he not only aims at this, (which is implied in having a single eye,) but actually attains it. His business and refreshments, as well as his prayers, all serve this great end. Whether he sit in his house or walk by the way, whether he lie down or rise up, he is promoting, in all he speaks or does, the one business of his life; whether he put on his apparel, or labour, or eat and drink, or divert himself from too wasting labour, it all tends to advance the glory of God, by peace and good will among men. His one invariable rule is this, "Whatsoever ye do, in word or deed, do it all in the name of the Lord Jesus, giving thanks to God the Father by him."[49]

Hymnically, Charles Wesley expresses the matter thus:

> Forth in thy name, O Lord, I go,
> My daily labour to pursue,
> Thee, only thee, resolved to know
> In all I think, or speak, or do.

The task thy wisdom hath assigned
O let me cheerfully fulfil,
In all my works thy presence find,
And prove thy acceptable will.

Thee may I set at my right hand,
Whose eyes my inmost substance see,
And labour on at thy command,
And offer all my works to thee.

Give me to bear thy easy yoke,
And every moment watch and pray,
And still to things eternal look,
And hasten to thy glorious day:

For thee delightfully employ
Whate'er thy bounteous grace hath given,
And run my course with even joy,
And closely walk with thee to heaven.[50]

Thus the Wesleys fuse the euchological and the ethical: prayer and work are subsumed in a single doxology.

Two examples may now be briefly offered of convergence between Methodists and Benedictines in the compenetration of prayer and work. First, singing plays an important part in the worship of both traditions. Psalms and hymns figure prominently in the divine office of the Benedictines (*Rule*, 8–19), while it has been aptly said that "Methodism was born in song."[51] Singing is a liturgical action in which the body clearly works to raise the spirit towards God.

Second, the interplay between liturgy and ethics is well captured in Wesley's dictum echoing St. Augustine to the effect that the service of God is "to imitate him you worship" (*imitari quem colis*): "They who resemble [God] in the spirit of their minds are transformed into the same image. They are merciful even as he is merciful. . . . Yea, they are, like him, loving unto every man, and their mercy extends to all his works."[52] Benedictines share the Roman rite at the ordination of presbyters, where the priests are charged to "imitate what you handle" (*imitamini quod tractatis*); and, in fact, all who share in the sacramental body and blood of Christ are expected, as several post-communion prayers make clear (especially in the Easter season), to live conformably to his death and resurrection.

V. Grace, Faith, Prayer, and Work(s)

Behind discussion of prayer and work stands the theological question of the respective roles of God and humankind in the attainment of our salvation. This issue is perennially, or at least periodically, controversial. The period of monastic, and particularly Benedictine, origins saw the catholic struggle to exclude pelagianism and semipelagianism yet without endorsing an extreme Augustinianism. Within Protestantism, Lutherans and Calvinists, who themselves lay claim to St. Augustine, have often suspected Methodism of pelagian tendencies, and therefore of falling back into what they think of as "catholicism."[53] Now, Dom Cipriano Vagaggini has argued that St. Benedict, while aware of the problem, deliberately took no side in what came to be known as the semipelagian controversy: at times Benedict sounds semipelagian, but he can always be read in an orthodox way, and some of his phraseology bears strongly Augustinian marks.[54] For his part, Wesley clearly teaches in his Sermon 85, "On Working Out Our Own Salvation," that even our first movement towards God is a work of divine grace, and yet his exhortations to the hearer imply freedom of the will. It appears, therefore, that Benedictines and Methodists may on this delicate matter come close to convergence at a point in the evangelical, catholic, orthodox faith.

A first approach may be made by way of Benedict's and Wesley's attitudes towards reading, and particularly towards the Scriptures. For to recognize the primacy of the Scriptures is to recognize the priority of divine Revelation and of the history of redemption in any account of the provision of salvation; and to highlight the process of reading is to discern an instance of the "active receptivity" that properly characterizes the human appropriation of salvation.

Reading figures prominently—as part of the divine office (8–18), at meals (38), and as individual responsibility (48)—in the *Rule* of St. Benedict, whose prologue and opening chapters are themselves largely a tissue of scriptural texts. The reading of the Scriptures takes pride of place, followed by the Fathers who help in its interpretation and application (see, typically, 9:8; 73:3-9). As meditation, reading may fall on the side of prayer; as study, it may fall on the side of work; in any case, the compenetration of prayer and work is thereby once more illustrated. The point that presently is of interest finds expression in a tripartite formula from some Carthusian "Statutes for Novices": *Nunc lege, nunc ora, nunc cum fervore labora.*[55] In calling my attention to that injunction to "read [the Scriptures and the patristic and spiritual writers]," my old friend Dom Otmar Bauer, of Engelberg and Mont Febë, commented: "Sans la lectio divina, il n'y a pas l'intégralité du monachisme bénédictin."[56]

John Wesley called himself "a man of one Book" (*homo unius libri*). Here is how he valued the Scriptures:

> I have thought, I am a creature of a day, passing through life as an arrow through the air [cf. Wisdom 5:9-13]. I am a spirit come from God, and returning to God [cf. Ecclesiastes 12:7]: Just hovering over the great gulf; till, a few moments hence, I am no more seen [cf. Psalm 39:13]—I drop into an unchangeable eternity! I want to know one thing, the way to heaven—how to land safe on that happy shore. God himself has condescended to teach the way: for this very end he came from heaven. He hath written it down in a book. O give me that book! At any price, give me the book of God! I have it: Here is knowledge enough for me. Let me be *homo unius libri*.[57]

The "one Book" of the Holy Scriptures constituted for Wesley not so much the "boundary of his reading" as "the center of gravity in his thinking."[58] On account of their scriptural faithfulness, he assembled from the writings of the early Fathers and the spiritual writers a fifty-volume "Christian Library" for his Methodist people.[59]

To stress the "lectio divina" is, then, to acknowledge the primacy and priority of grace in all soteriology while calling also for the human response. According to St. Benedict, the purpose of the monks' life is to "magnify the Lord at work in them" (*operantem in se Dominum magnificare*):

> Those who fear the Lord do not become proud of their good deeds but, considering that what is good in them cannot come from themselves but from the Lord, they magnify the Lord at work in them, saying with the prophet, "Not to us, Lord, not to us, but to your name give the glory" [Psalm 115:1], just as the Apostle Paul, too, claimed nothing for his own preaching but said: "By the grace of God I am what I am" [1 Corinthians 15:10] and "Whoever glories should glory in the Lord" [2 Corinthians 10:17].[60]

"To magnify the Lord at work in you" would in fact have constituted a suitable motto for John Wesley's Sermon 55, "On Working Out Our Own Salvation," which is in fact based in the Pauline text "Work out your own salvation with fear and trembling; for it is God that worketh in you, both to will and to do of his good pleasure" (Philippians 2:12-13).[61]

The Pauline text, says Wesley, "gives God the whole glory of his own work": "If we are thoroughly sensible that we have nothing which we have not received, how can we glory as if we had not received it [cf. 1 Cor. 4:7]? If we know and feel that the very first motion of God is from above, as well as the power which conducts it to the end—if it is God that not only infuses every good desire, but that accomplishes and follows it, else

101

it vanishes away—then it evdently follows that 'he who glorieth must glory in the Lord' [1 Cor. 1:31]."[62]

Wesley then goes on to trace the several stages in the appropriation of salvation:

> Salvation begins with what is usually termed (and very properly) "preventing grace"; including the first wish to please God, the first dawn of light concerning his will, and the first slight, transient conviction of having sinned against him. All these imply some tendency toward life, some degree of salvation, the beginning of a deliverance from a blind, unfeeling heart, quite insensible of God and the things of God.[63]
>
> Salvation is carried on by "convincing grace," usually in Scripture termed "repentance," which brings a larger measure of self-knowledge, and a farther deliverance from the heart of stone [cf. Ezekiel 11:19].
>
> Afterwards we experience the proper Christian salvation, whereby "through grace" we "are saved by faith" [Ephesians 2:8], consisting of those two grand branches, justification and sanctification. By justification we are saved from the guilt of sin, and restored to the favour of God; by sanctification we are saved from the power and root of sin, and restored to the image of God.[64]

Wesley goes on to show that there is no contradiction in saying "God works; therefore do ye work," but rather the closest connection: "For, first, God works; therefore you *can* work. Secondly, God works; therefore you *must* work."[65]

As to the ability to work: Christ truly said, "Without Me ye can do nothing" (John 15:5), yet every believer can say "I can do all things through Christ that strengtheneth me" (Philippians 4:13).[66]

As to the necessity of working:

> You must be "workers together with God" (they are the very words of the Apostle [2 Corinthians 6:1]); otherwise he will cease working. The general rule on which his gracious dispensations invariably proceed is this: "Unto him that hath shall be given, but from him that hath not," that does not improve the grace already given, "shall be taken away what he assuredly hath" [Luke 8:18] (so the words ought to be rendered). Even St. Augustine, who is generally supposed to favour the contrary doctrine, makes that just remark, *Qui fecit nos sine nobis, non salvabit nos sine nobis*: "he that made us without ourselves, will not save us without ourselves."[67] He will not save us unless we "save ourselves from this untoward generation" [cf. Acts 2:40]; unless we ourselves "fight the good fight, and lay hold on eternal life" [1 Timothy 6:12]; unless we "agonize to enter in at the

strait gate" [Luke 13:24], "deny ourselves and take up our cross daily" [Luke 9:23], and labour, by every possible means, to "make our own calling and election sure" [cf. 2 Peter 1:10].[68]

And the peroration of Wesley's sermon "On Working Out Our Own Salvation" becomes a catena of New Testament texts exhorting believers to work:

> "Labour" then, brethren, "not for the meat that perisheth, but for that which endureth to everlasting life." Say with our blessed Lord, though in a somewhat different sense, "My Father worketh hitherto, and I work" [John 5:17]. In consideration that he still worketh in you, be never "weary of well-doing" [cf. Galatians 6:9; 2 Thessalonians 3:13]. Go on, in virtue of the grace of God preventing, accompanying, and following you, in "the work of faith, in the patience of hope, and in the labour of love" [cf. 1 Thessalonians 1:3]. "Be ye steadfast and immovable; always abounding in the work of the Lord" [cf. 1 Corinthians 15:58]. And "the God of peace, who brought again from the dead the great Shepherd of the sheep",—Jesus—"make you perfect in every good work to do his will, working in you what is well-pleasing in his sight, through Jesus Christ, to whom be glory for ever and ever!" [Hebrews 13:20-21].[69]

In a different literary genre, the Methodist sense of these delicate matters of grace, prayer, faith and work(s) is captured in the tensions between and within the following two hymns by Charles Wesley:

> Behold the servant of the Lord!
> I wait thy guiding eye to feel,
> To hear and keep thy every word,
> To prove and do thy perfect will,
> Joyful from my own works to cease,
> Glad to fulfil all righteousness.
>
> Me, if thy grace vouchsafe to use,
> Meanest of all thy creatures, me:
> The deed, the time, the manner choose,
> Let all my fruit be found of thee;
> Let all my works in thee be wrought,
> By thee to full perfection brought.
>
> My every weak, though good design,
> O'errule, or change, as seems thee meet;
> Jesus, let all my work be thine!
> Thy work, O Lord, is all complete,

103

> And pleasing in thy Father's sight;
> Thou only hast done all things right.
>
> Here then to thee thy own I leave;
> Mould as thou wilt thy passive clay;
> But let me all thy stamp receive,
> But let me all thy words obey,
> Serve with a single heart and eye,
> And to thy glory live and die.[70]

And then:

> A charge to keep I have,
> A God to glorify,
> A never-dying soul to save,
> And fit it for the sky:
>
> To serve the present age,
> My calling to fulfil:
> O may it all my powers engage
> To do my Master's will!
>
> Arm me with jealous care,
> As in thy sight to live;
> And O thy servant, Lord, prepare
> A strict account to give!
>
> Help me to watch and pray,
> And on thyself rely,
> Assured, if I my trust betray,
> I shall for ever die.[71]

If one were to reflect more fully than John Wesley did on the theological implications for ecclesiology of this view of the appropriation of salvation, it would land Wesley rather on the "Catholic" side in the debates concerning the instrumentality of the Church, in which some contemporary ecumenists have located "the basic difference" between Roman Catholics and Protestants.[72] In its active reception of the gospel, the Church is by that same motion launched on its task of transmitting it. In practical terms, the early and traditional Methodist institutions of the annual conference and the quarterly meeting illustrate in communal form the concomitance of grace, faith, prayer, and work(s): there the Methodists at appropriate geographical levels gathered in faith to pray, to sing, to partake in the Lord's Supper and the love-feast, and to hold "conversation on the work of God," by which they meant what God was doing among them and through their mission in the world. A nice historical example is found in the conference service of a small Methodist denomination in Britain for the sending of missionaries overseas (with even a quotation, in garbled form, of our "ancient Benedictine motto"!):

> There are diversities of operations, but it is the same God that worketh in all [cf. 1 Corinthians 12:6]. This truth is nowhere shown more clearly than in the field of Foreign Missions. Some are called to be preachers of the Gospel, some to be teachers in schools, some to be translators of the Scriptures, some to the ministry of healing, whilst others are engaged in industrial, or agricultural work. All these forms of service are necessary; all are sacred; work done in the right spirit is a form of worship. It was truly said in old times: "To labour is to pray."[73]

That practice of mission to lands overseas—which has been strongly characteristic of historic Methodism—rejoins the evangelizing endeavors of the early medieval Benedictines, whereby Pope Gregory I had sent Augustine to the English, and in turn the insular figures of Willibrord and Boniface became apostles to the Netherlands and to central Germany.[74]

VI. Mutual Recognition?

In the foregoing, it has chiefly been a matter of the "ideal," whether Benedictine or Wesleyan. In ecumenical affairs, it is always important to compare either ideal with ideal, or actual with actual. The greater difficulty, for the ecumenical utility of the present exercise, resides therefore rather in the differences between the kinds of entity under comparison: on the one hand, a religious order within the Roman Catholic Church, wherein (according to its own claim) the sole Church of Christ "subsists" (Vatican II, *Lumen Gentium*, 8); and on the other hand, a denominational family of Methodist Churches which claim their own place within the Body of Christ that is held to include others also. Yet a Roman Catholic writer has felt able to compare Methodism's relationship to Wesley with the way in which "a religious order or spiritual family, within the Roman Catholic Church, owes its spirit to its founder."[75] And the late Methodist historian Albert Outler wanted to see Methodism as an "evangelical order of witness and worship, discipline and nurture" that needs "a catholic church" within which to function.[76] In searching for possible "ways of being one Church," the Joint Commission between the Roman Catholic Church and the World Methodist Council has noted an analogy between John Wesley's Methodist movement and figures such as Benedict of Norcia "whose divine calling was similarly to a spiritual reform," "which

105

gave rise to religious orders, characterized by special forms of life and prayer, work, evangelization and their own internal organization."[77]

If contemporary Methodists could find renewal according to the Wesleyan ideal, it is possible that they might encounter supporters among the Benedictines to advocate their recognition within the Church catholic. Certainly there are Methodists who have discovered, as I have done, striking embodiments of the Benedictine ideal within living monastic communities and have thereby been helped in our recognition of the ecclesiality of Roman Catholicism.

Let me leave you with a memory, which may also be an anticipation of the future. From the time of the Methodist celebrations in May 1988 of the two-hundred-and-fiftieth anniversary of the evangelical conversions of the Wesley brothers, it is the sight of the Cardinal Archbishop of Westminster and former Abbot of Ampleforth, Dom Basil Hume, coming to Wesley's Chapel, City Road, London, dressed in the simple habit of a Benedictine monk, and kneeling in silent prayer at the tomb of John Wesley.

METHODISTS AND LUTHERANS

CHAPTER FIVE

Ecclesiological Tendencies in Luther and Wesley

Methodists and Lutherans have no particular fondness for each other. Perhaps the Moravians of Herrnhut may take the blame for that. On his unhappy journey to America John Wesley had made contact with the Moravians, and these links were maintained after his return to London and played an important part in his so-called "evangelical conversion" of 24 May 1738. That experience of Wesley's not only set him off on a fifty-year career of tireless evangelism, it also became a prototype of spirituality for the Methodists who owed their (new) life to the preaching of Wesley and his helpers: the rather "pietistic" character of Methodism is therefore understandable.[1] So such a "true" Lutheran as Dietrich Bonhoeffer could consider "Methodism" the religious analogue to the pernicious existentialist philosophers and the psychotherapists.[2]

On the other hand, Wesley's conversion occurred, it is true, while a text from Luther's own hand was being read, namely his *Preface to the Romans*, which describes faith and the works of love which flow from it in exactly the same way as Wesley also would preach them to the end of his life. But the Luther whom Wesley got to know during and after his visit to Germany from June to September 1738 was the Luther of the Moravians. A practical separation was to take place between Wesley and the Moravians on account of the doctrine of mystical "stillness" or "quiet," which came to rule in the Moravian congregation in London with the arrival of Philip Molther and was then defended against Wesley's criticism of it by Zinzendorf himself.[3] Meanwhile Wesley came across Luther's large commentary on Galatians (1531–35), which he rejected after too quick reading during a coach ride. "With some justification he recognized in Luther," says Martin Schmidt, "the source of the mystical indifference of the Herrnhuters which caused him so much concern."[4] With some justification? It would doubtless be unfair to accuse the Reformer of underestimating the instituted means of grace and the good works of the justified; but we shall have to take note of the passivity in the Lutheran understanding of salvation. Evidently this tendency did not please the more actively minded Wesley.[5]

It may be that the Moravian intermediaries are in part responsible for mutual misunderstandings between Lutherans and Methodists. Two British Methodists, E. G. Rupp and P. S. Watson, now figure among the most respected Luther scholars in the English-speaking world; both have interpreted the Reformer sympathetically, without giving up their love for Wesley.[6] In the other direction, Franz Hildebrandt—a Lutheran convert to Methodism in the chance circumstances of the Second World War—has interpreted John Wesley in a very Lutheran and "unpietistic" way.[7] Nevertheless the bilateral conversations between the Lutheran World Federation and the World Methodist Council have had to recognize "important divergences" in matters of salvation.[8] Questions of salvation are of their very nature questions of ecclesiology.

Let us begin phenomenologically. The German Reformer sought the renewal of the (western) church. Such a renewal was to be achieved only through a theologically radical critique of existing church practice, since the practical life of the church was but the outcrop of false views of God, human beings, and salvation. Reactions to Luther's program of reformation varied with geography and led to church separations. Where the program was carried through with the cooperation of godly princes, Lutheranism took over the role of the *corpus christianum*. Two hundred years later, Wesley sought the renewal of an evangelical Church of England with which, on the surface at least, he had no theological quarrel: he appeals to its confessional writings from the Reformation period (Thirty-nine Articles, Book of Common Prayer, Homilies, Catechism) and tries to prevent his Methodist societies from thinking or behaving in a separatist way (for example, they are not allowed to hold "competitive" meetings at the hours of parish worship).[9] After the separation of the English Methodists from the Anglican Church—which had not been wished by Wesley and which took place only after his death, and then only gradually—Methodists were probably nowhere in danger of becoming a state church or even a folk church.[10] The end of the eighteenth century was no doubt too late for that, purely on grounds of secular history.[11] Although there is no proof of direct links with the left wing of the Reformation, Howard A. Snyder has recently shown how problematic the "Constantinian turn" was for the "radical Wesley": Wesley spoke several times of "that evil hour, when Constantine the Great called himself a Christian."[12] For Wesley it was not only a matter of the authority of "established" bishops who hindered his work of evangelism; it was more (though the two are connected) a matter of the great gap, in both quantity and quality, between the officially Christian population of England and "the congregation of

English believers."[13] With the ambiguous and controversial notion of "nominal Christians" (*Taufchristen*) we now come directly to theology.

So let us begin theologically with baptism. Luther preserved from medieval Christendom the generalized practice of infant baptism. Social and political considerations contributed to its maintenance.[14] But the relationship between infant baptism and justification through faith was not without its problems. The various and fluctuating arguments with which Luther over the years defends infant baptism impress one less as an *embarras de richesses* than as a *testimonium paupertatis*.[15] In Wesley there is a tension between infant baptism, which he kept in practice, and the deliberate emphasis on a personally experienced faith.[16] This tension is scarcely tackled by Wesley in a theological way; but neither does he establish a positive relation between its two poles. To the end of his life, Wesley looked on infant baptism as sacramental regeneration;[17] but he also held that by the age of nine or ten one had "sinned away" one's baptism and needed a (new) new birth for salvation. He preached: "Lean no more on the staff of that broken reed, that ye *were* born again in baptism."[18] How that offends Lutheran ears accustomed to the *baptizatus sum*! Luther was thinking of the believer faced by temptation, Wesley was exhorting the unbeliever or the no longer believing: is the difference in context sufficient to allow a reconciliation between Luther and Wesley?

When modern Methodists expound infant baptism, they think first of "prevenient grace," for which infant baptism is said to be an effective, or at least a useful, sign.[19] Wesley taught the universal occurrence of prevenient grace on account of the world-redeeming Cross of Christ; such grace enables the positive acceptance of the gospel in response to preaching. Correspondingly, Methodists have a more active conception of faith than is usual among Lutherans. Thus Edmund Schlink, for example, defends infant baptism in terms of the "pure passivity" of faith.[20] Although the Methodist Churches practice infant baptism, and although their theologians stress prevenient grace in the Wesleyan sense, yet Methodist talk of faith probably sounds Pelagian in Lutheran ears: there is an excess of human activity.[21] For my part as a Methodist, I would say that it is a permanent part of the Lutheran ecumenical task to warn others against exaggerating that grain of truth which the great Tradition at least secretly allows to Pelagianism, namely a certain "synergism" which raises human beings without diminishing God.

The question of baptism is itself the question of church membership. As a definition of the church Wesley several times quotes Anglican Article 19, which is strongly reminiscent of the Augsburg Confession, 7: "The visible Church of Christ is a congregation of faithful men, in which the pure Word of God is preached, and the sacraments be duly administered."

111

Wesley emphasized the *coetus credentium*.[22] He wanted to bring English people back to a "living faith." Where Methodist preachers worked, Methodists did not only gather among themselves but also went to the parish church, to hear where possible the word of God and, since Wesley harbored no Donatist scruples about evil-living Anglican parsons as ministers of grace (cf. Augsburg Confession, 8), to receive the sacraments. But faith works by love (Gal. 5:6 was a favorite text of Wesley); and those who did not produce fruits of the Spirit but fell back into the works of the flesh were then no longer admitted into Methodist societies (the penitent were naturally welcomed back with joy).[23] In all of this Wesley was saying nothing one way or the other about people's official membership in the Church of England. But at the very point where he is at his most ecumenical (say in the "Letter to a Roman Catholic"), he denies the name of Christian to those whom the apostle also excommunicates, such as whoremongers, blasphemers, drunkards, cheats (cf. 1 Cor. 5:11).[24] Faced with such passages, even such an admirer of Wesley as A.C. Outler speaks of "Montanism."[25] Lutherans often suspect Methodists of "moralism." For all the dangers of hypocrisy I would rather interpret the phenomenon as "ethical seriousness." Wesley saw it to be Methodism's providential call to "spread scriptural holiness through the land."

Willy-nilly, the Methodist societies and the Wesleyan "Connexion" of the eighteenth century turned into a "Church," in the fragmentary sense which that word bears when it stands for a "denomination." Membership discipline gradually relaxed, yet without ever disappearing altogether. A persistent trace of our societary origin is found in the distinction we make between (simple) members (by baptism children are recognized as belonging to "Christ's flock") and "full members," that is, those who have publicly professed their faith and take part in the Lord's Supper.[26] Lutherans see such a terminology as derogatory to baptism.

Baptism, church membership: the ecclesiological question can also be put from the closely related viewpoint of justification. In Lutheran eyes, the proper doctrine of justification is the *articulus stantis et cadentis ecclesiae*. Following Luther and the Anglican confessional writings Wesley considered justification through faith as the distinguishing mark of the gospel over against the Roman Catholic Church.[27] Between Luther and Wesley, between Lutheranism and Methodism, the accents are, however, unmistakably different. That is connected with our respective beginnings as a folk church and as a society or free church. On both sides we have to examine ourselves in the light of the gospel. Therein lies the importance of the correction brought from within Paul's writings themselves by the German Methodist exegete Walter Klaiber to the one-sided emphasis which his Lutheran teacher Ernst Käsemann places on the justification of the godless. Klaiber closes his "study of Paul's understanding of the Church" with these words: "That justification of the godless is justification of the believer and *vice versa* marks the poles of the tension in which the Church must take shape. This must prevent the folk church from appealing to the *justificatio impii* in order to justify a 'religion without decision'; it must also warn the free church against allowing the congregation of believers to become an 'association of the religiously qualified.'"[28]

The best possibility for Lutherans and Methodists to reach ecclesiological agreement is probably offered by the eucharist. Wesley esteemed the sacrament as highly as Luther did. For Wesley as for Luther, "the worship of the congregation gathered in the name of Jesus," to use Peter Brunner's expression, was the concrete form of the church.[29] An eschatologically oriented Lord's Supper was for Wesley the privileged place of a doxological communion of the saints on earth as in heaven:[30]

> Happy the souls to Jesus joined,
> And saved by grace alone;
> Walking in all Thy ways we find
> Our heaven on earth begun.
>
> The Church triumphant in Thy love,
> Their mighty joys we know;
> They sing the Lamb in hymns above,
> And we in hymns below.
>
> Thee in Thy glorious realm they praise,
> And bow before Thy throne;
> We in the kingdom of Thy grace,
> The kingdoms are but one.
>
> The holy to the holiest leads,
> From hence our spirits rise,
> And he that in Thy statutes treads
> Shall meet Thee in the skies.

The rediscovery in the seventeenth and eighteenth centuries of old liturgical texts from the eastern church allowed Wesley to reach conceptions of presence and sacrifice, anamnesis and epiclesis, which anticipate the Lima text of Faith and Order.[31] In our century, the liturgical and ecumenical movements have helped both Lutherans and Methodists move towards a renewal of eucharistic forms and sacramental practice.[32]

From a Methodist viewpoint, eucharistic unity demands corresponding churchly structures at all geographical levels, in order that "all in each place," in "churches which are themselves truly united," may be "united with the whole Christian fellowship in all places and all ages."[33] Methodists, particularly of British origin, retain from their origins an ecclesiologically significant sense of the "provisional" character of their own existence.[34] For that reason, Methodists of the British kind (though much less so the American, who took for themselves an ecclesial autonomy from Anglicanism at a very early stage) have almost always been willing to enter into organic unions with other churches.[35] As a concrete movement for reformation, Luther and the first Lutherans were in principle "provisional," too. Yet because in the sixteenth century nothing less than the truth was at stake, they quickly acquired a marked "confessional" identity, which characterizes Lutheranism to this day. If now an ecumenical consensus in faith, in all *quod ad unitatem requiritur et sufficit*, is coming within reach, then Lutherans too should be prepared, in the service of a *unitas fratrum* to be realized at local and universal levels, to surrender their purely "denominational" structures.[36]

CHAPTER SIX

Uniting What Was Never Divided:
The Next Steps
for Lutherans and Methodists

I. Strangers Beginning to Meet

It is not as though there had ever been an active division between Methodists and Lutherans, either doctrinally or ecclesiastically. Rather their different historical, geographical and cultural origins have simply kept them apart. In Britain there are a few Lutheran seamen's missions. In Scandinavia there are some small Methodist communities originating with returning emigrants from the USA. On overseas mission fields, informal comity arrangements distributed the work of Lutheran and Methodist agencies.

It is perhaps in Germany that the most significant interaction between Lutheran and Methodist churches has taken place. There, smallish Methodist communities, whether looking originally to Britain or to America, have been a rather more notable presence in the midst of the Lutheran or United *Landeskirchen*. On Michaelmas Day 1987, after a decade of quiet and careful preparation, pulpit and altar fellowship was declared and celebrated in St. Lawrence's, Nuremberg, between the Evangelisch-methodistische Kirche (EmK) and the churches of the Evangelische Kirche in Deutschland (EKD). The stimulus had been the statement in an official Lutheran handbook as late as 1978 advising Lutherans *not* to receive communion at Methodist hands. Discussions began between the VELKD (Vereinigte Evangelisch-Lutherische Kirche Deutschlands) and the EmK, which came to involve also other *Landeskirchen* that were party to the Arnoldshain Conference and the Leuenberg Concordat. The West German agreement of Michaelmas 1987, joined in 1990 by a similar one in East Germany, establishes the mutual acceptability of ministrations, while renouncing "organizational union" and retaining the canonical disciplines of the respective churches.[1]

In the United States, population mobility and ecumenical openness have brought Lutherans and Methodists into increasing contact. Theological conversations between the United Methodist Church and the Lutheran Council in the USA resulted in "common statements" on baptism (1979) and episcopacy (1988), but these have not (so far as I know) been legislatively enacted.[2] Would a move at the level of interchurch relations, similar to those made in Germany, now be possible and desirable between the UMC and the ELCA? The German work had been done in interaction with the international dialogue between the Lutheran World Federation and the World Methodist Council, whose "final report" under the title of *The Church: Community of Grace* had been accepted by the LWF at Budapest in 1984 and by the WMC at Nairobi in 1986.[3] This report recommended that "our churches take steps to declare and establish full fellowship of word and sacrament," seeing as a "first and important step" the official provision of "pulpit exchanges and mutual hospitality at the table of the Lord." For the inclination and resolve of our particular churches to be strengthened in this direction, a demonstration of some advantages might be helpful.

II. What Mutual Advantage?

The international joint commission considered that sufficient agreement could be shown on "the authority of the scriptures," "salvation by grace through faith," "the church," the "means of grace," and "the mission of the church." Among issues meriting "further exploration and discussion . . . in appropriate settings," however, were certain "aspects of anthropology." Anthropology, which of course never lacks *soteriological* reference, is an exercise ground for mutual suspicion between Methodists and Lutherans who are at the same time insufficiently familiar with one another and yet perhaps not totally mistaken in their respective perceptions of the other. Methodists with a little theological learning fear that Lutheranism is at least theoretically antinomian, while Lutherans overhear pelagianism in Methodist talk of free will and perfection. If different tendencies and emphases are viewed as *underlying* the characteristic configurations of Lutheranism and Methodism, the danger is that they will also *undermine* the dogmatic agreements that can be recognized and established. It may therefore be better if discussion of such themes be understood as *theological* clarification and debate within a commonly accepted *doctrinal* framework. But in either case, "exploration" of some anthropological/soteriological issues could be an important part of developing relations between Lutheran and Methodist churches. It is at any rate

116

my wager that each side can be helped by the other in its submission to, and grasp of, the gospel.

As a Methodist, let me begin from the Methodist side. Robert E. Chiles has traced over the long haul a significant, and *deleterious*, "theological transition in American Methodism."[4] According to Chiles, there has been a shift "from revelation to reason," "from sinful man to moral man," and "from free grace to free will." I would put it briefly this way: What had been secondary poles in a Wesleyan ellipse—"reason," "the moral character," and "free will"—took over from the primary poles, whereas they find their proper place in a Christian understanding of the human condition and divine salvation only when they stand in subordinate relation to the primary foci of "revelation," "the sinful predicament," and "free grace." The hypertrophy of the secondary elements in Methodism during the 19th and 20th centuries has doubtless been favored by the persisting ideology of the American Enlightenment, which is (at most) deistic in its theological options. Engagement with the more resistant Lutheranism could help Methodism towards a recovery of the Reformation priorites that still marked Wesley. In the other direction, if I may now be so bold: Methodist questioning of Lutherans in a Wesleyan spirit might help Lutherans to avoid the unilateralisms that tend to result from the corrective role which Luther necessarily played in the Western church of the 16th century.

III. Reshaping the Ellipse

Let us look at the need for, and possible course of, such interaction between Lutherans and Methodisms, starting again from the Methodist side with the three internal polarities already mentioned. First, reason and revelation. Perhaps the most regettable feature in the formulation of "Doctrinal Standards and Our Theological Task" in the 1988 United Methodist *Book of Discipline* is the panegyric to "reason" (¶68):

> By reason we read and interpret Scripture.
>
> By reason we determine whether our Christian witness is clear.
>
> By reason we ask questions of faith and seek to understand God's action and will.
>
> By reason we organize the understandings that compose our witness and render them internally coherent.
>
> By reason we test the congruence of our witness to the biblical testimony and to the traditions which mediate that testimony to us.
>
> By reason we relate our witness to the full range of human knowledge, experience, and service.

117

True, there is some recognition that "God's revelation and our experiences of God's grace surpass the scope of human language and reason," and some acknowledgement of "the limits and distortions characteristic of human knowledge." But one misses the sense, so strong in Luther, that the gospel "is being revealed" in "the preaching of Christ crucified," which is "foolishness to the Greeks."

Next, the moral character and the sinful predicament. Modern Methodists speak less of personal sanctification than their forebears, but they talk and act all the more as though human society as a whole could be turned in a salvific direction by their efforts. A recovery of the doctrine of original sin (still a key in Wesley as in the Reformers) and a greater appreciation of the distinction between the "two kingdoms" (another theme that needs further study, according to the international report) could help the Methodists towards more modesty in their social activism while also setting them free to resume the pursuit of a "Christian perfection" whose living signs are perhaps more present these days among Lutherans than among Methodists, *despite* (as Methodists might see it) the "simul iustus et peccator" understood as unremitting paradox.

And third, free will and free grace. If freedom of the will is taken absolutely (in what Wesley would call its "vulgar" sense), then one line leading from it could end up in a universalization of the "pro-choice" ideology, the destructive and self-destructive individualism rampant in modern Methodism as elsewhere. Wesley held that the measure of freedom needed to accept the gospel is itself a gracious restoration on the part of God towards humankind in virtue of Christ's redemptive work and for the sake of God's kingdom in which human salvation consists. Rubbing up against Lutherans and Luther as the "fifth evangelist" could help Methodists regain a sense of the awesome grace of God.

And now, again, in return: some recognition of the properly secondary poles in the Wesleyan configuration could protect Lutherans from that divine monergism which they have systematized on the basis of Luther's historically necessary rejection of works-righteousness. Doxologically, all Christians confess that God does *everything* for their salvation. Reflectively, Christians in the orthodox and catholic tradition then perceive that God does not work *alone* but graciously enables and invites our active acceptance and our continuing cooperation. That is what Wesley recognized in a will freed to accept the gospel, the call to growth in holiness, and even the use of a renewed mind.

IV. Justification and the Ecumenical Vision

With the last point I realize that I have hit the nerve center: the understanding of justification by grace through faith (alone). The 1989 working statement of the ELCA concerning its "ecumenical vision" endorses the Lutheran confessions when they "stress justification by grace through faith alone as the criterion for judging all church doctrine and life."[5] If there is disagreement on this issue (both as to justification itself and as regards its criteriological function), then it may be that the difference is, in Lutheran eyes, so *fundamental* that it does, after all, *sap* whatever other dogmatic agreements there may be. Perhaps, then, on their own terms, the Missouri Synod participants were right to refrain from subscribing the "Lutheran-United Methodist Statement on Baptism" of 1979.[6]

But, first, let us look again, however briefly and inadequately, at justification. For Wesley believed that he held the Reformation doctrine, at least as it was mediated to him through the Anglican Articles, Prayer Book, and Homilies; and Wesley's own teaching is enshrined in the "doctrinal standards" of Methodism.

The ELCA "vision" declares that the Gospel "is unconditional in that it announces the sure and certain promise of God who in Christ justifies the ungodly by grace through faith apart from works, and without partiality intends this for all people." With two hesitations or perhaps requests for clarification (to which I will return), I could as a Methodist accept that formulation. It does not, apart from the same reservations, go beyond the "fundamental affirmation" agreed in the national dialogue between Lutherans and Roman Catholics on "Justification by Faith" (1983): "Our entire hope of justification and salvation rests on Christ Jesus and on the gospel whereby the good news of God's merciful action in Christ is made known; we do not place our ultimate trust in anything other than God's promise and saving work in Christ" (§§4, 157).[7]

Now that affirmation is *not* claimed to be "fully equivalent to the Reformation teaching on justification" (§157). My own reservations concerning Lutheran formulations are close to some of those expressed by the Roman Catholics in the full report and are, I think, also Wesleyan. They are first attracted by the word "unconditional," which appears both in the ELCA vision and in Lutheran paragraphs in the Lutheran-Roman Catholic dialogue report. Faith is surely *necessary* to salvation (*sola fide* cannot mean *sine fide*) and is therefore in some sense a "condition." Reconciliation and justification are relational terms and are not realized until they are accepted. And the faith which accepts is, as Luther put it in his "Preface to the Romans" which was instrumental in John Wesley's "evangelical conversion," a "living, creative, active, powerful thing." This faith, while possible only by God's grace, is so active that it can even be called, according to such a self-consciously Lutheran theologian as Eilert Herms in his interpretation of Luther's "Sermon von den guten Werken," "a human deed and a good work," the first and foundational work of the Christian life.[8] Hence also my uneasiness at the extension of "apart from works" beyond the initial Pauline polemical context of "without the works *of the law.*"

It is, of course, for official ecclesiastical bodies to decide what degree of church fellowship is allowed and required by the continuing debate on justification. The theologians who signed the international report on *The Church: Community of Grace*, and those who subscribed *A Lutheran-United Methodist Statement on Baptism*, judged there to be (sufficient) agreement on salvation by grace through faith. My own hope is that Lutherans and Methodists will consider their mutual relationship to be at least as important, and advantageous, as their respective bilateral relationships with Roman Catholics, with Anglicans, and with the Reformed; and that all will continue to pursue unity (and its appropriate "forms," which are themselves, as the international Lutheran-Methodist dialogue recognized, a matter for further search) in the even wider multilateral context that includes also the Orthodox and the Baptists (to name only those).

CHAPTER SEVEN

Reason and Religion:
A Wesleyan Analogue to Grundtvig on
Modernity and the Christian Tradition

In the Anglican church Grundtvig found only rigid torpor
and empty forms. On his last English visit, in 1843, it was if
anything the Methodists who interested him. (Hal Koch,
Grundtvig [Yellow Springs, Ohio: Antioch Press, 1952],
103.)

I. Locating the Conversation Partners

As a Christian theologian, N. F. S. Grundtvig engaged with modernity
through recourse to the tradition of the Church; and he was able to do
so, precisely because modernity itself was, at least in part, an effect of
Christianity, a product of the *Wirkungsgeschichte* of the faith. Tensions
arise, however, between Christianity and modernity because modernity
has *also* other sources than the Christian faith, and these in turn can have
a distorting effect on the way Christianity is viewed and indeed held (as
would have been the case with the "rationalist Protestantism" of Professor
H. N. Clausen that combined a *sola Scriptura* position with an admission
of the "uncertain" and "contradictory" character of the Scriptures). The
trick, for Grundtvig in his time and for us in ours, must be to affirm and
integrate those features of our culture that derive from Christianity and
may enrich the Christian tradition, while at the same time we reject the
anti-Christian elements and demonstrate their wrongness. This twofold
(or fourfold) procedure—of assimilation and refusal (or affirmation and
integration, rejection and rebuttal)—is necessary for apologetics, evangelism and doxology, if the way is to be cleared, humanly speaking, for the
grace of God to abound to more and more people and for the eucharistic
chorus thereby to swell (cf. 2 Corinthians 4:15).[1] It requires us in our

generation, like the Church in each generation, to clarify the nature of the gospel and the faith; to discern the diachronic and synchronic identity of the believing and proclaiming community; and to risk making judgments as to where the kingdom of God is to be found. It is perhaps the principal duty of reflective theology to assist the Church and its pastoral leaders in these tasks.

Temporally to delimit "modernity," *die Neuzeit*, is difficult. In some intellectual and artistic circles on both sides of the North Atlantic, it is currently fashionable to speak of the "postmodern," and some would even say that we have already entered the next stage after that, however denominated; but such acceleration in journalistic historiography is to overprivilege—even granted an ostensibly unprecedented rapidity in superficial change—the ephemeral (and precisely *our* day in the sun) against the deeper and slower-moving "period" or "epoch" (*Konjunktur*) of "modernity," let alone the deepest levels of the human story, where anthropology is constant or nearly so.[2] My wager, for the purposes of present reflection, is that Grundtvig and ourselves live in what can still be significantly called a single period of history, and indeed that this period stretches back at least as far as John Wesley.[3]

It would, of course, be unwise to ignore altogether the differences of time and place. Philosophically, Wesley (1703–91) both was affected by and responded to the Enlightenment in its English form, characterized as it was by a Lockean empiricism and a Deistic worldview; religiously, Wesley was both helped by and became critical of German pietism in a Moravian or Herrnhut version; ecclesiastically, Wesley inherited the Reformation in its Anglican variant and sought to revitalize the Church of England according to the Prayer Book and the Homilies. Grundtvig's Denmark, two or even three generations later (1783–1872), was in some ways undergoing an Enlightenment that, across the German border, had both taken a Kantian turn and suffered a Romantic reaction. His church and people had been stamped by the Lutheran Reformation, and the vision which Grundtvig sought to implement for the Church of Denmark and the Danish nation would inevitably bear certain characteristics of Luther and his reception northwards. We live two hundred years after Wesley's death, and one hundred and twenty after Grundtvig's. Denmark is separated from Britain by the North Sea, and both are separated from the United States by the Atlantic Ocean, two stretches of water where the weather can be notoriously rough. My own situation is further complicated by the fact that I was raised a British Methodist and remain a minister of the British Methodist Church, even while living for the past decade and a half in a country where, at least since American independence, Wesley has been "received" in an ecclesiastical and cultural context that differs in complexity and style from his native land and mine. For all these reasons, the most that can be expected is an "analogy" between Grundtvig and Wesley, coming from a theologian who constantly struggles to keep Wesley's mark upon the latter's only half-intended ecclesiastical progeny (Wesley sought to remain Anglican, even while his para-church structures made an eventual ecclesial autonomy almost inevitable), while at the same time displaying that ecumenical openness and concern that is evinced precisely in, say, Wesley's sermon on the "Catholic Spirit" or in his "Letter to a Roman Catholic."[4] A sufficient commonality between Grundtvig and Wesley, while not neglecting certain differences between them, may help us to discern a viable range of nuanced options for ecclesial practice amid the modernity that continues to affect and challenge us all.

Wesley has recently been presented, in a rather controversial intellectual and theological biography, as a "reasonable enthusiast."[5] In that title, Henry Rack certainly links—in a tension-laden though hopefully not oxymoronic way—two characteristics of Wesley that Wesley himself might almost have preferred to designate according to the titles of his two apologetic "Appeals" to "Men of *Reason* and *Religion*."[6] "Enthusiasm" was what Wesley's high-and-dry critics in his own day accused him of, when he saw himself rather as simply encouraging "vital religion" or "real Christian experience," whose "reasonable" nature he himself was persuaded of—provided, of course, "reason" was not limited, as by the very definition of some of his contemporaries, in such a way as to exclude transcendent revelation and grace. The original and normative gospel and faith were to be found, according to Wesley, in the Scriptures (one of the most important of all his sermons expounded "The Scripture Way of Salvation"[7]), to which, above all, the earliest centuries and the English Reformers had been faithful. Methodism was but "the true old Christianity,"[8] partly recovered at the Reformation and now commendable to all "men of reason and religion" in face of its regrettable decline in the England of his day.

Scripture, tradition, reason, and experience: those are the four factors which recent scholarship has detected in the shaping of Wesley's thinking and practice. In setting the standards for "our theological task," the 1972 *Discipline* of the United Methodist Church in turn noted that the Methodist pioneers believed there to be "a 'marrow' of Christian truth that can be identified and that must be conserved. This living core, as they believed, stands revealed in *Scripture*, illuminated by *tradition*, vivified in personal *experience*, and confirmed by *reason*."[9] For a brief while in the 1970s and 1980s, this fourfold strand became popularly known in American Methodism as the Wesleyan or Methodist "quadrilateral" (no less a figure than Cardinal Ratzinger told the present writer he had heard of the Methodist

Viereck); but in so far as this expression may suggest an equal authority given to all four on a level plane, it is historically and theologically misleading, and much more careful attention is needed concerning the complex interplay and permutations among the four "sources" or "authorities." Nevertheless, this fourfold formulation, of Wesleyan or Methodist provenance, will be used, in an admittedly oversimple way, to identify some features by which Wesley and Grundtvig may be compared in their approaches to the issues of Christianity and modernity, with a view to detecting the range of tolerable options open to us as their respective heirs. Given the limitations of my own knowledge of Grundtvig, the weight will fall on the Wesleyan side of the analogy, and it will be up to those more familiar with Grundtvig, and especially those Danish readers who understand themselves in his line, to complement and correct what I say of Grundtvig[10] and to judge how far the range of compatible attitudes to modernity really extends for us at present.

We shall begin with reason and experience, for it is in those areas that the challenge of modernity is usually first encountered. Then we shall look at scripture and tradition, for those are the inherited resources upon which Christianity must draw if it is to retain its historic identity.

II. *The Status and Use of Reason*

Wesley's life spanned a century that considered itself the Age of Reason, even if it was only in 1793 that Reason became cultically enthroned for a few months in the cathedral of Notre Dame in Paris. That apotheosis, signifying the self-worship of humankind in its immanent powers, was but the logical entailment of the relegation of God from the world undertaken by the English Deists at the beginning of the century (John Toland's *Christianity Not Mysterious*, 1696; Matthew Tindal's *Christianity as Old as Creation*, 1730). Wesley would have no truck with the Deists and the dismissal of God to which their reasonings brought them: true Christianity was distinguished from Deism by the Atonement, by the original sin which made the latter needed, and by the incarnation through which the Triune God made it possible. Thus Wesley wrote to Mary Bishop in a letter of February 7, 1778: "Nothing in the Christian system is of greater consequence than the doctrine of Atonement. It is properly the distinguishing point between Deism and Christianity. . . . Give up the Atonement, and the Deists are agreed with us. . . . What saith the Scripture? It says, 'God was in Christ, reconciling the world unto Himself'; that 'He made Him, who knew no sin, to be a sin-offering for us'. . . . But undoubtedly, as long as the world stands, there will be a thousand objections to this scriptural doctrine. For still the preaching of Christ crucified will be foolishness to the wise men of the world. However, let *us* hold the precious truth fast in our heart as well as in our understanding; and we shall find by happy experience that this is to us the wisdom of God and the power of God."[11]

The reference to "understanding" suffices to show that Wesley was not thereby abandoning intelligence. To the contrary: in his "Earnest Appeal" to "Men of Reason" he acknowledged and affirmed that "so far as [a man] departs from true genuine reason, so far he departs from Christianity."[12] That is because Christianity is "a religion evidently founded on, and every way agreeable to, eternal reason, to the essential nature of things. Its foundation stands on the nature of God and the nature of man, together with their mutual relations. And it is every way suitable thereto. To the nature of God, for it begins in knowing him—and where but in the true knowledge of God can you conceive true religion to begin? It goes on in loving him and all mankind—for you cannot but imitate whom you love. It ends in serving him, in doing his will, in obeying him whom we know and love. It is in every way suited to the nature of man, for it begins in man's knowing himself: knowing himself to be what he really is—foolish, vicious, miserable. It goes on to point out the remedy for this, to make him truly wise, virtuous, and happy, as every thinking mind (perhaps from some implicit remembrance of what it originally was) longs to be. It finishes all by restoring the due relations between God and man, by uniting for ever the tender father and the grateful, obedient son; the great Lord of all and the faithful servant, doing not his own will but the will of him that sent him."[13]

Within that divinely-posed ontological context of "eternal reason," reason may appropriately denote the human "faculty of reasoning, of inferring one thing from another."[14] In matters of religion, all depends then on the right use of reason, which is a God-enabled use of a God-given faculty: "We therefore not only allow, but earnestly exhort all who seek after true religion to use all the reason which God hath given them in searching out the things of God. But your *reasoning justly*, not only on this but on any subject whatsoever, presupposes *true judgments* already formed whereon to ground your argumentation. . . . [And] before it is possible for you to form a true judgment of them, it is absolutely necessary that you have a *clear apprehension* of the things of God. . . . And seeing our ideas are not innate, but must all originally come from our senses, it is certainly necessary that you have senses capable of discerning objects of this kind—not those only which are called 'natural senses,' which in this respect profit nothing, as being altogether incapable of discerning objects of a spiritual kind, but *spiritual* senses, exercised to discern spiritual good and evil. It is necessary that you have the *hearing* ear and the *seeing* eye, emphatically so called. . . . And till you have these internal senses, till the eyes of your understanding are opened, you can have no apprehesnsion of divine things, no idea of them at all. Nor consequently, till then, can you either judge truly or reason justly concerning them, seeing your reason has no ground whereon to stand, no materials to work upon."[15] Once the Holy Spirit has revealed the things of God and bestowed the gift of faith, there is room for the believing mind to engage in more particular "chains of reasoning or argumentation, so close, so solid, so regularly connected" as may be found, for example, in the Epistle to the Hebrews.[16]

Doxologically, faith is maximized in comparison with unaided sense and reason:

> Author of faith, eternal Word,
> Whose Spirit breathes the active flame;
> Faith, like its Finisher and Lord,
> Today as yesterday the same:
>
> To Thee our humble hearts aspire,
> And ask the gift unspeakable;
> Increase in us the kindled fire,
> In us the work of faith fulfil.
>
> . . . .
>
> The things unknown to feeble sense,
> Unseen by reason's glimmering ray,
> With strong, commanding evidence
> Their heavenly origin display.
>
> Faith lends its realizing light,
> The clouds disperse, the shadows fly;
> Th' Invisible appears in sight,
> And God is seen by mortal eye.[17]

None of the above, adapted as it is from a Lockean epistemology, may be too far from Grundtvig. Grundtvig rejected "abstract philosophical rationalism" (Schjørring); he set "true reason," which recognizes the "older" truth, against "autonomous" or "false, mortal reason" (Jørgensen). And what Grundtvig had to say anthropologically about language may, in its theological application, give a better account than Wesley himself—if there is in him a tendency finally to depreciate the physical senses—of the part played by preaching, and by the responsive confession of faith, in the juncture of body and spirit and in the communication between God and man: "Through the sense of hearing we experience not only something physical, the sound, but also something spiritual, the word."[18] Then, too, according to Grundtvig, theological reasoning has its place, within the framework of the "rule of faith" (*regula fidei*), in the refutation of heretics (as Schjørring recalls in connection with Grundtvig's translation of the fifth book of Irenaeus' *Adversus Haereses*).

In the self-criticism of the modern which (I bet) the "postmodern" represents, rationality has once again become an important issue. "According to *which* rationality?" is a question that Alasdair MacIntyre has shown always needs to be asked, when reason is invoked or reasoning is practiced.[19] Against any too facile claims made by the Enlightenment in favor of an empirically universal reason, MacIntyre rightly argues that reasoning is always diachronically and synchronically "situated"—in a tradition and a community. Taken too far, however, that line could lead precisely to the epistemological scepticism that results from overprivileging the alleged "interest" of a putative knower over against what is there to be known, or to the spatial and temporal fragmentation of thinking that makes many "postmoderns" finally irrationalist.

The Christian story and confession offers rather a framework within which to account for the ontological consistency of true reasoning (thanks to the creative work of the Logos of the unique and universal Creator), the empirical distortions of knowledge and argument that are due to the self-interest of human thinkers (which manifests original sin and its persistence), and the hope for a final harmony between all true knowers and the truly known (when the reconciliation wrought through the redemptive work of Christ will have extended according to the fulness of God's purposes). According to the Christian faith, the *universality* which was too abstractly and unproblematically assumed by the Enlightenment and the *particularity* which the "postmoderns" exalt at the expense of coherence meet in the *concrete universal* of the Word made flesh as Jesus of Nazareth. Of all contemporary theologians, T. F. Torrance has perhaps done most to show the correspondence—when both are seen as participation in the given structures of being—between the Christian faith and the procedures of the natural sciences which have produced the most significant achievements of modernity.[20] Torrance indeed holds that modern scientific method is historically dependent upon an attitude to the world that derives from the biblical faith. Persuasively proposed, such a connaturality, or even dependence, between faith and science affords a promising instrument for apologetics and evangelism amid modernity. And in turn, whatever in the fruit of modern science will pass muster by an evangelical ethic can be integrated into the Christian tradition.

Finally under reason may be mentioned an issue which is internal to Christianity and chiefly concerns the latter's "modernist" practitioners. It is the relation of what Wesley calls "doctrine" and "opinion," which broadly overlaps the question that Grundtvig might designate as "faith" and "theology." It must at once be stated that by "doctrine" Wesley does not mean what Grundtvig might call a "dead system" (or "mere orthodoxy," as Wesley might put it); rather "doctrine" for Wesley is "the faith which is believed" (*fides quae creditur*), the content of the "faith which believes" (*fides quâ creditur*), which is itself a living faith. In matters of theology, Wesley is largely content to "think and let think"—but only "in *opinions* that do not strike at the root of Christianity."[21] On the other (or rather the same) hand, in a generously ecumenical text Wesley declares that "a man of truly catholic spirit is fixed as the sun in his judgment concerning the main branches of Christian *doctrine*."[22] This appears quite close to what Grundtvig means by letting the Church rest on the "firm, unshakeable foundations" of the apostolic faith, while allowing "freedom of thought in the school of theology" (Schjørring), tolerating and even encouraging "all theological difference that is reconcilable with the fundamental Christian faith" (Jørgensen).

Such views certainly permit the "exploratory" work that is dear to modern theologians as they seek to engage with the (relatively) "new" questions put by the changes in culture. But it is also clear that, for disciples of Wesley and Grundtvig, a Christian theologian will stay within the ground-plan of the *regula fidei*, and that speculative construction must not exceed what the apostolic foundations of faith and doctrine will support, nor must these foundations be undermined by critical cavils drawn from an essentially different world-view.

III. *The Place and Value of Experience*

According to Jørgensen, faith for Grundtvig "must be a matter of experience, because it concerns the salvation and thus the integrity of the individual. . . . The Christian faith must be verifiable in the life experience of the individual. . . . It is a precondition that man's autonomy be accepted. Man can only endorse what he can recognize as truth from his inner conviction." Faith is "the individual's most fundamental act of life." Yet the arbitrariness of individualism is avoided: "The autonomy of the heart, understood as its immediacy to God, is matched by God's sovereignty in His approach by virtue of His Word, which is Christ"; and that "brightly-alive" Word comes to humans in the historic community which it continues to create, namely the Church. The certainty of faith thus has its origin outside the believing individual—in the "external Word" (*verbum externum*), which is Christ himself who comes to expression in the Apostolic Confession and the Means of Grace.

For Wesley, too, Christianity is, in eighteenth-century terminology, "an experimental religion." Whereas Grundtvig at times appears to locate at the level of creation the human freedom to receive the gospel (as may be implied in what he has to say about the gift of language or in the polyvalent motto "first a man, then a Christian"), Wesley sees fallen humanity dependent, for its openness to accept the gospel, upon a sufficient restoration of freedom that has taken place only in virtue of the redemptive work of Christ: "Every man has a measure of free will *restored* to him by grace."[23] Although there may then be different "degrees of faith" (the fearful "faith of a servant," the confident "faith of a son"), it is, according to Wesley, "the general privilege of believers" to be "assured" of their present state of salvation (which is no guarantee against backsliding or forfeiture). That assurance is given by "the witness of the Spirit with our spirit, that we are children of God, whereby we cry 'Abba, Father'" (Romans 8:15f. is a frequently cited text). Wesley can, of course, also speak in christological terms of Christ living in the believer and the believer's being conformed to Christ.[24]

Doxologically, the most significant expression of Wesleyan experientialism is the principal and resumptive *Collection of Hymns for the Use of the People called Methodists* (1780), where "the hymns are not carelessly jumbled together, but carefully ranged under proper heads, according to the experience of real Christians. So that this book is in effect a little body of experimental and practical divinity."[25] The introductory first part is given to "exhorting and beseeching to return to God," "describing the pleasantness of religion, the goodness of God, death, judgment, heaven, hell," and "praying for a blessing." Part two briefly contrasts "formal religion" and "inward religion." Then the heart of the book comes in the next two sections: part three is devoted to "praying for repentance, for mourners convinced of sin, brought to the birth, convinced of backsliding, recovered," and part four to prayer "for believers rejoicing, fighting, praying, watching, working, suffering, groaning for full redemption, brought to the birth, saved, interceding for the world." The fifth and final part is "for the Society, meeting, giving thanks, praying, parting." Thus the emphasis falls on the way in which, within the fellowship of the Methodist Society, the individual is brought from sin through faith to salvation, corresponding to Wesley's statement that "our main doctrines, which include all the rest, are three, that of repentance, of faith, and of holiness."[26] In the 1780 *Collection*, the objective existence, work and presence of God are literally "taken for granted," and the interest centers on their achievement in the believer's justification and sanctification. Even in the many hymns, published in other collections, which Charles Wesley wrote for the great festivals that celebrate the Nativity, Passion, Resurrection and Ascension of Christ and the gift of the Holy Spirit at Pentecost, the present engagement of the worshipping believer is always prominent.

In his "Earnest Appeal" to "Men of Religion," Wesley is concerned that they pass from "the form" to "the power of godliness."[27] Correspondingly, he will not remain content with accurate statement of doctrines or with intellectual assent to them. With regard to the Trinity, for example, he endeavours to show, more experientially, that "the knowledge of the Three-One God is interwoven with all true Christian faith, with all vital religion": "I know not how anyone can be a Christian believer till 'he hath' (as St. John speaks) 'the witness in himself'; till 'the Spirit of God witnesses with his spirit that he is a child of God'—that is, in effect, till God the Holy Ghost witnesses that God the Father has accepted him through the merits of God the Son—and having this witness he honours the Son and the blessed Spirit 'even as he honours the Father.' Not that every Christian believer *adverts* to this; perhaps at first not one in twenty; but if you ask any of them a few questions you will easily find it is implied in what he believes."[28]

Now experience, whether empirical or existential, has been much valued in modernity, and it might appear that Wesley and Grundtvig were, in their insistence on the experiential dimension of faith, not only children of their age but also (and thereby) apt for apologetics and evangelism in the service and line of the Christian tradition. But matters are not quite so simple: much depends on the precise place of experience in historic Christianity. George Lindbeck has recently argued that there is, in typically "modern" Christianity, an experience with experience that in fact *reverses* the sequence and priorities of an older, more original and therefore more authentic, Christianity. In modernity, religious interests easily "take the experiential-expressive form of individual quests for personal meaning": "The structures of modernity press individuals to meet God first in the depths of their souls and then, perhaps, if they find something personally congenial, to become part of a tradition or join a church."[29] In my judgment, both Grundtvig and Wesley remain exempt from this flaw on account of their firm recognition of the divine origination of faith "outside of ourselves" (*extra nos*); and both of them can be accommodated within the "cultural-linguistic" understanding and practice of Christianity which Lindbeck advocates as both ancient and *post*-modern, but the demonstration of that will have to await an exposition of their views on scripture and tradition in the next two parts of this chapter.

Meanwhile it may just be necessary to reaffirm, in face of some forms of would-be *post*-modernism, that the individual and his or her personal experience were important in Wesley and Grundtvig and *will always remain so* in a faith which believes that even the hairs of our head are numbered by God. The "decentring of the subject" occurs, for Christianity, not in the subject's fragmentation or even dissolution but rather by the coming of one "from outside" to visit and dwell "within us":

> Vi ere, vi bleve,
> Vi røres, vi leve
> I Christus, Guds levende Ord;
> Tag Ordet i Munden,
> Og elsk det fra Grunden!
> Da hos dig i Navnet han boer.[30]

—and that presence is a transformative one:

> Heavenly Adam, Life divine,
> Change my nature into Thine;
> Move and spead throughout my soul,
> Actuate and fill the whole;
> Be it I no longer now
> Living in the flesh, but Thou.[31]

IV. The Sufficiency or Subservience of Scripture

Wesley called himself "a man of one book" (*homo unius libri*). That "one book" of the Bible constituted for Wesley not so much the "boundary of his reading" as "the center of gravity in his thinking,"[32] and there can be no doubt that he attributed a strong instrumentality to the Scriptures in the process of salvation: "I am creature of a day, passing through life as an arrow through the air. I am a spirit come from God and returning to God; just hovering over the great gulf, till a few moments hence I am no more seen—I drop into an unchangeable eternity! I want to know one thing, the way to heaven—how to land safe on that happy shore. God himself has condescended to teach the way: for this very end he came from heaven. He hath written it down in a book. O give me that book! At any price give me the Book of God! I have it. Here is knowledge enough for me. Let me be *homo unius libri*."[33] The written word remains subordinate to the work of the incarnate Word ("he came from heaven"), and it is significant that the passage just quoted comes from the preface to Wesley's *Sermons*, for in preaching, the "living voice of the gospel" (*viva vox evangelii*) is heard.[34] Yet scripture itself, as Wesley retained from the Anglican Articles of Religion, "containeth all things necessary to salvation."

Being already over seventy years old when Lessing published the

131

Wolfenbüttel fragments of Reimarus, Wesley remained largely innocent of the "higher criticism." He knew, however, that the scriptures needed exegesis, and to help his preachers and his people he produced his *Explanatory Notes upon the Old Testament* and, in a text that became constitutionally embedded in Methodism, the *Explanatory Notes upon the New Testament*.[35] Where any text appeared "dark or intricate," Wesley followed the traditional procedures for seeking understanding as he had outlined them in the preface to his *Sermons*: first he prayed to the Father of lights for illumination, and then "I search after and consider parallel passages of Scripture, 'comparing spiritual things with spiritual'. I meditate thereon, with all the attention and earnestness of which my mind is capable. If any doubt still remains, I consult those who are experienced in the things of God, and then the writings whereby, being dead, they yet speak. And what I thus learn, that I teach."[36]

This pre-critical approach easily allowed for the doxological use of the scriptures in hymns, in which interwoven texts depict the basic patterns of the Christian faith in ever-changing varieties of color. The following example from Charles Wesley's "Spirit of faith, come down" (of 1746) is characteristic:[37]

No man can truly say	
That Jesus is the Lord,	[1 Cor. 12:3]
Unless Thou take the veil away,	[2 Cor. 3:12-18]
And breathe the living word;	[Matt. 4:4;
Then, only then, we feel	John 20:22]
Our interest in His blood,	
And cry with joy unspeakable:	[1 Pet. 1:8]
Thou art my Lord, my God!	[John 20:28]

Such procedures also allow the scriptures to be read for their fourfold meaning, as in the medieval senses of the historical, the doctrinal, the moral and the anagogical.

For Grundtvig, too, sermons and hymns, "the preaching and the songs of praise," were vital to the communication of God's Word, although (according to the interpretation of both Jørgensen and Schjørring) he appears to make the scriptures subservient to the ancient creeds and the continuing confession in ways that would have struck Wesley (I think) as tending to undermine the normativity of the scriptures themselves over against any subsequent witness to Christ. Perhaps, by his positive emphasis on tradition, Grundtvig was already also, on the defensive front, making moves to counter the problems that would arise when the combination of a *sola scriptura* position with a critical approach to the Bible, occurring already in Clausen, would finally expose Protestantism to the revisionary proposals of a D. F. Strauss. In any case, Grundtvig apparently felt confident enough to be "open to the historical interpretation of biblical texts" even when this displayed "a tendency towards modern criticism" (Schjørring). Lessing's historical and hermeneutical "ditch" could be bridged by the living presence of Christ, by the traditionary process of the Church, and by an anthropological constancy that allowed biblical personages to figure as "examples of basic human characteristics" whose stories thereby remained susceptible to an "existential interpretation" (Schjørring).

The difference between Grundtvig and Wesley may be epitomized in the fact that Wesley calls the Bible "the Book of God" (and speaks in strong terms of the divine "inspiration" of the writings), whereas Grundtvig, even (or precisely) when he is dealing with the rationalistic criticism of "our present-day scholars," sees the historical books of the New Testament as "first and foremost . . . a human testimony about the founding of the Christian church." As "the oldest church history," they provide "a truthful and dependable history of the life and teachings of Jesus Christ and his chief apostles, and of the initial beginning of the expansion of their teaching."[38] While it is possible to interpret Wesley and Grundtvig in a convergent way (by stressing the congruence between the divine revelation or inspiration and the human witness or record), they clearly make a difference of emphasis—and Grundtvig's "church-historical" approach facilitates his high valuation of the Apostles' Creed and later confessions and prepares the way for a more "continuous" view of the Christian tradition than Wesley, as we shall see, allows.

How, now, may Wesley and Grundtvig offer us common or distinctive help for the appropriation of the scriptures in modernity or post-modernity? I would judge that modernity has precluded any return to a method of dealing with the scriptures that *ignores* historical investigation. Here Grundtvig's "openness to the historical investigation of biblical texts" is basically correct. Belief in the Incarnation makes it both necessary and possible to seek out "how things really were" (*wie es eigentlich gewesen*). But such investigation need not, and should not, be constrained by Humean or Troeltschean limits that rule out "miracle" by a combination of scepticism and a closed-causality view of reality. W. Pannenberg's treatment of the Resurrection provides an excellent example of better procedures.[39]

Yet I should not wish to follow Grundtvig too readily in his seeming "demotion" of the scriptures in relation to ancient creeds and continuing confession—precisely because the scriptures have proved themselves better guardians of the traditional faith than either a creed left drifting from its scriptural moorings or typically modern attempts to "save" the gospel by "demythologization." Although, historically, oral and practical tradition preceded the New Testament scriptures, and although the confession and preaching of the apostolic faith developed in parallel with the development of those scriptures, yet I judge (standing in the line of Wesley) that ancient creedal confessions and epitomes of the apostolic preaching must, theologically, be seen as summaries of the scriptures before they can be seen, as it were independently, as their hermeneutical key. Otherwise the creeds, by their very brevity, become too easy game, in the modern period at least, for the reductionism inherent in "doctrinal criticism" (so, on the Anglican side, G. F. Woods, M. F. Wiles, and, yes, D. Cupitt); and the "rule of faith" or "canon of truth" of an Irenaeus, by its selective concision, might seem to excuse (on the Lutheran side) a Bultmann's procedure of narrowing the kerygma to (say) justification by faith, now modernized as authentic existence. The thick and complex texture of the scriptures themselves keeps them resistant to truncation and allows them to go on providing a variety of resources for contemporary proclamation and confession.

Several features currently seen as characteristic of "post-modernity" should help to regain a hearing for a view of the scriptures in some ways closer to the Wesleyan (although, of course, secular scholars would want to prescind from questions of the divine inspiration and salvific purpose of the Bible). Interest in "text," and particularly in the integral form of texts, meshes with the "canon criticism" by which some North American exegetes have sought again to read the parts of scripture according to their place in the ecclesially received whole.[40] Reader-response criticism allows new attention to the *Wirkungsgeschichte* of the scriptures (remember G. Ebeling's thesis of "church history as the history of the exegesis of holy scripture"![41]) and opens up the possibility of multiple "readings" along the lines of the four medieval "senses" of scripture. Without seeking to turn the clock back,[42] there is now an available option to penetrate through and beyond historical criticism to a "second naïveté" (P. Ricoeur). In any case, the notion of myth is enjoying something of an intellectual comeback in post-modernity, even (and indeed most significantly) among the natural sciences.[43] George Lindbeck, in his "cultural-linguistic" approach to Christianity, has boldly revived the notion of a scriptural world being able to absorb the universe: "For those who are steeped in them, no world is more real than the ones [the canonical scriptures] create. . . . [A scriptural world] supplies the interpretive framework within which believers seek to live their lives and interpret reality."[44] According to Lindbeck, ecclesial doctrine then functions to set the "rules" by which this should take place; and therewith we return to the notion of the *regula fidei* and the tradition of the Church.

V. The Promise and Problem of Tradition

Grundtvig, it is generally agreed, held a strong view of ecclesial tradition. Behind "the historical continuity of the Church," the "long chain of tradition," lies a "divine power," the signs of whose presence and the means of whose action are principally the Apostolic Confession and the Means of Grace; these "essentials of the Church are safeguards of what is primordial, unchangeable and recognizable in the Church" (Schjørring). As Jørgensen points out, this comes very close to article VII of the Augustana: "Est autem ecclesia congregatio sanctorum, in qua evangelium pure docetur et recte administrantur sacramenta." Grundtvig's favorite witnesses in and to Church tradition were Irenaeus, Luther and "our Lutheran forefathers," although his hymn-translations show him willing to draw doxologically upon Christians from a very wide range of times and places.

Living as he did before the Romantic movement, Wesley did not hold such an "organic" view of ecclesial tradition as may be found in J. A. Möhler, J. H. Newman, and perhaps N. F. S. Grundtvig.[45] True, he retained the Apostolicum doxologically from the *Book of Common Prayer* in the morning and evening prayer of *The Sunday Service of the Methodists* prepared for North America; and he respected and used the Nicaenum and the Athanasianum doctrinally as the formal and substantive "rules" of the Christian faith: his exposition of "the faith of a true Protestant" in the *Letter to a Roman Catholic* consists in an expansion on the Nicene-Constantinopolitan creed;[46] and he valued the Athanasian Creed's "explication" of the Trinity as "the best I ever saw."[47] Wesley also appealed to the writings (incorporating some of them into his *Christian Library*, 50 volumes, 1747–55) and life of the "Primitive Church" of the first *three* centuries as a period of great, though not total, purity which the English Reformers had sought to repristinate.[48] Moreover, in the "Earnest Appeal to Men of Reason and Religion," Wesley draws on Anglican Article XIX (so close to CA VII) to define the Church as essentially "a company of faithful (or believing) people, *coetus credentium*," with the properties "that the pure word of God be preached therein, and the sacraments duly administered." "Assembling together," they are "visible"; "scattered abroad," "dispersed up and down," they are (curiously, in Wesley's terminology) "invisible." In any case, "the Church of England" is "the *faithful people*, the *true believers* of England."[49] Yet those words, which Wesley himself italicizes, start to hint at a different ecclesiology, and a different view of tradition, than Grundtvig's. While without the preaching and hearing of the pure word of God "faith would languish and die," and while the sacraments are "the ordinary means whereby God increases

135

faith," yet the essence is a "living faith, without which indeed there can be no church at all"—and, for Wesley, "living faith" has as its *indispensable expression* Christian character and works.[50]

Wesley, in fact, largely shared the "radical" view of a fall, or at least a precipitous decline, of the Church that set in at "that evil hour when Constantine the Great called himself a Christian."[51] A sermon on "The Mystery of Iniquity" declares that "persecution never did, nor could give any lasting wound to genuine Christianity. But the greatest it ever received, the grand blow which was struck at the very root of that humble, gentle, patient love, which is the fulfilling of the Christian law, the whole essence of true religion, was struck in the fourth century by Constantine the Great, when he called himself a Christian, and poured in a flood of riches, honours, and power upon the Christians, more especially upon the clergy. . . . When the fear of persecution was removed, and wealth and honour attended the Christian profession, the Christians did not gradually sink, but rushed headlong into all manner of vices. . . . Such has been the deplorable state of the Christian Church from the time of Constantine till the Reformation. A Christian nation, a Christian city . . . was nowhere to be seen; but every city and country, a few individuals excepted, was plunged in all manner of wickedness."[52] The Reformation itself, according to Wesley, was only partially successful. Then his "Farther Appeal to Men of Reason and Religion" contains, in its second part, a descriptive catalogue of the vices that currently abounded in England and, in the third part, an account of the "call to repentance" with which Methodism began to execute its vocation to "spread scriptural holiness through the land," and some evidence of its success.[53] All this makes for a much more "episodic" view of the history of Christianity than is suggested by Grundtvig's "historical continuity" and "the long chain of tradition."[54]

Since baptism is generally regarded as the sacramental initiation into the tradition, the differences between Wesley and Grundtvig on tradition may be expected to come to significant expression in their respective views on baptism, and some clarification on this matter may also help the English and Danish churches as to the policies they pursue in a social, cultural and religious situation that is at least as problematic as those obtaining in the days of Wesley and Grundtvig respectively. In Grundtvig, baptism always figures in tandem with communion as "means of grace," and he appears never to call in question the general practice of baptizing infants in a multitudinist folk-church. Wesley, too, accepted the Anglican practice of infant baptism and appears never to have abandoned the belief that its subjects were thereby sacramentally regenerated.[55] But the stress in his preaching on the empirical need for *post*-baptismal "new birth" always shocks Lutherans accustomed to the "Baptizatus sum." Thus: "Say not then in your heart, I *was once* baptized; therefore I *am now* a child of God. Alas, that consequence will by no means hold. How many are the baptized gluttons and drunkards, the baptized liars and common swearers, the baptized railers and evil-speakers, the baptized whoremongers, thieves, extortioners! . . . To say then that ye cannot be born again, that there is no new birth but in baptism, is to seal you all under damnation, to consign you to hell, without any help, without hope. . . . Lean no more on the staff of that broken reed, that ye *were* born again in baptism. Who denies that ye were then made 'children of God, and heirs of the kingdom of heaven'? But notwithstanding this, ye are now children of the devil; therefore ye must be born again."[56]

On a visit to Denmark just a few years ago, I was told there were three things one must never question: NATO, the Queen, and infant baptism. Is then the Church of Denmark (still—if it ever was) able to count on a kind of delayed catechesis being provided in the free-schools, folk-high-schools, and finally church-institutions in order to initiate growing children and young adults into the liturgical and moral existence for which their baptism in infancy marked them out (first baptized, then human, finally Christian—as it were)?[57] In England, at least, modernity has brought a far greater disruption to any such pattern: the number of infant baptisms among Anglicans per 1,000 live births in the general population fell from 672 in 1950, to 554 in 1960, to 466 in 1970, to 365 in 1980, to 288 in 1988. Over the same period, the number of Easter communicants has also declined, although at a noticeably slower rate on account of the time-lag, from 2 million (of a total population aged fifteen and over of 32.3 million) in 1950 to 1.58 million (of 38.8 million) in 1988.[58] In an effort to close the gap between the number of the baptized (which is any case shrinking on account of social and cultural factors) and the number of believing and practicing Christians, some voices in the Church of England are calling for greater discipline in baptismal use; but other Anglicans reject any move which might seem to turn the Church of England into a mere voluntarist "denomination" like (say) the Methodists. Meanwhile, on the Western side of the Atlantic, a parish priest in the Orthodox Church of America tells me his practice is to baptize infants only when he would be willing to baptize their parents or sponsors (were they not baptized already). That may be a lesson for Danes, English and Americans, Lutherans, Anglicans and Methodists, to relearn from the Ancient Church that was so much admired by Wesley and by Grundtvig in their respective ways.

VI. *Identifying a Eucharistic Church*

Between Grundtvig and Wesley we have discovered both commonalities and differences in respect of reason, experience, scripture and tradition and the place of these in the engagement between Christianity and modernity. In conclusion, it may be suggested that the commonalities come to best expression in the sacrament of the Lord's Supper, which, in addition, provides not only a framework in which the differences between Wesley and Grundtvig can be moderated but also a paradigm of understanding and practice for the Church in its cultural, worldly setting.

The Lord's Supper was vitally important for both Wesley and Grundtvig. Wesley's lifelong observance and advocacy of "constant communion" was merely sealed when, in writing in 1784 to the "brethren in North America", he advised "the elders to administer the Supper of the Lord on every Lord's day."[59] In 1745, John and Charles Wesley produced a collection of 166 *Hymns on the Lord's Supper* to enhance the Prayer Book order.[60] At a time when the Danish church, in its pietism or its rationalism, failed to show much interest in the sacraments, Grundtvig insisted on baptism and the supper as dominical means of grace, and his hymns abound with references to "bath and board," "font and table."

Let us then attempt the constructive statement of a eucharistic ecclesiology that incorporates and reconciles some of the strongest features of Wesley and Grundtvig: At the Lord's Supper, as the baptized and believing congregation gathers in the Lord's name, the combination and interplay of scripture reading, preaching, confession of faith and prayer allow the living Word to be heard. Here, in Christ, the congregation finds itself in communion with the whole company of heaven and all those who at all times and in all places have joined in the unending songs of praise. Here every believer, in the fellowship of the Church, may have his or her experience shaped, and character formed, by the scriptural and traditional experience of the Christian community as it receives the Father's blessings through Christ in the Holy Spirit and, as sons and daughters in the Son, by the Holy Spirit cries "Abba, Father" and produces the fruit of the Spirit to God's glory; here participants are fed body and soul by Christ and taste in advance the joys of heaven.[61] Here Christians learn doxological thinking, in which their reasoning is trained by the Logós, who became incarnate in Jesus Christ and was crucified and raised, and they learn to discern the signs of God's kingdom and corresponding ways of action in the world.[62]

In the last generation or two, there has occurred a growing ecumenical awareness and practice of a eucharistic ecclesiology that must rejoice the hearts of Wesley and of Grundtvig. While, in this life, a eucharistic community may always run the risk of self-righteousness, which needs to be countered by the remembrance that participants come as forgiven sinners, penitent and believing, yet the sharpening of the contours of ecclesial identity that takes place at the Lord's Supper has great potential for the clarity of the Church's witness to the world, whether ancient or modern.[63]

METHODISTS AND REFORMED

CHAPTER EIGHT

Perfect Salvation
in the Teaching of Wesley and Calvin

I. *Mutual and Common Learning*

Calvin already taught Christian perfection, as Wesley was to. Partly as a result of differences of emphasis in definition, however, they differ on the time it may be attained; and these differences point to substantive problems. A particular weakness in Wesley's teaching on perfection—at the divine end of the scale—might be corrected by attention to Calvin's doctrine of the perseverance of the saints, which Wesley rejected. Calvin's doctrine of the perseverance of the saints depends, however, on his doctrine of predestination, which Wesley severely criticized. Some of Wesley's criticisms could usefully qualify that doctrine, so that, in turn, a modified doctrine of perseverance might strengthen Wesley's own teaching on perfection.

The common interest of Calvin and Wesley in the restoration of God's image in humanity provides an area of convergence in their doctrine of salvation. At this point, both of them could profit from a recovery of some features in the medieval notion of *habitus*. In particular, a certain weakness in Calvin's teaching on perfection—at the human end of the scale—might be corrected.

My assignment was to treat Wesley's doctrine of perfection. That is where I will concentrate, but in fact this doctrine cannot be abstracted from the larger anthropological and soteriological picture. Moreover, it seemed sensible, for the sake of our dialogue, to relate Wesley directly to Calvin in comparison and contrast. In its historical aspects, the following account depends heavily on the work of others for their discrete studies on the figures and themes involved; but, in addition to bringing Calvin and Wesley together, I have not shunned the systematician's task of engaging in critical and constructive reflection. The historical and systematic theses which are to be expounded have now already been stated.

143

II. Perfection

First, Calvin and Wesley will be compared for their views on perfection, within the broader doctrine of sanctification.

1. Calvin

In the amply documented book of R. S. Wallace, *Calvin's Doctrine of the Christian Life*,[1] the penultimate chapter is entitled "Progress Towards Perfection." The author summarizes Calvin's teaching under seven heads:

(A) *Christian perfection means a wholehearted response to the grace of God.* God's perfection consists in his "free and pure kindness" in overcoming human malice and ingratitude. Our aim must be to respond fittingly in our own humble sphere to this perfect grace in which God has presented himself to us (Commentary on Matt. 5:48). The perfection of faith will express itself in wholehearted self-denial, in conforming ourselves to the will of God, and in bearing the yoke of affliction without rebellion (Sermon on Gal. 5:22-26). Job is described in some translations of scripture as a "perfect man." Calvin prefers the terms *rondeur* or *intégrité* for the dedication, such as Job's, of the whole heart and mind to God with one single aim (Serm. on Job 1:1). To approve ourselves to God means to conform our whole life to God, not in one or two particulars, but without making any reserve whatever the cost. Our lives should wholly correspond to the Word of God (Serm. on Deut. 5:28-33).

(B) *Though such perfection is unattainable in this life, we must strive towards it.* That Jesus washed his disciples' feet is a sign that, because we are involved in the life of this present sinful world, we are bound to be involved constantly in its sin, and therefore "Christ always finds in us something to cleanse" (Comm. on John 13:9). We are never truly wholehearted in our response to Jesus Christ; the Holy Spirit is never able to occupy the whole of us (ibid.). We are required to make constant progress, and "so long as there is daily progress, there cannot be perfection" (Comm. on Eph. 5:27). Moreover, "the more eminently anyone excels in holiness, the farther he feels from perfect righteousness, and the more clearly he perceives that he can trust in nothing but the mercy of God alone" (Comm. on Ps. 32:1). The perfect Christian is one who, conscious of his or her sin and misery, has learned to live by grace (Serm. on Eph. 1:4-6).

Confident belief in the attainability of perfection is a devilish device, but we are nevertheless "not to labour feebly or coldly in urging perfection" or in striving towards it (*Institutes* IV.1.20). "The highest perfection of the godly in this life is an earnest desire to make progress" (Comm. on Eph. 3:16). "Our own narrowness is what hinders God from pouring upon us an abundance of his blessings," for God "accommodates his liberality to the measure of our expectations" (Comm. on Ps. 65:4-5). Here Wesley will be found, for once, less willing than Calvin to set limits to the grace of God.

The Christian life is no "settled state" (Comm. on Acts 1:1-4). Our complete justification can take place at one moment of time, so that there and then we are accounted as wholly righteous before God, but our sanctification is a process that is more and more completed throughout the whole course of our lives, to be perfected only through death (Comm. on John 17:17).

(C) *There is a state of achieved victory over sin and wholehearted surrender which by the grace of God may be called "perfection."* Although still active, Satan has been deprived of "dominion" in the heart of the Christian (Comm. on John 13:9). Calvin's strongest positive statements occur in his commentary on 1 John 3:9: "Whoever is born of God can lead a holy life, because the Spirit of God restrains the lusting of sin." The government of the Spirit can indeed be so effectual that our hearts are given an "inflexible disposition" (*affectus*) to follow his guidance: "The power of the Spirit is so effectual that it necessarily retains us in continual obedience to righteousness." In the sermons on Deuteronomy, Calvin says there can be a wholehearted surrender to God and "un accord et comme une mélodie" between us and God, when we seek to give the grace of God the chief place in our life (Serm. on Deut. 1:34-40). In this case we may be said to serve God with true *rondeur de cœur*, for he does not impute to us the weaknesses that still remain in us (Serm. on Deut. 26:16-19). To be thus wholehearted is to be on the way to attaining the goal of purity and holiness, and is to have perfection attributed to us (*Institutes* IV.1.17). It will be noticed later that Wesley also admits lingering frailties among those whom he less guardedly than Calvin calls perfect, and we may wonder about the kind and status of those weaknesses in Calvin and Wesley respectively.

(D) *Yet we continually fail, and progress is slow.* "Even though we have experienced the victory by the grace of God, and sin has not reigned within us, yet it still dwells within us always, and there are stains and spots on our life. We must groan, then, and we must groan in such a way that it drives us on to do our duty. . . . and we must not be discouraged. Even though each day we see a million faults within us, yet we must always seek to get beyond" (Serm. on Deut. 5:21). Even after progress and victory, there will come times when we find ourselves completely swept off our feet, and unable to stand or control ourselves, and will be forced to cast ourselves in desperation on the help and mercy of God (Serm. on Job 3:11-19). Our progress is progress made always limping rather than running: "Quand encores nous tendrons au bien, ce sera toujours en clochant, au lieu de courir" (Serm. on Matt. 5:11-12).

(E) *Christian growth is primarily growth in faith.* "As our faith is never perfect, it follows that we are partly unbelievers; but God forgives us and exercises such forbearance towards us as to reckon us believers on account of a small proportion of faith. It is our duty in the meantime carefully to shake off the remnants of infidelity which adhere to us, to strive against them, to pray to God to correct them" (Comm. on Mark 9:24).

(F) *Faith grows in stability and clarity as it increasingly apprehends the exaltation of Christ.* In its imperfect state, faith suffers from a "twofold weakness" (*duplex debilitas*): it suffers from both ignorance (*ignorantia*) and instability (*dubitatio*), and it requires to be both illuminated and established (Comm. on Rom. 4:19). Paul's prayer for the Galatians is that the exalted Christ may be "formed" within them (Comm. on John 20:3).

(G) *Growth of faith is accompanied by a deepening experience of Christ and a progressive transformation of life.* Repentance "is never perfect at the start, but after God planes us, he also needs to polish us" (Serm. on Job 42:1-5). As our faith increases, we are able more and more to inherit the glorious liberty of the children of God (Comm. on John 8:32); we are able to receive "fresh additions of the Spirit of God," which are given "according to the measure of faith" (Comm. on John 7:38), and thus we make progress towards "fulness of life" (Comm. on John 10:10). With the increase of faith, our union with Christ is increased "until we are fully united to Jesus Christ" (Serm. on Acts 1:1-4). Growth in faith must be accompanied by a growing measure of sanctification. "The true stages in the growth of Christians are when they make progress in knowledge and understanding, and afterwards in love" (Comm. on Phil. 1:9). "True knowledge of God is a living and not a dead thing, and it will manifest itself and bear fruit in our whole way of living" (Serm. on Titus 1:15-16).

2. Wesley

Always controversial during his lifetime, Wesley's doctrine is summed up in *A Plain Account of Christian Perfection.* Here Wesley, with ample self-quotation, sets out the general consistency and detailed development of what he has "believed and taught for these forty years, from the year 1725 to the year 1765." The *Plain Account* includes a brief text of 1764, with eleven "short propositions"[2] and also succinct replies to several objections. It will be simplest to reproduce this text of 1764 directly. First, the propositions:

(1) There is such a thing as perfection; for it is again and again mentioned in Scripture.

(2) It is not so early as justification; for justified persons are to "go on unto perfection" (Heb. 6:1).

(3) It is not so late as death; for St. Paul speaks of living men that were perfect (Phil. 3:15).

(4) It is not absolute. Absolute perfection belongs not to man, nor to angels, but to God alone.

(5) It does not make a man infallible: None is infallible, while he remains in the body.

(6) Is it sinless? It is not worth while to contend for a term. It is "salvation from sin."

(7) It is "perfect love" (1 John 4:18). This is the essence of it; its properties, or inseparable fruits, are, rejoicing evermore, praying without ceasing, and in everything giving thanks (1 Thess. 5:16, etc.).

(8) It is improvable. It is so far from lying in an indivisible point, from being incapable of increase, that one perfected in love may grow in grace far swifter than he did before.

(9) It is amissible, capable of being lost; of which we have numerous instances. But we were not thoroughly convinced of this, till five or six years ago.

(10) It is constantly both preceded and followed by a gradual work.

(11) But is it in itself instantaneous or not? In examining this, let us go step by step.

An instantaneous change has been wrought in some believers: none can deny this.

Since that change, they enjoy perfect love; this feel this, and this alone; they "rejoice evermore, pray without ceasing, and in everything give thanks." Now, this is all that I mean by perfection; therefore, these are witnesses of the perfection which I preach.

And then the objections, with Wesley's answers:

"But in some this change was not instantaneous." They did not perceive the instant when it was wrought. It is often difficult to perceive the instant when a man dies; yet there is an instant in which life ceases. And if ever sin ceases, there must be a last moment of its existence, and a first moment of our deliverance from it.

"But if they have this love now, they will lose it." They may; but they need not. And whether they do or no, they have it now; they now experience what we teach. They now are all love; they now rejoice, pray, and praise without ceasing.

"However, sin is only suspended in them; it is not destroyed." Call it what you please. They are all love today; and they take no thought for the morrow.

147

"But this doctrine has been much abused." So has that of justification by faith. But that is no reason for giving up either this or any other scriptural doctrine. "When you wash your child," as one speaks, "throw away the water; but do not throw away the child."

"But those who think they are saved from sin say they have no need of the merits of Christ." They say just the contrary. Their language is:

> Every moment, Lord, I want
> The merit of thy death.

They never before had so deep, so unspeakable, a conviction of the need of Christ in all his offices as they have now.

Therefore, all our Preachers should make a point of preaching perfection to believers constantly, strongly, and explicitly; and all believers should mind this one thing, and continually agonize for it.[3]

Perhaps there only needs to be added, from Wesley's sermon on "The Scripture Way of Salvation" (1765), his conviction that "what God hath promised" in this matter—Wesley cites "the ancient promise" of Deuteronomy 30:6 that "I will circumcize thy heart, and the heart of thy seed, to love the Lord thy God will all thy heart and with all thy soul"—"He is *able* to perform," and that God is indeed "both able and willing to sanctify us *now*" so as to "cleanse us from all sin" (1 John 1:7, cf. 9—an epistle on which Wesley relies heavily in his teaching on perfection, and which we saw Calvin was unable to ignore, either).[4]

3. Calvin and Wesley

As long as we remain on the doctrine of sanctification broadly understood, there is a good measure of agreement between Wesley and Calvin. Wesley considered Calvin far superior to Luther on the matter. Both Calvin and Wesley see ongoing sanctification, begun in regeneration, as "the great work which God does *in* us."[5] According to both of them, sanctification is, by trinitarian appropriation, chiefly the work of the Holy Spirit; but Wesley can also, as we already found Calvin doing, very often speak in terms of the present work of Christ: the sanctified, even the perfect, "still need Christ as their king, for God does not give them a stock of holiness."[6] Both Wesley and Calvin say that God does *everything* for our salvation (*Allwirksamkeit Gottes*); and happily Calvin was perhaps not quite so insistent—see, for example, *Institutes* III.14.20-21—as caricatural Lutheranism on God's doing everything *alone* (in German, *Gottes All-ein-wirksamkeit*). Calvin might not have been pleased with Wesley's recurrent use of Augustine's maxim "He who made us without ourselves will not save us without ourselves"[7]; but if Wesley preached "On working out our own salvation,"[8] Calvin also could appreciate the text of Philippians 2:12, since its summons is grounded in the declaration that "God is at work in you" (cf. Comm. on Matt. 26:23; Wallace, p. 306).

Even on perfection there is considerable agreement. "Singleness" of eye and heart is also a Wesleyan expression. Calvin also could look on the fulfillment of the great dual commandment to love God and neighbor as the aim of the Christian life (cf. Wallace, pp. 114–16). Wesley allowed that the most saintly were most aware of how far they still had to go, and that there remained need and room for growth even in the perfect. But the fact that Calvin preferred to reserve perfection for the point of death betrays a substantive difference between him and Wesley.

This side of death, Calvin allows at least an *intentional* attainment of perfection; God *imputes* perfection to those on the way. Wesley preached and taught that "entire sanctification" might really be given and achieved in this life. The root of their difference appears to reside in the gravity of their respective restrictions upon what is attainable here below. Wesley certainly held that even the perfect were not exempt from the errors that came from the ignorance and weakness consequent upon the Fall. But these were not included in the definition of sin he used in the context of his teaching on perfection, namely "the voluntary transgression of a known law." Calvin, on the other hand, appears to consider the remaining effects of the Fall as more strictly "sin": they are equated with "unbelief." Digging further at the root, the difference between Calvin and Wesley may consist in their views of the human will. Wesley held that, in virtue of Christ's universally atoning work, "every man has a measure of free-will restored to him by grace"[9]—and not only that, but apparently also the capacity to choose the gospel when it is presented, and to remain in that choice for God. For Calvin, the correction and renewal of a human will amid a fallen humankind appears to regularly require a much more specifically directed and maintained act of sovereign grace.

Historically, we may suspect Wesley of sharing too far in the individualistic and voluntaristic view of humanity characteristic of the Enlightenment; and certainly depth-psychology should have made us suspicious of a naïve trust in the conscious will. Here Calvin's more total view of the profundity, range, persistence and solidary character of original sin may seem to come back into its own. But then the scheme of salvation which Calvin thought necessary if the Fall was to be overcome has proved repugnant to many moderns, is incompatible with several traditional versions of the Christian faith in both East and West, and enjoys far from uncontested exegetical support in the Scriptures. In part, at least, the problem lies in its deterministic cast. To Wesley, as to others, genuine acceptance of the gospel entails the liberty to refuse it. While the true use of creaturely freedom leads to the enjoyment of God, it is hard to see how, short of the definitive condition of the blessed in heaven where the "impossibility of sinning" (the *non posse peccare*) will not be restraint but liberation, we could be said to have freedom at all with regard to God, were we not able to refuse God.

We shall return to that question, but first we must face another possible weakness in Wesley's doctrine of perfection: its amissibility or the fact that it can be lost, and what that implies concerning particularly its divine donor.

III. Perseverance

Here the strengths and difficulties of Calvin's doctrine of perseverance are to be discerned in relation to Wesley's objections to the doctrine.

1. Wesley

The mature Wesley held, we saw in point 9 of his own summary, that perfection is "amissible, capable of being lost." So defensive was Wesley at times regarding his teaching on perfection that he almost welcomed the opportunity to introduce qualifications. On the basis of "numerous instances" he finally became "thoroughly convinced" that perfection could be lost. That is bound to reflect on the profundity of a transformation that might have rather prematurely been designated "perfection." A similar cause for concern may be found in Wesley's admission that "an instantaneous change"—in a stronger sense than imperceptible graduation—"has been wrought in some believers": "Since that change, they enjoy perfect love; they feel this, and this alone; they 'rejoice evermore, pray without ceasing, and in everything give thanks.' Now, this is all I mean by perfection" (point 10 and 11 in Wesley's summary). Can something so "easily" given—and then lost—really be perfection?

Now Wesley did teach that the perfect, like all the faithful, needed to persevere. But perseverance was simply continuance in faith—or in (perfect) love. It was therefore dependent on the believer's own acceptance of, and cooperation with, justifying and sanctifying grace. Perseverance was not an added gift, let alone an unconditional one.

Over perseverance, Wesley came into sharp conflict with Calvinism and Calvin. But it may nevertheless be that some corrective is to be found, precisely in a more—if not totally—Calvinist doctrine of the perseverance of the saints, for the shallowness and uncertainty that threaten the "punctiliar" character of an instantaneous and amissible perfection, and so reflect on the God who gives it.

2. Calvin

Again, we may turn for help to Wallace's study, where the last chapter is entitled "perseverance to the end." Five points are made:

(A) *The trial of faith is long and severe.* In the battle with Satan, "Christ will have no discharged soldiers except those who have conquered death itself" (Comm. on Heb. 12:4). "If [Christ] is possessed by faith, we must persevere in it, so that he may be our perpetual possession" (Comm. on Heb. 3:14). Closer fellowship with Christ is a reward that Christ bestows upon perseverance (Comm. on John 8:32).

(B) *Perseverance requires much patience and virtue.* "The chief virtue of the faithful is a patient endurance of the cross and mortification by which they calmly submit themselves to God" (Comm. on Luke 7:29). Patience involves believers in the constant exercise of humility, which does not despise the small steps by which faith is increased (ibid.).

(C) *Our faith is bound to persevere since God is bound to see us through.* The grace of God not only "prevents" or precedes believers but sustains them all their life and confirms them in their perseverance (Comm. on Ps. 68:29). "It is not enough to be able to rely on God's help only for today. I must also be fully persuaded that he will help me tomorrow, and right on to the end" (Serm. on Deut. 20:2-9). What God has begun he is bound to complete (Comm. on Ps. 138:8). Faith perseveres, not because some new strength of character has been worked up within the believer's psychological make-up by the grace of God, nor because some new-found and unshakable strength has been imparted to the human will, but only because God never goes back on his call and never disappoints in his promise of perseverance to the end: "Our salvation is certain because it is in the hand of God; for our faith is weak and we are prone to waver" (Comm. on John 10:29). Here a critic might wonder whether such a stark pair of alternatives are the only possibility. May one not expect a real change and growth in character among believers?

(D) *Regeneration is an incorruptible seed of life.* Calvin found further assurance about the "inflexible perseverance" of the elect in the thought that the "seed communicated when God regenerates the elect, since it is incorruptible, retains its virtue perpetually" (Comm. on 1 John 3:9). While faith may be choked, it is never wholly extinguished (Comm. on John 20:28). "God restrains his elect by a secret bridle that they may not fall into destruction" (ibid.). "It is right for the saints, when they have fallen into sin and have thus done what they could to repudiate the grace of God, to feel anxiety; but it is their duty to hold fast the truth that grace is the incorruptible seed of God which can never perish where it has once been bestowed" (Comm. on Ps. 51:12). If we believe in God's faithfulness, we must "keep pace with God in the steadfastness of our faith"; this is not in man's power, but it can be accomplished by the grace of God, and believers must strive towards it (Comm. on 2 Cor. 1:21). It is precisely because God will continue from day to day to perfect what he has begun that believers too must continue to the end without falling away from his obedience (Serm. on Luke 1:73-78).

(E) *Our confidence in our perseverance must be accompanied by effort, and fear and trembling.* To persevere in the grace of God requires "striving and vigilance" (Comm. on Heb. 12:15). The Psalmist showed an example of "perseverance combined with severe and arduous effort" (Comm. on Ps. 119:123). Even for the believer, nothing is so evanescent as faith (Serm. on Luke 1:69-72), and "nothing flows away so easily as love" (Comm. on Heb. 13:1). Even the slightest fall on our part should be a sign to us that we would soon fall to destruction were we not continually upheld by the hand of God (Comm. on Ps. 37:24). The confidence of the godly is the confidence of those who know that their life "hangs only by a thread and is encompassed by a thousand deaths" (Comm. on Rom. 4:19).

3. Calvin and Wesley

In a direct attack on Calvinist doctrine—"Serious Thoughts upon the Perseverance of the Saints"[10]—Wesley seeks to establish exegetically that even true believers may make shipwreck of the faith (1 Tim. 1:18f.), that those who are grafted into the good olive tree, or are branches of the true vine, may nevertheless so fall from God as to perish everlastingly (Rom. 11:17, 20-22; John 15:1-6), that those who were once enlightened may fall away without possibility of restoration (Heb. 6:4-6; cf. 10:26-29, 38). As in the sermons on "The New Birth," Wesley denies that regeneration cannot be lost. While God's promises are sure, they are conditional: they apply as long as one *continues a believer*.

What Wesley might have learnt from Calvin was both the sheer difficulty of perseverance and perfection and also the need for an active determination on God's part to see us through to the goal of permanent and complete holiness. Perhaps the whole thing is both higher and deeper than Wesley perceived. As the Scottish Methodist I. H. Marshall put it in a study which was sympathetic to Calvinist concerns but finally remained Arminian: "If entire sanctification is a dubious possibility, is complete apostasy also an impossibilty in the Christian life?"[11]

For Wesley, Calvin's doctrine was vitiated by its rootage in predestination. This was the target of Wesley's severest criticisms, and to this question we must now turn.

IV. Election

Here we reach the heart of the tension between Wesley and Calvin, the question of predestination—and look to Karl Barth as a mediator.

1. Wesley and Calvin

One of Wesley's most sustained theological treatises is his "Predestination Calmly Considered."[12] The idea of double predestination (and, as Wesley well knew, Calvin recognized that the "passing over" of whatever number was tantamount to their reprobation) was held by Wesley to be morally intolerable in the case of God and morally undermining in the case of human beings. It makes God an arbitrary and cruel tyrant; it can drive people to license or despair. Wesley argues that it corresponds better to the divine wisdom and love in creation and redemption that God's way should be "to save man as man; to set life and death before him, and then persuade (not force) him to choose life."[13]

Wesley's treatise illustrates a classic deadlock in Protestant theology. The twentieth century has been fortunate enough to enjoy at least the beginnings of a release.

2. Karl Barth

As is well known, Karl Barth operated an internal revolution in the Calvinist tradition on this matter. As is less often realized, he thereby provided a deeper and firmer background for Wesleyan values in the area of salvation.

From being categories that fixed individuals from the start and for ever, Barth turned election and reprobation into a dialectical process that focused on Christ—the eternal Son and the inclusive head of a human race called to communion with God, redeemed after its fall, and having the gates of reconciliation open before it. This universal covenant of salvation, rooted in the very life of God, makes for a stronger grip of God on the whole process than the ever so slightly deistic impression sometimes given by Wesley of a God who, in universal prevenience, simply makes grace "available." Yet, while Barth emphasized the surplus of grace over the negative side of human history, he stopped short of programmatic universalism, i.e. the belief that all will certainly be saved. He thereby left room for the exercise of that human freedom which, while its true use leads to the enjoyment of God, must, unless and until it is finally and permanently won over, be capable of refusing God. Wesley clearly saw that freedom belongs not only to God but also to the human creature, if the relationship between Creator and creature is to be a personal one.

Now, that "grip" of God allows God to be more searching, persistent and resourceful in winning the sinner, while yet respecting human freedom, than Wesley's theology was sometimes able to recognize. Because God has actively called all, God can direct his attention to each. John Wesley knew that in his preaching. Charles Wesley knew it in his hymns:

> Tis mercy all, immense and free,
> For, O my God, it found out me.[14]

> So wide it never passed by one,
> Or it had passed by me.[15]

Yet Wesley was perhaps too willing theologically to treat as "exempt cases" the individual experience of sovereign grace. Wesley was, I think, right to insist, in his "Thoughts upon God's Sovereignty," that "every individual may, after all that God has done, either improve his grace, or make it of none effect."[16] But he could perhaps have emphasized more the *persistence* of God in his gifts, whether of faith or love, and so have come up with a stronger doctrine of perseverance, whether in justification or in sanctification, than his repugnance towards predestinationism allowed.

V. *Imago Dei*

While Wesley and Calvin may differ on the depth and lasting effects of the Fall (though Wesley was prepared to talk of "total depravity," and Calvin could detect "some remaining traces of the image of God" [*Institutes* II.12-17] in fallen humankind), they join in seeing the restoration or renewal of the image of God in humanity as a major category for describing salvation. This would actually allow them to use more fully the medieval notion of "habitus" in ways that would strengthen their respective doctrines of perfection.

1. Calvin

Again we find help in Wallace (pp. 103–11, 332). Largely by reading back from Jesus Christ, who is the "living image of God his Father" (Serm. on Job 1:6-8), Calvin finds that "for Adam to have been made in the image of God meant that he should live in an ordered integrity and righteousness, in dependence on the grace of his Creator, rising ever into communion with God through the Word of God, which his mind was made to reflect, and through the glory of created things, meditating on the heavenly life, and living in a truly ordered relation to his fellow creatures and his environment" (Wallace's summary, p. 105). The work of Christ is to restore to humankind what was lost in Adam: "Adam was first created after the image of God, and reflected as in a mirror the divine righteousness; but that image, having been defaced by sin, must now be restored in Christ. The regeneration of the godly is indeed . . . nothing else than the formation anew of the image of God in them. . . . The design contemplated by regeneration is to recall us from our wanderings to that end for which we were created" (Comm. on Eph. 4:24). The work of the Spirit in human hearts is to "begin to reform us to the image of God" (Comm. on Luke 17:20).

That human lives be conformed to the image of God means a real effort to follow the example of the forgiving, gentle and generous love of God as we see it reflected in Jesus Christ, remembering that to be the children of God involves likeness in behavior and attitude to the heavenly Father (Serm. on Gal. 6:1-2). There is nothing in which we more truly resemble God than in doing good to others, and in this respect we are to seek to reproduce in ourselves the Father's disposition (*ingenium*) (Comm. on Ps. 30:5). "What God is in heaven, such he bids us to be in this world" (Comm. on 1 John 4:17). Calvin also sees in the humanity of Jesus the banishment of all excess or *ataxia*, and a perfect pattern of order, of true moderation and harmony.

When faith looks on the glory of God revealed in the gospel, it is no dead contemplation but one that transforms believers into the image of God. Calvin quotes 2 Corinthians 3:18 as a reminder that the future glory is promised to none but those in whom the image of God already shines and who are being transformed by it into continued advance of glory (Comm. on Matt. 13:43); and as a reminder that if this process has already begun within the godly, even in a feeble way, then it is bound to go on all their life with increasing force and fulness, for it promises ultimately their entire restoration into the image of God (Serm. on 1 Tim. 1:5-7; Comm. on Luke 17:20). These are by far the strongest statements Calvin makes on the real transformation of believers in this life.

2. Wesley

The most valuable study here is that of Jürgen Weissbach on "the new humanity in the theological thought of John Wesley," which detects a leading role for the notion of the *imago Dei* in Wesley's theology.[17]

155

From the anthropological end, Wesley describes the work of human salvation thus: "This, then, is the treasure which they have received; a faith of the operation of God; . . . the love of God shed abroad in their hearts, with love to every child of man, and a renewal in the whole image of God, in all righteousness and true holiness."[18] This renewal is a matter of daily growth: "The soul shall be renewed day by day, after the image of him that created it. . . . We are more and more filled with the love of God and man."[19] According to Wesley, the continuing "royal" work of Christ as the "federal head of all mankind" consists in "restoring those to the image of God, whom he had first reinstated in His favour; reigning in all believing hearts until he has subdued all things to himself, until he hath utterly cast out all sin, and brought in everlasting righteousness."[20] Already in 1734, he defined religion as "a renewal of our minds in the image of God, a recovery of the divine likeness, a still-increasing conformity of heart and life to the pattern of our most holy Redeemer."[21] Wesley often equates the image with "the mind of Christ," and that is expressed in "walking as He also walked."[22]

Sanctification, to which regeneration opens the door, "restores us . . . to the image of God"[23]: it is "what [God] works *in* us by his Spirit."[24] "By sanctification we are saved from the power and root of sin, and restored to the image of God."[25]

Imputed righteousness is worked out in imparted holiness:

> The righteousness of Christ is doubtless necessary for any soul that enters into glory. But so is personal holiness too, for every child of man. But it is highly needful to be observed, that they are necessary in different respects. The former is necessary to *entitle* us to heaven; the latter to *qualify* us for it. Without the righteousness of Christ we could have no *claim* to glory; without holiness we could have no *fitness* for it. By the former we become members of Christ, children of God, and heirs of the kingdom of heaven. By the latter "we are made meet to be partakers of the inheritance of the saints in light."[26]

Love reigns in the renewed person. "The love of God has purified his heart from all revengeful passions, from envy, malice and wrath, from every unkind temper or malign influence."[27] "In a Christian believer *love* sits upon the throne which is erected in the inmost soul; namely, love of God and man, which fills the whole heart, and reigns without a rival. In a circle near the throne are all holy tempers—longsuffering, gentleness, meekness, fidelity, temperance, and if any other were comprised in 'the mind which was in Christ Jesus.'"[28]

As we already saw Calvin doing, it is noteworthy that Wesley frequently bases his teaching of perfection on Jesus' exhortation to emulate the heavenly Father: "Be perfect / merciful, as your Father in heaven is perfect / merciful" (Matt. 5:48 / Luke 6:36). "A third thing we are to understand by serving God is, to *resemble* or *imitate* him. So the ancient father: *Optimus Dei cultus, imitari quem colis.* . . . We here speak of imitating or resembling him in the spirit of our minds; for here the true Christian imitation of God begins. . . . Now God is love: therefore, they who resemble him in the spirit of their minds are transformed into the same image."[29]

3. Habit

The word *habitus* received a bad press in the Reformation, where it was seen as proof that the Scholastics were Pelagians. As Gérard Philips has piquantly shown,[30] the notion originally served rather as a safeguard *against* pelagianism. It found a middle way between, on the one hand, the simple identification made by Peter Lombard of the indwelling Holy Spirit with the "virtue" of charity and, on the other hand, the separation between the Holy Spirit and his gifts which Abelard accentuated. It thus ensures that the works of believers *remain* the *gift of the Holy Spirit*, while allowing for a *real change* in the *continuing person of the believer*. Sometimes called "created grace," the notion of "habit" would help Wesley to maintain the *constancy* of the Holy Spirit's self-gift, making for a deeper and more permanent transformation of the believer without the fear of a loss dependent upon more superficial psychological fluctuations (the "punctiliarism" of which I spoke). It would help Calvin to see more consistently that God's gifts to us really become *ours*, so that while the imputation of Christ's merits is never left behind, our sanctification by the Spirit is intrinsic to our being, and the "rewards" of glory will be the "perfection" of the persons we have started to become (this against the flavor of mere "imputationism" that lingers on in Calvin from the Lutheran beginnings of the Reformation). The American Methodist Stanley Hauerwas is able to draw on both Wesley and Calvin against an implicit medieval (and Aristotelian!) background in developing his own most interesting "ethics of character" to counter the "situationism" still rampant in "mainstream Protestantism" in the United States.[31]

VI. Fears and Safeguards

To understand a controversy, it is often helpful to see what each party *fears* about the implications and consequences of the other's position. Calvinists and Wesleyans attack the *presumptuousness* of "perfection" and "predestination/perseverance" respectively, but that is not the heart of the matter. Wesley fears the *antinomianism*, whether of license or despair, to which unalterable election or reprobation can lead; and he fears the *loss of personality* in God and humankind which seems implied in the divine arbitrariness and the absence of human freedom apparently denoted by predestination. Positively put, Wesley is concerned for the *moral and spiritual perfection* of human persons in communion with the tripersonal God. Faced by Wesleyanism, Calvinists fear for *God's sovereignty* over against a promethean man which might imaginably frustrate God's purpose; and for the *uncertainty* to believers that would result from the abandonment of the "most comfortable" doctrines of predestination and consequent perseverance. Positively, Calvinists are concerned for the *originating and ongoing grace of God*, without which there is absolutely no salvation for humankind.

With that grace, perfection is *possible*—and *promised*—to believers, beginning *here* and completed *hereafter*. That may be both a necessary and a sufficient agreement to allow pious Calvinists, according to the *mot* of A. Mitchell Hunter, to continue to preach like Arminians, and pious Arminians to pray like Calvinists.[32]

METHODISTS AND ORTHODOX

CHAPTER NINE

Tradition and the Spirit of Faith: Methodists Address the Orthodox

In June 1992, there took place in Oxford, England, the first in a series of theological conversations sponsored by the Ecumenical Patriarchate and the World Methodist Council with a view to the eventual establishment of an official international dialogue between all the Orthodox Churches and the Churches of Methodism. During that first meeting, the Orthodox and Methodist representatives alike were deeply saddened by the news of Father John Meyendorff's sudden illness and rapid passing. Twenty years earlier, Father John had delivered a memorable lecture on "The Holy Spirit as God" to the Fifth Oxford Institute of Methodist Theological Studies. Now the Orthodox-Methodist ecclesiastical conversations were to take up the Pneumatological theme in its ecclesiological and anthropological aspects: how do Orthodox and Methodists understand the work of the Holy Spirit as the shaper of the Christian community across time as well as the source of faith for each believer in every present moment?

Meyendorff had written that the Eastern doctrine of salvation as *theosis* (or "divinization") by the Holy Spirit "implies a religion of *personal experience*" and that "the Orthodox East admits the *saints* as authoritative witnesses of truth." The personal faith of the believer and the evidentiary authority of the saints, he continued, are, in Orthodox understanding, located within a community which "the Spirit maintains through history" and in which "the Spirit created the apostolic ministry at Pentecost." "The true, 'catholic' tradition of Christianity," said Meyendorff, "is the one where institutional and charismatic leaderships are able *to recognize in each other the same Spirit*." For both an episcopal, priestly ministry and a charismatic, prophetic testimony, if authentic, are alike "founded in participation in the same divine Spirit granted to the Church at Pentecost, distributed in baptism, and always working at the 'building-up' of the Body of Christ."[1]

In the Oxford conversations of 1992 it appeared that the Orthodox representatives could hear the Methodist testimony to the present experience of the Holy Spirit in the life of the individual Christian but found it less clear how Methodists as an ecclesial body might see themselves, and indeed be, part of an historic Church founded upon the apostles at Pentecost and indwelt by the Holy Spirit ever since. The present chapter was, therefore, originally prepared for the second Orthodox-Methodist meeting, at Constantinople in July 1993, as an account of how Methodists, as Christians and as a denominational family, view their own relation to the great Tradition of the Church catholic. It is an attempt by a Methodist theologian to describe the sense in which Methodists see the historic Church as the location and instrument of the gospel and the faith, while considering every authentic present experience of faith and testimony to the gospel as the maintenance and renewal of the Tradition—and all of this, of course, in and under the Holy Spirit.[2]

The presentation begins with a statement of the constitutional claims made by Methodist Churches to belong to the Church catholic as the Body of Christ, even while deliberately acknowledging the particular origins of the Methodist movement. Since Methodists ascribe a founding role in their own history to John Wesley, a second section examines the way in which Wesley himself understood Methodism in relation to the patristic Church—a matter of great importance in any Methodist-Orthodox dialogue, given the significance of the early Fathers in the Orthodox understanding of the Tradition. A third section then looks at the ways in which John Wesley in turn has assumed the role of a father in the particular Methodist tradition, remembering that the Orthodox have an extended tradition of fatherhood which does not rest only with the great theologians of the early centuries but also includes the later founders of local Churches and the continuing exercise of pastoral (episcopal) and spiritual (monastic and saintly) direction. The fourth part takes examples from the liturgical repertory of Methodism, the *lex orandi*, to illustrate the content of the faith, the manners of its transmission, and the styles of its experience, as these occur characteristically within Methodism; and here the ongoing Wesleyan character again appears. A concluding section summarizes the most recent official theological statement on the theme of Tradition as the United Methodist Church, by far the largest Methodist denomination, has set it in relation to Scripture, experience and reason as in various senses "sources" and "criteria" of the Christian faith.

I. *The Constitutional Self-Understanding of Methodism*

The Methodist ecclesial family, which today numbers some sixty million adherents around the world, considers itself part of the entire mystery and history of salvation that begins and ends in the Triune God revealed in Jesus Christ. Methodism's particular origins date from the evangelistic, spiritual and moral revival led by John Wesley and his brother Charles within the Church of England in the eighteenth century. Both the broader and the narrower aspects of Methodist self-understanding are characteristically expressed in the constitutional documents of the British Methodist Church:

> The Methodist Church claims and cherishes its place in the Holy Catholic Church which is the Body of Christ. It rejoices in the inheritance of the Apostolic Faith and loyally accepts the fundamental principles of the historic creeds and of the Protestant Reformation. It ever remembers that in the Providence of God Methodism was raised up to spread Scriptural Holiness through the land by the proclamation of the Evangelical Faith and declares its unfaltering resolve to be true to its Divinely appointed mission.
>
> The Doctrines of the Evangelical Faith which Methodism has held from the beginning and still holds are based upon the Divine revelation recorded in the Holy Scriptures. The Methodist Church acknowledges this revelation as the supreme rule of faith and practice. These Evangelical Doctrines to which the Preachers of the Methodist Church both Ministers and Laymen are pledged are contained in Wesley's Notes on the New Testament and the first four volumes of his sermons.[3]

Similarly, the United Methodist Church, which chiefly results from the spread of the Wesleyan movement to North America, declares in its *Book of Discipline* that

> United Methodists profess the historic Christian faith in God, incarnate in Jesus Christ for our salvation and ever at work in human history in the Holy Spirit. Living in a covenant of grace under the Lordship of Jesus Christ, we participate in the first fruits of God's coming reign and pray in hope for its full realization on earth as in heaven.[4]

Claiming "a common heritage with Christians of every age and nation," United Methodists find this heritage "grounded in the apostolic witness to Jesus Christ as Savior and Lord, which is the source and measure of all valid Christian teaching." In the work of the "leaders of the early Church" to "specify the core of Christian belief in order to ensure the soundness of Christian teaching," a special place is recognized to "the determination of the canon of Christian Scripture and the adoption of ecumenical creeds" (Nicaea and Chalcedon are mentioned along with the Apostles' Creed). The Protestant Reformers attempted to "recover the authentic biblical witness" that had been "classical Christian teaching." Then, in their own day, the "early Methodists claimed to preach the scriptural doctrines of the Church of England as contained in the Articles of Religion, the Homilies, and the Book of Common Prayer." Wesley, it is said, "considered doctrinal matters primarily in terms of their significance for Christian discipleship." The "distinctive Wesleyan emphases" include "prevenient grace," "justification and assurance," "sanctification and perfection," "faith and good works," "mission and service," and "fellowship in the Church." As "our doctrinal standards and general rules," the *Book of Discipline* then cites the Articles of Religion (based on John Wesley's abbreviation of the Anglican Articles), the Confession of Faith of the Evangelical United Brethren Church,[5] the "Standard Sermons" of Wesley, Wesley's *Explanatory Notes upon the New Testament*, and the General Rules (based on Wesley's advice in practical ecclesiology and Christian living).[6]

Parts of the extended Methodist family look, in addition, to important figures in their own early history (this is notably true of those originally German speaking communities in North America deriving from Jacob Albright's Evangelical Association and Philip William Otterbein's United Brethren, and of the African Methodist Episcopal Church that followed Richard Allen, and of the other historically Black or African American bodies, the African Methodist Episcopal Zion and Christian Methodist Episcopal Churches). But the Methodist family as a whole undoubtedly regards John Wesley as its founding father.

II. *Wesley on the Fathers*

While holding, with the Anglican Articles of Religion, that "Holy Scripture containeth all things necessary to salvation,"[7] Wesley considered the early Christian writers to be "the most authentic commentators on Scripture, as being both nearest the fountain, and eminently endued with that Spirit by whom all Scripture was given."[8] He often supported his own exegesis of the Scriptures by appeal to patristic interpretations of the biblical passages.[9] The Apostolic Fathers were special favorites of Wesley on the grounds revealed by his endorsement of Archbishop Wake's judgement of them which he quoted when he published his own translation of them in the first volume of his *Christian Library*: "The authors of the following collection were contemporaries of the holy Apostles. . . . We cannot therefore doubt, but what they deliver to us is the pure Doctrine of the Gospel; what Christ and his Apostles taught, and what these holy men had themselves received from their own mouths."[10] Wesley esteemed "the writings of the first three centuries, not equal with, but next to, the Scriptures."[11] He had learned from the Manchester Non-Jurors[12] that the "agreement of the ancients: what had been believed by all, everywhere, and always" (*consensus veterum: quod ab omnibus, quod ubique, quod semper creditum*) was "a sure rule of interpreting Scripture," although this should not lead to the mistake of "making antiquity a co-ordinate rather than a subordinate rule with Scripture."[13] In particular, "well-meaning men" had shown "weakness" in relying on what allegedly "had been orally delivered down from the Apostles."[14] Wesley affirmed, as true interpretations of Scripture, the Nicene-Constantinopolitan Creed, the Chalcedonian definition of the one person and two natures of Christ, and the Trinitarian theology of the so-called Athanasian Creed.[15] He upheld, and polemically invoked, the teachings of the early Church against the revival in his own time of the ancient heresies of Sabellianism and Arianism.[16]

In liturgical matters, Wesley was willing to invoke, first in a precise sense and later rather more generally, the precedent and example of the early Church. In the early to middle 1730s, when he still accepted the authenticity of the so-called *Apostolic Constitutions* and *Canons*, he wrote in a notebook:

> I believe myself it a duty to observe, so far as I can without breaking communion with my own church:
> 1. To baptize by immersion.
> 2. To use water [i.e. the mixed chalice], oblation of elements, and alms, invocation [i.e. epiclesis], and a prothesis, in the Eucharist.
> 3. To pray for the faithful departed.
> 4. To pray standing on Sunday and in Pentecost.
> 5. To observe Saturday, Sunday and Pentecost as festival.
> 6. To abstain from blood and things strangled.
> I think it prudent (our own church not considered):
> 1. To observe the stations [fasting Wednesday and Friday].
> 2. Lent, especially the Holy Week.
> 3. To turn to the east at the Creed.[17]

It seems that Wesley originally intended to be guided by these practices as part of his attempt in the North American colony of Georgia to restore "primitive Christianity in the wilderness."[18] Later in his career, as the Methodist movement developed in England, Wesley appealed more generally to the early Church to justify and encourage such practices as the love-feast (agape) and the watchnight (vigil). Above all, he saw his own custom of frequent communion as an emulation of the early Church. At Christmas 1774 he wrote:

> During the twelve festival days we had the Lord's Supper daily; a little emblem of the Primitive Church. May we be followers of them in all things, as they were of Christ![19]

And at Easter 1777:

> Easter Day was a solemn and comfortable day, wherein God was remarkably present with His people. During the Octave I administered the Lord's Supper every morning, after the example of the Primitive Church.[20]

When, in 1784, Wesley was making provision for the Methodist Episcopal Church in the newly independent United States, he "advise[d] the elders to administer the Supper of the Lord on every Lord's Day"—thus displaying awareness of the patristic connection between Sunday and the Eucharist.[21]

In fact, from the very early days of the Methodist movement in England in the 1740s, John Wesley observed similarities between its developing organization and the early Church. Sometimes he applied a patristic model programmatically; sometimes he called attention to the patristic precedents only after the event. Thus in *A Plain Account of the People Called Methodists* of 1748–49, he noticed that Methodist institutions "generally found, in looking back, something in Christian antiquity likewise, very nearly parallel": the Methodist societies for "seekers after salvation" corresponded, he thought, to ancient catechetical classes; Methodist "class tickets" for identification of membership, to *symbola* or *tesserae*, as the ancients termed them, being of just the same force with the *epistolai systatikai*, commendatory letters, mentioned by the Apostle"; the Methodist penitent bands, to the segregation of penitents in the early Church; the offices of deaconess and widows, to primitive orders.[22] When finally, in 1784, Wesley, a presbyter of the Church of England, felt driven to ordain a ministry to oversee the Methodist work in North America, he appealed to studies of the ancient Church which claimed that bishops and presbyters were essentially of the same order; considering himself "as much a scriptural *episcopos* as any man in Europe," he judged that the emergency situation in America warranted his exercising the sacramental power of ordination which had hitherto been held in check only by limits of jurisdiction.[23]

In all of this, Wesley's favor fell chiefly on the Church of the first three centuries. He admired its courage under persecution and its persistence in propagating the gospel.[24] Nevertheless, "before the end of the third century the Church was greatly degenerated from its first purity," and Cyprian's testimony was cited for evidence of degeneration.[25] The greatest fall from grace, however, followed on the conversion of Constantine. A grave moral decline resulted from the Emperor's gifts of wealth and honors to the Church, especially to the clergy.[26] Wesley regretted the building of churches, the homage paid to images, and the multiplication of ritual.[27] He agrees with his correspondent Dr. Conyers Middleton that "after the Empire became Christian, a general corruption both of faith and morals infected the Christian Church, which, by that revolution, as St. Jerome says, 'lost as much of her virtue, as it had gained of wealth and power.'"[28] Wesley was also disgusted by the polemics and intrigues surrounding conciliar gatherings, even while accepting the dogmatic decisions of the ecumenical councils.[29]

It was doubtless chiefly in reaction against the perceived moral decline of the "great Church" that Wesley showed sympathy with a number of both earlier and later figures and groups on account of their ostensible spiritual and ethical seriousness. Thus he has positive things to say about the Montanists ("real, scriptural Christians"),[30] the Novatianists, and the Donatists ("I suspect they were the real Christians of that age, and were therefore served by St. Augustine and his warm adherents as the Methodists are now by their zealous adversaries").[31] Pelagius, wrote Wesley to his friend John Fletcher, "very probably held no other heresy than you and I do now."[32]

Wesley held that a genuine Christianity remained alive even under the Empire. He recommended for their spiritual quality the reading of St. Basil and St. John Chrysostom, of "Macarius the Egyptian" and "above all, the man of a broken heart, Ephraem Syrus."[33] He recommended familiarity with the lives of early Christians on account of their exemplary moral character in contrast with the sorry state of many professing Christians in his own time.[34]

To end this section, let me refer to Wesley's citation of St. John Chrysostom in exegesis of Romans 8:15-16, a favorite passage of Wesley's concerning the Spirit of faith and adoption. In the *Farther Appeal to Men of Reason and Religion*, Wesley is out to prove that the "testimony of the Spirit," far from being a specially miraculous gift reserved to the apostolic age, is "among those ordinary gifts of the Spirit of Christ, which if a man have not he is none of his" (cf. Rom. 8:9). He takes Chrysostom's Fourteenth Homily on Romans to show that the Spirit of adoption comes with the New Covenant as such. By the Spirit of adoption we cry "Abba,

Father," and Wesley quotes Chrysostom on this Pauline phrase and translates him thus: "This is the first word we utter after those amazing throes (or birth-pangs) and that strange and wonderful manner of bringing forth."[35] This witness of the Holy Spirit is thus, Wesley holds with Chrysostom, "the ordinary privilege of all Christians."

While Orthodox Christians will be gratified by Wesley's evident respect for the earliest Church and its Fathers, they will doubtless have problems with some of his historical interpretations (as, for example, in the matter of episcopacy). Most difficult perhaps will be his insistence on some of the nefarious effects of Constantine's adoption of Christianity, but it should not be forgotten that the Tradition of Orthodoxy also includes the strands of prophetic criticism, spiritual freedom, and moral renewal.

III. Wesley as a Father

A sympathetic observer is able to recognize in the continuing Methodist family the mark of spiritual identity left upon it by John Wesley.[36] In the newly independent United States, the Methodist Episcopal Church was constituted at the Christmas Conference of 1784 held in Baltimore.[37] In Britain, the embryonic Methodist denomination emerged more gradually from the Anglican womb, and it was not until the late nineteenth century that the principal Wesleyan body officially called itself the "Wesleyan Methodist Church" as distinct from a "Connexion" (a term deriving from the Conference of Preachers "in connexion with Mr. Wesley"). From early days, however, Methodists on both sides of the Atlantic looked on John Wesley with affection and respect as their "father" (although perhaps Francis Asbury, one of the first two bishops in America, went exceptionally far when he called Wesley "our dear old Daddy."[38])

It may be illuminating in our Methodist-Orthodox dialogue if I can convey a sense of the fatherly position which John Wesley occupies in Methodism. No disrespect is thereby intended to those early Fathers whom Wesley himself held in high regard. In certain ways, Orthodoxy itself has regarded some later-comers as continuing a patristic role in the founding of Churches and the exercise of dogmatic, pastoral and spiritual teaching and direction. Wesley has in fact been viewed by Methodists as a father in at least four respects: (1) his work of evangelism has begotten us in the gospel; (2) we have sought to be his obedient children and collaborators under God; (3) he has been our teacher in the Christian faith and life; and (4) he has bequeathed us a liturgical heritage.

1. Our Spiritual Progenitor

In the Minutes of the Methodist Conference held at Bristol in 1745, Wesley offers an account of "the origin of church government" which shows how ecclesial order derives from the commission to preach the gospel and the consequent rise of congregations of believers. The passage can be read stereoscopically as a description of both apostolic times and the origins of Methodism:

> Christ sends forth a preacher of the gospel. Some who hear him repent and believe the gospel. They then desire him to watch over them, to build them up in the faith and to guide their souls in the paths of righteousness. . . . If it please God to raise another flock in [a] new place, before [the evangelist] leaves [the first place] he appoint[s] one whom God has fitted for the work to watch over [their] souls also. In like manner, in every place where it pleases God to gather a little flock by His Word, [the evangelist] appoints one in his absence to take the oversight of the rest and to assist them of the ability which God giveth. These . . . look on their first pastor as their common father. And all these congregations regard him in the same light and esteem him still as the shepherd of their souls.[39]

While in the primary sense it is God the Father who begets believers (1 Peter 1:3), the apostle Paul could look on his own work of evangelism as the fathering of faith (1 Corinthians 4:15). Commenting on the Pauline text in his *Explanatory Notes upon the New Testament*, Wesley remarks that "the relation between a spiritual father and his children brings with it an inexpressible nearness and affection."

It is not surprising that subsequent generations should look on those who evangelized them as their "fathers in the gospel."[40] That is how Methodists have considered John Wesley. A nice early example can be found in the letter written from Baltimore on 1 November 1796 to "The General Conference of the People called Methodists in Great Britain" by Bishops Thomas Coke and Francis Asbury on behalf of "The American General Conference," "Your affectionate and younger Brethren in the Gospel": "We [cannot] possibly," they write, "be too thankful to our adorable Lord, for that highly honoured instrument of his grace, your and our late Father in the Gospel, the Rev. John Wesley."[41]

2. Our Senior Evangelist

The spiritual offspring of the evangelist seek to obey their parent. How the matter appeared from Wesley's side emerges from the following question and answer in the Minutes of the Methodist Conference of 1766 meeting at Leeds:

> Q. But what power is this which you exercise over all the Methodists in Great Britain and Ireland?
>
> A. To me the preachers have engaged themselves to submit, to "serve me as sons in the Gospel." But they are not thus engaged to any man, or number of men besides. To me the people in general will submit. But they will not yet submit to any other.[42]

Commenting on Philippians 2:22, from which he made an inexact citation in the text above, Wesley in his *Explanatory Notes upon the New Testament* observed the "elegance" of St. Paul's phrase concerning Timothy: the Apostle speaks of St. Timothy "partly as of a son, partly as of a fellow labourer." That is sufficient to remove any unpleasant edge from the notions of service and obedience to the senior evangelist.

That Wesley's disciplinary oversight was felt to continue after his death appears from a letter written at Leeds by the President (Thomas Coke) and Secretary (Samuel Bradburn) on behalf of the British Methodist Conference of 1797 to the Methodist Societies: the affairs of the Connexion were to be conducted according to "all our ancient rules, which were made before the death of our late venerable Father in the Gospel, the Rev. Mr. Wesley, which are essential rules, or prudential at this present time."[43] This applied even to such matters as the discouragement of complex tunes and anthems in favor of hymns in which "the whole congregation can in general join," on which "our late venerable Father in Christ, Mr. Wesley" first "printed a Minute."[44]

3. Our Doctrinal and Moral Teacher

Mention has already been made of the constitutional status of texts emanating from Wesley as permanent standards for doctrine and practice in Methodist churches. In the British Methodist Church, all candidates for the preaching ministry, whether ordained or lay, are required to have read, and to undergo examination on, the "Standard Sermons" of Wesley and his *Explanatory Notes upon the New Testament*. In the United Methodist Church, ordinands and their recommenders must answer a series of questions that derive in large part from the questions which Mr. Wesley put to his preachers from the beginning:

> Do they know God as a pardoning God? Have they the love of God abiding in them? Do they desire nothing but God? Are they holy in all manner of conversation? Have they gifts, as well as evidence of God's grace, for the work? Have they a clear, sound understanding;

a right judgment in the things of God; a just conception of salvation by faith?

Have you faith in Christ? Are you going on to perfection? Are you resolved to devote yourself wholly to God and his work? Do you know the General Rules of our Church? Will you keep them? Have you studied the doctrines of the United Methodist Church? Will you preach and maintain them?[45]

In these ways, Wesley continues to instruct the Methodist preachers and members of the Methodist churches.

In academic and even popular theology, Methodists have of course been affected by changing cultural fashions.[46] But periodic Wesleyan revivals arise through returns to the eighteenth-century sources.[47] The more significant of these revivals invoke not simply a Wesleyan method in theology but Wesleyan doctrinal substance.[48]

4. Our Liturgist and Hymnographer(s)

Ancient Fathers left their names on liturgies that at least in part derive from them: so with St. Basil and St. John Chysostom, not to mention other cases in the lesser Eastern Churches. Some patristic saints are honored for their hymn writing: so Ambrose, Ephraim, John of Damascus (whose "Day of Resurrection" appears in twentieth-century Methodist hymnals), and even the ninth-century "St. Joseph the Hymnographer" (familiar to modern Methodists through his "Happy Band of Pilgrims").

John Wesley provided the Methodists with a *Sunday Service*. Destined first for North America (1784), then for the British Dominions overseas (1786), and finally issued without restriction (1788), it was closely based on the Anglican *Book of Common Prayer* (1662). In the United States, the Methodists between 1784 and 1792 referred to it as "our Prayer Book."[49] In England, it became known as "our venerable father's abridgement" (a phrase used in the "Plan of Pacification" of 1795 as part of the efforts to regulate Methodist liturgical practice in the difficult years of transition after Wesley's death). On both sides of the Atlantic, it underwent several revisions in the nineteenth and twentieth centuries; and although it was overtaken by less formal orders of worship for Sunday morning preaching services, it remained the basis for sacramental rites and pastoral offices.[50] In the second half of the twentieth century, Methodist service books and practice have been greatly influenced by the modern ecumenical and liturgical movements, which have made the ritual structures more patristic in shape while at the same time turning the language of worship more towards contemporary speech patterns. Nevertheless, something of the "Cranmerian" style of Wesley is retained at least in a fragmentary way or as allowed variants (as in the 1784/1882/1936 Order for the Lord's Supper in the British *Methodist Service Book* of 1975 and in Word and Table Service IV in the United Methodist *Book of Worship* of 1992).

It is, however, chiefly through hymnody that the Wesleyan stamp has been put on Methodist worship. Charles Wesley was the principal hymn writer, although John also composed some texts, translated others notably from the German, and edited his brother's when collections appeared under their joint names. Their 166 *Hymns on the Lord's Supper* of 1745 guided the eucharistic understanding and devotion of the early Methodists, and some of the best of these hymns have been maintained or reintroduced in subsequent Methodist hymnals.[51]

Finally, it was the more general *Collection of Hymns for the Use of the People called Methodists*, which Wesley published in 1780, that provided the structure and the vast bulk of all official hymnals of the British Wesleyans and the Methodist Episcopal Churches in America throughout the nineteenth century. In the preface, Wesley claimed that this collection was sufficient to "contain all the important truths of our most holy religion, whether speculative or practical; yea, to illustrate them all, and to prove them both by Scripture and reason. And this is done in a regular order. The hymns are not carelessly jumbled together, but carefully ranged under proper heads, according to the experience of real Christians. So that this book is in effect a little body of experimental and practical divinity."[52]

In the twentieth century, Methodists have widened the ecumenical range of their hymnody in both time and space, while the Wesleys have remained their chief source (most abundantly so in Britain, where the 1904 *Methodist Hymn Book* contained over 400 Wesleyan texts, the 1933 some 268, and the 1983 *Hymns and Psalms: A Methodist and Ecumenical Hymn Book* still some 173). If many Wesleyan hymns from the 1780 *Collection* have been lost to usage, others of a dogmatic and festival kind have been added from other Wesleyan sources.

The *United Methodist Hymnal* of 1989 arranged its hymns according to a structure that follows closely the ancient ecumenical creeds:

> The Glory of the Triune God (Praise and Thanksgiving; God's Nature; Providence; Creation).

> The Grace of Jesus Christ (In Praise of Christ; Christ's Gracious Life: Promised Coming; Birth and Baptism; Life and Teaching; Passion and death; Resurrection and Exaltation).

> The Power of the Holy Spirit (In Praise of the Holy Spirit; Prevenient Grace; Justifying Grace; Sanctifying and Perfecting Grace).

The Community of Faith (The Nature of the Church; The Book of the Church—Holy Scripture; The Sacraments and Rites of the Church; Particular Times of Worship).

A New Heaven and a New Earth (Death and Eternal Life; Communion of the Saints; Return and Reign of the Lord; The Completion of Creation—The City of God).

It would be a great enrichment if more hymns from the Orthodox Tradition could be made available for singing by Methodists.[53] Might some of the best Wesleyan hymns even find their way into Orthodox worship, so that a Wesleyan voice could contribute to the great symphony?[54] It is, in any case, to the existing Methodist hymnic *lex orandi* that we shall turn for a couple of examples concerning "the Spirit of faith" in the Wesleyan tradition.

IV. *"Spirit of Faith," "Remembrancer Divine"*

"Spirit of faith, come down": This pneumatological epiclesis of a hymn was contained as number 83 of the 525 hymns in the 1780 *Collection*. It has maintained its place in the current British and United Methodist hymnals of 1983 and 1989 respectively.

A full quotation of it will illustrate a number of Wesleyan characteristics. First, the tissue of biblical phrases and allusions demonstrate a use of the Scriptures as the canonical book of the Church's faith and life. Second, the Scriptures are read according to a hermeneutical grid given by the Church's dogmatic understanding concerning the persons and work of the Holy Trinity and the Church's classic proclamation and confession of the gospel of salvation for humankind. Third, this hymn brings together the "faith which is believed" and the "faith which believes," the *fides quae creditur* and the *fides quâ creditur*, in a fusion of living faith, of incandescent orthodoxy.

Here is invoked the Holy Spirit, whose gift is the fruit of Christ's redemptive work and the beginning of our salvation, who has shaped the Christian community throughout its existence and brings God home in the personal experience of the believer. Let the hymn speak, or sing, for itself:

Spirit of faith, come down,	[1 Cor. 2:12]
Reveal the things of God,	[2 Cor. 4:13]
And make to us the Godhead known,	
And witness with the blood:	[1 John 5:8]

'Tis Thine the blood to apply,
And give us eyes to see,
Who did for every sinner die   [Rom. 5:8]
Hath surely died for me.

No man can truly say   [1 Cor. 12:3]
That Jesus is the Lord
Unless Thou take the veil away,   [2 Cor. 3:12-18]
And breathe the living word;   [Matt. 4:4;
Then, only then we feel   John 20:22]
Our interest in His blood,   [1 John 1:7]
And cry with joy unspeakable,   [1 Pet. 1:8]
Thou art my Lord, my God!   [John 20:28]

O that the world might know
The all-atoning Lamb!   [John 1:29]
Spirit of faith, descend, and show
The virtue of His name;   [Acts 4:12]
The grace which all may find,
The saving power impart,
And testify to all mankind,
And speak in every heart!

Inspire the living faith
(Which whoso'er receives,
The witness in himself he hath,   [1 John 5:10;
And consciously believes),   Rom. 8:15]
The faith that conquers all,   [1 John 5:4]
And doth the mountain move,   [Mark 11:23]
And saves whoe'er on Jesus call,   [Rom. 10:13]
And perfects them in love.   [1 John 4:17]

That is how, at the heart of their life together, Methodists typically preach, receive, teach, learn, confess and celebrate the Christian faith. That hymn constitutes the "tradition of the faith" in Wesleyan substance and mode.

A second example comes from the Wesley brothers' *Hymns on the Lord's Supper*, where it figured as number 16; it has been included in all British Methodist hymn books of the twentieth century. "Come, Thou everlasting Spirit" is a eucharistic epiclesis whose key image is drawn from a phrase at the epiclesis in the liturgy of the eighth book of the *Apostolic Constitutions*, where the Holy Spirit is called "the Witness of the sufferings of the Lord Jesus." Invoking the Holy Spirit also as the "Recorder" of Christ's passion and the divine "Remembrancer," the Wesleys link anamnesis and epiclesis in a very traditional way that has also been recovered in such modern ecumenical texts as the Lima document of Faith and Order on *Baptism, Eucharist and Ministry*.[55] Again, the Holy Spirit appears as the bringer of the gospel, the source of living faith, and the power of Christian experience:

> Come, Thou everlasting Spirit,
> Bring to every thankful mind
> All the Saviour's dying merit,
> All His sufferings for mankind.
>
> True Recorder of His passion,
> Now the living faith impart,
> Now reveal His great salvation,
> Preach His gospel to our heart.
>
> Come, Thou Witness of His dying,
> Come, Remembrancer Divine,
> Let us feel Thy power applying
> Christ to every soul and mine.

Clearly, for Wesleyans as for the Orthodox, the eucharist embodies the content and a means of the evangelical Tradition and of the Christian faith—all in and under the Holy Spirit. Historically, later Methodists have not been able to match the Wesleys for frequency of sacramental celebration, while the more frequent celebrations in the Orthodox Churches still fail to attract the regular Sunday communion of the faithful such as marked the Church of the earliest centuries. Both Orthodox and Methodists may have something to learn from John Wesley's sermon, written for his Oxford students in 1732 and published by him in 1787–88, on "The Duty of Constant Communion."[56]

V. Scripture, Tradition, Experience, and Reason

The 1972 *Book of Discipline* of the United Methodist Church, in the more discursive parts of its treatment of "Doctrine and Doctrinal Statements and the General Rules," declared, in phraseology widely attributed to Albert C. Outler, that the "living core" of "Christian truth," according to Methodist belief, "stands revealed in scripture, illumined by tradition, vivified in personal experience, and confirmed by reason." Informally, the four elements of Scripture, tradition, experience and reason quickly became dubbed "the Methodist, or the Wesleyan, Quadrilateral." Unfortunately, that designation evoked a mental image of four equal sides, with

175

the carefully nuanced verbs of "revealed, illumined, vivified, and confirmed" lost from sight.

The underlying problematic emerged more clearly in the 1980s, when the theological Evangelicals began to ask for a firmer declaration of the primacy of Scripture (Wesley called himself "a man of one book," *homo unius libri*, which meant that the Scriptures constituted, in the neat phrase of George Croft Cell, not so much "the boundary of his reading" as "the center of gravity in his thinking"), while the theological Liberals prized "reason" and "experience" for the latitude it allowed their quest for contemporary relevance.[57] That most parties were keen to show the "Wesleyan" character of the "quadrilateral," or at least of their version of it, is itself an interesting indication of the role of Wesley among Methodists.

The one element among the four that received by far the least attention in the recent debate was Tradition.[58] For our present purposes, the most useful procedure now will be to see what, after the preceding debate, the General Conference of 1992 put into the *Book of Discipline* concerning Tradition in its relation to Scripture, experience, and reason. It must be emphasized that the section on "Our Theological Task" (68) in which this discursive treatment occurs, like the sections on "Our Doctrinal Heritage" (65) and "Our Doctrinal History" (66) but unlike "Our Doctrinal Standards and General Rules" (67), are mere "legislative enactments and neither part of the Constitution nor under the Restrictive Rules"; in other words, they are readily subject to improvement. It must further be stressed that the 1992 text maintains, on the whole, a clearer distinction than the 1972 text did between (stable) "doctrine" and (more ephemeral) "theology": "the Church considers its doctrinal affirmations a central feature of its identity," whereas the "theological task" is much more concerned with "interpretation" and "application" in the changing daily contexts. The theological task serves above all the cause of authentic Christian witness in particular situations.

This, then, is the gist of what the 1992 General Conference, under "Theological Guidelines: Sources and Criteria," stated particularly with reference to Scripture and to Tradition:[59]

> Scripture is primary, revealing the Word of God "so far as it is necessary for our salvation." . . .
>
> Tradition provides both a source and a measure of authentic Christian witness, though its authority derives from its faithfulness to the biblical message. . . .
>
> The Christian witness, even when grounded in Scripture and mediated by tradition, is ineffectual unless understood and appropriated by the individual. To become our witness, it must make sense in terms of our own reason and experience.

176

Scripture, as the constitutive witness to the wellsprings of our faith, occupies a place of primary authority. . . .

More particularly under the heading of "Scripture":

Through Scripture the living Christ meets us in the expereience of redeeming grace. . . .

The biblical authors, illumined by the Holy Spirit, bear witness that in Christ the world is reconciled to God. The Bible bears authentic terstimony to God's self-disclosure in the life, death, and resurrection of Jesus Christ as well as in God's work of creation, in the pilgrimage of Israel, and in the Holy Spirit's ongoing activity in human history. . . .

The Bible is sacred canon for Christian people, formally acknowledged as such by historic ecumenical councils of the Church. . . .

We properly read Scripture within the believing community, informed by the tradition of that community. . . .

The close relationship of tradition, experience, and reason appears in the Bible itself. Scripture witnesses to a variety of diverse traditions, some of which reflect tensions in interpretation within the early Judeo-Christian heritage. However, these traditions are woven together in the Bible in a manner that expresses the fundamental unity of God's revelation as received and experienced by people in the diversity of their own lives.

And then directly under the heading of "Tradition":

The theological task does not start anew in each age or each person. Christianity does not leap from New Testament times to the present as though nothing were to be learned from that great cloud of witnesses in between. For centuries Christians have sought to interpret the truth of the gospel for their time.

In these attempts, tradition, understood both in terms of process and form, has played an important role. The passing on and receiving of the gospel among persons, regions, and generations constitutes a dynamic element of Christian history. The formulations and practices that grew out of specific circumstances constitute the legacy of the corporate experience of earlier Christian communities.

These traditions are found in many cultures around the globe. But the history of Christianity includes a mixture of ignorance, misguided zeal, and sin. Scripture remains the norm by which all traditions are judged.

The story of the Church reflects the most basic sense of tradition, the continuing activity of God's Spirit transforming human life. Tradition is the history of that continuing environment of grace in and by which all Christians live, God's self-giving love in Jesus Christ.

177

As such, tradition transcends the story of particular traditions.

In this deeper sense of tradition, all Christians share a common history. Within that history, Christian tradition precedes Scripture, and yet Scripture comes to be the focal expression of the tradition. As United Methodists, we pursue our theological task in openness to the richness of both the form and power of tradition.

The multiplicity of traditions furnishes a richly varied source for theological reflection and construction. For United Methodists, certain strands of tradition have special importance as the historic foundation of our doctrinal heritage and the distinctive expressions of our communal existence.

We are now challenged by traditions from around the world which accent dimensions of Christian understanding that grow out of the sufferings and victories of the downtrodden [and so on for seven or eight more sentences].

Although this United Methodist text contains several important insights, it does not appear to be controlled by what it itself calls the "deeper" or "most basic" sense of Tradition as the entire life of the Church in so far as it bears the gospel—an understanding that has gradually made its way ecumenically since the World Conference on Faith and Order at Montreal in 1963 and is characteristic of Orthodoxy.[60] The Methodist hesitancy in this regard may be due to the more episodic view of Church history which characterizes not only Wesley but Protestants more generally. On the other hand, the United Methodist emphasis on the authoritative primacy of Scripture might valuably prompt Methodists to ask Orthodox Christians what account they too can give of how the Scriptures, as a very special part of the Tradition, serve as a critical norm for the entire life of the historical Church—a view which marked the Reformation in the sixteenth century, the Wesleyan revival in the eighteenth, and the confessing Church in the twentieth. How do the Orthodox account for failings in the life of the Church?

Both Orthodox and Methodists will affirm, as the Fathers and Wesley likewise did, that authentic Tradition is found only where the Spirit of faith is present. A subject for exploration in their dialogue may well be the criteria by which the Spirit of faith and authentic Tradition are discerned.

CHAPTER TEN

The Orthodox Role
in the Ecumenical Movement:
A Protestant Perception

Having started all our sessions with "Christ is risen: He is risen indeed," let us begin this time with an Easter greeting from the Methodist tradition. The response at the end of each line is "Alleluia":

> Christ the Lord is risen today: Alleluia.
> Sons of men and angels, say: Alleluia.
> Raise your songs and triumphs high: Alleluia.
> Sing, ye heavens; thou earth, reply: Alleluia.

Your Eminences, your Graces, fathers, sisters and brothers: Many Orthodox hierarchs and theologians have played an invaluable part in the modern ecumenical movement. Archbishop Jakovos is one of the outstanding examples. It is an honor for me to speak at a symposium to celebrate his thirty years as Archbishop of the Americas and the Oceans. I shall speak as a Protestant, and more particularly as a Methodist, who is persuaded that his own tradition, at least in its Wesleyan origins within the Church of England, is a recognizable instance of the great evangelical, catholic and orthodox Tradition. Under John and Charles Wesley, Methodism was a movement that brought together the preaching of the gospel, the creedal faith of the ancient church, the renewal of eucharistic life, an emphasis on personal and social sanctification, and a sustained philanthropy towards the poor and wretched. That tradition has, like much of Protestantism, sadly declined either into fundamentalism or, much more seriously, into liberalism. We have much to gain from the ecumenical movement, and particularly from the Orthodox. In what follows I want to highlight four themes or areas in which the Orthodox witness is vital and attractive. In each case I will (1) signal briefly the Orthodox contribution, (2) state why Protestantism needs it, and (3) suggest by way of

179

example one detailed issue where we can reflect and work, mutually and together, to facilitate the reception of the Orthodox witness on the issue.

I. *The Witness to Unity*

(1) My revered teacher, Nikos Nissiotis of blessed memory, wrote this for the Third Assembly of the World Council of Churches at New Delhi in 1961: "The unique contribution of Orthodoxy to the discussion on Church unity lies in its simple reminder [of] the unbroken continuity of the life of the historical Church. . . . Our very existence derives from the inseparable union between the three persons of the Holy Trinity given to us as a historic event on the day of Pentecost."[1] Metropolitan John Zizioulas has given a eucharistic focus to this notion: the holy communion, which constitutes the church sacramentally, comes from the very life and being of the Holy Trinity.[2] Orthodoxy thus witnesses to the *visibility* of the Church which is creedally confessed as "one," in harmony with the Word who was made *flesh* and the Holy Spirit who descended upon a *flesh-and-blood* community of believers. It witnesses also to the *fulness* of a perduring churchly body that belongs to Christ in whom the fulness of the Godhead dwelt bodily (Eph, 1:23; Col. 1:18-19).

(2) However unpalatable the Orthodox claim to be the one continuing *visible* and *complete* body of Christ may be to Protestants, we need to hear this witness. It challenges the insufficiency of any invisibilist, spiritualistic understanding of the Church, according to which all "true believers" are assumed to be one, even if they live institutionally and sacramentally isolated lives. True, a "visible" unity would be a mere façade, if it did not find a spiritual correspondence in an inward unity of faith, hope and love. But the alternative to visible unity is not spiritual unity; it is visible *dis*unity, which is a counter-witness to the gospel of reconciliation. Thus the Orthodox claim, which in strictness denies a place in the church to those outside Orthodoxy, should prevent Protestants from acquiescing in any (f)actual brokenness of the body of Christ. It should be a spur to efforts for the healing of the fractures that any Protestants who believe the Church to be greater than their own community are bound to recognize as afflicting a body that, on such a Protestant understanding, is in internal schism (a notion which, for their part, the Orthodox find repugnant).

(3) An issue on which Orthodox and Protestants might in this connection reflect and work, mutually and together, is the episcopate. The Orthodox themselves consider that the existence of "overlapping jurisdictions" within their own communion is at least a canonical anomaly. Protestants must be brought to recognize that separate structures of

pastoral government—the institutionally distinct "denominations"—are, even if they sometimes manage to be more cooperative than competitive, also an anomaly, for ultimately they betoken a claim to "independence" from other parts of the body of Christ. Now it needs to be recognized, on the one hand, that modern metropolitical life, in particular, is unlikely to be able to function under the same conditions as a small Mediterranean town in antiquity ("one city, one bishop"); and, on the other hand, that a principle of unity is needed for each local church, understood as all Christians in a given geographical area. Both Orthodox and Protestants might therefore bend their combined efforts to elaborating a pattern of "perichoretic" episcopacy, whereby a permanent "council" of bishops might take care of a composite local community in which there were no longer any barriers of faith or life but rather the possibilty of free circulation among various groups of Christians belonging to different cultural and/or liturgical traditions, united in doctrine and sacrament but continuing to express distinct theological and devotional styles.[3]

II. *The Witness to Worship*

(1) The recent celebrations of the millennium of Russian Christianity have brought once more to mind the famous story of the emissaries of Prince Vladimir who found Muslim worship frenzied and foul-smelling, and "beheld no glory" in the ceremonies of Western Christians. But in Constantinople

> the Greeks led us to the buildings where they worship their God, and we knew not whether we were in heaven or on earth. For on earth there is no such splendor or such beauty, and we are at a loss to describe it. We know only that God dwells there among men, and their service is fairer than the ceremonies of other nations.[4]

For many modern Protestants, their first significant encounter with Orthodoxy has been through its liturgy. My own dates back to 1963 when, as a student, I attended the Orthodox Seminar at the Ecumenical Institute of Bossey which prepared us for sharing in the Holy Week services at the St. Sergius Institute in Paris. We are attracted by the "mystery," both in the phenomenological sense of an epiphany of the sacred and, more importantly, in the scriptural sense of a revelation in Christ and the Holy Spirit of the Father's loving purpose for the salvation of the world.

(2) Protestants need this witness in face of the missing dimensions in our own worship. Even classical Protestantism, let alone its later developments, favored the didactic over the latreutic. We concentrated so much on the oral and the aural that we tended to forget that the Word of life is

given to be "seen with our eyes (. . .) and touched with our hands" (1 John 1:1), that the goodness of the Lord can be "tasted" (1 Peter 2:3) and the gospel is a "fragrance of life" to those who are being saved (cf. 2 Cor. 2:14-16). Protestant believers need a body-and-soul exposure to the richly sacramental practice of Orthodox worship. Moreover, our theologians and our moralists need to rediscover the doxological scope of doctrine and ethics that should both transcend and permeate the classroom and the workplace.[5]

(3) Dean Calivas' address at this symposium passionately expounded the nature and importance of worship, while indicating areas in which contemporary Orthodox liturgical practice requires reform and renewal. An area in which Orthodox and Protestants can reflect and work mutually and together is that of the holy communion. Orthodox churches celebrate the divine liturgy on Sundays and on the great feasts; but, in their responses to the Faith and Order text *Baptism, Eucharist and Ministry*, both from the Inter-Orthodox Symposium held at Holy Cross in June 1985 and on the part of the several autocephalies, most Orthodox churches have recognized a need for more frequent communion by the laity, provided proper spiritual and moral preparation takes place. On their side, most of the Protestant Reformers desired to restore the ancient practice of a weekly service of word and sacrament according to the pattern reported by St. Justin the Martyr in his *First Apology* (67); but a millennium of infrequent communion on the part of post-Constantinian Christians made the faithful loth to receive more often, and the Reformers were unwilling to hold the Lord's Supper without the full participation of the people, so that Protestantism became saddled with simply a preaching service as its regular Sunday fare. John Wesley hinted at the significance of the ancient pattern when he advised the Methodist elders in North America to "administer the Supper of the Lord on every Lord's day";[6] but Methodists have lagged behind several other Protestant churches in their recovery of a more frequent celebration of the eucharist in the twentieth century.

III. *The Witness to Dogma*

(1) The Orthodox liturgy abounds with references to "Christ our God" and with ascriptions of "Glory to the Father and to the Son and to the Holy Spirit." Here is a strong christocentrism within a firmly trinitarian framework. Orthodox dogma and theology bears continued witness to the "homoousion," which, as St. Athanasius expounded it, is the ontological grounding of the soteriological truth that only God can reveal God, and only God can save humankind. Orthodox theology exploits the

vision of the Cappadocian Fathers that the communion among the divine Persons is the source, model and goal for the saving communion of humans with God and among the redeemed.

(2) Liberal Protestants need this witness because they are always in danger of contemplating other "saviors." They tend to doubt the sufficiency of a Jesus who lived so long ago, in another cultural situation. They are apt to turn their new heroes into demi-gods. They let themselves be enticed to the promethean task of "buiding the kingdom." Conservative Protestants, especially those of an experientialist outlook, run the risk of limiting themselves to an individualist and subjectivist understanding and practice of salvation, lacking an ecclesiological and ultimately trinitarian sense of persons-in-community.[7]

(3) Orthodox and Protestants can helpfully reflect and work, mutually and together, on the hermeneutics of dogma. Kosuke Koyama, the Japanese theologian at Union Theological Seminary in New York, recently spoke at a meeting of the American Theological Society to the effect that a Japanese Christian can easily grasp, in terms of a Greek vocabulary, what the Nicene Creed means by confessing the Son to be *homoousios* with the Father. The challenge is to find a way of expressing that in a Japanese vocabulary. Orthodox and Protestants are already engaged together in the WCC Faith and Order study "Towards the Common Expression of the Apostolic Faith Today." The Orthodox contribution resides above all in their safe anchorage upon a steady dogmatic base, although already at the Odessa consultation of 1981 Metropolitan Filaret of Kiev recognized that "the human expression of the unchangeable divine content reflects the language, the way of thinking and the culture of this or that epoch. . . . The dogmatical formulations have a historically conditioned character, but this by no means diminishes the significance of the contents of these formulations. All this testifies to the fact that the Church, in principle, has a possibility of new dogmatical formulations and definitions; but by their contents they should remain self-identical to the one divine Truth kept by the Church and existing outside and beyond history."[8] Protestants, having passed through the critical fires of the Enlightenment, have perhaps a greater sense of the problems posed by historical and cultural change, and a sharper sensitivity to the needs of the "receptor" language into which the faith has to be newly put; but several Protestant participants in the study have already regained admiration for the achievements of the Fathers and a conviction that the Christian faith substantially stands or falls with them.

IV. The Witness to Tradition

(1) The Orthodox sense of an uninterrupted history of unity, worship and dogma names vital elements in the great Tradition. This comprehensive notion designates the life of the Holy Spirit in the Church. The living Tradition is the continuing story of a people on its way to glory. It is conspicuously instantiated in the liturgical ikons, where Christ and his Mother are joined first by the biblical saints, next by the patristic, and then by figures from the later cloud of witnesses, so that the believing community of each generation is invited and welcomed into their company. In the words of Constantine Kalokyris: The worshipper "does not merely remember, but lives and actually partakes himself of the life of the Saviour and of His saints. . . . The sacred persons and events are represented in such a manner that they are *sunchronizomena* (contemporized) and appear as belonging to the eternal present, or, to put it otherwise, to eternity—introduced and lived in the present and in every time."[9]

(2) "To be deep in history is to cease to be a Protestant," said John Henry Newman, if I may quote one whose own path took him not to Orthodoxy but to Roman Catholicism.[10] While most of the major Protestant Reformers had a profound regard for the Church of the early centuries and were guided by patristic and conciliar interpretations of the Christian faith, it is unfortunately true that many of their successors have, on the "conservative" side, imagined that one could leap directly to the Scriptures and back, without much sense that this is the Book of *the Church*; while, on the "liberal" side, many have thought that the slogan of *semper reformanda* implies that the Church starts from scratch to "invent" its message as "new" occasions arise. I think it was at Holy Cross that I first heard the joke about Professor Dr. X. Y. Tzet, who "profoundly affected the history of Protestant theology from 3:40 to 3:45 p.m." on a particular and passing day. Mere "novelty" is too easily valued by liberal Protestants over the genuine "newness" of the gospel. They live in a permanent state of flux.

(3) The World Conference on Faith and Order at Montreal in 1963 registered some convergence between Orthodox and Protestants on the issue of Scripture and Tradition. They were able to speak together of "the *paradosis* of the *kerygma*." Scripture was seen as an internal norm to Tradition, and Tradition as the interpretative context of Scripture. Yet Montreal could only pose, without answering in detail, the criteriological questions that arise when it comes to discerning and expressing the truth of the Christian faith and embodying it in the life of the Church. Diachronically, we must aim at faithfulness to the witness of the prophets, apostles and martyrs. Synchronically, we need a conciliarity in which

common judgments can be made concerning the authentic expression and embodiment of the faith. How, ecumenically, are we to arrive at the condition of conciliarity in which the discernment of faithfulness can be made? How, concretely, are we to distinguish failures, deviations and witherings in the Christian witness from genuine and vital testimony? And to distinguish between "local" and "temporary" traditions and the great Tradition, and properly relate them? That last is the question of "culture" raised by this symposium in honor of Archbishop Jakovos. All these questions are recognized by Faith and Order as being placed on its agenda by the responses of the churches to the Lima text.[11] They are questions on which Protestants and Orthodox *and Roman Catholics* have to reflect mutually and together.

Let us end as we began, with another stanza from Charles Wesley's Easter hymn:

> Soar we now where Christ hath led: Alleluia.
> Following our exalted Head: Alleluia.
> Made like him, like him we rise: Alleluia.
> Ours the cross, the grave, the skies: Alleluia.

Methodists in
Multilateral Dialogue

CHAPTER ELEVEN

Methodism and the Apostolic Faith

It is tempting simply to declare that Methodism's best contribution to the World Council of Churches study on the Apostolic Faith would be to sit still and listen. But denominational honor requires that we participate more actively. The hope must be that the exercise will prove mutually beneficial to ourselves and to other participants.

The present chapter will correspondingly unfold in three stages. In the first part, we shall examine what Methodism might receive from the WCC Faith and Order project as it has been set up and is developing. In the second part, we shall suggest how Methodism might add to the project. In the third part, we shall try to discern more synthetically some possible results from the engagement in a common process.

In examining, in the first part, the Faith and Order program, we shall find the Apostolic Faith study to be marked by four characteristics that need to be restamped on contemporary Methodism. The study is: (a) creedal; (b) trinitarian; (c) ecumenical; (d) homological, that is, in the service of confessing the faith. These same four points will then also be used to structure Methodism's own potential contribution to the project (part two), and to discern some elements in a desired synthesis (part three).

In suggesting, in the second part, an authentic Methodist contribution to the project, we shall take as our paradigm John Wesley's *Letter to a Roman Catholic* of 1749. As is well known, this "olive branch," as Albert Outler calls it,[1] is not all that Wesley had to offer to the Romans: he could be polemical as well as irenical, as may be seen in "A Roman Catechism faithfully drawn out of the allowed writings of the Church of Rome, with a Reply thereto".[2] Nor is it claimed that Wesley was interested in relations with Roman Catholics to the exclusion of others. Our choice of paradigm depends on the fact that, in setting out "the faith of a true Protestant," Wesley proceeded by way of an expansion upon the Nicene-Constantinopolitan creed, the very procedure being followed in the Faith and Order study. The wider range of Wesley's ecumenical interests will be represented by our drawing also on his more generally intended sermon of 1750 on a "catholic spirit" (where the "c" is lower case).[3]

In the third, and more synthetic, part, we shall declare our desire that, in the give and take of study and the common pursuit, Methodism may be reconfirmed in a faith which is scriptural, patristic, Wesleyan, and (we hope) synchronically ecumenical. By its active and receptive participation in the Faith and Order project, Methodism may perhaps recover its Wesleyan heritage where we have abandoned it, reenter the catholic path where we have strayed from it, and maintain or restore Wesleyan impulses where the broader Christian Tradition needs them.

I. The Apostolic Faith Study

The current state of the WCC project "Towards the Common Expression of the Apostolic Faith Today" is represented in Faith and Order Paper No. 140, a study document which bears the title "*Confessing* One Faith: Towards an *Ecumenical* Explication of the Apostolic Faith as Expressed in the Nicene-Constantinopolitan *Creed* (381).[4] The words I have emphasized, coupled with the fact that the councils of Nicea and Constantinople settled precisely the *trinitarian* faith of the Church, provide the four characteristics highlighted in our description. The project is, first, creedal.

1. Creedal

The Nicene-Constantinopolitan Creed [= NC], not to the exclusion of the Apostles' Creed, is taken as "the theological basis and methodological tool for the explication of the apostolic faith" (Introduction, 11). The creed was chosen for these purposes after a lengthy debate involving such questions as: (a) why not simply take the Scriptures? (b) why fix on such an antique formulation as part of confessing the faith today? (c) why be bound to a form that some have experienced as authoritarian? Answers were reached along the following lines respectively:

(A) The "decision was taken in the conviction that this Creed represents an exemplary and authentic summary of the apostolic faith" (Intro., 11), "the same apostolic faith that was expressed in Holy Scriptures and summarized in the Creeds of the Early Church" (Intro., 8). The councils of the fourth century would have preferred to stick entirely to scriptural language but needed to include a minimum of other terminology (e.g. the *homoousion*) in order to reject mistaken interpretations of the biblical witness. In any case, in the present project each phrase of NC has its "biblical foundation" carefully laid out (see Intro., 11–12).

(B) "The decision was also taken in the recognition that the Nicene Creed served as an expression of unity of the Early Church and is, therefore, also of great importance for our contemporary quest for the unity of Christ's Church" (Intro., 11). The project is thus employing NC as part of the recognized ecumenical technique of getting back behind divisions to common ground, of rediscovering and reappropriating "common roots" (Intro., 4). This procedure has enjoyed considerable success in the liturgical movement of our century and in such doctrinal convergences as are expressed in the Lima document on "Baptism, Eucharist and Ministry."[5]

(C) An anecdote may help. A Jamaican Baptist began by expressing all the suspicions which his cultural and denominational background would naturally lead him to entertain towards the "Greek metaphysical" vocabulary and "imperially oppressive" uses of NC; but he came to value its substantial affirmation of the deity and sovereignty of Christ over against theological liberalism.

As Methodists, we need to recover our creedal inheritance, and participation in the Faith and Order study can help us to do so. It is true that Wesley omitted Article VIII ("Of the Three Creeds") in his selection of the Anglican Articles for American Methodism (we know that he particularly disliked the damnatory clauses of the so-called Athanasian Creed), and that he removed NC in his abridgement of the Prayer Book communion order in *The Sunday Service*. He had, however, no quarrel with the substance of NC, as we shall see; and he retained the Apostles' Creed in his American service book. The "inheritance of the apostolic faith" and "the fundamental principles of the historic creeds" are part of the constitutional basis of the British Methodist Church. The Apostles' and Nicene Creeds figure in the current liturgical books of Methodism on both sides of the Atlantic and in many other parts of the world. We should make better use of them, both in the recitation of them, as a "performative act" of our faith, and in the evangelistic and catechetical tasks of *explicating* the faith (the need for which the WCC study fully recognizes).

2. Trinitarian

The Faith and Order project is necessarily trinitarian if it follows NC in substance and in structure. For the council of Nicea declared the Son of the Father to be "true God from true God," and the council of Constantinople proclaimed the sovereignty of the Holy Spirit who is worshiped and adored with the Father and the Son. And NC follows the threefold pattern common to creeds based on the baptismal interrogations that match the triune Name.

191

The tripartite structure of "Confessing One Faith" is in fact as follows:

I. We believe in one God.
II. We believe in one Lord Jesus Christ.
III. We believe in the Holy Spirit, the Church and the life of the world to come.

Substantially, the text stresses the oneness of God, which is a unity of tripersonal communion, with the First Person as "the eternal source of that living trinitarian communion of love" (I/18). It is insisted that the Father is always the Father of the Son, and the Son is always the Son of the Father (e.g. I/52; II/93); and the only Holy Spirit is "the Spirit [who] belongs to the eternal being of the Trinity" (III/180) and is never "dissociated . . . from the work of Christ in the economy of God's salvation" (III/188).

The *doctrine* of the Trinity, as bound to the *reality* of the Trinity, is vital to our knowledge of God and to our salvation. As Athanasius and the Cappadocians argued at the various stages of the Arian controversy: only God can reveal God, only God can redeem, and only God can give participation in God. In our time and place, Methodists must not acquiesce in, let alone create, patterns of understanding, speech and prayer that some are proposing in an effort to overcome "patriarchy" but which in fact threaten the Trinity.

Quite apart from the difficulty of principle in knowing whether one has lighted on a formulation just as good as, or now even preferable to, the divine Name used by Jesus and the writers of the New Testament, the alternatives or substitutes concretely proposed appear unsatisfactory in the light of the Christian doctrinal tradition. "Creator, Christ and Spirit" has an Arian ring; and, by reducing Christ and the Spirit to creatures, we should, as Athanasius and the Cappadocians argued, be undermining our salvation. "Creator, Redeemer, Sustainer" sounds Sabellian and is in any case purely functional, forfeiting the internal divine communion in which salvation gives us a share. Even at his most "catholic spirited," Wesley refused his hand to Arians, semi-Arians, Socinians and Deists, for their heart was not right with his heart.[6]

A denomination which in practice allows baptisms to be performed under a divine name changed at the discretion of the minister or the candidate will, in the longer historical term and on the wider geographical scene, eventually bring all its baptisms into disrepute. This appears to be the danger being run by the United Methodist Church in the United States at the moment.[7] Nor is it a matter of baptism alone, fundamental as that is. An isolated use of "Father, Son, and Holy Spirit" in baptism would lead to its becoming a petrified, or even a magical, formula. Father, Son and

Holy Spirit need to be named as the story is told, as the word is preached, as candidates are baptized, as the congregation prays, as the eucharist is offered, as ministers are ordained, and as the people are blessed. As Methodists in America, we in particular need to regain the confidence to do that.

3. Ecumenical

The Faith and Order project also grounds its employment of NC in (a) widespread existing usage, and (b) the ecumenical aim:

(A) NC is "officially recognized and used by many churches within the ecumenical movement"; "the main content" of NC and the Apostles' Creed "is also present in the thinking and life of churches which do not explicitly recognize these Creeds or use them in their teaching and worship" (Intro., 11). Here again the study is following a familiar principle in ecumenical work, this time that of building on what the churches already have in common. The need now is for what is called, in an ungainly expression, the "re-reception" of the ancient creeds. For that reason, the *explication* of the creeds is important, even internally to the Christian community, let alone vis-à-vis the world (a point to which I shall return).

(B) The aim of the Faith and Order project is ecumenical in the classical sense of the ecumenical movement. It "serves the primary function and purpose of the WCC 'to call the churches to the goal of visible unity in one faith and in one eucharistic fellowship' [Constitution of the WCC, III.1]. The common confession of the apostolic faith is one of the essential conditions and elements of visible unity" (Intro., 4; cf. 6).

As Methodists we should not jettison what we already hold in common with other Christians, either for the sake of emphasizing a "specific difference" or for the sake of a new will-o'-the-wisp that might bring us closer to other revisionists while severing the ties that bind us to the continuing historic Tradition. Rather we should find our strength in unity with others who hold fast to common Christianity.

As Methodists, again, we need to recommit ourselves to the goal of unity, "visible unity" as the 1986 Nairobi Report of the Joint Commission between the World Methodist Council and the Roman Catholic Church puts it; and to the search for appropriate models and means to realize that unity. In the 1970s and 1980s, British Methodists were frustrated by failures in the plans for reunion with the Church of England and for a covenant with other churches in England; American Methodists show little enthusiasm for the various proposals that have emerged from the Consultation on Church Union (COCU). What lessons, positive and negative, are to be drawn from Methodist participation in the United

Church of Canada, the Church of South India, the Uniting Church in Australia? How are we to respect both the truly local and the truly universal dimensions of the unity to which the Church is called? In any case, agreement "in the faith" is required for visible unity; and NC, as a common global text for common particular explication, appears to provide the best hope for progress in that direction.

4. Homological

In the title of the Faith and Order project, the broader term "common *expression*" is employed, but the elemental form of expression is the *confession* of the faith. Common confession of the faith is needed for united worship, life and mission. Made both before God and before humankind, *coram Deo* and *coram hominibus*, confession is at once (a) doxological, (b) evangelistic, and (c) ethical, in intention and scope. The Faith and Order document brings this out:

(A) The commentary to I/10 speaks of "the mystery of the triune God celebrated in the liturgy of the Church." Under pneumatology and ecclesiology, the doxological vision is extended to what the Orthodox have taken to calling "the liturgy after the Liturgy":

> Christians, therefore, glorify the triune God through prayer, common worship and *the daily service which is their acceptable sacrifice* (cf. Rom. 12:1f.). (III/191)

> The Church is the eucharistic community . . . whose basic calling is the glorification of the triune God in worship and service. (III/213)

(B) The WCC study shows a strong awareness that the apostolic faith expressed in NC has to be "explicated" in relation to the "challenges"—perennial and contemporary—that it faces. In appropriate circumstances, evangelism may be served either by direct proclamation of the gospel, or by apologetic, or by learning from outside critiques.

(C) The explication exemplified in Faith and Order Paper 140 also relates "doctrinal affirmations to ethical problems" (Intro., 13). Thus the project is linked to other ecumenical concerns for peace, justice, and the integrity of creation.

As Methodists, we need to recover the Wesleyan fusion of confession *coram Deo* and *coram hominibus*. One of the most remarkable features of the Wesleyan revival was in fact the combination of hymnography, eucharistic observance, evangelistic preaching, changed lives, and charitable action.

II. The Wesleyan Paradigm

Apart from a few ill-formulated sentences scattered in his writings, Wesley did not minimize orthodoxy of belief. When he writes, for instance, that "orthodoxy, or right opinions, is at best a slender part of religion, if it can be allowed to be any part at all,"[8] it must be remembered, first, that Wesley was prepared to "think and let think" only in those matters of theological "opinion" that did not "strike at the root of Christianity";[9] and second, that orthodoxy in the stricter sense of doctrine was, for Wesley, not so much unnecessary as insufficient—if it was not believed, experienced, and lived.

1. Creedal

Attention to Wesley could help the Faith and Order project to keep together "the faith which is believed" and "the faith which believes," the *fides quae creditur* and the *fides quâ creditur*. Wesley's *Letter to a Roman Catholic* [= *LRC*] first sets out the *content* of "the faith of a true Protestant," and then goes on to the *attitude*, *act* and *conduct* of faith.

That Wesley's substantive statement of faith is based on NC, rather than the Apostles' Creed alone, receives confirmation at several points:

- The fuller form of "*one* God, the Father, the Almighty, maker of heaven and earth, *of all things visible and invisible*" appears to provide more ground for Wesley's "I believe that this one God is the Father of all things, especially of angels and men"; and it may even be that the Greek *pantokratora*, rather than the Latin *omnipotentem*, stands behind Wesley's ensuing "I believe this Father of all not only to be able to do whatsoever pleaseth him but also to have an eternal right of making what and when and how pleaseth; and of possessing and disposing of all that he has made; and that he of his own goodness created heaven and earth, and all that is therein" (*LRC* 6).

- The Nicene phrases concerning the eternity and consubstantiality of the Son are repeated in Wesley's "the Father of his only Son, whom he hath begotten from eternity" (*LRC* 6), "the proper, natural Son of God, God of God, very God of very God" (*LRC* 7).

- The Nicene "who for us human beings and for our salvation" is expanded by Wesley's reference to the threefold office, prophet, priest and king, of "the Saviour of the world" (*LRC* 7).

- The Nicene *sarkôthenta* is given Chalcedonian precision by Wesley's "I believe that he was made man, joining the human nature with the divine in one person, being conceived by the singular operation of the Holy Ghost and born of the Blessed Virgin Mary" (*LRC* 7).

• When Wesley explicitly makes the Spirit "equal with the Father and the Son" (*LRC* 8), he is benefiting from the council of Constantinople.

Then Wesley describes the *fides quâ creditur* in this way:

> A true Protestant believes in God, has a full confidence in his mercy, fears him with a filial fear, and loves him with all his soul. He worships God in spirit and in truth, in everything gives him thanks, calls upon him with his heart as well as his lips, at all times and in all places, honours his holy Name and his Word, and serves him truly all the days of his life. (*LRC* 13)

The integration of the *fides quae creditur* and the *fides quâ creditur* is even more clearly and powerfully expressed in the sermon on "A Catholic Spirit," when he sets out in section I what he means by the question "Is thine heart right, as my heart is with thy heart?"

> [12.] . . . Is thy heart right with God? Dost thou believe his being and his perfections, his eternity, immensity, wisdom, power, his justice, mercy and truth? Dost thou believe that he now "upholdeth all things by the word of his power" [Heb. 1:3], and that he governs even the most minute, even the most noxious, to his own glory and the good of them that love him [cf. Rom. 8:28]? Hast thou a divine evidence, a supernatural conviction, of the things of God [cf. Heb. 11:1]? Dost thou "walk by faith, not by sight," looking not at temporal things but things eternal [2 Cor. 5:7; cf. 4:18]?
>
> [13.] Dost thou believe in the Lord Jesus Christ, "God over all, blessed for ever" [Rom. 9:5]? Is he revealed in thy soul [cf. Gal. 1:15]? Dost thou "know Jesus Christ and him crucified" [1 Cor. 2:2]? Does he "dwell in thee and thou in him" [1 John 4:13, 15]? Is he "formed in thy heart by faith" [Gal. 4:19; cf. Eph. 3:17]? Having absolutely disclaimed all thy own works, thy own righteousness, hast thou "submitted thyself unto the righteousness of God" [Rom. 10:3], which is by faith in Christ Jesus? Art thou "found in him, not having thy own righteousness, but the righteousness which is by faith" [Phil. 3:9]? And art thou, through him, "fighting the good fight of faith, and laying hold of eternal life" [1 Tim. 6:12]?
>
> [14.] Is thy faith *energoumenê di agapês*, "filled with the energy of love" [Gal. 5:6] ? Dost thou love God—I do not say "above all things," for it is both an unscriptural and ambiguous expression, but—"with all thy heart, and with all thy mind, and with all thy soul, and with all thy strength" [Luke 10:27]? Dost thou seek all thy happiness in him alone? And dost thou find what thou seekest

[cf. Matt. 7:8]? Does thy soul continually "magnify the Lord, and thy spirit rejoice in God thy Saviour" [Luke 1:46f.]? Having learned "in everything to give thanks" [1 Thess. 5:18], dost thou find "it is a joyful and pleasant thing to be thankful" [Ps. 147:1]? Is God the centre of thy soul, the sum of all thy desires? Art thou accordingly "laying up" thy "treasure in heaven" [Matt. 6:20] and "counting all things else dung" and dross [Phil. 3:8]? Hath the love of God cast the love of the world out of thy soul? Then thou art "crucified to the world" [Gal. 6:14]; thou art dead to all below and thy "life is hid with Christ in God" [Col. 3:3].

The trinitarian structure of these three paragraphs is clear, particularly when it is remembered, in connexion with paragraph 14, that "the love of God is shed abroad in our hearts *by the Holy Spirit*" (Rom. 5:5). Wesley then continues in similar vein with questions concerning the service of God, love of neighbor, and good works.[10]

2. Trinitarian

Wesley refused to speculate on *how*, while firmly believing *that*, Father, Son and Holy Spirit are one God. Although he sometimes hesitated to impose the terms "person" and "Trinity" (apparently on account of their not being directly scriptural), he knew that the game would be lost with a surrender to mere functionalism: "The quaint device of styling them three offices rather than persons," he wrote to Jane Catherine March on 3 August 1771, "gives up the whole doctrine."[11] Wesley knew that the divine work in the world, the experience of believers, and the final kingdom all found their basis and implicate in the ontological reality of "the Three-One God."

Wesley's trinitarian preaching carries a strong soteriological interest. Listen to a sermon of 1775 directly "On the Trinity," in which he shows how "knowledge of the Three-One God is interwoven with all true Christian faith, with all vital religion":

I know not how anyone can be a Christian believer till "he hath" (as St. John speaks) "the witness in himself"; till "the Spirit of God witnesses with his spirit that he is a child of God"—that is, in effect, till God the Holy Ghost witnesses that God the Father has accepted him through the merits of God the Son—and having this witness he honours the Son and the blessed Spirit "even as he honours the Father." Not every Christian believer *adverts* to this; perhaps at first not one in twenty; but if you ask any of them a few questions you will easily find it is implied in what he believes.[12]

197

And again, in the final salvation envisioned in a sermon of 1785 on "The New Creation":

> And to crown all, there will be a deep, an intimate, an uninterrupted union with God; a constant communion with the Father and his Son Jesus Christ, through the Spirit; a continual enjoyment of the Three-One God, and of all the creatures in him.[13]

In Wesley's *Letter to a Roman Catholic*, this soteriological dimension of the doctrine and reality of the Trinity comes to the fore already in the exposition of the first article of NC:

> I believe that this one God . . . is in a peculiar manner the Father of those whom he regenerates by his Spirit, whom he adopts in his Son as coheirs with him and crowns with an eternal inheritance. (*LRC* 6)

The insertion of the *munus triplex* in the second article has already been referred to:

> I believe that Jesus of Nazareth was the Saviour of the world, the Messiah so long foretold; that, being anointed with the Holy Ghost, he was a *prophet*, revealing to us the whole will of God; that he was a *priest*, who gave himself a sacrifice for sin, and still makes intercession for transgressors; that he is a *king*, who has all power in heaven and in earth, and will reign till he has subdued all things to himself. (*LRC* 7)

Christ's sovereignty is likewise presented soteriologically:

> I believe . . . that he is Lord of all, having absolute, supreme, universal dominion over all things; but more particularly *our* Lord (who believe in him), both by conquest, purchase, and voluntary obligation. (*LRC* 7)

The soteriological orientation of Wesley's confession concerning the Holy Spirit will appear in a moment.

In Faith and Order Paper 140, the soteriological orientation of the exposition of the second article emerges clearly from the titles of the sections on the Son:

> A. Jesus Christ, incarnate for our salvation.
> B. Jesus Christ, suffering and crucified for us.
> C. Jesus Christ, risen to overcome evil powers.

Perhaps the explication concerning the Holy Spirit could be clearer in its soteriology, not only in the paragraph headings but in the substantive connections made between the divine ontology and human salvation. True, the ecclesiological section includes a paragraph on the Church as "communion of saints in the Spirit." But many Evangelicals, and not they alone, would be helped by a corresponding emphasis on the direct work of the Holy Spirit in the heart and lives of believers. Wesley shows the way in *LRC*:

> I believe the infinite and eternal Spirit of God, equal with the Father and the Son, to be not only perfectly holy in himself, but the immediate cause of all holiness in us: enlightening our understandings, rectifying our wills and affections, renewing our natures, uniting our persons to Christ, assuring us of the adoption of sons, leading us in our actions, purifying and sanctifying our souls and bodies to a full and eternal enjoyment of God. (*LRC* 8)

3. Ecumenical

Wesley's *LRC* can set an example for the conduct of the Faith and Order dialogue in at least three ways:

(A) The *human, and Christian, respect and concern* which are shown towards one's conversation partners. Wesley considered the Roman Catholic Church to be in doctrinal error on a number of important points; but he could at times regard it as at least *part* of the Church catholic, and certainly he recognized individual Roman Catholics as Christian. In *LRC* Wesley grounds his regard for his interlocutor not only in the universally creative and redemptive work of God but also in the Christian intention of serious Roman Catholics:

> I think you deserve the tenderest regard I can show, were it only because the same God hath raised you and me from the dust of the earth and has made us both capable of loving and enjoying him to eternity; were it only because the Son of God has bought you and me with his own blood. How much more, if you are a person fearing God (as without question many of you are) and studying to have a conscience void of offence towards God and towards man? (*LRC* 4)

The partners ought at the least never to hurt one another deliberately, either in deed, word, or thought:

> In the name, then, and in the strength of God, let us resolve, first, not to hurt one another, to do nothing unkind or unfriendly to each other, nothing which we would not have done to ourselves. Rather let us endeavour after every instance of a kind, friendly and Christian behaviour towards each other.
>
> Let us resolve, secondly, God being our helper, to speak nothing harsh or unkind of each other. The sure way to avoid this is to say all the good we can, both of and to one another; in all our conversa-

tion, either with or concerning each other, to use only the language of love. . . .

Let us, thirdly, resolve to harbour no unkind thought, no un-friendly temper towards each other. Let us lay the axe to the root of the tree, let us examine all that rises in our heart and suffer no disposition there which is contrary to tender affection. (*LRC* 17)

More positively yet:

If God still loveth us, we ought also to love one another. We ought . . . to provoke one another to love and to good works. (*LRC* 16)

The goal is eschatological:

Let us . . . endeavour to help each other on in whatever we are agreed leads to the kingdom. (*LRC* 17)

I hope to see *you* in heaven. (*LRC* 16)

(B) Wesley sets *a methodological and hermeneutical principle* by his distinction between vital "doctrines," on the one hand, and the "opinions" on which theological schools may differ as long as they do so on the same basis of faith. "I say not a word to you about your opinions," writes Wesley to the Roman Catholic (*LRC* 13), and calls for a stop to the "endless jangling about opinions" (*LRC* 16). True, the distinction between doctrine and opinion is not always easy to make; but all Christian traditions do in fact make such distinctions *within* their own fellowship (Molinists vs. Thomists within the Roman Catholic Church, for example), and there is no reason why the propriety and inevitability of making such distinctions should not be recognized *across* confessional boundaries from the very start of the search for agreement in the faith.

Similarly, Wesley allows variety in "outward manner of worship" in a way which would allow diversity of "rites" within a single communion:

Be your form of worship what it will, but in every thing give him thanks; else it is all but lost labour. Use whatever outward observances you please, but put your whole trust in him, but honour his holy Name and his Word, and serve him truly all the days of your life. (*LRC* 13)

Again, it is not always easy to draw the limits of possible and welcome variety within a worship that is to remain solidly scriptural and trinitarian; but distinctions of the kind that were made between doctrine and opinion with respect to the *lex credendi* are surely allowable between, say, a sacrament and the ceremonial manner of its observance in the *lex orandi*.

(C) There is the matter of *openness to other traditions*. Wesley was

200

prepared to make what may at first blush appear to be "accommodations," even in matters of significant doctrine and practice; but it could well turn out that Wesley was bringing forward in dialogue with the Roman Catholic certain items that had not entirely disappeared from Protestantism, and whose recovery might even now help Methodism's settlement in the catholic tradition of both East and West. Thus he confesses Christ to be "born of the Blessed Virgin Mary, who, as well after as before she brought him forth, continued a pure and unspotted virgin" (*LRC* 7). And he believes that Christians "have fellowship with the holy angels who constantly minister to these heirs of salvation, and with all the living members of Christ on earth, as well as all who are departed this life in his faith and fear" (*LRC* 9). Participants in the Faith and Order study on the apostolic faith should be willing to open themselves to treasures that have been better preserved, insights that have been more vitally lived, in other parts of the great Christian Tradition than their own.

4. Homological

Wesley's *LRC* instantiates the same three aspects of confessing the faith as we noted in Faith and Order Paper 140: (a) doxological; (b) evangelistic; (c) ethical. Wesley's example and exhortations concerning process and goal could be heeded by all participants in the WCC project:

(A) with regard to glorifying God:

> All worship is an abomination to the Lord unless you worship him in spirit and in truth, with your heart as well as your lips, with your spirit and your understanding also. (*LRC* 13)

> Do you do all as unto the Lord, as a sacrifice unto God, acceptable in Christ Jesus? (*LRC* 15)

(B) All Wesley's evangelistic activity is set under the initiative of the *missio Dei* and the free grace of God, as confessed by Wesley to the Roman Catholic:

> I believe that Christ and his Apostles gathered unto himself a church to which he has continually added such as shall be saved. . . . (*LRC* 9)

> I believe that God forgives all the sins of them that truly repent and unfeignedly believe his holy gospel. . . . (*LRC* 10)

Evangelism was not directly Wesley's theme in writing to the Roman Catholic, but it is interesting for Faith and Order purposes that his language in the Letter may at times reflect an awareness of contemporary philosophico-theological controversies, if not an apologetic intent. In the

201

century of the Enlightenment, he precedes his credo with a subordinate clause: "As I am assured that there is an infinite and independent Being and that it is impossible that there should be more than one, so I believe that this one God is [the Holy Trinity]" (*LRC* 6). The same issues live on in the efforts of Faith and Order Paper 140 to situate the God confessed by Christians in relation to Judaism, to Islam, to the religious search of humankind, to idolatry, and to atheism (I/6–8; 21–34).

(C) Wesley writes that "a true Protestant loves his neighbour (that is, every man, friend or enemy, good or bad) as himself, as he loves himself, as he loves his own soul, as Christ loved us. And as Christ laid down his life for us, so he is ready to lay down his life for his brethren" (*LRC* 14). It is important that the WCC, in its battle against systemic evil, should not neglect to address the sanctification of the believer as part of Christian witness. If the dimension of personal conduct finds little place in the present study, many Evangelicals, and not they alone, will find it difficult to recognize the description of the apostolic faith.

III. Hopes For Unity

We saw, first, some needs of contemporary Methodism, which participation in the Apostolic Faith project might help to meet. We offered, second, a Wesleyan paradigm which might both encourage Methodist participation in the Faith and Order study and provide substantive and procedural help for the whole project. In this third part, it is now time to express more synthetically some further hopes concerning the results of the Faith and Order exercise for both Methodism and the Church universal.

1. Creedal

The focus on the creeds allows an understanding and practice of the relation between Scripture and Tradition in ways that were convergently expressed by the Fourth World Conference on Faith and Order at Montreal in 1963 and the near-simultaneous Vatican II text on "Divine Revelation" (*Dei Verbum*). Scripture was there understood as the internal norm of Tradition, and Tradition as the immediate interpretative context of Scripture. Now the traditional creeds are grounded in the same apostolic faith as comes to expression in the Scriptures:

- they provide a summary of the biblical story of creation, redemption, and consummation;

- they clarify the implied ontological basis of the story in the reality of God;

- they engage the believing Church in the transmission of the story and the reality through reception and proclamation.

Thus the creeds and the study of them provide both content and methodological model for all controversial questions where the relation of Scripture and Tradition is at stake.

Participation in the present project should help all partners to understand better (certainly some Methodist responses show a lack in this regard) the procedures that were followed in producing the Lima text on "Baptism, Eucharist and Ministry," and perhaps to improve on the results achieved in the Lima document. The kind of interplay between Scripture and Tradition represented by the Apostolic Faith study should prove fundamentally congenial to Methodists. That Wesley was "a man of one book" (*homo unius libri*), namely the Scriptures, does not indicate a "boundary of his reading" so much as "the center of gravity in his thinking."[14] He sought thereby to live in the continuing Tradition of the apostolic faith. The creedal basis and method of the Faith and Order project should allow the churches to grow together into a commonly accepted understanding and practice of Scripture and Tradition.

2. Trinitarian

The trinitarian shape and content of the WCC project brings us to the most vital point of action at the level of fundamental faith. The signs are that the doctrine of the Trinity is becoming once again, as it was in the fourth century, the *articulus stantis et cadentis ecclesiae*. For the doctrine expresses who the God is, who is the source, sustenance and goal of the redemption of humankind. At stake is the identity of God, and the nature of God's presence and action in the world.

To take only one case: Western liberal Christianity, or in U.S. terms the "mainline churches," are for various reasons in danger of losing their grasp on the understanding and practice of the triune God. Evidence can be found in recent liturgical compositions. The 1986 *Book of Worship* of the United Church of Christ practically limits the use of the scriptural and traditional name of Father, Son and Holy Spirit to baptism. The successive revisions leading to the United Methodist *Book of Services* (1985) manifest an increasingly feeble grasp of the Trinity (although, happily, the 1988 *Hymnal* fares better). The same is true of the "Supplemental Liturgical Resources" in the Presbyterian Church in the U.S.A. (although, as an invited advisor, I was able to restore a few modest trinitarian references in the eucharistic prayers for *The Service for the Lord's Day* of 1984).

To touch on the most neuralgic point: the Faith and Order text, while sensitive to the motherly as well as the fatherly aspects of God's care for us, roundly declares:

> In Jesus' language about God, "Father" is not only an image, it is primarily the *name* of the God to whom he relates in his mission and whose kingdom he proclaims. It is the name used to address God in prayer. In its function as a name, the name of God in Jesus' own teaching and prayer, the word "Father" cannot be replaced by another one. It would no longer be the God of Jesus to whom we relate if we were to exclude the name Jesus himself used. (I/51; cf. I/43)

Deeper reflection, in the context of the ecumenical study, might help the truly liberating character of God to emerge from the overlay of obfuscating and oppressive practices of "patriarchalism":

> Paul indicates that God is our Father because he is first the Father of Jesus, who graciously allows us to share by adoption in that unique Father-Son relationship. Furthermore, it is the Spirit who unites us with the Son and who sets us free as his sisters and brothers, to call God "Abba." What Paul says of "sons" he says also of daughters (2 Cor. 6:16-18): communion with the Father is open to all human beings without differentiation (cf. Rom. 8:14-15; Gal. 4:6). (I/44)

This, again, should be congenial to Methodists. For Wesley, "adoption" was a major soteriological category. To call God "Abba, Father" was the privilege of believers, not an alien imposition. One of the Wesleys' greatest hymns runs as follows:

> Since the Son hath made me free,
> Let me taste my liberty;
> Thee behold with open face,
> Triumph in thy saving grace,
> Thy great will delight to prove,
> Glory in thy perfect love.
>
> Abba, Father, hear thy child,
> Late in Jesus reconciled;
> Hear, and all the graces shower,
> All the joy, and peace, and power,
> All my Saviour asks above,
> All the life and heaven of love.

Heavenly Adam, Life divine,
Change my nature into thine;
Move and spread throughout my soul,
Actuate and fill the whole;
Be it I no longer now
Living in the flesh, but thou.

Holy Ghost, no more delay;
Come, and in thy temple stay;
Now thine inward witness bear,
Strong, and permanent, and clear;
Spring of life, thyself impart,
Rise eternal in my heart.

3. Ecumenical

The Apostolic Faith study sets the wider dogmatic context for particular doctrinal discussions in Faith and Order—a context whose inescapability was in fact recognized as early as the First World Conference on Faith and Order at Lausanne in 1927. Renewed attention to the full scope of Christian belief, as expressed in the creeds, would "correct" what some, including some Methodists, have felt to be the "narrow" sacramentalism of *Baptism, Eucharist and Ministry*. (Carefully read, *BEM* covers a wider dogmatic range, since the sacraments themselves are there shown to have—as, say, the Wesleys' *Hymns on the Lord's Supper* make clear—trinitarian, christological, ecclesiological and eschatological reference.)

The Apostolic Faith study is valuable, too, in so far as it provides the multilateral context needed to keep all the churches honest in their respective bilateral dialogues. It should prevent them from saying contradictory things to and with different partners. This is an important consideration for the World Methodist Council in its various dialogues with the Roman Catholics, the Lutherans, and the Reformed.

Finally, the Apostolic Faith study should help all churches together to rediscover what Wesley understood by the *analogia fidei,* the "proportion of the faith"—the place and connection of the main elements of belief within a range of patterns that are recognizably ecumenical in time and space.

4. Homological

By combining the doxological, kerygmatic and ethical components in the confession of faith, the WCC project should help to hold together the varying dominant interests of particular groups within Methodism and

205

across the confessional board: the liturgical, the evangelistic, and the social-activist. This is vital to the integrity of a denominational tradition that looks to Wesley, and to the rounded prosecution of its calling by the whole Church universal. We need to ensure that it is the *same faith* which is being confessed in the *various modes* of worship, mission and service.

Last of all, the gathering of Christians from the four winds around the theme of the Apostolic Faith should facilitate that proclamation and embodiment of the *one gospel* in *diverse cultural circumstances* which have been the aim of Christianity, and of Methodism, since their beginnings.

CHAPTER TWELVE

Methodists Respond to *BEM*

I. The Preparation and Reception of the Lima Text

In January 1982, at Lima in Peru, the Faith and Order Commission of the World Council of Churches unanimously declared its text on *Baptism, Eucharist and Ministry* to have reached a "stage of maturity" sufficient for it to be transmitted to the churches with a request for their evaluative responses "at the highest appropriate level of authority."[1] The remote preparation of the Lima document dated from the First World Conference on Faith and Order in Lausanne, Switzerland, in 1927; the proximate preparation began in the 1960s.[2] Now *Baptism, Eucharist and Ministry*,[3] quickly abbreviated to *BEM*, would in 1982 be dispatched to all member churches of the WCC as well as to the Roman Catholic Church and other bodies which also participate in the work of Faith and Order. It would provoke a degree of interest unprecedented in an ecumenical text, running into some twenty-five official printings in English and being translated into some thirty-five other languages. Almost two hundred formal responses from the churches were gathered into six volumes over the next six years.[4] Then an analytical synopsis of the responses was made, on the basis of which "clarifications" and "comments" regarding critical points in the original text were drafted and "major issues demanding further study" formulated.[5] The provisional closure of the study has allowed *BEM* to become integrated into the continuing wider program of Faith and Order[6] and absorbed into the life of the churches at the levels of doctrinal dialogues, theological education, catechetical instruction, and liturgical composition.

Methodists have played an active part in Faith and Order from the start, and in the creation of *Baptism, Eucharist and Ministry* in particular. The text, of course, was not such as any one of us, whether as individuals or as churches, would have produced had we been working alone. Rather, individuals and churches, starting from many different points, have converged in the construction of a document which seeks to express, with the greatest attainable measure of internal consistency, "the faith of the Church through the ages" such as it is discernable together on these topics in fidelity to the Scriptures and authentic Tradition. For my part, I belonged to the small core group that, in the light of many intervening comments from churches, faculties, and individual theologians, reworked the text between the Accra (Ghana) version of 1974, *One Baptism, One Eucharist, and a Mutually Recognized Ministry*,[7] and the final form of *BEM*; I chaired the *BEM* sections of the full Faith and Order Commission meetings at Bangalore in 1978 and Lima in 1982; and I continued on the steering and drafting team that formulated the response to the responses.

Methodist and related churches were quite forthcoming in their responses to *BEM*. The Methodist Church of New Zealand, characteristically for the people of the Land of the Long White Cloud who by virtue of their position in relation to the international date line like to be among the early birds in all things, managed to get their response into the very first volume of *Churches Respond to BEM*. Ten others, including the United Methodist Church, the Methodist Church of Great Britain, and the Methodist Church in Ireland, followed in volume two. Six more came in the subsequent volumes. These figures include united and uniting churches with a Methodist component (Canada, Japan, North India, South India, Australia, Belgium, and the joint synod of Waldensians and Methodists in Italy). Continental Europe was present through the Evangelical Methodist Churches of the former Democratic and Federal Republics of Germany and the Conference of Central and Southern Europe. Replies from the Methodist Church of Southern Africa (notably "sympathetic" rather than "defensive"), the Protestant Methodist Church of Benin, and the Jamaica District of the Methodist Church of the Caribbean and the Americas were among the disappointingly few of any denomination to come from their parts of the world.

II. The Response of The United Methodist Church

The response of the United Methodist Church to *BEM* was issued by the Council of Bishops under the date of 30 April 1986.[8] It was among the longest and most thorough of all responses. While critical at several points, it offered in general a benevolent reading of the text, and its overall judgment of the document was strongly affirmative. Let me now present that United Methodist response, as glossed by one who is not himself a United Methodist but stands within the Methodist tradition.

1. The Wesleyan Reference

Openly declaring, just as the Roman Catholics, the Orthodox, the Lutherans, the Reformed, the Anglicans, and others do, the confessional stance from which they speak, the United Methodists make Wesleyan claims for what they will say in their response to *BEM*. The Wesleyan reference is made at four levels: the criteria to be used for evaluation in matters of faith, doctrine and theology; the teaching and practice of the Wesleys as instances of the positions now recorded in *BEM*; the self-critical assessment of later and current Methodism, and corresponding moves towards the recovery of an authentic Wesleyan heritage as helped by ecumenical renewal; and the suggestions which Methodists can offer for the continuing work of Faith and Order.

First, evaluative criteria. The UM bishops deliberately intend their examination of the Lima text to be accomplished in the light of the "four Wesleyan criteria" of Scripture, Tradition, experience, and reason. (Here it must be remembered that the UM response was written in the midst of a decade of intense internal discussion in the United Methodist Church around what was informally and misleadingly called for a time the Wesleyan or Methodist "quadrilateral," and before the General Conference of 1988 had reasserted a "primacy of Scripture" more in accord with Wesley as *homo unius libri*.) Thus with regard to baptism, the UM response judges that *"BEM*'s text is clearly derived from the Scriptures, is representative of Tradition and varying traditions, while including the experiential dimension and providing reasonable interpretation and recognizing some unresolved questions for the still divided churches. . . . [*BEM*'s exposition of the meaning and effect of baptism is] derived from explicit teachings of the New Testament as well as from the Church's long history of preaching, formulating liturgies, and instructing catechumens for baptism. *BEM* itself belongs to that history, and is a most significant contemporary witness to the apostolic Christian faith."[9] With regard to the eucharist as the "work of the Triune God," bringing together "eternity and time, spirit and matter, redemption and creation," the UM response considers that *"BEM* deftly unites the truths and testimonies of the New Testament and the ecumenical creeds."[10] The opening paragraphs of *BEM*'s section on Ministry—"The Calling of the Whole People of God"— are judged to be "a superb retelling of the biblical history of God's saving work, extended beyond apostolic times to all history." As far as "the experiential dimension" is concerned, the UM response is "gratified to note how *BEM* points to the personal and social implications of the Holy Communion for ethical guidance of Christians active in society"; but experience is also turned as a critical tool on the practice, and even the doctrine, of the churches (as reflected in *BEM* itself), when reference is made by the UM response to the "history of discrimination against women and peoples of color" and a call is made for a clearer affirmation of "mission" to "every place of need, oppression, poverty and exploitation."

Second, Wesleyan anticipations of *BEM*. With regard to Christ's presence in the eucharist, the UM response welcomes *BEM*'s appropriation of the scriptural and traditional understanding recovered by twentieth-century liturgical scholarship and focused in the Greek terms *anamnesis* (dynamic conjoining of Christ past, present, and future) and *epiklesis* (the effective invocation of the Holy Spirit, to "realize the sign"—as the Wesleys would say in their *Hymns on the Lord's Supper*, no. 72); and notes: "All this we find explicitly taught by John and Charles Wesley, who knew and respected the apostolic, patristic and reformed faith of the Church." With regard to the sacrificial aspect of the eucharist, the UM response argues that "Jesus' words of institution at the Last Supper" justify the fact that "throughout Christian history the concept of the sacrifical and atoning death of Jesus Christ has been closely related to the sacrifice of worshipping Christians in the context of the Lord's Supper," even while recognizing that "just how that relationship is to be acknowledged and interpreted theologically is a question much disputed by Catholics and Protestants, though less by Orthodox"; and, with especially the Wesleys' *Hymns on the Lord's Supper* no doubt again in mind, the witness and judgment are made that "as Wesleyans, we are accustomed to the language of sacrifice, and we find *BEM*'s statements to be in accord with the Church's Tradition and with ours."

With regard to baptism, the very ambiguity of the Wesleyan heritage is put to positive effect. The UM response recognizes that "John Wesley's own teachings can be construed to support each of three positions as conditioned by varying stages of the denomination's life in America": "First, the traditional Wesleyan interpretation of infant baptism emphasizes very personally such doctrines as original sin, universal atonement, and prevenient grace. Second, the more churchly emphasis is based upon a covenant theology and corporate fellowship in Christ. Third, some United Methodists accept the presuppositions underlying believer's baptism only, interpreting it in clearly voluntaristic terms." This mixed heritage is used by the UM response to justify the kind of variety in baptismal understanding and practice which *BEM* itself recognizes and commends, embracing both the baptism of infants and the baptism of professing believers within the context of a faithful community that looks for commitment and growth on the part of all. Acknowledging the virtual ignorance of confirmation in early Methodism and the current "uncertainty" about it in the United Methodist Church, the UM response rightly notes that "*BEM*'s reticence about confirmation is itself a reflection of the existing confusion in many churches"; it suggests that baptism and its renewals are best seen as the expression of "the extended working of" (in a characteristically Wesleyan formulation) "God's prevenient, justifying and sanctifying grace by the Holy Spirit."

With regard to the third main theme of *BEM*, that of ministry, the UM response notes that "the Wesleyan theological heritage provides no singular pattern"; yet the pattern which has characterized American Methodism since 1784—of bishop/superintendent, presbyter/elder, and deacon, within a recognition of "the ministry of all members in diverse functions and services"—is felt to match the pattern which "has prevailed since the second century, even though the exact definition of the function and character of each has never achieved a fully ecumenical consensus," and so to place the United Methodist Church within the flow of *BEM*'s recommendations concerning mutual recognition of ministries. While, however, the importance of the "orderly transmission" of ministries is acknowledged, the UM response has nothing directly to say about *BEM*'s notion of "the episcopal succession as a sign, though not a guarantee, of the continuity and unity of the Church."[11]

Third, self-criticism and recovery. Particularly with regard to the Lord's Supper, the UM response to *BEM* reads Methodist history this way: "The Wesleyan renewal movement within and beyond the Church of England was as much sacramental as it was evangelical. The Wesleys had the highest respect for eucharistic worship, and expounded in sermons and hymns a substantial eucharistic theology. In America, however, during a century and a half after Wesley's death in 1791, the place of the Holy Communion in Methodist worship declined, and the beliefs about it lost continuity with the traditional doctrines which the Wesleys espoused. . . . As we United Methodists regard the Church's practice through the ages, we can recognize how our own usage has fallen short of the fullness of the Holy Communion." Yet recent years have seen the beginnings of a recovery of the Wesleyan tradition as part of Methodism's sharing in "the vigorous renewal of liturgical theology and practice in the ecumenical movement." And now the UM response is able to declare *BEM* to be "right" in considering the eucharist, as it "effectively unites word and sacrament," to be "the central act of the Church's worship." (In fact, the Methodist text then formulates the point in its own way in one of the finest sentences in all the responses to *BEM*: "God's effectual word is there [in the central act of the Church's worship] revealed, proclaimed, heard, seen, and tasted.") And "as for the frequency of celebration of Communion, we can only cite John Wesley's call to 'constant communion' and his own faithful witness to the importance of this sacrament for personal faith

211

and ecclesial vitality. Although we fall short of a weekly celebration, we acknowledge that the Church's long experience shows it to be normative. We intend to urge our congregations to a more frequent, regular observance of the sacrament." Sagely, it is acknowledged that "we United Methodists need to recover the belief that the Holy Communion is central in our worship and life together before some other churches will honor our statements of theological concord."

Fourth, suggestions for continuing study. At two points in particular, Wesleyan emphases are invoked as a contribution to future work in Faith and Order on the themes of *BEM* as part of the move "Towards the Common Expression of the Apostolic Faith Today." Under the heading of "new birth," the UM response opines that "*BEM* is unduly tentative about the Spirit's work of recreating persons in their struggle against sin. It says that baptism 'has ethical implications' which 'call for personal sanctification.' Along with evangelical Christians of all centuries, United Methodists urge the presenting of apostolic faith in terms of the personal experience of new birth by the indwelling Spirit, being conformed to the image of Christ, and showing forth the nine-fold fruit of the Spirit in daily life (Gal. 5:22)." And then, while recognizing that Wesley's designation of the Lord's Supper as a "converting ordinance" did not occur outside of the context of baptism, the UM response calls for "relating the sacrament [of the Lord's Supper] to evangelization."[12]

2. Points of Tension

Besides its deliberate intention to be Wesleyan, the other particularly interesting feature of the United Methodist response to *BEM* consists in the way it puts its finger on, and sometimes seeks to resolve, certain points of tension in the United Methodist Church or Methodism more generally or within and between churches on the broader ecumenical scene. Five such may be listed: divine initiative and human response; the individual and the community; unity and diversity; the universal and the particular; and the status and role of women.

First, divine initiative and human response. In the matter of understanding "how divine action and personal human response come together," in "the perennial and complementary interplay of objective-sacramental and subjective-commitmental elements," the UM text affirms what *BEM* says in the test case of baptism as "both God's gift and our human response to that gift" (Baptism, 8), emphasizing (in the UM formulation) "the *priority* of the objective-theocentric-sacramental dimension of baptism, and the *secondary* or *consequential* character of the subjective-anthropocentric-confessional dimension." That is correctly said in distinction from accounts given by some Baptists. But one might wish that the UM response had been slightly more guarded in its ensuing statement that "from our Wesleyan perspective, we want . . . to derive understanding of baptism from the objectivity of universal atonement and prevenient grace, and then bind its subjective, personal appropriation to God's whole work in Christ of salvation, justification and sanctification through the Holy Spirit." I am not sure of the precise meaning of the second half of that sentence; but I have observed that modern Methodists, from the universal sufficiency of Christ's atoning work (agreed by all Christians), and indeed (in Methodist eyes) the universal availability of prevenient grace, often jump too quickly to the conclusion that the general practice of infant baptism—as though unconditionally for the whole human race—is an appropriate sacramental expression of these things. In Georgia, Wesley early received advice from the American Indian Tomo Chachi concerning the baptism of the uncatechized: "We would not be made Christians as the Spaniards make Christians; we would be taught before we are baptized";[13] and the prevenience of grace which Wesley invoked in his own rationale for the baptism of infants was that manifested to "the infants of believers" under "the gospel covenant."[14] One must therefore welcome the stress which the UM response to *BEM*, in conformity with recent liturgical revisions within Methodism, places on the covenant community as the "context" of baptism. That should open up again a possibility of dialogue about election with Methodism's historic foes the Calvinists; and it should not too readily be assumed that Methodists hold all the answers, and the Reformed none.[15]

Second, the individual and the community. This tension is often linked in the UM response with the previous one. There are several repudiations of "individualistic voluntarism." Stress is placed on "the Church's organic, communal character." Yet it is equally recognized that gospel and faith are to be appropriated in personal experience and responsibility. This balance seems to accord well with the importance of fellowship in early Methodism, expressed in "connection," "society," "classes," and "bands." It is a contribution offered by Methodism to ecumenical ecclesiology.

Third, unity and diversity. The UM response repudiates "theological indifferentism" but recognizes and affirms certain cases of variety in understanding and practice, both within Methodism and in the Church at large. In classic Wesleyan terms, it is the question of "doctrine" and "opinions";[16] there is a perpetual need, both confessionally and ecumenically, to discern both the values and the limits of diversity.[17] The UM response to *BEM* shows from the start a welcome continuing commitment to the visibility of Christian unity and views the *BEM* process as an

213

important contribution towards that end. It recognizes the inadequacy of "the denominational model of church organization," views intercommunion as "an interim goal," and looks forward to a "full union" whose form continues to be the subject of ecumenical exploration.

Fourth, the universal and the particular. The UM response speaks of "the inevitable problem of particularity and universality": "Baptism, eucharist and ministry are particularly derived from Jesus Christ and have their meaning in him. They are quite obviously, likewise, the particular institutions of the Church. Even so, *BEM* does not hesitate to make universal claims for them, relating all three in some ways to the salvation of humanity and even to all creation." That is said by the UM text to be only "one side of the matter." The "other side" includes "the manifest spiritual and moral values of various other religions." The UM response regrets *BEM*'s "lack of expressed concern about the new relation of Christianity to other faiths." This criticism comes perhaps from a different perspective than the Roman Catholic and Lutheran responses that note the absence in *BEM* of a position on the necessity of baptism for salvation; but all these responses raise an issue that the Church has yet again to face.[18]

Fifth, the status and role of women. Noting that "a deep gulf separates the churches which ordain women to ministry from those which do not," the UM response to *BEM* declares that "just as the Roman Catholic and Orthodox churches have allowed no concession to ordaining women, we Wesleyans allow no refusal to do so. . . . Neither will we desist from witnessing to the theological integrity and manifest beneficence of our non-discriminatory ordinations." A helpful approach might be through the assertion which the UM response virtually makes that the ordination of women is the *development* of a truth inherent in the gospel. The testing of that development, and its reception in other parts of Christianity, may depend to a considerable extent on the success with which churches that ordain women are perceived to hold fast to the apostolic faith across the broad range of dogma. It is, therefore, somewhat disturbing that the UM response should link its affirmation of women's ordination so closely with its remarks on "the sexist flaws within the fabric of the Church's language," when these are seen to go beyond the question of "inclusive language" to the trinitarian Name itself of Father, Son and Holy Spirit. At one point in the UM response, the "Father-Son image" is apparently not considered "immutably normative for the language of worship, preaching and theology," while in connection with "the biblical and traditional formula" for baptizing "in the name of the Father, the Son, and the Holy Spirit," the rather ambiguous comment had already been passed that "we do not urge abandoning or changing it. Nevertheless, with the heightened sensitivity to the disproportionate masculinity of liturgical language, we are compelled to sense a certain reserve about perpetuating this form of the Trinitarian name of the Triune God."[19]

III. *The British Methodist Response*

In a distinction between British and American Methodism which has become increasingly noticeable in recent years, the British response to *BEM* mentions the name of Wesley only twice. One occurrence is the oblique reference to "Wesley's Notes on the New Testament and the first four volumes of his Sermons" by way of the Deed of Union which established the Methodist Church of Great Britain in 1932 and declares that the doctrines of the faith are to be found in those Wesleyan texts. The British response to *BEM* proceeds in the apparent confidence that it is operating within these "doctrinal standards."

The British text is in fact a smoothly, even elegantly, written piece of discursive theology. It rejoices in the convergences which *BEM* marks and sees these as part of a necessarily continuing process, without however admitting that a "final and complete" statement of doctrine is a possible or desirable goal, even in that "visible unity" which the Methodist Church remains "firmly committed to search for."[20] The British Methodist judgment on *BEM* is "basically positive": in the exposition of baptism and eucharist "we find the essential matter of the faith through the ages," while the response on ministry, though "in general positive," is tempered by some "serious reservations." While they are sometimes formulated with characteristic understatement, the British Methodist "reservations" on ministry and some other matters point towards difficulties found in *BEM* by some other Methodist Churches, and indeed by other bodies with a concern for what they consider the Protestant witness (although the angles of approach may be variably liberal or conservative).

Three areas may be specially mentioned, for these are the three that are taken up in Faith and Order's own 1990 synoptic analysis of the churches' responses as matters that need further study: the relation between Scripture and Tradition; the understanding of sacramentality; and implied ecclesiology. It is important to recognize that these are matters raised not only by those Protestant Churches, variably liberal or conservative, which suspect *BEM* of a "catholicizing" tendency[21] but also by the Roman Catholic and Orthodox responses that find *BEM* (without using the term) too "protestant" at points.

First, Scripture and Tradition. The British response does not doubt that "the method employed [in *BEM*] falls within the broad agreement regarding Scripture and Tradition reached by the Fourth World Conference on Faith and Order at Montreal in 1963" but finds no clarity in its methodological application. In particular, *BEM* leaves unclear "what approach to the authority and use of Scripture is being adopted." Speaking for itself, the British response says that "the authority of the New Testament over our church life today may be accepted in principle, but what kind of authority this is, how it is to be applied, and how it is to be related to our understanding of the continued work of the Holy Spirit, are questions that need to be addressed."[22] And, while eschewing pure relativism, the British call for greater attention to "the cultural context of both theology and ecclesiastical structures."[23]

Second, sacramentality. It is particularly in regard to baptism that the British response asks for clarity about sacramental efficacy: "Is it being said [by *BEM*] that the rite 'effects' these things ['incorporation into Christ,' 'washing away of sin,' 'new birth,' etc.], or simply that it 'signifies' them as being important elements in the Christian life into which the baptised person is initiated?"[24] Methodists, say the British, "would want to emphasise that the efficacy of the sacraments depends upon God and not upon any supposed automatism in the rite."[25] It would, surely, be common Christian teaching to stress the importance of the faithful performance of what God has instituted. The more delicate question concerns the "moment" of a sacrament's efficacy. While continuing to affirm the practice of infant baptism (and even suggesting that the theological arguments in its favor are stronger than *BEM*'s "muted" statement of them allows), the British response recognizes that infant baptism in particular poses difficulties regarding what might be called the timing of a sacrament's results.

A further question about sacramentality finds symptomatic expression in the British questioning of the statement in *BEM* that "Christ's mode of presence in the eucharist is unique." "Unique" is rejected, if it means "superior to all others": "Methodism, in common with those Churches that look to the Reformation for inspiration, has always prized preaching as a vehicle for the divine Word. Through the Holy Spirit Christ is present to the congregation in the word of the preacher."[26] Historical and practical reasons are cited by the British for the greater frequency in Methodism of preaching services without Communion (it is recognized that "John Wesley"—in the second reference to him—"was firm in his belief in regular and frequent communion," but the eventual separation between Methodism and the Church of England made provision for the eucharist difficult), and it is affirmed that "Methodists have learnt to nourish themselves on that kind of worship." In recent years, Methodism has, by its participation in the ecumenical and liturgical movements, come closer to its founder in the matter of eucharistic frequency, but many would still argue that "infrequency of celebration actually heightens the sense of the eucharist's importance."[27]

Third, ecclesiology. In a sense, ecclesiology is an implicit issue throughout *BEM*.[28] It emerges explicitly at three points at least in the British Methodist response. With regard to baptism, the British Methodist response considers "fraught with danger" the suggestion made in *BEM* that it may be possible to treat the infant-baptist and the believer-baptist patterns of initiation as "equivalent alternatives" in a single Church, even while promising to observe with the closest attention the attempt made to do so in the United Reformed Church since the union with the Churches of Christ (Disciples). The Methodists wonder whether it may not be a question of "two different, and perhaps competing, ecclesiologies."

Then the British response hesitates over the (in any case, tentative) remarks in the Ministry section of *BEM* about priesthood. The question is "whether the ordained minister contributes to the eucharist in his/her own person some essential element other than the right to preside at it": Is the eucharist "the offering of the people presided over by the ordained minister," or is it "the offering of the people presided over by the ordained minister *and specifically activated by the minister's presence*"? The latter case would imply "a *distinction of kind* between the priestly service of the ordained ministry and the priestliness of the laity" such as the Methodist Deed of Union denies. A way to overcome the false dilemma encoded in the unfortunate phraseology of Vatican II (*Lumen Gentium*, 10) about a difference *essentiâ et non gradu tantum* might, as I have written elsewhere, be found in the development of British Methodism's own notion, found in the Conference Statement on Ordination of 1974, of "representative ministry": "Precisely as *representatives* of Christ and his Church, the ordained ministers are *distinct*, but *what* they represent is *not other* than the character and mission of the whole Church, and this itself is *nothing other* than participation, by the grace of the Holy Spirit, in the ministry of Christ the Savior and Head of the Church."[29]

Perhaps the most sensitive ecclesiological issue of all, for British Methodism, turns on episcopal ministry in a claimed apostolic succession. The response to *BEM* factually notes that "the Methodist Conference has ruled that acceptance of the historic episcopate would not violate our doctrinal standards, and indeed has shown itself ready to embrace the threefold ministry to advance the cause of visible unity"—yet insists that all this depends on a recognition on the part of others that the existing forms of British Methodism do not constitute a lack or deprivation. Despite "much that is conciliatory to non-episcopal traditions" and "many instances of balanced judgment in the text [Ministry, 35–38]," *BEM* is found to show "too great a leaning towards the threefold ministry" and not fully to recognize that the apostolic tradition has also been adequately maintained in some cases without the historic episcopate.[30]

IV. Responses from United and Uniting Churches

It may be questioned how far "united and uniting churches" represents a coherent category, even though WCC Faith and Order has from time to time sponsored consultations bringing such bodies together. From a confessional standpoint, much depends on historical origins of the parties to the union. For our present purposes of reviewing Methodist responses to *BEM*, the questions are those of the original and continuing strength of the Methodist components in such unions, and of the forms of the association between the particular united and uniting churches and the World Methodist Council. Briefly, however, we may note two features that are common to several of the respones made to *BEM* by such churches which themselves have a varied relationship to the Methodist tradition. First, these responses relate *BEM* to issues that reflect the efforts to embody unity within the constitutionally united and uniting churches. Second, several of these responses are notable for raising, at least tentatively, matters to do with the Christian faith and other religions.

1. Internal Unity

The United Church of Canada, which dates from the 1925 union between Methodists, Presbyterians and Congregationalists, notes some tensions in its own life; but these seem to have less to do with classic historic oppositions among the original traditions than with differences that cut across in more recent times that entire swathe of Anglo-Saxon Protestantism. With regard to "infant or adult baptism," for instance, "for us, the issue is as much one of internal dialogue as it is of dialogue with churches which exclusively practise adult baptism." Then there are the debates occasioned by the provision for otherwise "unchurched people" of "rites of passage, particularly baptisms, weddings and funerals." Or there is gratitude for "the warning [in *BEM*] against the minimization" of material elements, and yet a complaint that *BEM* is "insufficiently sensitive to the relatively 'low church' understandings of the sacramental that we have inherited." And for some in the United Church of Canada, "the centrality of the eucharist and its normative character," where admitted, "do not necessarily imply its frequent celebration," whereas others "would encourage the more frequent celebration of the Lord's Supper in the congregations of our Church." Recognizing that "ecclesiology and sacra-

218

mental theology have a different place on the ecumenical agenda for different Churches," the United Church of Canada in sum declares that it "traditionally has not seen agreement on these matters as being as crucial for Christian unity as they have been regarded by some other Churches." Characterizing its own position on the matters addressed by *BEM* as "flexible or liberal," the United Church of Canada is yet able to glimpse the risk of "confusing openness with laxity" in ways that may give offense to other Churches.[31]

The Uniting Church in Australia came into being in 1977 with an original confessional composition very similar to the United Church of Canada. Its strikingly positive response to *BEM* relates the statements in the Lima text very carefully to the founding doctrinal constitution of the Uniting Church itself, the efforts to produce which were no doubt still fresh in the memories of its members.[32] *BEM* is measured, and not found wanting, for consistency with the "reformed" tradition of the gospel, which must here be considered as shared by those of Presbyterian, Congregational, and Methodist background. At just a few places, the Australian response hints that issues addressed by *BEM* are also matters of tension in the UCA (for example, the relation between grace and faith in respect of baptism, the understanding of priestly ministry, and—curiously and perhaps marginally—the need for ordination at all). The most developed point concerns different understandings of the real presence of Christ in the eucharist, which "are held in the UCA as a direct consequence of the theological traditions that were brought into union" (and that do not always, I suspect, coincide with former denominational boundaries): "Down through the ages, and particularly since the Reformation, the Church has been bitterly divided on this issue, those holding one view refusing to discern in those holding the other 'the faith of the Church through the ages.' The UCA, along with other Churches, is now challenged to affirm this diversity and not to unchurch those who take the other view of the real presence."

In the responses of the synod of the Waldensian and Methodist Churches in Italy[33] and of the synod of the United Protestant Church of Belgium[34] the overwhelming tendency is to see themselves as representing on all relevant issues a unified "Protestant," and particularly "Reformed," position in sharp distinction from Roman Catholicism.

The Church of North India, which united in 1970, includes "former Anglicans, Baptists, Brethren, Disciples, Methodists (British and Australasian), Presbyterians and Congregationalists." Its response finds *BEM* to be in general agreement with its own faith and order.[35] Particularly with regard to "the effort to overcome differences concerning the ordained ministry," but one might also mention differences over baptism, the North

Indian response notes that the discussions in *BEM* "recall our own experience in the negotiations that led to the formation of the CNI and the early years of the Church's life." An effective reception of *BEM* should "help the Churches to think and review the traditional formulations of faith (which were often shaped in contexts of controversy) along the lines proposed in this document [i.e. *BEM*]."

2. The Christian Faith and Other Religions

United in 1947, the Church of South India brought together Anglicans, Methodists (British and Australasian), Presbyterians, and Congregationalists. Its response to *BEM*[36] deplores the shift that has taken place from baptism as "a means of liberation from the age-old, dehumanizing caste system, untouchability and entry into a state of new identity with a new community" to baptism now experienced as "a narrow communal rite" that is apparently viewed by many as no longer worth the cost of separation from the "culture and tradition of our country." Attempts are, however, being made to "include healthy cultural practices in the Christian community." Those facts mark the changed context for one instance of the question regarding the Christian faith and other religions: "If an earnest, devoted Hindu seeker comes to the holy table, are we justified in denying the holy sacrament to him? Why do non-Christians desire the eucharist so much, while they do not show the same desire with regard to baptism?" Similarly, the United Church of Christ in Japan, noting its own location, "amidst non-Christian cultural traditions and climate, on the one hand, and a secularized modern society, on the other," observes and asks: "A matter of deep concern in the Japanese church, where so many non-Christians (seekers) are present in worship, is how we can best understand and celebrate the eucharist as part of worship. What should we do when unbaptized persons wish to communicate?"[37]

The Indian and Japanese responses are concerned to maintain the connection between the sacraments of baptism and eucharist and Christ's universal work of salvation, even while not wishing to limit God's grace necessarily to the church as defined by those sacraments. These are among the voices that the United Church of Canada will need to listen to as it looks, in its own "increasingly pluralistic" context and in what its response to *BEM* perhaps too easily (in light of the "many 'gods' and many 'lords'" of 1 Corinthians 8:4-6) calls "a world of many sacraments," for help to "those Churches which have lived for centuries as minorities among non-Christian neighbors."

Conclusion

At stake in *BEM* are questions concerning the nature, identity, and boundaries of the Church. As is shown by the almost unanimous welcome given by the responding Churches to the opening paragraphs of the Ministry section on "The Calling of the Whole People of God," it has become fairly easy for Churches involved in the classical ecumenical movement to agree on *"what the Church is* and *what the Church is for*: it is 'people of God,' 'body of Christ,' 'community of the Holy Spirit,' privileged with anticipating God's kingdom in its worship (*leitourgia*) and meanwhile charged with proclaiming the gospel to the world (*martyria*, witness) and serving the needy among humankind (*diakonia*)."[38] It is much more difficult for the churches to agree in identifying *who are the Church*. The crucial doctrinal issue which Methodists must face in common with others was very well formulated by the Uniting Church in Australia in its opening comment on the first question to which *BEM* invited a response: "Clearly the question of 'the extent to which the faith of the Church can be discerned in the text' must be taken as both historical and normative, i.e. about what the Church should be confessing as well as what she has confessed, and that already points to the underlying issues of authority and ecclesiology which constantly surfaced in the Commission's discussions but which are not directly addressed in the document. Those issues arise because down through the ages there has been a variety of expressions of faith among those who claim to belong to the Church and therefore to answer only the historical question, 'is there a precedent somewhere in the Church's history for this expression of faith?' would be of little value in pressing on to the ecumenical goal. But the normative question 'what ought the Church to believe?' already implies that some expressions of the faith of the Church are unacceptable. Some people hold that the Church can believe a wrong thing and be in error, others that one cannot believe the wrong thing and be the Church. So the inter-relationship between the issues of authority and ecclesiology becomes apparent in the questions that emerge from the one the *BEM* document asks, *viz.*, by what authority is the validity of the Church's faith and practice to be tested? How is what genuinely belongs to the faith of the Church to be determined?" Clearly, there is still work for Faith and Order to do in the areas of Scripture, Tradition, hermeneutics, and ecclesiology.[39]

CHAPTER THIRTEEN

Ecclesial Identity:
Basic Agreements and Basic Differences

Ecumenical dialogues, especially of the bilateral kind, have often established convergences between the partners in which a "basic agreement" is recognized or established but also a remaining "basic difference" discerned that suffices to prevent the fulness of consensus judged necessary for unity. Given the stubbornness of the alleged basic differences, and their shifting character (different writers locate them differently, and they have a habit of resurfacing elsewhere after supposedly being settled), it may be wondered whether attempts to detect them are at all of service to the ecumenical cause; and yet some way must be found to overcome divisive differences. The frustration of ecumenists might be lessened if the matter of agreements and differences were set in the more organic context of a whole form of life and self-understanding on the part of the various communities claiming to be Church.[1]

A fruitful approach may perhaps be found in the notion of ecclesial "identity," in the senses both of *character* or *profile* and also of *consistency* or *continuity*. What, we may ask, do the several putatively Christian communities consider to be features necessary and sufficient for remaining "true to type," a faithful Church? The next step would then be to inquire what model of unity is implied by their answers and what account they respectively give of such other communities as do not meet the test of ecclesiality.[2]

To the synchronic question of where is *now* the Church of Christ, John Henry Newman took a diachronic approach in his *Essay on the Development of Christian Doctrine*.[3] There were seven "notes" that marked the "genuine development of an Idea" in contrast with its "corruptions" (granted that, for Newman, an "Idea" was not limited to the intellectual but included its institutional embodiments): (1) preservation of its type ("young birds do not grow into fishes"); (2) continuity of its systematic principles, i.e. of the axioms underlying any particular doctrines, or of the spirit inspiring any particular act; (3) its power of assimilation, i.e. its ability to "heal," "mould" and "absorb" external material; (4) its logical sequence, even if the growth precede its rational justification; (5) anticipation of its future (the boy Athanasius "is elected bishop by his playfellows"; "evidence of the faithfulness of an ultimate development is its *definite anticipation* in an early period of the history of the idea to which it belongs"); (6) conservative action upon its past, i.e. it protects, rather than contradicts or reverses, "the acquisitions gained in its previous history"; (7) its chronic vigor, or tenacity ("the course of heresies is always short," or a corrupt institution slowly decays). This was the kind of argumentation which led Newman to see in Roman Catholicism the Church of Jesus Christ and of the apostles. Whether the Church of Rome was the exclusive, or merely the best, locus of Christianity, its claims were certainly sufficient in Newman's judgment to provoke and sustain his own conversion to it from Anglicanism.

Here I want, with a minimum of substantive prejudice in concrete matters of doctrinal or ecclesiological truth, to make what will, for reasons of brevity, necessarily be rather crude use of Newman's notion of a consistency of type. We may also rejoin, again with little substantive prejudice, Cardinal Willebrands' notion of a variety of ecclesial *typoi*, or "types" of ecclesial community, each with a liturgical, spiritual, theological and disciplinary tradition (though unity would require agreement in faith, dogma, sacrament and fundamental ecclesial structure).[4] My question would then be: can one discern, among the respective communities making some claim to be "church," certain features—or even a single feature—that is held by those who have it (whether, in their own estimation, exclusively or not) to be indispensable to Christian identity, and therefore to ecclesiality? Let us try a few examples. In the first three cases, it will be fairly easy, *prima facie*, to pick out the distinguishing feature. In the other three, the distinguishing feature itself is rather complex or even diffuse.

I. Roman Catholicism

In the bull *Unam Sanctam* of 1302, Boniface VIII declared that "it is altogether necessary to salvation for every human being to be subject to the Roman Pontiff." Rome is no longer so quick to damn, or even to unchurch, others. Nevertheless, Cardinal Ratzinger, in commenting upon the work of the Anglican-Roman Catholic International Commission, still speaks of "the indispensability of the Petrine principle."[5] The Vatican I dogma is only a "symptom" of "the overall problem of authority in the Church," and "the way one views the structure of Christianity will necessarily affect in some measure, great or small, one's attitude to various particular matters contained within the whole."[6] "It is necessary," says Cardinal Ratzinger, "to contradict the ARCIC Report where it says 'The Second Vatican Council allows it to be said that a Church out of communion with the Roman See may lack nothing from the viewpoint of the Roman Catholic Church except that it does not belong to the visible manifestation of full Christian communion'. With such an assertion wrongly claiming the support of Vatican II, church unity is debased to an unnecessary, if desirable, externality, and the character of the universal Church is reduced to mere outward representation, of little significance in constituting what is ecclesial."[7] Here, true ecumenism means the return or restoration to communion with Rome. This communion of faith and life can be declared only by the bishops *una cum* the pope. It is observable that every ecumenical conversation in which Rome is engaged comes sooner or later to look, in the light of Scripture and history, at the question of whether a Petrine office, and of what kind and where, has been present all along.

II. Lutheranism

From the sixteenth century, Lutheranism has considered the doctrine of justification to be the "point at which the Church stands or falls" (*articulus stantis et cadentis ecclesiae*). Cardinal Ratzinger agrees that Luther's doctrine of justification by faith alone continues to be what sets Lutheranism apart from the Catholic Church. Lutherans appeal principally to the primary writings of St. Paul but find their doctrine also in the records of Jesus' table fellowship with sinners and the parable of the publican and the sinner, for example. Justification by faith alone is the "center of Scripture," the "canon within the canon." It renders such matters as the forms of ministry adiaphora or not divisive. At stake is the gospel, which is proclaimed by the word and communicated in the dominical sacraments. It is the function of theology, concretely therefore of theologians, to discern and maintain the purity of the gospel. Some Lutheran theologians hold that the "unconditionality of the gospel" is such that not even faith is a condition of salvation.

III. Baptists

Whatever concessions they may make by "economy" or out of pastoral generosity, Baptists hold that membership of the Church in the fullest sense comes by way of baptism upon profession of faith. They find this to

225

be the sole practice of the New Testament and the presupposition of the apostolic doctrine of baptism. It is clear that a different anthropology and a different soteriology are here at work than in communities where infant baptism is the practical, or (a fortiori) also the theoretical, norm. In terms of ecumenical vision, Baptists do not say much about how each covenanted congregation of professed believers is (to be) related to other such congregations.

IV. *Orthodoxy*

The distinguishing characteristic of Orthodoxy is its intentional maintenance of what Georges Florovsky called "the patristic synthesis," as it is seen to be embodied in dogma, sacraments, canonical order, and hierarchy.[8] Necessary to this synthesis was both closeness to the original revelation in Christ and also time for the revelation to find a mature historical expression. Roman Catholicism is seen to have offended by adding to this synthesis, Protestantism by having—partly by a "Western overcorrection"—subtracted from it. The process of ecumenism is here understood as a growth in substantive orthodoxy, which will eventually be recognized as such by the churches that have historically remained Orthodox.

V. *Anglicanism*

Anglicanism is characterised by its "comprehensiveness." This characteristic has its origins in the diversity of responses to the call to Reformation and in the consequent need to include the broadest range possible within a particular territorial and political unit, the English realm. "Holy Scripture containeth all things necessary to salvation" (Article VI), but little is said about a "center" of Scripture or its internal coherence (despite the clue in Article VII that "both in the Old and New Testament everlasting life is offered to mankind by Christ, who is the only mediator between God and man, being both God and man"); and whatever is not forbidden by Scripture gets tolerated. If, in the terms of S.W. Sykes, being "an essentially contested concept" belongs to "the identity of Christianity,"[9] then the question becomes: How much internal tension can be contained in, and sustained by, this single community or communion without disrupting "the integrity of Anglicanism"?[10] Does "comprehensiveness" provide a viable model for a "coming great Church" in which a greater variety of "traditions" is likely to provide even greater tensions?

226

VI. Methodism

Methodism has overstretched Wesley's notion of the Lord's Supper as a "converting ordinance" into a characteristic practice of admitting to eucharistic communion any and all who are "seeking the Lord."[11] Appeal may be made to the generosity of Jesus in welcoming the crowds, an enactment of the universal offer of salvation on God's part. But since, in ecclesial terms, participation in the receiving community is, by the same token, participation in the celebrating community, the identity of the church and the message it proclaims becomes fluid. The "half-Christian" is being taken as an authentic witness to the faith. Is it really a paradox, then, that those Methodist churches/denominations which have practiced the most open communion are those which by now are in decline?

Conclusion

I have undoubtedly annoyed, and probably infuriated, my audience by these caricatures. The point of a caricature is that its truth resides in its falsehood. The exaggeration of a characteristic enables one to see what is in truth more subtly distinctive of the subject. It deliberately minimizes what the subject may have in common with others. My purpose has been to suggest that differences among communities making some claim to be church are a matter of complex configurations, to which either a detailed feature or a general pattern may provide the clue.

The respective "identities" of the various communities have a diachronic dimension. Each would claim an origin in primitive Christianity, whether in historic continuity or (if "interruptions" have necessitated "reforms") in recovered substantive fidelity. Certainly each has been affected, in various ways, by the passage of time. Some have been shaped, in part, by oppositional stances towards (some) others. All have interacted, in various ways, with their particular ambient cultures.

Phenomenologically, each of our six examples may be called a "type" in Newman's sense. Internally, each may be examined, whether by Newman's or similar criteria, for truth to itself. Ecumenically, the question is whether, or how far, they may legitimately be regarded as sub-types of a single Type (Christianity): what is required of any, each or all before they can properly be seen as *typoi*, in Willebrands' benign sense, within a single Church?

The difficulty of mutual comparability among these complex identities is obvious, even where particular relationships have been (at certain times and over some issues) confrontational. The way forward may depend on a common will toward conformity to the commonly professed Lord, who is also the True Man—the Son who is the *charaktèr* of the Father's *hypostasis* (Hebrews 1:3). The difference in starting points, or hermeneutical perspectives, makes the execution of such an intention arduous and problematic. Our hope must reside in the sufficiency of grace.

METHODIST PRINCIPLES OF ECUMENISM

CHAPTER FOURTEEN

Doctrine, Opinions, and Christian Unity: A Wesleyan and Methodist Perspective

Liberal Methodists isolate Wesley's dictum that "we think and let think" and make him the patron of sentimental ecumenism or even religious indifferentism. They forget that Wesley's magnanimity was limited to "opinions that do not strike at the root of Christianity."[1] In his generous sermon on a "Catholic Spirit," in which he reached out to Baptists and Romans (to name only those) in a plea for mutual respect and love, Wesley declares that "a man of truly catholic spirit is fixed as the sun in his judgment concerning the main branches of Christian doctrine" and supposes that the practitioners of a catholic spirit have in common at least "the first elements of the gospel of Christ."[2] In his "Letter to a Roman Catholic" Wesley expressed the faith of "a true Protestant" in words that amount to an expansion of the Nicene-Constantinopolitan creed.[3] At the anthropological end of the scale, Wesley stated in "The Principles of a Methodist Farther Explained" that "our main doctrines, which include all the rest, are three, that of repentance, of faith, and of holiness"[4]; and behind these stood, as Wesley shows in a lengthy treatise on "The Doctrine of Original Sin," original sin and the gratuitous work of Christ and the Spirit:

> A denial of original sin contradicts the main design of the gospel, which is to humble vain man, and to ascribe to God's free grace the whole of his salvation. Nor, indeed, can we let this doctrine go without giving up, at the same time, the greatest part, if not all, of the essential doctrines of the Christian faith. If we give this up, we cannot defend either justification by the merits of Christ, or the renewal of our natures by his Spirit.[5]

In all this Wesley adhered wholeheartedly to the official teachings of the Church of England, and he expected his preachers and his people to

231

do the same. As a simple presbyter of the Anglican Church, he was not in a position either to declare or to break ecclesial communion. But he sought for Methodists both friendly association and practical cooperation, whether within the Church of England or beyond it. There were, however, certain conditions set on his side. Thus, soon after his own "evangelical conversion" in which the Moravians had been instrumental, Wesley ceased to meet with them on account of their teaching on "stillness": the quietistic attitude that those awaiting full assurance of faith should meanwhile abstain from the means of grace. And in 1741 he broke off evangelistic collaboration with his younger friend George Whitefield on account of the latter's Calvinistic teaching on predestination. In his ferocious sermon of 1739–40 on "Free Grace" (which was never included among his "Standard Sermons"), Wesley berated predestinationism as "a direct and manifest tendency to overthrow the whole Christian Revelation."[6]

From the 1740s Wesley was dealing with Methodism as an embryonic denomination, not yet out of the womb of Anglicanism. The separation took place slowly, and indeed it was not until the end of the *nineteenth* century that the British Wesleyans took to themselves the name of church as distinct from "connexion." By Christmas 1784, however, the Americans had constituted themselves the Methodist Episcopal Church. Besides the Standard Sermons and the *Explanatory Notes upon the New Testament* which Wesley by the law of England set up as doctrinal guidance for his conference and connexion, Wesley also gave to the American Methodists his reduction of the Thirty-Nine Articles to Twenty-Four and his own abridgment of the Book of Common Prayer ("The Sunday Service"). He bequeathed to both sides of the Atlantic, although it nowhere attained constitutional status, *A Collection of Hymns for the Use of the People called Methodists* (1780), which Wesley saw as containing "all the important truths of our most holy religion, whether speculative or practical."[7]

Since these documents belong to various literary and theological genres, it is not in fact easy to distill from them a single comprehensive statement that would declare what is necessary and sufficient Methodist doctrine. But it seems clear enough that Wesley intended to maintain and propagate the scriptural, creedal, patristic, orthodox, catholic faith as this had been reformed in the Church of England. As "essential" to Christianity (he used the word), he clearly held to God the Holy Trinity, origin and goal of human salvation; the work of Christ and of the Holy Spirit in our redemption and its application; and the human condition, need, and calling, involving original sin, the justification of believers, and their sanctification and glorification. If Methodist denominations ever declined constitutionally from those doctrines, they could no longer legitimately claim to be Wesleyan.

That is the substantial heritage which Methodist denominations have had at their disposal for their life and mission and with which they have ever since Wesley had to negotiate, theoretically and practically, their own ecumenical relationships. Inherent in those substantive doctrines and in Wesley's understanding and practice concerning them are also certain distinctions and goals that come into play when the substance has to be dynamically interpreted in the ongoing life of the Methodist denominations and, which is our chief concern here, in their ecumenical interactions with other ecclesial bodies in the search for Christian unity.

The first of these is the distinction between doctrine and opinions. The former admits no difference; the latter may vary. Thus Wesley later admitted that, at the time of his break with Whitefield, he considered Calvinist teaching on predestination "not as an opinion, but as a dangerous mistake." It is, however, interesting that by the time of his letter of 14 May 1765 to John Newton, Wesley was prepared to rank it among those matters of "opinion" where Christians might vary as long as they were "compatible with a love to Christ and a work of grace." Wesley had been persuaded to reclassify the matter through acquaintance with Calvinists, including Newton himself, who "have real Christian experience." With fine evenhandedness, incidentally, Wesley was prepared to qualify as an "opinion" his own teaching on perfection, which he told Newton was "the main point between you and me."[8] These particular examples of predestination and perfection assume their full importance when it is realized that the most frequent partner with Methodists in church union plans and achievements have been denominations in the Reformed family. However particular negotiations turn out to distribute items between "doctrine"and "opinions" (and obviously a maximal consistency must be aimed at—that is why "multilateral" dialogues are so important), the distinction remains an important one of principle in the cause of Christian unity.

The second indication Methodists will be liable to take from Wesley concerns the importance of soteriological considerations. It is this, for example, which will cause Wesley to refuse his hand to Arians, semi-Arians and Socinians, and to insist on full trinitarianism. Listen to his late sermon "On the Trinity":

> There are ten thousand mistakes which may consist with real religion; with regard to which every candid, considerate man will think and let think. But there are some truths more important than others. It seems there are some which are of deep importance. I do not term them "fundamental" truths; because that is an ambiguous word. And hence there have been so many warm disputes about the number of "fundamentals." But surely there are some which it nearly concerns us to know, as having a close connexion with vital religion. And

233

doubtless we may rank among these that contained in the words above cited: "There are three that bear record in heaven, the Father, the Word, and the Holy Ghost. And these three are one". . . .

The knowledge of the Three-One God is interwoven with all true Christian faith, with all vital religion. . . . I know not how anyone can be a Christian believer till "he hath" (as St. John speaks) "the witness in himself"; till "the Spirit of God witnesses with his spirit that he is a child of God"—that is, in effect, till God the Holy Ghost witnesses that God the Father has accepted him through the merits of God the Son—and having this witness he honours the Son and the blessed Spirit "even as he honours the Father." Not that every Christian believer *adverts* to this; perhaps at first not one in twenty; but if you ask any of them a few questions, you will easily find it is implied in what he believes.[9]

That example is not without substantive interest to us at a time when the doctrine of the Trinity is for various reasons under threat and bids fair to become once more, as in the fourth century (where the argumentation of Athanasius and Basil was also basically soteriological!), the *articulus stantis et cadentis ecclesiae*. In fact, in all issues of doctrine or opinion Wesley displayed a strong soteriological interest in the content of the gospel, its proclamation, its reception, and its end in that holiness without which no one shall see the Lord.

The third Wesleyan indication will encourage Methodists to stretch their tolerance to the limits for the sake of unity in evangelism and mission. That approach was shown by Wesley in his letter of 19 April 1764 to "various clergymen" of Calvinist persuasion in the Church of England, wherein he sought, though without success, to win them for a missionary alliance.[10] The same attitude governed his views on church order, as expressed in his letter of 25 June 1746 to "John Smith":

What is the end of all ecclesiastical order? Is it not to bring souls from the power of Satan to God; and to build them up in his fear and love? Order, then, is so far valuable, as it serves these ends, and if it answers them not, it is nothing worth.[11]

Methodists have been sympathetic to the modern ecumenical motto *ut omnes unum sint*, "in order that the world may believe." It is above all this missionary motivation which has prompted Methodist participation, both British and American, in the World Council of Churches, and which has pushed churches of British Methodist origin in particular in the direction of organic unity with churches of other confessional traditions.

It would now be appropriate to examine how well Methodist bodies have used their doctrinal deposit and followed the Wesleyan guidelines in their application of it to ecumenical situations. If space allowed, we could look in detail at union plans (failed, successful, and continuing), at the reports of bilateral dialogues between Methodists and others, and at Methodist responses to the Lima text on *Baptism, Eucharist and Ministry*. The most significant unions have probably been those of the United Church of Canada (1925), the Church of South India (1947), and the Uniting Church in Australia (1977). The first and the third brought Methodists together with Presbyterians and Congregationalists; the second joined Methodists of British origin not only to Christians of Reformed background but also to Anglicans. One would need to look at the "Basis of Union" in these three cases to see how the historically controversial matters of doctrine and order were dealt with. In England, in connection with the finally unsuccessful plan of 1982 for a "covenant" between Methodists, Moravians, United Reformed, and Anglicans, the Church of England declared itself satisfied with the doctrinal assurances it had already received from the Methodist Church at the time of the earlier, and unadopted, plan of union in 1969 and 1972. In the United States, all four Methodist denominations in the Consultation on Church Union have given affirmative answers to questions on the "theological basis" for a "covenant" put forward by COCU in 1984.

As to bilateral dialogues, the World Methodist Council's oldest is with the Roman Catholic Church, which began in 1967 and still continues to produce reports every five years. Whereas Wesley in the historical circumstances of the eighteenth century had looked upon individual Roman Catholics as Christians *in spite of* their allegiance to their church (and Wesley wrote several tracts against certain Roman doctrines, along the lines of the Anglican Articles of Religion), the Nairobi Report of 1986 (*Towards a Statement on the Church*) declares joint commitment to a "goal of full communion in faith, mission and sacramental life." The first twenty-eight paragraphs of the Nairobi text are a completely agreed statement on many matters of ecclesiology, and the succeeding long discussion on authority concludes that "in any case Catholics and Methodists are agreed on the need for an authoritative way of being sure, beyond doubt, concerning God's action insofar as it is crucial for our salvation."[12]

The "final report" produced in 1984 by the joint commission between the World Methodist Council and the Lutheran World Federation on "The Church: Community of Grace" was able to recommend that "our churches take steps to declare and establish full fellowship of Word and sacrament" and that "as a first and important step our churches officially provide for pulpit exchange and mutual hospitality at the table of the Lord." While recognizing continuing characteristic "emphases," the report reaffirms the "basic common convictions" present from the start. It "witnesses to important agreements and convergences" and "indicates the ways in which we express our common faith differently."[13]

Two points may be made in conclusion. The first is to admit the great internal variety within the United Methodist Church, in the United States in particular. The 1972 *Book of Discipline* sandwiched the "foundation documents" between a statement on their "historical background" and a reflection on "our theological task." It declared that the Methodist pioneers believed there to be "a 'marrow' of Christian truth that can be identified and that must be conserved. This living core, as they believed, stands revealed in *Scripture*, illumined by *tradition*, vivified in personal *experience*, and confirmed by *reason*."[14] Since then there has been much debate concerning the relationships and respective functions of the four terms in this "quadrilateral." Unfortunately the 1972 text used the words "doctrine" and "theology" very loosely so that it is difficult to know where the church stands on the matter of a theological pluralism that does not sink into doctrinal laxity. The 1988 *Book of Discipline* contained a revised statement on "Doctrinal Standards and Our Theological Task" which the General Conference mandated for a four-year study in the church at large.[15]

The second concluding point returns to Methodist origins. For the Wesleys it was clear that Christian doctrine and Christian unity subserved the upbuilding of the church in truth and love. Therein resides human salvation, which is to the glory of God.[16]

CHAPTER FIFTEEN

Wesley and the Communion of Saints

It is gratifying for a Methodist to note that John Wesley's place in the communion of the saints has received increasing ecumenical recognition in recent decades. In the calendar of the North American *Lutheran Book of Worship* (1978), John and Charles Wesley are commemorated—as "renewers of the Church"—on March 2nd, the date of John's death. For Anglicans, that date has been pre-empted by St. Chad of Lichfield, and so the Wesleys—"John and Charles Wesley, priests"—are allocated to March 3rd in the 1979 *Book of Common Prayer* of the Episcopal Church in the USA and also—as "priests, hymn-writers, and founders of Methodism"—in *An Australian Prayer Book* of 1978. With rare tact, the 1980 *Alternative Service Book* of the Church of England ignores the traditional principle of celebrating a saint on his death-day as his "birthday" to eternal life and, instead of commemorating John Wesley on the day of his passing, keeps the feast of the Wesleys—"John and Charles Wesley, priests, poets, teachers of the faith"—on May 24th, the most popular occasion of Methodist celebration, being the date of John Wesley's evangelical conversion or "new birth" in 1738. That is also the date chosen for the Wesleys—"reformers of the Church"—by the Uniting Church in Australia in its bold move, for a body resulting from Reformed and Methodist traditions, of introducing a "calendar of commemorations" into its service-book, *Uniting in Worship* (1988).

Given this widespread "reception" of the Wesleys into the calendars of the churches, it will be a worthwhile exercise to examine the teaching and practice of the Wesleys themselves concerning the communion of saints, and to consider at each point how contemporary Methodists might continue or re-appropriate that inheritance. Each point will be set into the context of Methodist dialogue with other Christian families, so that we ourselves shall be facing the challenge of ecumenical learning. That will constitute the bulk of this chapter. A brief conclusion will look in return at the wider ecclesiological implications of the adoption of the Wesleys beyond the bounds of Methodism.

I. *The Festival of All the Saints*

We may begin with an entry in John Wesley's *Journal* for November 1st, 1767:

> Being All-Saints' Day (a festival I dearly love), I could not but observe the admirable propriety with which the Collect, Epistle, and Gospel for the day are suited to each other.[1]

In the 1662 Book of Common Prayer, the collect of All Saints' Day runs thus:

> O almighty God, who hast knit together thine elect in one communion and fellowship, in the mystical body of thy Son Christ our Lord: Grant us grace so to follow thy blessed Saints in all virtuous and godly living, that we may come to those unspeakable joys, which thou hast prepared for them that unfeignedly love thee; through Jesus Christ our Lord. Amen.

The scripture appointed for the Epistle is Revelation 7:2-12, which describes St. John's heavenly vision of a great multitude from every nation, clothed with white robes and palms in their hands, crying with a loud voice, "Salvation to our God, which sitteth upon the throne, and unto the Lamb." And the whole company of heaven worships God, saying "Amen. Blessing, and glory, and wisdom, and thanksgiving, and honour, and power, and might, be unto our God for ever and ever. Amen." The Gospel of All Saints' Day is St. Matthew 5:1-12. In the Beatitudes, Jesus there promises to the pure in heart the vision of God, and the various other blessings of God's kingdom to those who manifest its characteristics.

These three texts whose mutual appropriateness Wesley admired—the collect, Epistle and Gospel of All Saints' Day—provide us with the necessary themes for examining the Wesleys' teaching and practice concerning the communion of saints. First, the address of the collect stresses fellowship in the body of Christ. Then the Epistle suggests that this is a fellowship of praise to God's glory. The Gospel reveals the nature of sanctification and sainthood. And on this path to perfection and the final kingdom of divine glory and our joy, we have—the collect again reminds us—the example of the blessed saints. Let us take each of those points in turn.

II. *Fellowship in the Body of Christ*

In his contribution to *Northern Catholicism*, the centenary volume of the Oxford Movement, Robert Newton Flew reckoned the communion of saints among the first "re-discoveries" made by Methodism in advance

238

of Pusey, Newman and company.[2] "From being an article in the creed," says Flew, this became "for multitudes a present possession." To them, "conversion meant immediate entrance into a fellowship unknown before. . . . The early band-meetings and society classes of Methodism were the instruments used by this new passion for fellowship." Flew here focuses on the local and temporal units in an interlocking fellowship that extends across the world and beyond death. Wesley himself, in his exposition of the ecclesiological clauses in the creeds offered in his *Letter to a Roman Catholic*, recognizes the global and transcendent dimensions of the communion of the saints. The "catholic (that is, universal) Church" comprises "such as shall be saved," from "all nations and all ages": "Its members . . . have fellowship with God the Father, Son and Holy Ghost . . . and with all the living members of Christ on earth, as well as all who are departed in his faith and fear."[3]

It is the transcendence of time which interests us principally in this essay. The Wesleyan sense of it is captured in Charles's great funeral hymn which is familar to non-Methodists in its bowdlerized form "Let saints on earth in concert sing" (as though every schoolchild did not know the word "terrestrial"). Let us recall the more authentic version found in Methodist hymnals:[4]

> Come, let us join our friends above
> That have obtained the prize,
> And on the eagle wings of love
> To joys celestial rise:
> Let all the saints terrestrial sing
> With those to glory gone;
> For all the servants of our King,
> In earth and heaven, are one.
>
> One family we dwell in him,
> One church, above, beneath,
> Though now divided by the stream,
> The narrow stream of death:
> One army of the living God,
> To his command we bow;
> Part of his host have crossed the flood,
> And part are crossing now.
>
> Ten thousand to their endless home
> This solemn moment fly;
> And we are to the margin come,
> And we expect to die;

239

Ev'n now by faith we join our hands
With those that went before,
And greet the blood-besprinkled bands
On the eternal shore.

Our spirits too shall quickly join,
Like theirs with glory crowned,
And shout to see our captain's sign,
To hear his trumpet sound.
O that we now might grasp our guide!
O that the word were given!
Come, Lord of hosts, the waves divide,
And land us all in heaven.

This Wesleyan notion of "one family," of "one Church, above, beneath," of a single "army of the living God" on the march to the "eternal shore," can help us in our ecumenical endeavours to envision and realize Christian unity. It lends dynamism to the classic description of church unity proposed from the New Delhi assembly of the World Council of Churches in 1961, according to which the currently divided churches aim at being "united with the whole Christian fellowship in all places and all ages in such wise that ministry and members are accepted by all."[5]

To take the example of Methodists' relations with Roman Catholics: the joint commission between the Roman Catholic Church and the World Methodist Council produced for presentation to the Vatican and to the Singapore 1991 meeting of the WMC, its report on "The Apostolic Tradition."[6] The commission tackled this theme in order to fill the "gap" perceptible in the 1986 Nairobi Report between a general description of the Church, which could be largely agreed on a New Testament basis, and the doctrinal and practical division between Methodists and Catholics concretized in the papacy.[7] It was felt that closer agreement on the apostolic tradition, both as content and as process, would, if attainable, provide a promising context in which to examine the controversial questions of episcopal succession and a petrine office. The lodestone of the commission's work in the quinquennium 1986–91 turned out to be the understanding of apostolic tradition as "koinonia in time," a concept clearly related to our theme of the communion of saints.[8]

This approach is not foreign to Methodism. To revert to Robert Newton Flew: in that same chapter on "Methodism and the Catholic Tradition" he speaks thus of "the evangelical succession": "The bread of life is the gift of God, but it is broken from hand to hand. Almost always there is some human intermediary in the bringing of a soul to walk with God." And then our Methodist author neatly quotes Newman in support:

240

The Apostles were such men. . . . Each receives and transmits the sacred flame, trimming it in rivalry of his predecessor, and fully purposed to send it on as bright as it has reached him; and thus the selfsame fire, once kindled on Moriah, though seeming at intervals to fail, has at last reached us in safety, and will in like manner as we trust be carried forward even to the end.

"These words," said Flew, "would be accepted by Methodists as a description of the essential work of the Church. This nexus of Christian personalities, all learning the secret of God's personal dealing with us, and passing it on again to others, *is* the Church."[9]

In the international Roman Catholic-Methodist dialogue the commission has sought to discern, in a Church confessed to be constituted by the Word and sustained by the Spirit, a constant, time-transcending "pattern of Christian faith, Christian life, and Christian community." "Our knowledge of the past life of the people of God, witnessing to their experience of God's action among them, enables us," says the Singapore report (¶6), "to recognize and to comprehend the risen Christ as he speaks to us today." Next to the witness of the first apostles—with "the written word of Scripture" as "permanent norm" (¶16)—"an important place is given to those theologians who provided the earliest elucidations of the faith" (¶34). This matches nicely Wesley's allegiance to "the Book of God," his respect for the early Fathers, and his acceptance of the doctrinal decisions of the first ecumenical councils.[10] The joint commission goes on to say that "when Christians recite the Creed, . . . they identify themselves with that great company 'whose lives are hid with Christ in God' (Col. 3:4)" (¶37).

This secret location of all Christian believers—"hid with Christ in God"—means that the witness of past generations is not confined to what they said and did in their own times and places: "The saints who have passed into the fulness of the mystery of God's grace are forever part of the community: the witness and examples of the past continue to be cherished; the saints in heaven are held as instances of Christ's 'closest love' and as present tokens of the ultimate fulfillment of all God's promises" (¶75). Moreover, the saints "watch from heaven and encourage us" (¶47).

This perspective of a "koinonia in time" may help in the difficult question of ministries. In both Catholicism and Methodism, ministers are appointed who, their respective churches believe, "inherit the apostolic function of oversight in the community" (¶74): "The transmission of the Gospel is the work of the whole assembly of the faithful under the guidance and with the encouragement of their pastors" (¶76). In a Catholic understanding, "the succession of bishops through the generations serves the continued unity of the Church in the faith handed on from the apostles" (¶93). In the Methodist tradition, Wesley also accepted the need for *episcopé*; and, prolonging his own supervision of the Methodist societies in Britain, "his appointment of Francis Asbury and Thomas Coke to the superintendency in America was rooted in his belief that the Holy Spirit wished to bestow the gift of *episcopé* at that time and in that place for the sake of maintaining unity of faith with the Church of all ages" (¶93). If the Roman Catholic Church could arrive at a full endorsement of the very next sentence in the Singapore report, prospects for the mutual recognition of our two communities in the communion of saints would greatly increase: 'It [that is, Wesley's action] was part of a fresh and extraordinary outpouring of the gift of the Spirit who never ceases to enliven and unify the Church" (ibid.). The divine inspiration of the Wesleyan movement being thus recognized, Methodists would immediately become more open to hearing the Catholic claim that "the teaching of a common faith by the college of bishops in union with the successor of Peter ensures unity in the Truth" (¶93). For, given a communion of the saints now acknowledged to include both St. Peter and John Wesley, Methodists might acquire a stronger sense of the apostolic tradition as "koinonia in time" and so come to a deeper appreciation of the acclamation made at the council of Chalcedon, "This is the faith of the fathers; this is the faith of the apostles; this is the faith of us all; Peter has spoken through Leo"[11]—and perhaps an understanding of the medieval title of the bishop of Rome as "vicar of Peter" as well as the more recent proposal of J.-M. R. Tillard to consider the petrine ministry as an "anamnesis" of the apostle.[12]

III. A Fellowship of Praise

Returning to the broader theme of the communion of the saints, let us look a little more closely at some of the ways in which, according to the Wesleys, the Church "beneath" is even now "joined" to the Church "above" ("to join" is a thrice repeated verb in the hymn "Come, let us join our friends above").

The Epistle of All Saints' Day pictures the life of heaven as praise to God's glory. In their *Hymns on the Lord's Supper* (1745), John and Charles Wesley depict and enact the doxology that is already common to the kingdom of grace and the kingdom of glory. Thus, for instance:

> Happy the souls to Jesus join'd,
> And saved by grace alone;
> Walking in all thy ways we find
> Our heaven on earth begun.

The church triumphant in thy love
Their mighty joys we know;
They sing the Lamb in hymns above,
And we in hymns below.

Thee in thy glorious realm they praise,
And bow before thy throne;
We in the kingdom of thy grace,
The kingdoms are but one.

The holy to the holiest leads,
From hence our spirits rise,
And he that in thy statutes treads
Shall meet thee in the skies.[13]

By the *Sursum corda*, we are invited to join "all the company of heaven" in singing the *Sanctus*. For *dignum et iustum est*: "Meet and right it is to sing. . . ."—

Vying with that happy choir,
Who chant thy praise above,
We on eagles' wings aspire,
The wings of faith and love:
Thee they sing with glory crowned,
We extol the slaughtered Lamb;
Lower if our voices sound,
Our subject is the same.

Father, God, thy love we praise,
Which gave thy Son to die;
Jesus, full of truth and grace,
Alike we glorify;
Spirit, Comforter divine,
Praise by all to thee be given;
Till we in full chorus join,
And earth is turned to heaven.[14]

This doxological thrust in the Wesleyan practice of the communion of the saints should bring Methodists close to the Eastern Orthodox. Might it be possible to consider "our hymns" (as Methodists like to say)—now drawn from a vast range of times and places—as a kind of musical iconography, analogous to the way in which the Orthodox, themselves no mean lovers of hymnody, by the liturgical use of icons enact the presence of the saints so that the joy of heaven may be known upon earth? Certainly the liturgical expression of the communion of saints could

243

eventually become an interesting theme for exploration in the theological conversations that the Ecumenical Patriarchate in 1990 agreed to begin with the World Methodist Council under the rubric of ecclesiology.

It would then become necessary for Methodists to consider again the questions of prayer for the dead and the invocation of the saints. In his *Collection of Forms of Prayer for Every Day in the Week* (1733), John Wesley includes a number of texts, of which the following are typical:

> O let it be thy good pleasure shortly to put a period to sin and misery, to infirmity and death, to complete the number of thine elect, and to hasten thy kingdom; that we, and all that wait for thy salvation, may eternally love and praise thee [*Sunday evening*].

> Visit in mercy all the children of affliction. . . . and at length bring them and us, with those that already rest from their labours, into the joy of our Lord [*Monday evening*].

> Unite us all to one another by mutual love, and to thyself by constant holiness; that we, together with all those who went before us in thy faith and fear, may find a merciful acceptance in the last day [*Thursday morning*].

Most interesting is a prayer—for Saturday evening—that Wesley began to add in the 1740 edition, with the explicit annotation "The words of the ancient liturgy, commonly called St. Mark's":

> O Lord, thou God of spirits and of all flesh, be mindful of thy faithful from Abel the just even unto this day. Grant them to rest in the region of the living, in thy kingdom, in the delights of paradise, where there is no grief, sorrow or sighing, where the light of thy countenance perpetually shines. And for thy Son's sake give to them and us, in thy due time, a happy resurrection, and a glorious rest at thy right hand for evermore.[15]

In defense of such prayers against the attacks of Dr. Conyers Middleton and Bishop George Lavington of Exeter,[16] Wesley appeals to a range of authorities: dominical ("'Thy kingdom come' manifestly concerns the saints in paradise as well as those upon earth"); scriptural (prayer "that God would shortly accomplish the number of his elect and hasten his kingdom" derives from Revelation 6:11 and 2 Peter 3:12); patristic ("the words of an ancient liturgy," from "earliest antiquity"); and Anglican (Wesley notes the prayer in the burial service of the Book of Common Prayer, "that we, with all those who are departed in thy faith and fear, may have our perfect consummation and bliss, both in body and soul"). Wesley clearly accepts and practices what he calls "this kind of general prayer for the faithful departed," for those who have died in the Lord and are believed to be even now in paradise.[17] While obviously reluctant to "name names" in these "general" prayers for the dead, Wesley continued to expound, as Albert Outler puts it, "an Eastern Orthodox view of an 'intermediate state' wherein the saved foretaste the heavenly state to come and the unsaved foretaste their final damnation."[18]

What, then, of invoking the saints for their prayers on our behalf? Wesley grimly notes a single biblical example—the cry of the rich man to Abraham in the parable at Luke 16:24:

> It cannot be denied but here is one precedent in Scripture of praying to departed saints: but who is it that prays, and with what success? Will any, who considers this, be fond of copying after him?[19]

Wesley's discouragement of the practice of calling on the saints for their prayers may again be due to a reluctance to name names in the case of the departed, even with persons of conspicuous sanctity whose bliss might reasonably be supposed. An even stronger motive here, however, may be the association of the invocation of saints with a cult of relics and a treasury of merit that Wesley found to reproach in the Roman Catholic Church.[20] At this point we might find ecumenical help again from the Eastern Orthodox Churches.

IV. The Nature of Sanctity

In his exposition of the Beatitudes, the Gospel of All Saints' Day, Wesley teaches that sanctity itself and its intrinsic rewards—holiness and happiness—are alike the "gifts of God." In the *Explanatory Notes upon the New Testament*, he writes thus at the beginning of the Sermon on the Mount (Matt. 5:2):

> To bless men, to make men happy, was the great business for which our Lord came into the world. And accordingly he pronounces eight blessings together, annexing them to so many steps in Christianity. Knowing that happiness is our common aim, and that an innate instinct continually urges us to the pursuit of it, he in the kindest manner applies to that instinct, and directs it to its proper object.
>
> Though all men desire, yet few attain, happiness, because they seek it where it is not to be found. Our Lord therefore begins his divine institution, which is the complete art of happiness, by laying down, before all that have ears to hear, the true, and only, method of acquiring it.
>
> Observe the benevolent condescension of our Lord. He seems, as it were, to lay aside his supreme authority as our legislator, that he may the better act the part of our friend and saviour. Instead of using

245

the lofty style, in positive commands, he, in a more gentle and engaging way, insinuates his will and our duty, by pronouncing those happy who comply with it.

While Wesley certainly speaks of Christ *"showing* the way to heaven," he declares—in the fuller development found in his "Discourses upon our Lord's Sermon on the Mount"[21]—how the very "disposition" to receive salvation is itself a gift of God,[22] how righteousness and renewal are the work of the Holy Spirit in believers,[23] and how the future contains the "highest blessings of God in Christ Jesus"[24] and a "crown which the Lord . . . will give at that day."[25] Faith is "the life of God in the soul," and for the believer "heaven [is] already opened in the soul, the first springing up of those rivers of pleasure which flow at God's right hand for evermore."[26]

That all holiness and happiness is thus dependent on grace is a Wesleyan truth to which the dialogues with the Lutheran World Federation and the World Alliance of Reformed Churches may have helped recall Methodists. The Lutheran dialogue produced in 1984 a report entitled *The Church: Community of Grace;*[27] the 1987 report of the Reformed dialogue was called *Together in God's Grace.*[28] Methodists need reminding by these churches of the Reformation—Lutheran and Reformed—that Arminianism, even an *"evangelical* Arminianism," remains constantly exposed to the Pelagian temptation, as the *Minutes* of the notorious Methodist Conference of 1770 illustrate. Moreover, the communal, corporate, churchly dimensions of the documents from the conversations with the Lutherans and the Reformed is significant. For sanctity cannot fail to be communal, corporate, churchly ("No holiness but social holiness" was Wesley's watchword[29]). It is a shared partaking of the divine nature (cf. 2 Peter 1:4, the text Wesley encountered on the morning of 24 May 1738), a gracious participation in the family life of God, a communion of saints in and with the Holy Trinity. "To crown all," Wesley perorates in his sermon on "The New Creation," "there will be a deep, an intimate, an uninterrupted union with God; a constant communion with the Father and his Son Jesus Christ, through the Spirit; a continual enjoyment of the Three-One God, and of all the creatures in him!"[30]

Or in Charles Wesley's words (from the hymn "Love divine, all loves excelling"):

> Finish then thy new creation,
> Pure and spotless let us be;
> Let us see thy great salvation,
> Perfectly restored in thee;

246

> Changed from glory into glory,
> Till in heaven we take our place,
> Till we cast our crowns before thee,
> Lost in wonder, love, and praise![31]

Or again (from "All praise to our redeeming Lord"):

> And if our fellowship below
> In Jesus be so sweet,
> What heights of rapture shall we know
> When round his throne we meet![32]

V. The Example of the Saints

The Anglican collect of All Saints' Day, it will be remembered, asks God: "Grant us grace so to follow thy blessed saints in all virtuous and godly living, that we may come to those unspeakable joys, which thou hast prepared for them that unfeignedly love thee." The prayer for the Church militant may also be recalled from the communion office:

> And we also bless thy holy Name for all thy servants departed this life in thy faith and fear; beseeching thee to give us grace so to follow their good examples, that with them we may be partakers of thy heavenly kingdom: Grant this, O Father, for Jesus Christ's sake, our only Mediator and Advocate. Amen.

Without being limited to Anglicanism, the notion of following the example of the saints appears to be a characteristically prominent feature of the Anglican understanding of the *communio sanctorum*. As the World Methodist Council takes up the invitation from the Lambeth Conference of 1988 to a dialogue with the Anglican Consultative Council, this may be a theme on which its mother community has lessons for Methodism. In two matters in particular, it could be valuable to rejoin Wesley's practice in this area.

First, we know that Wesley not only "dearly loved" the festival of All Saints but also regularly observed the Prayer Book calendar whose "holy days" included the red-letter feasts of the biblical saints with their proper readings and texts. (What a pity that Charles Wesley did not anticipate John Keble's "Christian Year"!) The Prayer Book calendar's emphasis on biblical figures is good, while the celebration of All Saints' Day opens the door also to the modest commemoration of conspicuous men and women from the post-scriptural history of the Church which occurs on the black-letter saints' days. Those Protestant Churches which are now seeking to restore the lost practice of a *sanctorale* can turn for inspiration to

247

a sober Anglican tradition which has avoided the excesses of a luxuriating Catholicism.

Second, Wesley enjoyed the Anglican habit of spiritual reading; and by his publication of a "Christian Library" he encouraged the Methodist people to acquire it. By their writings the literate saints have given us access to their Christian experience and provided us with a means to follow their example. We are now in need of "lives" of other saints written in styles which avoid those that gave hagiography a bad name and yet (or rather) encourage us to emulation of their subjects.[33]

With that we come in fact to a question of some current ecumenical concern, namely the choice of "models of holiness"—both personal and social.[34]

VI. *Ecumenical Implications*

Rather than entering into detail over that latter task, let us in fact conclude with some possible consequences of the simple fact, gratefully noted at the beginning, that some churches beyond Methodism are starting to include the Wesleys in their calendar of saints.

The Anglicans might be thought thus to be reclaiming their own. The Lutherans are reaching out to figures of whom they have hitherto been ignorant or suspicious (it is interesting that the *The Lutheran Book of Worship* includes Calvin also in its calendar, but not Zwingli). In the calendar of the Uniting Church in Australia, the obvious inclusion of Methodist and Reformed figures represents a seal on the constituent traditions of that Church (Methodist, Presbyterian, and Independent or Congregationalist),[35] while the presence of more remote names serves to commemorate a former, broader unity or to anticipate an even greater unity still to come. At the end of his book *John Wesley and the Catholic Church,*[36] the Catholic layman John Todd confided that "as I have come to know Wesley, I have believed him to be in heaven and have prayed to God through him—not publicly as the Church prays through those declared to be saints—but privately as I pray for and to those who have been close to me." What would an official Roman Catholic recognition, as envisaged above, of the Methodist movement as an outpouring of the Holy Spirit do for Wesley's canonical status in the Catholic Church? Might the Orthodox even come to a similar position?

To recognize the saints of another community is in some way also to recognize their home community, and vice versa. The Roman Catholic-Methodist report on *The Apostolic Tradition* declares that "the 'cloud of witnesses' transcends denominational barriers" (para. 66). A French

Catholic pioneer of the modern ecumenical movement, Paul Couturier, was fond of the Russian dictum that "the walls of separation do not reach up to heaven." The prayers and witness of the saints—about membership in whose company there is apparently an increasing ecumenical agreement—must surely be allowed to influence our growing mutual recognition and our progress to greater ecclesial unity on earth.[37]

As Methodists, we should rejoice to share the Wesleys with other Christian communities. Our best expression of gratitude for their adoption of our particular founders will be to believe and live *as* the community of the Wesleys and *so* enrich the Church catholic in our times and in the future—with a fusion of faith that is both warm and orthodox, of evangelistic preaching, liturgical observance, social action, and holy living.[38]

Sancti Joannes et Carole, orate pro nobis.

CHAPTER SIXTEEN

"Sent to Disciple All Mankind": A Wesleyan and Biblical Theology of Mission

"Sent to disciple all mankind": This striking phrase comes from the great baptismal hymn contained in the Wesleys' *Collection of Hymns for the Use of the People called Methodists* of 1780. In its entirety the hymn runs as follows:

> Come, Father, Son, and Holy Ghost,
> Honour the means ordained by thee!
> Make good our apostolic boast,
> And own thy glorious ministry.
>
> We now thy promised presence claim;
> Sent to disciple all mankind,
> Sent to baptize into thy name,
> We now thy promised presence find.
>
> Father, in these reveal thy Son;
> In these for whom we seek thy face,
> The hidden mystery make known,
> The inward, pure, baptizing grace.
>
> Jesus, with us thou always art;
> Effectual make the sacred sign,
> The gift unspeakable impart,
> And bless the ordinance divine.
>
> Eternal Spirit, descend from high,
> Baptizer of our spirits thou!
> The sacramental seal apply,
> And witness with the water now.

O that the souls baptized therein
May now thy truth and mercy feel;
May rise and wash away their sin—
Come, Holy Ghost, their pardon seal![1]

That hymn is directly based on the great commission of the risen Lord recorded at the end of St. Matthew's gospel (Matt. 28:18-20):

Jesus came and said to [the eleven], "All authority in heaven and on earth has been given to me. Go therefore and make disciples of all nations, baptizing them in the name of the Father and of the Son and of the Holy Spirit, teaching them to observe all that I have commanded you; and lo, I am with you always, to the close of the age."

That scriptural passage, and the hymn deriving from it, will provide the main lines for the following sketch of a theology of mission that is both biblical and Wesleyan. Naturally, details will be filled in from other parts of the Scriptures and from the fuller expressions the founders of Methodism gave to their doctrine elsewhere. But the pattern will retain a shape suggested by the biblical text and by the hymn. First, we shall indicate the *authority* of the Christ who thus dispatched his followers on a universal mission. Second, we shall set forth the *trinitarian* dimensions of the Triune God's saving design for the world, of which the Christian mission is an instrument. Third, we shall see that the mission aims at a *discipleship* that is sustained by the teaching and power of Christ and sealed by baptism in the threefold Name. Fourth and last, we shall hint at the *ultimate* significance and scope of a mission that will not be completed before the age to come.

I. Commissioned by the Risen Lord

Since the time of Jesus Christ's life, death and resurrection, believers have acclaimed his person and his work as possessing a *unique* and *universal* significance. The core of the earliest Christian confession was that "Jesus Christ is Lord" (Philippians 2:11; cf. Romans 10:9; 1 Corinthians 12:3). He was hailed by his followers as "the Saviour of the world" (John 4:42). It was preached that "there is no other name under heaven given among men by which we must be saved" (Acts 4:12). It was this Lord who, in the record of St. Matthew's gospel, issued the great commission to his apostles to "disciple all mankind" to himself. We should recall the *ground* of that commission and the *need* for it.

The commission is grounded in the *personal authority* of Christ. To him "has been given" all authority in heaven and on earth. The passive voice is an oblique way of indicating that God the Father is the source of Christ's unique authority. In Christ we have to do with no less than God. Christ is the Son who, in the divine economy, was entrusted with the personal mission of God to the world. He is the Word who became flesh and dwelt among us (John 1:14). Taking human form, he remained faithful unto death and has therefore received the Name which is above every name (Philippians 2:5-11). According to Christian belief, "there is one God, the Father, from whom are all things and for whom we exist, and one Lord, Jesus Christ, through whom are all things and through whom we exist" (1 Corinthians 8:6). As Christ had himself been sent by the Father in the incarnation, so then after his resurrection he sent his apostles into the world with the gift of the Holy Spirit to forgive sins (John 20:21-23).

That the mission involves the forgiveness of sins is an indication of the world's need of *salvation*. "God so loved the world that he gave his only Son, that whoever believes in him should not perish but have eternal life" (John 3:16). A sign of the world's perishing is the presence in it of many so-called "gods" and "lords" (cf. 1 Corinthians 8:5). Exchanging the truth about God for a lie, humans have worshipped the creature rather than the Creator. Idols are ultimately emblems of ourselves. Turned in upon ourselves, we cut ourselves off from the divine source of life. Left to ourselves, we wallow in a chaos which ends up in death (Romans 1:18-32). But God has graciously provided for our rescue: "in Christ God was reconciling the world to himself" (2 Corinthians 5:19). To the apostles has been entrusted "the message of reconciliation": "We are ambassadors for Christ, God making his appeal through us. We beseech you on behalf of Christ, be reconciled to God" (2 Corinthians 5:20). So now it is possible, and enjoined, to turn "to God from idols, to serve a living and true God, and to wait for his Son from heaven, whom he raised from the dead, Jesus who delivers us from the wrath to come" (1 Thessalonians 1:9-10). According to Jesus's prayer to the Father: "This is eternal life, that they know thee the only true God, and Jesus Christ whom thou hast sent" (John 17:3).

The Lord who utters the great commission has the authority to do so, and when he instructs his apostles to make for him disciples of all nations, it is because he himself is the substantial means of meeting the world's need: he is the only Son of the Father, and in him is the world's salvation to be found. To waver from that belief would be to deviate from what has been Christian faith from its beginnings.

John Wesley clearly recognized, over against the contemporary Arians and Deists, that Christianity stands or falls with the full *divinity* of the Son, for only so is his redemptive work effective. Thus, in a letter of

February 7, 1778 to Mary Bishop, Wesley writes: "Nothing in the Christian system is of greater consequence than the doctrine of Atonement. It is properly the distinguishing point between Deism and Christianity. . . . Give up the Atonement, and the Deists are agreed with us. . . . What saith the Scripture? It says, 'God was in Christ, reconciling the world unto himself'."[2] And in the 1780 sermon on "Spiritual Worship" Wesley includes this among the many reasons for calling Christ "true God": "'The true God' is also the Redeemer of all the children of men. It pleased the Father to 'lay upon him the iniquities of us all,' that by the one oblation of himself once offered, when he tasted death for every man, he might make a full and sufficient sacrifice, oblation, and satisfaction for the sins of the whole world."[3] So Wesley recognized, too, that without the admission of the universally and all-pervasively *fallen* character of humanity, there would be no need of a gospel: "A denial of original sin," he writes, "contradicts the main design of the gospel, which is to humble vain man, and to ascribe to God's free grace the whole of his salvation. Nor, indeed, can we let this doctrine go without giving up, at the same time, the greatest part, if not all, of the essential doctrines of the Christian faith. If we give this up, we cannot defend either justification by the merits of Christ, or the renewal of our natures by his Spirit."[4]

II. *The Saving Design of the Triune God*

The saving design of God for the world is what the New Testament means by a phrase that occurs a dozen or so times, the "mystery of God" or the "mystery of the kingdom." Since Christ, this *mystery* is what Lesslie Newbigin, one of the outstanding missionary bishops and theologians of our century, calls an "open secret."[5] The trinitarian pattern of mission is described by Newbigin as "Proclaiming the Kingdom of the Father: Mission as Faith in Action," "Sharing the Life of the Son: Mission as Love in Action," and "Bearing the Witness of the Spirit: Mission as Hope in Action." Without at all claiming to improve on Newbigin (but I wanted to recommend the reading of his book), I will briefly make my own exposition of the trinitarian dimensions of the Christian mission, giving a Wesleyan slant to the presentation (Newbigin, after all, comes of Presbyterian stock, even though he exercised his ministry as a bishop in the Church of South India).

Returning to the "mystery," we find that what has been revealed in Christ is *God the Father*'s saving design for the entire world, which embraces therefore not only the people of Israel, which for many centuries carried alone the privileges and responsibilities of election, but also the whole host of the nations: so, for instance, Romans 16:25-27, Ephesians 3:4-12. Thus were brought to light again the implications of the creation of all mankind in Adam and Eve by the universal Creator (Genesis 1–3), of the promise of Yahweh to Abraham that in him all the families of the earth would be blessed (Genesis 12:3), of the message of Isaiah that the one and only Lord God invited "all the ends of the earth" to "turn to (him) and be saved" (Isaiah 45:22), of the vision of the apocalyptic writers that God's universal kingdom would one day be complete (e. g. Isaiah 25:6-9; cf. Revelation 10:7).

The universal scope of the saving purpose of God is sung in a Wesleyan hymn whose positive truths transcend the original anti-Calvinistic polemic:

> Father, whose everlasting love
> Thy only Son for sinners gave,
> Whose grace to all did freely move,
> And sent him down the world to save:
>
> Help us thy mercy to extol,
> Immense, unfathomed, unconfined;
> To praise the Lamb who died for all,
> The general Saviour of mankind.
>
> Thy undistinguishing regard
> Was cast on Adam's fallen race;
> For all thou hast in Christ prepared
> Sufficient, sovereign, saving grace.
>
> The world he suffered to redeem,
> For all he hath the atonement made,
> For those that will not come to him
> The ransom of his life was paid.
>
> Arise, O God, maintain thy cause!
> The fullness of the Gentiles call;
> Lift up the standard of thy Cross,
> And all shall own thou diedst for all.[6]

That God's purpose is a saving one—even and precisely in the face of human sin—is confirmed by the atoning work of *the Son*. The apostle Paul recognized that "all have sinned and fall short of the glory of God" (Romans 3:23). But he then went on to show the superabundance of God's grace which, in the redeeming work of Christ, far exceeds the power and effect of sin (Romans 5:15-21). In a world of sin and death, Christ held fast to his Father, and by his death he trampled down death and brought

255

life and immortality to light (2 Timothy 1:10; 1 Peter 2:9). As the one mediator between God and humankind (1 Timothy 2:5), Christ made the peace with God upon which all human peace depends (Ephesians 2:14-22). As the holy and righteous one (Acts 3:14; 1 John 2:1), Christ displayed the merciful justice of God which is the final standard for all human justice.

The Wesleys knew that—

> He left his Father's throne above
> (So free, so infinite his grace),
> Emptied himself of all but love,
> And bled for Adam's helpless race.[7]

And so they wanted "a thousand tongues" in order to "spread through all the earth abroad the honours of" the name of Jesus, for through them

> He speaks, and, listening to his voice,
> New life the dead receive,
> The mournful, broken hearts rejoice,
> The humble poor believe.[8]

God's saving purpose is continued in the work of *the Holy Spirit*. At the prayer of the risen and ascended Christ, the great pentecostal outpouring of the Spirit takes place (Acts 2:33; cf. John 14:16-17; 14:26; 15:26-27), so that Christ's followers may be his witnesses "to the end of the earth" (Acts 1:8) and preach "the gospel (. . .)to all nations" (Mark 13:9-11). Only by the Holy Spirit is it possible to confess that Jesus is Lord (1 Corinthians 12:3) and to pray in his name to the Father (Romans 8:15-27). The same Spirit empowers Christian preaching (1 Thessalonians 1:5), Christian virtues (Romans 5:1-5; Galatians 5:22-25), and the life in love (1 Corinthians 12:31—13:13) that all testify to Christ.

According to St. Athanasius and the great Cappadocian teachers of the fourth century who did most to bring trinitarian theology to its full development, every work of God towards the world begins with the Father, is mediated by the Son, and comes to completion in the Holy Spirit. While the New Testament writers largely confine the explicit work of the Holy Spirit to those who name the name of Jesus Christ, it may therefore be appropriate to ascribe to the Holy Spirit that active divine presence beyond the bounds of the church which Wesley calls *prevenient grace*. This works, for instance, through conscience, which Wesley links to the Son as "the true light, which enlighteneth every man which cometh into the world—And it is his Spirit who giveth thee an inward check, who causeth thee to feel uneasy, when thou walkest in any instance contrary to the light which he hath given thee".[9] "Salvation," said Wesley, "begins with what is usually termed preventing grace, including . . . the first transient conviction of having sinned against God."[10] It would seem, then, that the Christian mission may count on the preparatory work of the Holy Spirit at least in bringing people to conviction of sin. Then also the Spirit of faith in the fuller and positive sense must be invoked:

> O that the world might know
> The all-atoning Lamb!
> Spirit of faith, descend, and show
> The virtue of his name;
> The grace which all may find,
> The saving power impart;
> And testify to all mankind
> And speak in every heart.[11]

III. *The Mission Invites to Discipleship*

Those whom the risen Lord sends on mission are themselves already "disciples" (*mathetai*, Matthew 28:16). They are now to "disciple all mankind" (as Wesley translates the Greek verb *matheuo*, Matthew 28:19). In what does this *discipleship* consist, which is both the qualification for being sent and also the aim of mission?

It consists first of all in *confessing* Christ. In a saying that occurs in variant forms in the synoptic gospels, Jesus promises that "every one who acknowledges me before men, I also will acknowledge before my Father who is in heaven; but whoever denies me before men, I also will deny before my Father who is in heaven" (Matthew 10:32-33 = Luke 12:8-9; cf. Mark 8:38; Luke 9:26). When Jesus comes on the scene, the final judgment is being anticipated according as people acknowledge him or not. "If you confess with your lips that Jesus is Lord, and believe in your heart that God raised him from the dead, you will be saved" (Romans 10:9); and, as the apostle Paul goes on to acknowledge, to call on the name of the Lord supposes belief in him, and to believe in him requires having heard of him, and to hear of him requires a preacher, and a preacher can only be sent (Romans 10:14-17). The mission is intended to make confessing believers.

According to Jesus himself, however, it is not enough to invoke his name in mere lip service: "Not every one who says to me, 'Lord, Lord' shall enter the kingdom of heaven, but he who does the will of my Father who is in heaven" (Matthew 7:21). It is not only a matter of "hearing" the words of Jesus but also of "doing" them (Luke 6:46). The apostles are instructed by the risen Lord to "teach" the converts "to observe all that I have commanded you" (Matthew 28:20). The true disciple has a *faith that works by love*. John Wesley consistently cited that phrase from Galatians 5:6 to stress the need for continuing sanctification. We shall not finally be justified on account of our works (for salvation is entirely by God's grace), but we shall not be saved without good works (for they are the evidence and product of our faith).

The sacramental sign of believing, confessing, working discipleship is *baptism*. The mission aims at bringing people to baptism in the expectation that they will then go on to live the baptismal life of faith. To the end of his life, John Wesley maintained the Anglican doctrine that baptism is God's instrument of regeneration in infants, and many Methodist have since held that infant baptism is at least an appropriate sign of prevenient grace. But Wesley also clearly preached that baptism was a "broken reed" and not to be leaned on, if persons had fallen away from their baptism: "The question is not, what you was made in baptism . . . but what are you now? Is the Spirit of adoption now in you heart? . . . I ask not, whether you *was* born of water and of the Spirit, but are you *now* the temple of the Holy Ghost? . . . Who denies that you were then made children of God, and heirs of the kingdom of heaven? But, notwithstanding this, ye are children of the devil. Therefore, ye must be born again."[12] The notion of multiple rebirths is difficult (can a man enter a third time into his mother's womb, or a fourth, or a fifth . . . ?). Yet our situation in a declining Christendom requires that we at least recall to their baptism many who never entered into its existential implications or else fell away from them. And those whom the mission leads to faith without their having previously been baptized, we should bring to baptism as soon as they may responsibly profess their faith.

Baptism "in the name of the Father and of the Son and of the Holy Spirit" (not, be it noted, in the currently fashionable formula of Creator, Redeemer and Sustainer) was instituted, according to St. Matthew's gospel, by the risen Lord himself. It is the eminent sign of that salvation which Wesley loved to depict under the Pauline imagery of adoption: as sons and daughters in the Son, we through Christ and in the Spirit call upon God as "Abba, Father" (Romans 8:14-17; Galatians 4:4-7).

The life in Christ is sustained by word and sacrament in *the Lord's Supper*. The eucharistic prayer follows the pattern of Ephesians 2:18, whereby we have access to the Father through Christ in the Holy Spirit. The blessings of the Father reach us through Christ in the Holy Spirit as we feed on the words of the gospel and take into ourselves the signs of Christ's body and blood. As those who already share in the fellowship of the Lord's table, Christians have the mission of inviting all to prepare themselves for the great banquet of God's kingdom (Matthew 22:1-13).

IV. The Lasting Importance of the Mission

"Freely you have received, freely give" (Matthew 10:8, KJV). Those words addressed by Jesus to the apostles he sent out on mission during his earthly ministry summarize exactly the movement of the continuing mission also. Graced itself by God, the Christian church is to be what the Second Vatican Council called the "sign and instrument" that offers to the world the divine chance of eternal *salvation*, beginning now. As sinners forgiven by God, we must declare to others the divine forgiveness on which fallen humanity depends for the restoration of right relationships with God and neighbor. With "a thousand tongues" we must proclaim:

> Look unto him, ye nations, own
> Your God, ye fallen race;
> Look, and be saved through faith alone,
> Be justified by grace![13]

As those who have been started on the path of sanctification, we must urge upon others, by word and example, that "holiness without which no one shall see the Lord" (Hebrews 12:14, a favorite text of Wesley). For in the words of Charles's hymn "Father of Jesus Christ, my Lord":

> Eternal life to all mankind
> Thou hast in Jesus given,
> And all who seek, in him shall find
> The happiness of heaven.[14]

A generation ago, the Dutch missiologist Johannes Blauw pointed to the fact that the Christian mission marked a "great turning point" in the biblical history of salvation: Whereas the Old Testament was characterized by a "centripetal" vision of the nations flocking one day to Jerusalem, the New Testament is launched by the "centrifugal" impulse of the risen Christ sending his witnesses to the ends of the earth.[15] Therein lies, I would suggest, an indication of the *urgency* of the mission. Many have claimed to show roads to salvation. Some have proved false; with others the case may still be open. Christians trust only one, Jesus Christ who is himself "the way, the truth, and the life" (John 14:6). It is therefore incumbent on us to make him known to others. We may count on what the Sri Lankan evangelist Daniel Niles called "the previousness of Jesus."[16] The Word and the Spirit are already at work, as we saw, in prevenient grace. Those who go on mission as his witnesses are assured by the risen Lord that "lo, I am with you always, to the close of the age" (Matthew 28:20). He had already promised his apostles in his earthly ministry: "He who hears you hears me" (Luke 10:16).

Until "the close of the age," the Christian mission remains, in the words of the Anglican bishop Stephen Neill, "the unfinished task."[17] In mainstream Protestantism, the crisis of confidence in evangelistic mission across geographical boundaries is an indicator that many appear in practice to have given up on the job altogether, and certainly I have not found there in the last generation a source of much helpful theological reflection on mission either. But the Lord's commission to his followers remains *permanent*. For there will always be those to whom the gospel must be presented for the first time, and then no doubt again. The loss of what D. T. Niles called "the westernity of the base" should not perhaps surprise us, given what Johannes Blauw termed the "ex-centricity" of the mission. With the numerical weight of Christianity having shifted to the southern hemisphere, we ourselves may gratefully expect to receive the witness of Christians from the other side of the equator, as well as from such more recently evangelized nations as Korea or the recently liberated churches of the communist world. We shall not thereby be relieved of our own responsibility to spread the gospel at home and abroad.

For the gospel is finally about *eternal bliss*. "Thou hast made us for thyself," confessed St. Augustine to the Triune God, "and our hearts are restless until they find their rest in thee."[18] God wishes to share his holiness and his happiness with his human creatures: "The glory of God," said St. Irenaeus, "is living humanity, and the life of humanity is the vision of God."[19] The biblical picture of the heavenly city is that of praise and feasting, with every tear wiped dry. "And to crown all," said John Wesley in his sermon on "The New Creation," "there will be a deep, an intimate, an uninterrupted union with God; a constant communion with the Father and his Son Jesus Christ, though the Spirit; a continual enjoyment of the Three-One God, and of all the creatures in him!"[20]

CHAPTER SEVENTEEN

Why Wesley Was a Trinitarian

I. A Deliberate Trinitarian

"I know not," says Wesley in his sermon *On the Trinity* (1775), "how anyone can be a Christian believer till 'he hath' (as St. John speaks) 'the witness in himself'; till 'the Spirit of God witnesses with his spirit that he is a child of God'—that is, in effect, till God the Holy Ghost witnesses that God the Father has accepted him through the merits of God the Son—and having this witness he honours the Son and the blessed Spirit 'even as he honours the Father'. Not that every Christian believer adverts to this; perhaps at first not one in twenty; but if you ask any of them a few questions, you will easily find it is implied in what he believes."[1] In that passage one finds indicated the biblical basis, the soteriological grounding, and the doxological intention of Wesley's doctrine of the Trinity. Each of those will be expounded in a systematic way in what follows: the scriptural evidence of a trinitarian faith, its saving significance, and its importance for worship. But first of all, there is, in Wesley's case, a historical point to be made.

One can imagine an objector intruding at the outset: Of course Wesley was a trinitarian; at his juncture in the history of doctrine and ideas there was no real alternative to such an inherited belief. I have in fact heard the objection made, but it arises from (let us say) incomplete information. Wesley was well aware of the Deists, the Socinians, and the Arians among his contemporaries. John Toland's *Christianity not Mysterious* (1696) and Matthew Tindal's *Christianity as Old as Creation* (1730) had indeed been countered by Bishop Joseph Butler's *Analogy of Religion* (1736), but the Deistic stream that began as early as Lord Herbert of Cherbury (1583–1648) had certainly not dried up. Joseph Priestley advocated Socinianism in his *Appeal to the Serious and Candid Professors of Christianity* (1770), and in 1773 Theophilus Lindsey seceded from the Church of England to form a Unitarian congregation. John Wesley, in a letter of April 17, 1776 to Mary Bishop, strongly commended the book of William Jones (1726–

1800), *The Catholic Doctrine of a Trinity* (1756), which was written to refute the anti-trinitarian interpretation of the Scriptures launched by Samuel Clarke (1675–1729) and to combat "the attempt" by a late Bishop of Clogher "to propagate Arianism." In the same letter, Wesley recalls that the "application" of the doctrine to "our hearts" and "lives" is "abundantly supplied by my brother's *Hymns*."[2] Wesley is here referring, principally at least, to the *Hymns on the Trinity* published by Charles in 1767: this collection is structured in its first four parts according to Jones of Nayland's book ("The Divinity of Christ," "The Divinity of the Holy Ghost," "The Plurality and Trinity of Persons," and "The Trinity in Unity") and takes as its scriptural texts those adduced by Jones; and to these 136 hymns Charles Wesley then adds 52 more "Hymns and Prayers to the Trinity."

The seriousness with which John Wesley took anti-trinitarianism and opposed it is shown by the fact that even at his most "catholic spirited," he refused his hand to Arians, Socinians and Deists, for their heart was not right with his heart. (In the famous sermon on *Catholic Spirit*, Wesley rejected doctrinal "latitudinarianism," saying that "a man of a truly catholic spirit . . . is as fixed as the sun in his judgment concerning the main branches of Christian doctrine," and Wesley there set out the Christian faith in a trinitarian pattern.[3]) Thus in a letter of July 3, 1756 to James Clarke, Wesley writes: "And could any man answer these questions, 'Dost thou believe in the Lord Jesus Christ, God over all, blessed for evermore?' (which, indeed, no Arian, semi-Arian, or Socinian can do). . . . If, I say, any man could answer these questions in the affirmative, I would gladly give him my hand."[4] And, at the christological heart of trinitarianism, Wesley writes in *The Character of a Methodist* : "We believe Christ to be the eternal, supreme God; and herein we are distinguished from the Socinians and Arians. But as to all opinions which do not strike at the root of Christianity, we think and let think."[5] (Those Methodists who have declined into "Liberal Protestantism" are apt to quote only the last clause in isolation.) We shall see later why, in a positive way, Wesley judged faith in the Trinity to be essential to Christianity.

It should by now be clear that Wesley knew, and declined, some contemporary alternatives to the trinitarian faith. Let us therefore begin on our positive exposition, taking Wesley as partner and guide in the systematic work. We shall elaborate in turn on the biblical, soteriological, and doxological dimensions of the doctrine of the Trinity as these are found in Wesley.

II. The Scriptural Basis of Trinitarian Doctrine

Wesley claimed to be "a man of one book," *homo unius libri*.[6] In George Croft Cell's neat formulation, this meant that the Holy Scriptures constituted not so much the "boundary of his reading" as "the center of gravity in his thinking."[7] We may therefore rightly expect that he would accept the doctrine of the Trinity if he was persuaded it was scriptural. Wesley did indeed declare that he "dare not insist upon anyone's using the word 'Trinity' or 'Person'" for an objector might maintain that he did "not find those terms in the Bible." Wesley for his part said, "I use them myself without any scruple, because I know of none better"; and so his occasional adoption of the phrase "the Three-One God" must be seen as a terminological accommodation to others.[8] But the substance of the doctrine, and of course the triune Name, Wesley did believe to be biblical.

Wesley's 1775 sermon *On the Trinity* was composed in Cork, Ireland, upon request, and the text proposed to him was "There are three that bear record in heaven, the Father, the Word, and the Holy Ghost: and these three are one." Wesley shows himself well aware that the textual authenticity of 1 John 5:7 was questionable, but he thinks that Bengel has proved its genuineness. Not many modern scholars would agree with that judgment; but in any case, the passage we quoted at the outset makes it clear that Wesley had other biblical material at his disposal. As is characteristic of him whenever he defends the doctrine of the Trinity, Wesley looks to the Scriptures for, above all, the divinity of Christ and the work of Christ and of the Holy Spirit in our salvation. That, in fact, is one of the chief routes by which the early Church historically established the doctrine of the Trinity, and the biblical basis remains exegetically defensible and indeed persuasive. Let us look at the conclusions of two or three respected New Testament scholars among our own contemporaries.

The Roman Catholic Raymond E. Brown faces the most narrowly formulated question, "Does the New Testament call Jesus God?"[9] Of the texts that are leading candidates for allowing an affirmative answer, almost all present textual, grammatical, syntactical or exegetical problems. Brown allows five "probable" cases: (1) John 1:18, taking the manuscript reading "No one has ever seen God; the only *God* [not Son], who is in the bosom of the Father, he has made him known"; (2) Romans 9:5, punctuating so as to get "Christ, who is God over all, blessed for ever" (this was a favorite text of Wesley's in this connexion, and the corresponding punctuation has lately been meticulously defended by Bruce M. Metzger[10]); (3) Titus 2:13, construing "our great *God and Savior* Jesus Christ"; (4) 2 Peter 1:1, similarly construing "our *God and Savior* Jesus Christ"; and (5) 1 John 5:20, taking "his Son Jesus Christ" as the referent for "This is the true

God." These five "probable" cases are outbid by three that are "certain" in Brown's estimation: (1) John 1:1, where the absence of a definite article is not considered significant in the predicate "And the Word was *God*"; (2) Hebrews 1:8-9, where "Thy throne, O God" from Psalm 45:6 is applied to "the Son"; and (3) John 20:28, where Thomas' acclamation of the risen Christ as "My Lord and my God" was the one text which even R. Bultmann allowed in his critical essay on the confession of Jesus Christ as "God and Savior" in the membership Basis of the World Council of Churches. While that is hardly a rich harvest, and each case has to be argued and can be contested individually, the liturgical settings or resonances of several of the above texts point us to the most important factor in an assessment of whether there is a recognition of Christ's "divinity" in the New Testament, namely the fact that he was confessed and worshipped as "Lord." That most frequent title appears to be both a baptismal confession (e. g. Rom. 10:9; 1 Cor. 12:3) and a hymnic acclamation (it is particularly striking that the hymn of Philippians 2:5-11 uses the strongly monotheistic language of Isaiah 45:23 in calling Jesus Christ "Lord" while not neglecting "the glory of God the Father").

The doxological recognition of Christ's divinity has certain broader presuppositions and implications for his person and work in a trinitarian context according to the New Testament. Here we may turn to another contemporary biblical scholar and this time a Methodist, namely Arthur W. Wainwright, the author of *The Trinity in the New Testament*.[11] (When I receive congratulations on the grounds of my namesake's excellent book on the Trinity, I try to accept the compliments gracefully, and I can only hope that Arthur does the same when people attribute my writings to him.) Arthur Wainwright's importance in this connection resides especially in his demonstration that the New Testament writers' recognition of Christ's divinity consists also in their attribution of divine *functions* to him. He is given a part in jobs that belong to God alone. Christ has a role in creation (1 Cor. 8:6; Col. 1:16; Heb. 1:2; John 1:1); in judgment (Matt. 3:12 = Luke 3:17; Mark 8:38; cf. Matt. 1:32-33 = Luke 12:8-9; Matt. 25:31-46; John 5:22,27,30; 12:47-48; Acts 10:42; 17:31; Rom. 2:16; 1 Cor. 4:4-5; 2 Cor. 5:10; 2 Tim. 4:1; Rev. 22:12); and in salvation (Matt. 1:21; Mark 2:10; Luke 7:48, 19:9-10; John 3:17; 11:25; 12:47; Acts 2:21; 4:12; 5:31; 13:23; 15:11; Gal. 1:4; 3:13; 5:1; Eph. 2:16; 1 Thess. 1:10; 1 Tim. 1:15; 2 Tim. 1:10; Titus 2:13-14; Heb. 9:28; 2 Peter 1:1,11; 2:20; 3:2,18). It may of course be that the protological, cosmic and eschatological functions of Christ are here extrapolated from present experiences of salvation in him, but that itself would be positive testimony to the strength of conviction among the earliest Christians concerning his divine identity.

As I said, one of the chief routes by which the early Church established the doctrine of the Trinity was the recognition of Christ's divinity and the parts played by him and by the Holy Spirit in our salvation (more will be said about the Holy Spirit shortly). With what proved to be conclusive force, St. Athanasius argued in the first place from the fact that Christ was an object of worship on the Church's part, and it would be an unthinkable idolatry if he were not God; and in the second place, only God can save us, and so we should be lost if the putative agents of our salvation were not divine.[12] The explicitation of New Testament faith into developed trinitarian doctrine has lately been legitimized once again by our third biblical scholar, who is another Methodist, namely Leander E. Keck, in an article on "The New Testament and Nicea."[13] That this track is taken by a professional *Neutestamentler*, rather than (say) a historian of doctrine or a dogmatician, is particularly important. For, as Keck himself writes, "it can hardly be stated too strongly that 'Nicea' plays no role whatever in historical-critical New Testament study. . . . In fact, to a considerable degree, often unacknowledged, the engine of historical criticism was driven by a revolt against the influence of Nicea (and Chalcedon) on the interpretation of the New Testament. That is to say, historical criticism undertook to liberate the texts from the dogmatic reading of scripture which Nicea represents."

Keck maintains the preexistence of Christ in "the hymnic/creedal passages" of Philippians 2:5-11, Colossians 1:15-20, Hebrews 1:3, and John 1:1-18. (Interestingly, he does this over against J. D. G. Dunn, who is a British Methodist. James Dunn has apparently not yet removed all traces of the Presbyterianism from which he came to us: it will be remembered that that tradition was a seedbed for Unitarianism!) Even more importantly, Keck brings the preexistence and divine identity of Christ into relation with his saving work. Keck admits that there is a superficial plausibility to Arian interpretations of certain passages in the New Testament, particularly where Christ is in view as teacher and example. But he recognizes that "a superficial view of Jesus cannot deal with a profound view of sin." He finds an awareness of this above all in Paul, in the Letter to the Hebrews, and in the Fourth Gospel. To take only Paul, Keck writes that "in Romans, the fullest christological statement appears in Rom. 8:1-11, where Paul not only shifts from relational language ("no condemnation," v. 1) to the participatory language associated with redemption, but presents the Christ-event as the radical solution to the radical anthropology to which he penetrated in chapter 7; and of Galatians 3:23 to 4:11 (which culminates in "When the time had fully, God sent forth his Son, born of woman, born under law, to redeem those who were under law"), Keck comments that "here it is even clearer that redemption depends on the Son's entering into the human plight." Keck concludes that a "thread that runs through Paul's diverse ways of regarding the situation of the unredeemed, unrectified self, is the self's inability to save itself. . . . Athanasius too held a radical view of human nature and its salvation. And it was precisely this radical need that he sought to satisfy by insisting that the savior was nothing less than *homoousios* with the Father. No one less would do, could do, what needed to be done. Does the same logic lie latent in Paul's understanding? . . . In deepening the inherited theology of rectification to redemption, Paul—in his own way— seems to have sensed this." Thus Keck reinforces the argument of the Anglican New Testament scholar Reginald H. Fuller who, in the heyday of "functional" christologies, claimed that nothing less than an ontology would correspond to the New Testament witness.[14]

There was a second, complementary route by which the early Church established the doctrine of the Trinity. A. W. Wainwright points to a striking number of "triadic" passages in the New Testament: Matt. 28:19; Luke 1:35; 24:49; John 1:33-34; 14:16; 14:26; 16:15; 20:21-22; Acts 2:33; 2:38-39; Rom. 14:17-18; 15:16; 15:30; 1 Cor. 12:4-6; 2 Cor. 1:21-22; 3:3; 13:14; Gal. 3:11-14; 4:6; Eph. 2:18; 2:20-22; 3:14-16; Phil. 3:3; Col. 1:6-8; 2 Thess. 2:13-14; Titus 3:4-6; Heb. 6:4-6; 1 Peter 1:2; 4:14; 1 John 4:2; 4:13-14; Jude 20–21. While many of these "threefold" passages simply reveal unreflectingly something about their writers' "background of worship and thought," some of them start to face what Wainwright calls the "problem of the mutual relationship of Father, Son and Spirit," and all of them provided building-blocks for the patristic Church to construct its developed doctrine of the Trinity.

The continuing groundplan was supplied chiefly by the practice of baptism in the threefold Name of Father, Son, and Holy Spirit. St. Athanasius insists that Christians professed that faith at their baptism and were baptized in that Name: their very salvation was therefore at stake in the divinity of the Three, since only God could save.[15] Closely allied to the baptismal use was the address of eucharist and doxology "to the Father through the Son in the Holy Spirit," or as St. Basil also shows in his treatise *On the Holy Spirit*, "to the Father with the Son and with the Holy Spirit" or "to the Father and to the Son and to the Holy Spirit." Thus the Council of Constantinople in 381 was finally able to declare Christian belief in "the Holy Spirit, the Lord and Life-giver, . . . who with the Father and the Son together is worshiped and glorified." That such as declaration took so long in coming was doubtless due to the fact that the Spirit's divinity did not need to be argued for, until the Spirit's distinct personality had been fully recognized; and then in that case, very similar arguments could be advanced as were advanced by the Nicenes in favor of the divinity of the Son.

When John Wesley, in his *Letter to a Roman Catholic* (1749), set forth the faith of "a true Protestant," this *homo unius libri* did not in fact invoke the *sola Scriptura*.[16] Rather he based his exposition on the Nicene-Constantinopolitan creed.[17] He could do so because he was obviously satisfied with that trinitarian creed as a summary of the biblical faith. It is equally obvious that Wesley, throughout his works, in turn uses that trinitarian creed as a hermeneutical grid for the reading of the Scriptures. In both directions Wesley is aligned with the vast majority of Christians who have ever been.

We move now to insist even more directly on the Trinity in the substantive history and experience of salvation, lest it be mistakenly thought that so far we had been engaged in a merely formal exercise of scriptural "proof-texting."

III. The Soteriological Grounding of Trinitarian Doctrine

Returning once again to the passage from Wesley's sermon *On the Trinity* with which we began, we find that Wesley starts with the available experience of the Holy Spirit, the witness of the Spirit of God with the spirit of the Christian believer that he or she is a child of God. In his *Letter to a Roman Catholic*, Wesley expounds more fully the work of the Holy Spirit in believers: "I believe the infinite and eternal Spirit of God, equal with the Father and the Son, to be not only perfectly holy in himself, but the immediate cause of all holiness in us: enlightening our understandings, rectifying our wills and affections, renewing our natures, uniting our persons to Christ, assuring us of the adoption of sons, leading us in our actions, purifying and sanctifying our souls and bodies to a full and eternal enjoyment of God." Notice that it is only as fully God that the Holy Spirit can do these things; and that the Holy Spirit does these things "immediately" in us, that is to say by personal presence. Our salvation depends on, and consists in, our being made "partakers of the divine nature," to use the phrase of 2 Peter 1:4 that Wesley lighted upon on the morning of his conversion in 1738. The appropriate agent is God the Holy Spirit.

Then again, in the sermon *On the Trinity*, the witness of the Holy Spirit is to the effect that the believer "is a child of God," that "God the Father has accepted him through the merits of God the Son." We become "sons and daughters in the Son" (*filii et filiae in Filio*). As Wesley writes in the *Letter to a Roman Catholic*, "the one God . . . is in a peculiar manner the Father of those whom he regenerates by his Spirit, whom he adopts in his Son as co-heirs with him and crowns with an eternal inheritance." (Notice, of course, that this is not a detraction from, but

267

rather a confirmation of, the uniqueness of Christ, who is, says Wesley following Nicea, "the proper, natural Son of God, God of God, very God of very God," whom "the Father . . . hath begotten from eternity.") The "adoption" of believers is, for Wesley, a major soteriological category. It is, therefore, disturbing to see it neglected in the statement on Doctrine and Theology of the 1988 General Conference of the United Methodist Church; and since that neglect probably derives from the extreme difficulty which the statement appears to find in naming "the Father," it may be useful here to say a word about the name of the First Person of the Trinity.

Christian linguistic usage depends principally on Jesus, who presumably knew best the character of the One who sent him, and how that One was named and should be addressed. Apart from the cry of dereliction, all the recorded prayers of Jesus have him addressing "Abba, Father," and the Christian use of that form (Luke 11:2 = Matt. 6:9; Rom. 8:15; Gal. 4:6) is a *privilege* (not an imposition, in either direction), a privilege afforded to adoptive sons and daughters who are thus graciously given a share with the Jesus whom the gospels can present as speaking in sovereign and free terms of "the Son" and "the Father" (Matt. 11:25-27 = Luke 10:21-22; Mark 13:32; and often in John). Moreover, when Jesus teaches on the fatherhood of God, it is not in terms of a despot, but rather of a Father, who feeds the birds of the air—"Are you not of more value than they?" (Matt. 6:26), a Father without whom not a sparrow falls to the ground; but "even the hairs of your head are all numbered. Fear not, therefore; you are of more value than many sparrows" (Matt. 10:29-31). John Wesley spent thirteen of his "standard sermons" expounding the Sermon on the Mount. Every day of his life as an ordained minister he would say the second collect of Morning Prayer which finds in the service of this God our "perfect freedom."

Remark again, in the sermon *On the Trinity*, that God the Father accepts believers "through the merits of God the Son." The redemptive death of the divine Son is recognized by Wesley to be indispensable to the Christian faith, as indeed to the world's salvation. That is obvious throughout his preaching, but let us just take one polemical statement as an example which bears very clearly on our trinitarian concern. In a letter of February 7, 1778 to Mary Bishop, Wesley writes: "Nothing in the Christian system is of greater consequence than the doctrine of Atonement. It is properly the distinguishing point between Deism and Christianity. . . . Give up the Atonement, and the Deists are agreed with us. . . . What saith the Scripture? It says, 'God was in Christ, reconciling the world unto Himself'; that 'He made Him, who knew no sin, to be a sin-offering for us'. . . . But undoubtedly, as long as the world stands, there will be a thousand objections to this scriptural doctrine. For still the preaching of Christ crucified will be foolishness to the wise men of the world. However, let *us* hold the precious truth fast in our heart as well as in our understanding; and we shall find by happy experience that this is to us the wisdom of God and the power of God."[18]

In sum, our salvation is for Wesley the differentiated but united work of the Three Persons of the Godhead; it sets us into an appropriate relation to each Person, and it gives us, as will shortly be insisted, a share in their divine communion. The Holy Trinity appears, therefore, as both the origin and goal of soteriology. That can meanwhile be expressed in a great trinitarian hymn of Charles Wesley from the *Hymns and Sacred Poems* of 1739 which figured continuously in the official British Methodist repertory until it was shamefully dropped in 1983:

> Since the Son hath made me free,
> Let me taste my liberty;
> Thee behold with open face,
> Triumph in thy saving grace,
> Thy great will delight to prove,
> Glory in thy perfect love.
>
> Abba, Father! hear thy child,
> Late in Jesus reconciled;
> Hear, and all the graces shower,
> All the joy, and peace, and power,
> All my Saviour asks above,
> All the life and heaven of love.
>
> . . . .
>
> Heavenly Adam, Life divine,
> Change my nature into thine!
> Move and spread throughout my soul,
> Actuate, and fill the whole!
> Be it I no longer now
> Living in the flesh, but thou.
>
> Holy Ghost, no more delay!
> Come, and in thy temple stay!
> Now thine inward witness bear,
> Strong, and permanent, and clear;
> Spring of life, thyself impart,
> Rise eternal in my heart!

269

With that hymn we may now move into the doxological dimension of faith in the Trinity.

IV. *The Doxological Intention of Trinitarian Doctrine*

In our passage from Wesley's sermon *On the Trinity*, the preacher says that the Christian believer "honours the Son and the blessed Spirit even as he honours the Father." The Johannine text which is there echoed (John 5:23) implies that it is a single worship which is offered the divine Persons even though they are distinctly named. We recall again the words of the Nicene-Constantinopolitan creed: ". . . . And in the Holy Spirit, . . . who with the Father and the Son together is worshiped and glorifed."

In his sermon of 1780 on *Spiritual Worship*, John Wesley expounds the First Letter of John in a trinitarian way.[19] He says the Epistle "treats, first, severally, of communion with the Father, chapter one, verses 5-10; of communion with the Son, chapters two and three; of communion with the Spirit, chapter four"; and "secondly, conjointly, of the testimony of the Father, Son, and Holy Ghost, on which faith in Christ, the being born of God, love to God and his children, the keeping his commandments, and victory over the world, are founded, chapter five, verses 1-12." The eternal life of which St. John speaks "commences when it pleases the Father to reveal his Son in our hearts; when we first know Christ, being enabled to 'call him Lord by the Holy Ghost' ; when we can testify, our conscience bearing us witness in the Holy Ghost, 'the life which I now live, I live by faith in the Son of God, who loved me and gave himself for me'. . . . Then it is that heaven is opened in the soul, that the proper heavenly state commences, while the love of God, as loving us, is shed abroad in the heart, . . . producing . . . an entire, clear, full acquiescence in the whole will of God, enabling us to 'rejoice evermore, and in everything to give thanks'." True religion, Wesley continues, "consists in the knowledge and love of God, as manifested in the Son of his love, through the eternal Spirit. And this naturally leads to every heavenly temper, and to every good word and work." Wesley concludes his sermon with the exhortation: "And this moment, and every moment, 'present yourselves a living sacrifice, holy, acceptable to God,' and 'glorify him with your body, and with your spirit, which are God's'." The trinitarian form, content and scope of "spiritual worship" according to Wesley could hardly be clearer.

When we look at the hymns composed and published by the Wesleys as evidence of their doxological practice, we find three main patterns of trinitarian reference. First, thanks and prayers may be addressed to the

Father through the Son in the Holy Spirit. Second, the divine Persons may be invoked either separately or in succession. Third, praise may be ascribed to all three Persons together. Each of these patterns has scriptural roots and emerges very early in the Christian tradition. As to the first pattern, we note that already Christ "through the eternal Spirit offered himself without blemish to God" (Heb. 9:14), and consequently "through him [Christ] we . . . have access in one Spirit to the Father" (Eph. 2:18). The fundamental structure of the eucharistic prayer in Christian liturgy is to address the Father through Christ in the Spirit. As to the second pattern, dying Stephen already called directly on "Lord Jesus" (Acts 7:59), the primitive church prayed him to come, "*Maranatha*" (1 Cor. 16:22; Rev. 22:20), and hymns addressed "to Christ as to a god" are certainly as early as Pliny's letter to Trajan, so there is early as well as ample precedent for Charles Wesley's "Christ, whose glory fills the skies" and the many other Wesleyan hymns that are christological in address. Prayers and hymns addressed to the Holy Spirit in particular are postscriptural, but once the distinct divine personality of the Holy Spirit had been recognized, the way was in principle open, and there are famous examples in the Byzantine Pentecostarion and in the Golden Sequence of the medieval West for pneumatologically addressed hymns (though it must be admitted that the proportion of them in Wesley's output is greater than in the tradition in general). One of the most interestingly structured of Wesleyan hymns for our purposes is the verse-paraphrase which John appends (its authorship is often ascribed to him rather than to Charles) to his sermon on the Lord's Prayer.[20] The hymn moves twice through a threefold sequence of address to Father, Son and Spirit, before finally addressing all together the "co-equal, co-eternal Three." It is the address of the three divine Persons in unity which constitutes the third principal pattern of trinitarian worship. This has embryonic scriptural warrant in the doxologies "to God and to the Lamb" of Revelation 5:13 and 7:10, but its fuller development, as is clear from Basil's treatise *On the Holy Spirit*, was part of the recognition of the distinct divine personality of the Holy Spirit.

What trinitarian doctrine does is to help the church worship God as God stands self-revealed and, therefore (since God does not deceive), as God is.[21] St. Basil points out that thanksgiving is appropriately made *to* the Father *through* the Son *in* the Holy Spirit, since that matches the way by which God's blessings reach us *from* the Father *through* the Son *in* the Spirit. But since God is thereby revealed to *be* Father, Son and Holy Spirit, it is appropriate that, when God is contemplated *per se*, praise should be offered conjointly *to* the Father *and to* the Son *and to* the Holy Spirit.

So far, we have seen how, according to Wesley and with reason, trinitarian doctrine corresponds to the scriptural witness, to the experience of salvation, and to true worship. In conclusion, we shall see how deep is the association between this deliberate trinitarianism and a personal communion.

V. A Personal Communion

In the sermon *On the Trinity*, Wesley declares that he neither knows nor needs to know *how* "God is Three and One," but believes only *that* "God is Three and One." It is just the same as with the incarnation: "'The word was made flesh.' I believe this fact also. . . . But as to the *manner*, *how* he was made flesh . . . I know nothing about it." But then, in a letter of August 3, 1771 to Jane Catherine March, while making the same point, Wesley immediately added: "The quaint device of styling them three offices rather than persons gives up the whole doctrine."[22]

Wesley was, of course, familiar with the Prayer Book catechism: "First, I learn to believe in God the Father, who hath made me, and all the world. Secondly, in God the Son, who hath redeemed me, and all mankind. Thirdly, in God the Holy Ghost, who sanctifieth me, and all the elect people of God." But clearly Wesley would not have considered that in listing "Creator, Redeemer, Sanctifier" he had thereby named the Trinity, for that would have been to reduce the "persons" to "offices." The appropriation of offices to persons can be done only in the context of a full trinitarian doctrine, such as Wesley found in the First, Second and Fifth Articles of Religion, and in the Athanasian Creed, for whose positive exposition Wesley had a high regard.[23] Such a doctrine affirms the personal relationships within the Trinity and consequently holds, in an Augustinian fashion, that "the works of God towards the outside are undivided," or, in the Cappadocian manner, that all God's works start from the Father, are mediated by the Son, and are completed in the Holy Spirit.[24]

It is both the being of God and our experience of salvation that are at stake in what Wesley calls "the quaint device of styling them three offices rather than persons." It is a matter of communion with God and within God. The word "person" is to be taken with full seriousness when used in connection either with the divine Trinity or with human beings. As the Greek Orthodox theologian John Zizioulas has recently recalled with great persuasion, a person, whether divine or human, lives only in relationship: "Being is communion."[25] John Wesley allowed that Christians might have, at particular points in their lives, a greater *sense* of communion with one or another of the divine persons.[26] But the Christian life was truly a communion with the Holy Trinity. Thus in his *Letter to a Roman Catholic* Wesley defined the church as those "who have fellowship with God the Father, Son and Holy Ghost."[27] Even more tellingly, perhaps, in his sermon on *The New Creation* he describes the final bliss in this way: "And to crown all, there will be a deep, an intimate, an uninterrupted union with God; a constant communion with the Father and his Son Jesus Christ, through the Spirit; a continual enjoyment of the Three-One God, and of all the creatures in him!"[28] Salvation thus consists in being given, by grace and in glory, a share in that divine communion of Father, Son and Holy Spirit such as had enacted our redemption in the incarnation, life, death and resurrection of Jesus Christ. We thereby attain our "chief end," which is "to glorify God and to enjoy him forever" (Westminster Catechism).

To sum up now in just a paragraph: Trinitarian doctrine corresponds, on the divine side, to what Wesley in another context called "The Scripture Way of Salvation"[29]: The Father saw the human need for redemption, the Son supplied it, the Holy Spirit applies it; and all this within their own loving communion, into which the Three-One God desires to bring us as our true worship. If Methodists are trinitarian, it is not primarily because Wesley was so. Rather we are grateful that, under God, Wesley transmitted to us what is quite simply the Christian faith. *Mutatis mutandis* we can endorse, as Wesley would have done, the words of St. Augustine at the start of his own treatise *On the Trinity*: "This is my faith, since it is also the catholic faith." This faith can be sung in Wesleyan words from the 1780 *Collection of Hymns for the Use of the People called Methodists*:

> Father of everlasting grace,
> Thy goodness and thy truth we praise,
> Thy goodness and thy truth we prove;
> Thou hast, in honour of thy Son,
> The gift unspeakable sent down,
> The Spir't of life, and power, and love.

> Send us the Spirit of thy Son
> To make the depths of Godhead known,
> To make us share the life divine;
> Send him the sprinkled blood t'apply,
> Send him our souls to sanctify,
> And show and seal us ever thine.

> So shall we pray, and never cease,
> So shall we thankfully confess
> Thy wisdom, truth, and power, and love,
> With joy unspeakable adore,

273

And bless, and praise thee evermore,
And serve thee as thy hosts above:

Till added to that heavenly choir
We raise our songs of triumph higher,
And praise thee in a bolder strain,
Outsoar the firstborn seraph's flight,
And sing, with all our friends in light,
Thy everlasting love to man.[30]

CONCLUSION

CONCLUSION

Continuing a Methodist Voice

In the preceding chapters it has been possible, I hope, to discern a consistent Methodist and Wesleyan voice. Sometimes the speaker has been an individual theologian writing in a scholarly capacity, sometimes such a theologian appointed to represent Methodism in an ecumenical context, sometimes a commission officially engaged in dialogue with other world Christian communions, sometimes a corporate body constitutionally charged with proclaiming and safeguarding Methodist doctrine in the Church catholic, sometimes a Wesleyan now joined to the heavenly company, sometimes John Wesley himself, or his brother Charles. Differences of opinion have occasionally been heard, but the ecclesial, spiritual, theological identity of the speakers is, I judge, unmistakable, even to people in other parts of the Christian world.

In ecumenical dialogue, it is important that we compare ideal with ideal, best with best, imperfect realization with imperfect realization. On the Methodist side, that means striking a strongly Wesleyan note. Even in its origins, the movement was, of course, wider than the Wesleys; others have joined the Methodist family at later points; and, in continuing developments, the degree of fidelity to the original vision of faith and pattern of action has been variable. But Methodism's dominant standards have been Wesleyan, and there have occurred periodic renewals of the Wesleyan spirit when slippage had become noticeable. Doctrinally and theologically, that has entailed at the formal level a recovery of the primacy of Scripture, a search for the authentic Tradition of Christianity, a cultivation of the experience of faith, and a disciplined use of our reasoning capacities in the service of Christ. At the substantive level, a Wesleyan renewal in doctrine and theology involves the affirmation, with Wesley, of the great tenets of the Church's belief: the transcendent Three-One God, Father, Son and Holy Spirit, one in deity and worship, three persons mutually indwelling and perfectly cooperating; the divine creation of the world and the vocation of humankind to holiness and happiness; the incarnation and atoning work of God the Son in Jesus Christ our Lord;

277

the Spirit of God, who is the source of all truth, renewal and communion; the need of fallen humankind to repent and believe the gospel; the divine provision of grace through word and sacrament; the summons to love of God and neighbor; the institution and gathering of a Church whose divine fellowship transcends time and space; the promise of a final judgment and victory, where all the redeemed will share in glorifying and enjoying God for ever.

If Methodism is to make a significant contribution to ecumenical dialogue into the future, it will be by virtue of what a distinctively Wesleyan voice can bring to the symphony of faith, as is indicated by the growing recognition accorded by Christians in other communions to John Wesley and his hymn-writer brother Charles. Indeed, Methodism's own place within a recognizably evangelical, catholic, orthodox Christianity may well depend on a deeper recovery and more vital renewal of Wesleyan form and substance.

Thirty-five years ago, the form and substance of the Christian faith in its Wesleyan perception was displayed by the Australian Methodist Colin W. Williams in a book whose arrangement largely followed the classic sources of fundamental theology and the classic topics of dogmatics, while giving a characteristically Wesleyan formulation to most of its chapter headings:

I. The Catholic Spirit: Doctrine and Opinion
II. Authority and Experience
III. The Order of Salvation: Prevenient Grace
IV. Original Sin
V. The Order of Salvation: Repentance and Justification
VI. The Atonement
VII. The Order of Salvation: The Work of the Holy Spirit
     in New Birth and Assurance
VIII. The Order of Salvation: Repentance in Believers
IX. The Doctrine of the Church
X. The Order of Salvation: Christian Perfection
XI. The Order of Salvation: Eschatology.[1]

Clearly, soteriology dominates (the Person of Christ and the Trinity, for instance, are treated under the Atonement), and that is faithful to Wesley. Indeed, the author's promise to present "John Wesley's Theology" is in general well kept. Williams's title further indicated an aim to present John Wesley's theology "Today." The contemporary significance of Wesley's theology was above all suggested in ecumenical applications at the end of each chapter. Williams was answering a call from within Methodism for help in articulating an authentic contribution to the search for Christian unity, and he sought to bring a Wesleyan approach and content to the discussion of questions that were current in the areas especially of faith and order.

Williams's book acquired a deserved popularity, and its wide use in seminary teaching served to give many students an appropriately simultaneous introduction to Wesley and to ecumenism. The task needs repeating a generation or two later. Since 1960, historical studies in aspects of Wesley's theology have multiplied,[2] and Wesley has been more recently "read" from various angles of interest.[3] The time is ripe for one or more new synopses of Wesley's entire theological vision and praxis, with an awareness of currently agitated ecumenical issues. Such studies would help to preserve and enhance Wesley's presence in the wider Christian Tradition and facilitate the job both of those who wish to continue speaking with a Methodist voice on the ecumenical scene and those who kindly agree to listen. These studies would provide a resource and supply a complement for the kind of *ad hoc* approach that characterizes most of the essays in the present book, where an ecumenical issue sets the agenda and Wesley is then invoked to help shape a characteristically Methodist response. (Of course, matters become ecumenical "issues" in the first place only because various Christian traditions are known or supposed to adopt different positions on them.)[4]

In my judgment, the ecumenical movement, and indeed the entire body of those who claim the name of Christ, is facing one large and comprehensive question that outcrops in many different ways and at many different levels. It is the matter of maintaining, in the presence of internal and external pressures, a recognizable continuing identity with historic Christianity. Of course, Christian history itself is multiform, and divisions among those who call themselves Christian render the whole notion problematic. But a principal aim, and partial achievement, of the modern ecumenical movement has been to discern the authentic Tradition of the dominical gospel and the apostolic faith in its historically, geographically, and culturally varied mainfestations.

At various levels, people are starting to display the sense of approaching a major fork in the road. To begin at the level of a single denomination in the United States, the Presbyterian Church (U.S.A.). Like several others, this Church experienced internal controversy following the November 1993 conference on "Re-imagining" that had gathered in Minneapolis under the banner of the Ecumenical Decade of Solidarity with Women. Historian Richard Lovelace, writing in *The Presbyterian Layman*, suggested that the availability of clear, widely distributed information, together with the economic realities of the dependence of denominational bureaucracies on financial support from the local congregations, put before laypeople and their pastors the opportunity to hear the call from Presbyterian scholars for fidelity to the classic Reformed heritage in face of institutional acquiescence in, and even approval of, the line represented by prominent speakers at the Minneapolis conference:

> Speakers rejected the transcendent holiness of God as presented in Scripture, opting instead for immanent pantheistic goddesses. One presenter offered three goddesses for worship, including Kali, the Hindu goddess of revenge who wears a necklace of skulls. Speakers denied the incarnation of Jesus as a Savior "from the top down," and recommended instead female human saviors who have worked their way up to the godhead "from the bottom up." The only doctrine of Atonement presented by the speakers was the imitation of these goddesses. The evangelistic mission of the Church was repeatedly rejected: instead of presenting Jesus Christ as Savior we were encouraged to learn from folk religions how to be polytheistic. Several speakers called for a "spirit-centered" faith as opposed to Christ-centered religion. Energy healing, acupuncture and the reincarnation of ancestral spirits were described as potential parts of this faith.[5]

Lovelace predicts that "the predominance of Liberalism, which has grown in our denomination since the 1920s, is about to collapse." If, "in a powerful convergence of informed theological conviction and economic action," mainstream Presbyterians insist upon a Reformation faith, they will seek "a leadership that can take them in a more biblical direction." The moral move for "the extreme Left" would be to "leave the denomination for organizations that share their views, such as the Metropolitan Community Church or the United Church of Christ."[6]

At the national level of the entire United States, the Princeton sociologist Robert Wuthnow has assembled evidence to show that, since the 1960s, denominationalism has declined as a stucturing factor in American religion, which is now more shaped by a realignment dividing "the left" from "the right," "religious liberals" from "religious conservatives."[7] These latter categories are theologically problematic (sociological surveys have a knack of begging too many theological questions in their formulations), but Wuthnow's presentation leaves the definite impression of a marked cleavage between those who, on doctrinal and moral issues, recognizably stick with the historic Christian Tradition and those who seek new ways. It is, of course, well known that membership is statistically in decline among what used to be considered the mainline denominations, especially towards the "liberal" end of the spectrum, and that the numbers grow among the more "conservative" bodies, including those which would identfy themselves as "independent" or "nondenominational."[8]

At the level of the Western world, Professor Wolfhart Pannenberg of the University of Munich in Germany, Lutheran author of the most intellectually distinguished and ecumenically rich systematic theology in the second half of the twentieth century,[9] sees the mainline Protestant Churches as wavering in their Christian identity, if not actually surrendering the substance of the Christian faith, thus becoming unable to present an alternative to the spiritual emptiness of erosive secularism. If the decline continues, Pannenberg forecasts that the only surviving communities in the third millennium will be Roman Catholic, Orthodox, and Protestant Evangelical.[10]

At the level of the largest Christian Church with the most universal presence, the leading Jesuit theologian Avery Dulles has suggested new strategies and forecast new alignments in ecumenical relations:

> The Churches that have held most steadfastly to the deposit of biblical and patristic faith, and those that have best resisted the allurements of modernity, may have most to offer to an age that is surfeited with the lax and the ephemeral. The time is ripe to welcome the more traditional and conservative Churches into the dialogue. For the Catholic Church it may not prove easy to reach a consensus with either the Orthodox or the conservative evangelicals, but these Churches and communities may have more to offer than some others because they have dared to be different. . . . Through earnest dialogue among communities that hold fast to their own heritage of faith, it may be possible to effect a new kind of fellowship, very valuable in its own way. A community of witnessing dialogue, cutting across denominational barriers, is one of the finest fruits of ecumenism. In such a community each Church can profit from listening to clear and unambiguous presentations of others' points of view; it stands to gain from hearing its own doctrines criticized from the perspective of outsiders. In this way individual believers may achieve a deeper realization of the ecclesial character of their own faith-commitments; the Churches can learn to formulate their distinctive doctrines more circumspectly, and all can acquire a deeper appreciation of other Christian traditions. As a result, the participating Churches may be able to find a path toward deeper convergence in the truth.[11]

At the level of the World Council of Churches, the Eighth Assembly, at Canberra in 1991, was literally set ablaze—in a fire ritual—by the Korean theologian Chung Hyun-Kyung; but it was above all the content of her speech on the theme of the assembly, "Come, Holy Spirit: Renew the Whole Creation" that became the spontaneous symbol of most of those trends in the World Council of Churches which provoked sharp reactions on the part of Orthodox and Evangelical participants.[12] The Eastern Orthodox and Oriental Orthodox statement reads in part:

> The Orthodox note that there has been an *increasing departure from the Basis* of the WCC. The latter has provided the framework for Orthodox participation in the World Council of Churches. Its text is: "The World Council of Churches is a fellowship of churches which confess the Lord Jesus Christ as God and Saviour according to the scriptures and therefore seek to fulfill together their common calling to the glory of the one God, Father, Son and Holy Spirit" (Constitution). Should the WCC not direct its future work along these lines, it would be in danger of ceasing to be an instrument aiming at the restoration of Christian unity and in that case it would tend to become a forum for an exchange of opinions without any specific Christian theological basis. In such a forum, common prayer will be increasingly difficult, and eventually will become impossible, since even a basic common theological vision will be lacking.
>
> The tendency to marginalize the Basis in WCC work has created some dangerous trends in the WCC. We miss from many WCC documents the affirmation that Jesus Christ is the world's Saviour. We perceive a growing *departure from biblically-based Christian understandings* of (a) the Trinitarian God; (b) salvation; (c) the "good news" of the gospel itself; (d) human beings as created in the image and likeness of God; and (e) the Church. . . .
>
> The Orthodox follow with interest, but also with a certain disquiet, the developments of the WCC towards the broadening of its aims in the direction of *relations with other religions*. The Orthodox support dialogue initiatives, particularly those aiming at the promotion of relations of openness, mutual respect and human cooperation with neighbours of other faiths. When dialogue takes place, Christians are called to bear witness to the integrity of their faith. A genuine dialogue involves greater theological efforts to express the Christian message in ways that speak to the various cultures of our world. All this, however, must occur on the basis of theological criteria which will define the limits of diversity. The biblical faith in God must not be changed. The definition of these criteria is a matter of theological study, and must constitute the first priority of the WCC in view of its desired broadening of aims.
>
> Thus, it is with alarm that the Orthodox have heard some presentations on the theme of this Assembly. With reference to the theme of the Assembly, the Orthodox still await the final texts. However, they observe that some people tend to affirm with very great ease the presence of the Holy Spirit in many movements and developments without discernment. The Orthodox wish to stress the factor of sin and error, which exists in every human action, and

separate the Holy Spirit from these. We must guard against a tendency *to substitute a "private" spirit, the spirit of the world or other spirits for the Holy Spirit* who proceeds from the Father and rests in the Son. Our tradition is rich in respect for local and national cultures, but we find it impossible to invoke the spirits of "earth, air, water and sea creatures." Pneumatology is inseparable from Christology or from the doctrine of the Holy Trinity confessed by the Church on the basis of Divine Revelation.

The Evangelicals' "Letter to Churches and Christians Worldwide" contained this passage:

> As the Assembly discussed the process of listening to the Spirit at work in every culture, we cautioned, with others, that discernment is required to identify the Spirit as the Spirit of Jesus Christ and thus to develop criteria for and limits to theological diversity. We argued for a high Christology to serve as the only authentic Christian base for dialogue with persons of other living faiths. . . .
>
> The ecumenical movement needs a theology rooted in the Christian revelation [as well as] relevant to contemporary problems. At present, there is insufficient clarity regarding the relationship between the confession of the Lord Jesus Christ as God and Saviour according to Scripture, the person and work of the Holy Spirit, and legitimate concerns which are part of the WCC agenda. We share many of these concerns, such as those related to justice, peace and the integrity of creation, to the contextualization (or inculturation) of the Gospel, and to religious pluralism. This theological deficit not only conspires against the work of the WCC as a Christian witness but also increases the tensions among its member churches.

These Orthodox and Evangelical voices are clearly calling the World Council of Churches back to the concerns of the classical ecumenical movement for Church unity and Christian mission based on the dominical gospel and the apostolic faith to which the Scriptures and authentic Tradition bear witness.[13]

Allowing for the lapse of two hundred years, there is a close correspondence between the classic ecumenical movement and the profile of John Wesley that informed Methodists, and others, would recognize. Wesley's vision, program, and praxis were marked by the following six principal features. First, he looked to the *Scriptures* as the primary and abiding testimony to the redemptive work of God in Christ. Second, he was utterly committed to the ministry of *evangelism*, where the gospel was to be preached to every creature and needed only to be accepted in faith. Third, he valued with respect to the Christian Tradition and the doctrine of the Church a *generous orthodoxy*, wherein theological opinions might

283

vary as long as they were consistent with the apostolic teaching.[14] Fourth, he expected *sanctification* to show itself in the moral earnestness and loving deeds of the believers. Fifth, he manifested and encouraged a *social concern* that was directed toward the neediest of neighbors. Sixth, he found in the *Lord's Supper* a sacramental sign of the fellowship graciously bestowed by the Triune God and the responsive sacrifice of praise and thanksgiving on the part of those who will glorify God and enjoy him for ever. These are the features which must be strengthened in contemporary Methodism, if we are to maintain our historic identity, speak with a significant voice on the ecumenical scene, and keep on a recognizably Christian track as the ways diverge.

Within the United Methodist Church in the United States, this will entail the deliberate reclamation of the historic doctrinal standards in practice as well as in theory, in substance as well as in form, necessitating a vital accountability to them on the part of bishops, preachers, administrators, seminary teachers, and candidates for ordination, and their use in nourishing the congregations and the courts of the Church.[15] In British Methodism and in some other parts of the Western world, a Wesleyan identity will need re-asserting in face of the inroads made by secular ideologies and practices such as we found Wolfhart Pannenberg lamenting in the case of Western Christianity more broadly.

Within the worldwide Methodist family, an aim should be to facilitate the appropriation of the Wesleyan heritage on the part particularly of those Churches in Asia, Africa and the Pacific which are growing rapidly and could become its chief transmitters into the future. Small but notable hints of this are found in the work of the World Methodist Historical Society, especially in its Singapore conference of 1991 and the joint conference with members of the Benedictine Order in the Roman Catholic Church on "Sanctification in the Benedictine and Methodist Traditions" (Rocca di Papa, 1994). The five-yearly Oxford Institute of Methodist Theological Studies has been rapidly broadening the geographical range of its participants. Events organized by several standing committees of the World Methodist Council are also significant (worship and liturgy, family life, and so on), as well as the major institutes and programs in evangelism. The gatherings of the World Methodist Council itself and the associated Conference could be put to even greater effect.

In relations with Christians of other communions, Methodists concerned for an authentic Wesleyan witness will find natural allies, in the United States for instance, among Lutherans concerned for an "evangelical catholicism" (represented in the periodical *Pro Ecclesia*) and among those Episcopalians from both the traditionally "catholic" and "evangelical" wings of Anglicanism who are gathering around such a document as the

Baltimore Declaration of 1991. At the international level, the continuing dialogue with the Roman Catholic Church and the impending dialogue with the Orthodox Churches may help shape the circumstances in which Methodism can, as Albert Outler hoped, best function according to its Wesleyan origins as an "evangelical order of witness and worship, discipline and nurture" within "an encompassing environment of catholicity."[16]

As the Churches approach that fork in the road, it is my hope that as many Methodists as possible will be Wesleyan enough to keep walking with historic Christianity. What exactly that will mean in institutional terms is not yet clear.

Abbreviations

Wesley's writings are cited, whenever possible, from the Bicentennial Edition of *The Works of John Wesley*. Older editions are cited if the relevant volumes have not yet been published in this series. To facilitate the use of multiple editions, I have cited section numbers as given by Wesley in some writings, especially the *Sermons* and *Appeals*, and provided dates for letters and for *Journal* entries. References to the *Explanatory Notes Upon the New Testament* are given by book, chapter, and verse.

Curnock *The Journal of the Rev. John Wesley, A.M.*, ed. Nehemiah Curnock, 8 vols. (London: Epworth Press, 1909–16).

Journal Refers to Wesley's *Journal*, in either Curnock or *Works*.

Letters *The Letters of the Rev. John Wesley, A.M.*, ed. John Telford, 8 vols. (London: Epworth Press, 1931).

NT Notes John Wesley, *Explanatory Notes Upon the New Testament* (London: William Bowyer, 1755; reprint London: Wesleyan-Methodist Book-Room, n.d.).

Works *The Works of John Wesley*; begun as "The Oxford Edition of The Works of John Wesley" (Oxford: Clarendon Press, 1975–1983); continued as "The Bicentennial Edition of The Works of John Wesley" (Nashville: Abingdon Press, 1984—); 14 of 35 vols. published to date.

Works [J] *The Works of John Wesley*, ed. Thomas Jackson, 14 vols. (London: Wesleyan Conference Office, 1872; reprint, Grand Rapids, MI: Zondervan, [1958–59]).

Notes

Notes to Introduction

1. "Letter to a Roman Catholic," *Works* [J] 10:80–86, in particular 84f.

2. Sermon 39, "Catholic Spirit," in *Works* 2:81–95. Ever since the Reformation, liturgy and ecclesiastical polity had been controverted within the Church of England, whether the attempted solutions veered towards uniformity, toleration, or comprehension.

3. The Orthodox and Roman Catholic Churches see the "dialogue of charity" as preparing the way for the "theological dialogue," without being superseded by it; cf. *Towards the Healing of Schism: The Sees of Rome and Constantinople: Public Statements and Correspondence between the Holy See and the Ecumenical Patriarchate 1958–1984*, ed. and trans. E. J. Stormon (New York: Paulist, 1987).

4. See C. H. Hopkins, *John R. Mott, 1865–1955: A Biography* (Geneva: W.C.C., 1979).

5. *World Missionary Conference, 1910: The History and Records of the Conference* (Edinburgh: Oliphant, and New York: Revell [no date]), 23.

6. *The Nature of the Church*, ed. R. Newton Flew (London: SCM, 1952). See Gordon S. Wakefield, *Robert Newton Flew 1886–1962* (London: Epworth, 1971).

7. See *The Wesleyan Theological Heritage: Essays of Albert C. Outler*, eds. Thomas C. Oden and Leicester R. Longden (Grand Rapids: Zondervan, 1991). These papers from three decades display the complete congruence between their author's commitment to Wesley and his commitment to ecumenism.

8. See *Report on Tradition and Traditions*, Faith and Order Paper No. 40 (Geneva: W.C.C., 1963), and *The Fourth World Conference on Faith and Order, Montreal 1963*, eds. P. C. Rodger and L. Vischer (London: SCM, 1964), 50–61.

9. (London: Lutterworth, 1962).

10. See M. Thurian (and G. Wainwright), "'Baptism, Eucharist and Ministry' (the 'Lima text')," in *Dictionary of the Ecumenical Movement*, eds. N. Lossky and others (Geneva: W.C.C., and Grand Rapids: Eerdmans, 1991), 80–83; and, in the same dictionary, the entries "Baptism" (E. Lanne), "Eucharist" (G. Wainwright), and "Ministry in the Church" (L. S. Mudge).

11. An idea of the complexity of the process by which nearly two hundred

289

Churches from every confessional family responded to the Lima text can be gained from *Baptism, Eucharist and Ministry 1982–1990: Report on the Process and Responses*, Faith and Order Paper No. 149 (Geneva: W.C.C., 1990). Illustratively, see G. Wainwright, "Word and Sacrament in the Churches' Responses to the Lima Text," *One in Christ* 24 (1988), 304–27, and "The Eucharist in the Churches' Responses to the Lima Text," *One in Christ* 25 (1989), 53–74.

12. See *On the Way to Fuller Koinonia: Official Report of the Fifth World Conference on Faith and Order, Santiago de Compostela 1993*, eds. Thomas F. Best and Günther Gassmann (Geneva: W.C.C., 1994), in particular 237–44. The paper on "Methodism and the Apostolic Faith" [chapter eleven in this book] was presented to the Eighth Oxford Institute of Methodist Theological Studies in 1987, when Günther Gassmann, director of W.C.C. Faith and Order, also gave a general introduction to the Faith and Order project; see *What Should Methodists Teach? Wesleyan Tradition and Modern Diversity*, ed. M. Douglas Meeks (Nashville: Kingswood Books, 1990), in particular 93–100 and 101–17.

13. Documentation of the W.C.C. projects that finally converged in the "Apostolic Faith Study" can be found, together with deeper background material, in *Apostolic Faith Today: A Handbook for Study*, Faith and Order Paper No. 124, ed. Hans-Georg Link (Geneva: W.C.C., 1985).

14. For insight into the development of the Faith and Order text, cf. *One God, One Lord, One Spirit: On the Explication of the Apostolic Faith Today*, Faith and Order Paper No. 139, ed. H.-G. Link (Geneva: W.C.C., 1988). The first complete draft of the text itself appeared as *Confessing One Faith: Towards an Ecumenical Explication of the Apostolic Faith as Expressed in the Nicene-Constantinopolitan Creed (381): Study Document*, Faith and Order Paper No. 140 (Geneva: W.C.C., 1987). The reworked text was published as *Confessing the One Faith: An Ecumenical Explication of the Apostolic Faith as it is Confessed in the Nicene-Constantinopolitan Creed (381)*, Faith and Order Paper No. 153 (Geneva: W.C.C., 1991).

15. G. Gassmann, "Towards the Common Expression of the Apostolic Faith Today," in Meeks, ed., *What Should Methodists Teach?*, 93–100, in particular 100.

16. See also my review, in *Modern Theology* 10 (1994), 413–15, of Robert W. Jenson's book, *Unbaptized God: The Basic Flaw in Ecumenical Theology* (Minneapolis: Fortress, 1992).

17. From the hymn, "Great is our redeeming Lord," first published only in the *Arminian Magazine* in 1797, but included in all British Methodist hymnbooks since 1877. See *The Poetical Works of John and Charles Wesley*, ed. G. Osborn, 13 vols. (London: Wesleyan-Methodist Conference Office, 1868–1872), 8:111–14.

18. *Towards a Statement on the Church: Report of the Joint Commission between the Roman Catholic Church and the World Methodist Council, 1982–1986 (Fourth Series)*, ¶74–75.

19. *The Wesleyan Theological Heritage*, 226.

20. *Towards a Statement on the Church*, ¶24.

21. *The Church: Community of Grace*, ¶¶8 and 9.

22. See *Reformed World* 39 (1986–87), 821–29.

23. In the Church of South India (1947), the union is made more complex by the participation of Anglicans, and in the Church of North India (1970), of Baptists, Brethren and Disciples as well. In Italy, the Methodists and the (Reformed) Waldensians have an integrated synod, while local congregations retain their respective identities; the historic theological tensions between Wesleyans and Calvinists may there remain in force (see, for example, Vittorio Subilia, *La Giustificazione per fede* (Brescia: Paideia, 1976), 317–22.

24. See also the little book of my Cato lecture delivered at the 1985 Assembly of the Uniting Church in Australia, *Geoffrey Wainwright on Wesley and Calvin: Sources for Theology, Liturgy and Spirituality* (Melbourne: Uniting Church Press, 1987).

25. Within the Methodist fold, Randy L. Maddox has recently suggested that there is room for reconsideration of my own detection of a certain "punctiliarism" in Wesley's view of salvation [see below, pp. 150f. and 157]: Maddox argues that in Wesley's notion of "[holy] tempers" there is already a possible equivalent of the "habitus." See R. L. Maddox, *Responsible Grace: John Wesley's Practical Theology* (Nashville: Kingswood Books, 1994), 69–70, 151–53, 329.

26. (London: Epworth, and New York: Oxford University Press, 1980).

27. Some individual Methodists have worked at the matter; see, for example, Brian Frost, *Living in Tension between East and West* (London: New World Publications, 1984); Randy L. Maddox, "John Wesley and Eastern Orthodoxy: Influences, Convergences, and Differences," *Asbury Theological Journal* 45 (1990), 29–53.

28. [No place, no date, but in fact London and Lake Junaluska, 1993.]

29. See G. Wainwright, "Rain Stopped Play? The Anglican Communion at Lambeth 1988," *Midstream* 28 (1989), 193–99.

30. For some broader philosophical and ecclesiological reflections on dialogue, see Peter Neuner, "Dialogue, intrafaith," in *Dictionary of the Ecumenical Movement*, eds. N. Lossky and others (Geneva: W.C.C., and Grand Rapids: Eerdmans, 1991), 287–91.

31. On the nature of difference, see G. Wainwright, "Is the Reformation over?" in *Theological Students Fellowship Bulletin* (May–June 1984), 2–5, and "Ecumenical Dimensions of George Lindbeck's 'Nature of Doctrine'," *Modern Theology* 4 (1987–88), 121–32.

32. See G. Wainwright, "Dialogue, multilateral," in *Dictionary of the Ecumenical Movement*, 291–93.

33. See, for example, A. Schmemann, *Church, World, Mission: Reflections on Orthodoxy in the West* (Crestwood, N.Y.: St. Vladimir's Seminary Press, 1979), 199–200.

34. Letter of uncertain date to James Hervey, in *Letters* 1:284–87 (but see *Works* 2:66f.); cf. the studies by the French Dominican ecumenist Yves Congar, *Vaste monde ma paroisse: vérité et dimensions du salut*, Foi vivante 27 (Paris: Témoignage chrétien, 1966), where Wesley's tag is employed to set evangelization within the broadest context of human history.

35. Sermon 64, "The New Creation," in *Works* 2:500–510, in particular 510.

36. See G. Wainwright, "The Doctrine of the Trinity: Where the Church Stands or Falls," *Interpretation* 45 (1991), 117–32.

Notes to Chapter One

1. *John Wesley's Letter to a Roman Catholic*, ed. Michael Hurley, S.J. (London and Dublin: Geoffrey Chapman, 1968). Hurley developed a particular theme in Wesley's thought in "Salvation Today and Wesley Today," in *The Place of Wesley in the Christian Tradition: Essays delivered at Drew University in celebration of the commencement of the publication of the Oxford Edition of the Works of John Wesley*, ed. Kenneth E. Rowe (Metuchen, N.J.: Scarecrow Press, 1976), 94–116.

2. Here Wesley anticipated the method of the ongoing W.C.C. Faith and Order study, "Towards the Common Expression of the Apostolic Faith Today." See G. Wainwright, "Methodism and the Apostolic Faith," in *What Should Methodists Teach?*, ed. M. Douglas Meeks (Nashville: Kingswood Books, 1990), 101–17 [chapter eleven in this book].

3. *Works* [J] 10:86–128 (extracted from Bishop John Williams). See also "Popery Calmly Considered," ibid., 10:140–58.

4. Thus, in his *Journal* for 25 March 1743, in reply to Bishop Richard Challoner's *The Grounds of the Old Religion* Wesley notes: "In the first thirty pages the author heaps up scriptures concerning the privileges of the Church. But all this is beating the air till he proves the Romanists to be the Church, that is, that a part is the whole" (*Works* 19:319f.).

5. See Sermon 74, "Of the Church" (1786), in *Works* 3:52.

6. Thus again to Bishop Challoner, in a letter of 17 February 1761 to the Editor of the "London Chronicle," Wesley countered: *"Whatever may be the case of some particular souls*, it must be said, if your own marks be true, the Roman Catholics in general are not 'the people of God'" (*Letters* 4:138).

7. *John Wesley's Letter to a Roman Catholic*, 7, citing *The Methodist Recorder*, 1 September 1966.

8. *The Apostolic Tradition: Report of the Joint Commission between the Roman Catholic Church and the World Methodist Council, Fifth Series 1986–1991*, ¶100. Published in *Proceedings of the Sixteenth World Methodist Conference, Singapore 1991*, ed. Joe Hale (Lake Junaluska, N.C.: World Methodist Council, 1992), 287–310, and as a separate brochure; in the Pontifical Council for Christian Unity's *Information Service*, no. 78 (1991/3–4), 212–25; in *Origins* (Washington, D.C.), vol. 21, no. 19 (September 19, 1991), 237–47; in *Catholic International* (Paris), vol. 3, no. 3 (1–14 February 1992), 106–20; and in *One in Christ* 28 (1992), 49–73.

9. *The Apostolic Tradition*, ¶100.

10. In addition to the international dialogue, bilateral dialogues have taken place in New Zealand, in Great Britain (where, for instance, studies were devoted to the eucharist, to ministry, to authority, to justification, and to the Blessed Virgin Mary), and in the United States (where reports have been issued on *Holiness and Spirituality of the Ordained Ministry*, 1976, *Eucharistic Celebration: Converging Theology, Divergent Practice*, 1981, and *Holy Living and Holy Dying*, 1989).

11. The first three reports can be conveniently located in *Growth in Agreement: Reports and Agreements of Ecumenical Conversations on a World Level*, eds. H. Meyer and L. Vischer (Ramsey, N.J.: Paulist Press, and Geneva:

W.C.C., 1984). Initial publications respectively in *Proceedings of the Twelfth World Methodist Conference, Denver, Colorado, 1971*, ed. Lee F. Tuttle (Nashville: Abingdon, 1972), 39–68, in *Proceedings of the Thirteenth World Methodist Conference, Dublin, Ireland, 1976*, ed. Joe Hale (Lake Junaluska, N.C.: World Methodist Council, 1977), 254–70, and in *Proceedings of the Fourteenth World Methodist Council, Honolulu, Hawaii, 1981*, ed. Joe Hale (Lake Junaluska, N.C.: World Methodist Council, 1982), 264–77; and in the Secretariat for Promoting Christian Unity's *Information Service*, no. 21 (1973/3), 22–38; no. 34 (1977/2), 8–20; and no. 46 (1981/2), 84–96. The Singapore 1991 report has been identified in note 8. The Nairobi 1986 report, *Towards a Statement on the Church*, was analogously published in *Proceedings of the Fifteenth World Methodist Conference*, ed. Joe Hale (Lake Junaluska, N.C.: World Methodist Council, 1987), 360–72, and as a separate brochure; the Secretariat for Promoting Christian Unity's *Information Service*, no. 62 (1986/4), 206–16; and *One in Christ* 22 (1986), 241–59. In view of the different editions, references will be given by paragraph number rather than by page.

12. I should perhaps declare my own hand and reveal that I have been a member of the Joint Commission since 1983 and its Methodist co-chairman since 1986.

13. Mention should also be made of attempts to deal with matters of moral theology that have been little treated in other international bilateral dialogues but figured between Catholics and Methodists: "Christian Home and Family," "Euthanasia". . . .

14. Albert Outler once described Wesley as "rather like the superior general of an evangelical order within a regional division of the church catholic," and he extended the idea into ecclesiological significance for Methodism: "We need a catholic church within which to function as a proper evangelical order of witness and worship, discipline and nurture." These ideas are developed within the context of a broader discussion in my own essay on Methodism's "ecclesial location and ecumenical vocation"; see G. Wainwright, *The Ecumenical Moment: Crisis and Opportunity for the Church* (Grand Rapids: Eerdmans, 1983), 189–221.

15. F. Frost, "Méthodisme," in *Catholicisme, hier, aujourd'hui, demain*, ed. G. Jacquemet (Paris: Letouzey et Ané, 1948ff.), vol. IX, cols. 48–71.

16. In the Roman Catholic-Methodist dialogue, the matter is made very complex by the long and varied tradition which Catholicism claims for itself, whereas Methodists tend to see themselves as starting in the eighteenth century. In another perspective, I would want to maintain that Catholics and Methodists share a common tradition at least until the sixteenth century. See G. Wainwright, *The Ecumenical Moment*, in particular (teasingly) 189.

17. For instance: *Salvation and the Church* (1987), and *Church as Communion* (1991), both by the Second Anglican-Roman Catholic International Commission (ARCIC II); *The Church: Community of Grace* (1984), by the Joint Commission between the Lutheran World Federation and the World Methodist Council; *Together in God's Grace* (1987), between the World Methodist Council and the World Alliance of Reformed Churches.

18. See *Baptism, Eucharist and Ministry 1982–1990: Report on the Process and Responses* (Geneva: W.C.C., 1990), especially 147–51.

19. In one of his celebrated *bons mots*, Raymond George, a member of the Joint Commission for its second, third and fourth rounds, launched the thought that "the Pope has spoken infallibly on only two occasions, and each time he was wrong."

20. See G. Wainwright, "The Assurance of Faith: A Methodist Approach to the Question Raised by the Roman Catholic Doctrine of Infallibility," in *One in Christ* 22 (1986), 44–61 [chapter two in this book].

21. J. M. R. Tillard, "Commentary on 'Towards a Statement on the Church'" in the Secretariat for Promoting Christian Unity's *Information Service*, no. 62 (1986/4), 216–19, and in *One in Christ* 22 (1986), 259–66.

22. G. Tavard, "Tradition as *Koinonia* in Historical Perspective," *One in Christ* 24 (1988), 97–111.

23. So far, the Joint Commission has done no more than register the recent divergence over the ordination of women (Dublin 1976, 102; Singapore 1991, 96–97).

24. For the response of the Methodist Church of Great Britain on this matter, see *Churches Respond to BEM: Official Responses to the "Baptism, Eucharist and Ministry" Text*, ed. Max Thurian, 6 vols. (Geneva: W.C.C., 1986–88), 6:32–33.

25. The practice of the World Methodist Council has been to give, without detailed discussion, a general welcome to the Commission's reports and extend its mandate; only at one point (Honolulu 1981), did the WMC express its "opinion," apropos of ¶19 of the report presented to it, that "baptism might more satisfactorily be stated to be *an* outward sign and means of grace and faith rather than *the* outward sign." At the Vatican, the customary procedure has been for the Secretariat (now Council) for Christian Unity to make a brief epistolary response to the co-chairmen, sometimes incorporating observations from the Congregation for the Doctrine of the Faith and offering suggestions for future work.

26. For Wicks's commentary, see the Pontifical Council for Promoting Christian Unity's *Information Service*, no. 78 (1991/3–4), 225–29, *One in Christ* 28 (1992), 74–81, or *Catholic International*, vol. 3, no. 3 (1–14 February 1992), 120–24.

27. See already Dublin 1976, 81–91, 104; Nairobi, 27, 29–38; Singapore, 92–94. Even in Singapore 1991, the treatment specifically of episcopacy remains, in Tillard's earlier phrase, largely "diagnostic." For a broad discussion from a Wesleyan and Methodist viewpoint, see G. Wainwright, "The End of All Ecclesiastical Order," *One in Christ* 27 (1991), 34–48 [chapter three in this book].

28. See already Honolulu, 19; Nairobi, 2, 11–16, 17; Singapore, 16, 26, 40–41, 46, 59–60, 63–66. Notice the late emergence of the theme. Nairobi spoke quite strongly of baptism and eucharist *together* as dominical sacraments and "effective signs of grace": "By the power of the Holy Spirit they bring into our lives the life-giving action and even the self-giving of Christ himself. It is Christ's action that is embodied and made manifest in the Church's actions which, responded to in faith, amount to a real encounter with the risen Jesus" (16). Of baptism in particular it was said that "neither of us believes that a non-baptized person is by that very fact excluded from salvation, nor that baptism automatically ensures perseverance unto salvation" (12, footnote 2).

Yet that very footnote acknowledged that "we must still examine and resolve persisting differences concerning the efficacy of baptism, particularly of infants." I remember just how gingerly the Commission had to tread in formulating ¶¶63–66 of Singapore 1991. The chief problem resides in the mixed heritage that Methodists received from Wesley and to which both "sacramentalists" and "experientialists" can appeal. On the one hand, Wesley endorsed a "high" view of baptism in republishing his father's treatise on the subject, and he never quite abandoned belief in the baptismal regeneration of infants, although he appears gradually to have phased away the mention of it. On the other hand, his standard sermons clearly show his opinion that one can "sin away" one's baptismal status and need to be "born again"—again! Wesley distinguished between water baptism, as the "outward and visible sign," and "the new birth" as the inner reality, but he failed to give a clear and consistent account of how the two were related. See Bernard G. Holland, *Baptism in Early Methodism* (London: Epworth, 1970), and O. E. Borgen, *John Wesley on the Sacraments* (Nashville: Abingdon, 1972). In turn, it seems fair that Methodists should press with Catholics the question of the ecclesiological status of the many baptized who never come to faith and practice or lapse from them.

Notes to Chapter Two

1. Informed Methodists are of course aware that the conditions under which the Pope is held in fact to speak infallibly are very restricted. Nevertheless they fear that the phenomenon of "creeping infallibility" may be not so much an abuse or exaggeration as rather the inevitable tendency of a position that is wrong from the outset.

2. The American Methodist Articles of Religion, following the Anglican, reject "the Romish doctrine concerning purgatory," the "sacrifice of masses," transubstantiation, works of supererogation, invocation of saints, and various usages with the eucharistic elements, relics and images. These and other doctrines and attendant practices were attacked by John Wesley in "A Roman Catechism faithfully drawn out of the allowed writings of the Church of Rome, with a Reply thereto"(*Works* [J] 10:86–128), and in "Popery Calmly Considered" (ibid., 140–58). The 1970 General Conference of the United Methodist Church declared that the polemical Articles should be "reconsidered and reassessed," and passed a "resolution of intent" to interpret all the denomination's standards of doctrine "in consonance with our best ecumenical insights and judgment." The substantive question is whether what Methodists have historically rejected is in fact Catholic doctrine, and whether in turn the Tridentine and other anathemas in fact hit Methodists. The answers would have to be nuanced according to the various matters in controversy: see my article "Is the Reformation over?" in *Theological Students Fellowship Bulletin* (May–June, 1984), 2–5. It is the Marian dogmas, unilaterally defined by Rome (and apparently more out of exuberance than because a vital doctrine was directly under threat), which these days cause the most obvious dogmatic difficulty for Methodists and most Protestants. It has more recently been wondered whether Catholics on the one hand and (say) Methodists on the

other could *agree*—in a way that made these matters no longer churchdividing—that such doctrines were *de fide* for Catholics but not for (say) Methodists. Yet many on both sides would deny that truth was optional. In that case, there can be no reconciliation without *substantive* agreement, although a certain *range of interpretation* might eventually come to accommodate both sides. For the merest beginnings of such an approach, see the chapter "Mary and Methodism" in my book *The Ecumenical Moment* (Grand Rapids: Eerdmans, 1983), 169–88.

    3. J. Hale (ed.), *Proceedings of the Fourteenth World Conference, Honolulu, Hawaii, July 21–28, 1981* (Lake Junaluska. N.C.: World Methodist Council, 1982), 264–77. The Report was published piecemeal in *One in Christ* 15 (1979)/3; 16 (1980)/3; 17 (1981)/4; and also as a separate booklet by the World Methodist Council.

    4. (London: Epworth, 1952), in particular 11.

    5. In a letter of 31 July 1747 John writes to Charles Wesley of "a distinct, explicit assurance that my sins are forgiven" as "the common privilege of real Christians" (*Works* 26:254f.). Forty years later, Wesley declared to Melville Horne "We preach assurance as we always did, as the common privilege of the children of God" (Robert Southey, *The Life of Wesley*, second edition, 2 vols. [London, 1820], 1:295).

    6. So already in opposition to the Moravians and their teaching on "stillness": see Wesley's *Journal* for 31 December 1739, 25 April 1740, and 22 June 1740. And again, for instance, in the epistolary debate of 1755–56 with Richard Tompson. On the latter debate, see *Works* 26:566–71, 574–80. The Baker edition of Wesley's letters (*Works* 25–26) has not yet reached the letter that most develops our phrase; for this, see meanwhile *Letters* 3:158–62 (letter of 5 February 1756).

    7. See the letter of 1 December 1760 to the Editor of Lloyd's Evening Post (*Letters* 4:116).

    8. See Yates, 61–68.

    9. Letter of 28 March 1768 to Dr. Rutherforth (*Letters* 5:359).

    10. Sermon 106, "On Faith" (in *Works* 3:492–501, in particular 497f.).

    11. Letter of 28 March 1768 to Dr. Rutherforth (*Letters* 5:358).

    12. *NT Notes*, Heb. 6:11.

    13. Letter of 10 April 1781 to Hetty Roe (*Letters* 7:57f.).

    14. Letter of December 1751 to Bishop G. Lavington of Exeter (*Letters* 3:305 and *Works* 11:398f.).

    15. Letter of 28 March 1768 to Dr. Rutherforth (*Letters* 5:358).

    16. *Letters* 7:58.

    17. J. Hale (ed.), *Proceedings of the Thirteenth World Methodist Conference, Dublin, Ireland, August 25–31, 1976* (Lake Junaluska, N.C.: World Methodist Council, 1977), 254–70, in particular 256. Whether Trent or Wesley properly appreciated the Calvinist doctrine of perseverance is a question that may need re-examination. It would in any case be interesting to see a Reformed theologian, in an experiment similar to the present one, try to relate "the perseverance of the saints" to Roman Catholic doctrine on the "indefectibility of the Church."

    18. No. 194 in *A Collection of Hymns for the Use of the People called Methodists*, in *Works* 7:325. This 1780 *Collection* has continued to be forma-

tive for Methodist hymnals and Methodist people, especially in the British tradition.

19. *A Collection of Hymns*, no. 93, *Works* 7:195.

20. The connexion between assurance and confidence or boldness is strongly made by the late nineteenth-century Methodist systematician, W. B. Pope. See his *Compendium of Christian Theology* (London, 1880), 3:117–20.

21. *A Collection of Hymns*, no. 93, *Works* 7:197.

22. Sermon 11, "The Witness of the Spirit, II," in *Works* 1:285–98, in particular 297.

23. *A Collection of Hymns*, no. 379, *Works* 7:552.

24. *A Collection of Hymns*, no. 354, *Works* 7:522.

25. Wesley had no difficulty with the idea that, with all due allowance for divine transcendence and ineffability, the revealed nature and works of God can be stated in propositions, and his faith was substantially creedal. In his "Letter to a Roman Catholic" of 1749, his statement of the faith of "a true Protestant" took the form of an expansion of the Nicene Creed (*Works* [J] 10:80–86). From his Sermon 39, on "Catholic Spirit" (1750), it emerges that if your heart was to be right with Wesley's heart, your faith had to be pretty orthodox: "A man of a truly catholic spirit . . . is as fixed as the sun in his judgment concerning the main branches of Christian doctrine" (*Works* 2:79–95, in particular 93). And when, in "The Character of a Methodist," it is stated that "we think and let think," this magnanimity is limited to "opinions which do not strike at the root of Christianity" (*Works* [J] 8:339–47, in particular 340). In so far as the mystery of God has been revealed in Jesus Christ, believers have open to them an "assurance of understanding, *plêrophoria syneseôs*" (Colossians 2:2), a text on which Wesley in the *NT Notes* makes the jejune comment: "That is, unto the fullest and clearest understanding and knowledge of the gospel." W. B. Pope (op. cit., 118) remarks more interestingly: "St Paul prays on behalf of the Colossians that they might add to the two other kinds of assurance an abounding and undimmed confidence of the understanding, *syneseôs*, in all the truths that belong to the mystery of God, which is Christ. It imports that it is the privilege of all who receive Christ to have an intellectual and experimental hold of Him, and of the whole circle of His doctrine. They know truth, as truth is in Jesus . . . They have the highest knowledge which is the knowledge of faith, they have such faith in this Object as makes it the certitude of knowledge." Wesley held that Christians cannot "*understand how* 'There are Three that bear record in heaven, the Father, the Son, and the Holy Spirit, and these Three are One' . . . or how the eternal Son of God 'took upon himself the form of a servant'" (Sermon 40, "Christian Perfection" [1741], in *Works* 2:101); but though their manner cannot be understood, such facts can be believed, as the Sermon 55, "On the Trinity" (1775), declares (*Works* 2:383f.).

26. Wesley's Sermon "On the Trinity," from which the phrases in the text are taken, is instructive here. He says: "The knowledge of the Three-One God is interwoven with all true Christian faith, with all vital religion . . . I do not know how anyone can be a Christian believer till 'he hath' (as St John speaks), 'the witness in himself'; till 'the Spirit of God witnesses with his spirit that he is a child of God'—that is, in effect, till God the Holy Ghost witnesses that God the Father has accepted him through the merits of God the Son—and having this witness he honours the Son and the blessed Spirit 'even as he

honours the Father.' Not that every Christian believer adverts to this; perhaps at first not one in twenty; but if you ask any of them a few questions you will easily find it is implied in what he believes" (*Works* 2:384f.). The lasting character of this trinitarian faith, both as *fides quâ creditur* and as *fides quae creditur*, is expressed in the conclusion of Sermon 64, "The New Creation" (1785): "To crown all, there will be a deep, an intimate, an uninterrupted union with God; a constant communion with the Father and his Son Jesus Christ, through the Spirit; a continual enjoyment of the Three-One God, and of all the creatures in him" (*Works* 3:510).

27. See note 3 above.

28. For a retrospective compendium of Wesley's teaching, see "A Plain Account of Christian Perfection" (1767), *Works* [J] 11:366–446.

29. "Our main doctrines, which include all the rest, are three, that of repentance, of faith, and of holiness. The first of these we account, as it were, the porch of religion, the next, the door; the third is religion itself." See "The Principles of a Methodist Farther Explained" (1746), *Works* [J] 8:414–81, in particular 472.

30. Sermon 40, "Christian Perfection" (1741), in *Works* 2:97–121, in particular 101f.

31. See G. Wainwright, "La confession et les confessions: vers l'unité confessionnelle et confessante des chrétiens," *Irénikon* 57 (1984), 5–26.

32. See note 3 above.

33. H. Küng, *The Church—Maintained in Truth* (London: SCM, 1980), 15.

34. To the Baptist Gilbert Boyce, Wesley wrote "The true Church of Christ . . . is but one, and contains all the true believers on earth" (letter of 22 May 1750; *Works* 26:424); and to the Roman Catholic bishop Richard Challoner he defined "the Catholic Church" as "the whole body of men, endued with faith working by love, dispersed over the whole earth, in Europe, Asia, Africa, and America" (*Journal*, 19 February 1761). In controversy with Calvinists, Wesley was prepared to adopt a distinction between "the outward, visible church" and "the spiritual, invisible church . . . consisting of holy believers" ("Predestination Calmly Considered," 1752, ¶71; *Works* [J] 10:204–59, in particular 244f.). Yet Wesley, as we shall see, also recognized the visible character of the "congregation of believers." For the complexities and tensions in Wesley's ecclesiology see the chapter "Ecclesial Location and Ecumenical Vocation" in my book *The Ecumenical Moment* (Grand Rapids: Eerdmans, 1983), 189–221, and also my essay "Ecclesiological Tendencies in Luther and Wesley" in P. Manns and H. Meyer (eds), *Luther's Ecumenical Significance* (Philadelphia: Fortress, 1984), 139–49 [chapter five in this book].

35. See *An Earnest Appeal to Men of Reason and Religion* (1743), §§76–78 (*Works* 11:45–90, in particular 77f.).

36. Wesley knew this at the pastoral level of the "religious society" (society, classes, bands), but the fuller ecclesiological consequences need to be drawn out.

37. "To be deep in history is to cease to be a Protestant" (J. H. Newman, *An Essay on the Development of Christian Doctrine*, edition of 1878, introduction, ¶5)!

38. See *The Book of Discipline of the United Methodist Church, 1972*

(Nashville: The United Methodist Publishing House, 1973), where the Landmark Documents (¶69) are sandwiched between "Historical Background" (¶68) and "Our Theological Task" (¶70). By the 1972 Statement I mean ¶¶68 and 70.

39. *Eucharist, Ministry, Authority: Statements agreed by Roman Catholics and Methodists* (Abbots Langley: Catholic Information Services, n.d.).

40. Contrast the *Minutes* of Wesley's own Conferences!

41. Interim Report of the Joint Commission between the Roman Catholic Church and the World Methodist Council (Milan, 1983): *Towards a Statement on the Church,* ¶12.

42. By hazarding the term "meta-dogma" I mean to suggest that 1870 itself may not be so much an addition to the faith, a "new item" to be believed—as rather an intended aid to belief in the dogmas of the faith. (*Mutatis mutandis,* biblical fundamentalists of whatever stripe can be asked: What is gained by requiring belief in scriptural inerrancy if *what* the Bible teaches as necessary to salvation is already believed?) That would still leave room for Methodists and Catholics to thrash out the question of *when,* concretely, the Pope has spoken, and may still speak, infallibly, or, in other words, of *what are* "all things essential" to the faith. Colin W. Williams has assembled convincing evidence to show that for Wesley the essential doctrines included original sin, the divinity and atoning work of Christ, justification by faith, the work of the Holy Spirit in regeneration and sanctification, and the Trinity (*John Wesley's Theology Today* [Nashville: Abingdon, 1960], 16f.). This list may be aligned with Wesley's recital of the faith of a true Protestant in the "Letter to a Roman Catholic" (see earlier, note 25).

Notes to Chapter Three

1. *Works* 26:197–207.

2. When, in this chapter, I use "sacramental" in a broader sense than for baptism and the Lord's Supper alone, I am following the hint in the 1986 Nairobi Report of the Joint Commission between the Roman Catholic Church and the World Methodist Council that "Methodists, while using the term 'sacrament' only of the two rites for which the Gospels explicitly record Christ's institution, do not thereby deny sacramental character to other rites" (¶13).

3. *Letters* 1:284–87. Wesley gives the letter in his *Journal* under June 11, 1739 and describes it as written "some time since" (see *Works* 19:66f.).

4. From hymns no. 507 and 508 in the 1780 *Collection of Hymns for the Use of the People Called Methodists* (*Works* 7:698–700).

5. Hymn no. 504 in the 1780 *Collection* (*Works* 7:693f.).

6. This hymn begins "Come, let us join our friends above." It was published in Charles Wesley's *Funeral Hymns* of 1759; see *The Poetical Works of John and Charles Wesley,* ed. G. Osborn, 13 vols. (London, 1868–1872), 6:215f.

7. "Methodism's Ecclesial Location and Ecumenical Vocation" in *One in Christ* 19 (1983), 104–34 (revised in G. Wainwright, *The Ecumenical Moment* [Grand Rapids: Eerdmans, 1983], 189–221).

8. " . . . that evil hour, when Constantine the Great called himself a Christian" (Sermon 121, *Works* 4:77; cf. Sermon 61, *Works* 2:463).

9. From the 1878 edition of the *Essay on the Development of Christian Doctrine*.

10. So the *Minutes* of the 1745 Methodist Conference, quoted from A. C. Outler, ed., *John Wesley* (New York: Oxford University Press, 1964), 154.

11. *Baptism, Eucharist and Ministry*, Faith and Order Paper No. 111 (Geneva: W.C.C., 1982).

12. *Letters* 7:284.

13. The best succinct account, and theological rationale, of Wesley's actions in September 1784 is in A. Raymond George's chapter on "Ordination" in R. Davies, A. R. George and G. Rupp (eds.), *A History of the Methodist Church in Great Britain*, vol. 2 (London: Epworth, 1978), 143–60.

14. *Journal* for 20 January 1746, in Curnock 3:232 and *Works* 20:112; cf. *Letters* 7:238.

15. Edgar W. Thompson, *Wesley: Apostolic Man. Some Reflections on Wesley's Consecration of Dr Thomas Coke* (London: Epworth, 1957).

16. *Letters* 7:262 (letter of March 25, 1785, to Barnabas Thomas).

17. *Towards a Statement on the Church: Report of the Joint Commission between the Roman Catholic Church and the World Methodist Council (1982–1986, Fourth series)*, ¶33.

18. George, "Ordination."

19. Minutes of the 1747 Methodist Conference, quoted from A. C. Outler (ed.), *John Wesley*, 173f.

20. *Letters* 7:239 (letter of 10 September 1784, to "Our Brethren in America").

21. Sermon 121, *Works* 4:72–84.

22. The 1974 British Methodist Conference's *Statement on Ordination* reads in part: "As a perpetual reminder of this calling [of the whole people of God to be the body of Christ] and as a means of being obedient to it, the Church sets apart men and women, specially called, in ordination. In their office the calling of the whole people of God is focused and represented, and it is their responsibilty as representative persons to lead the people to share with them in that calling. In this sense they are the sign of the presence and ministry of Christ in the Church, and through the Church to the world." More succinctly, the doctrinal statement of the Consultation in Church Union in the U.S.A. says: "Their ordination marks them as persons who represent to the Church its own identity and mission in Jesus Christ."

23. G. Wainwright, "Reconciliation in Ministry" in M. Thurian (ed.), *Ecumenical Perspectives on Baptism, Eucharist and Ministry* (Geneva: W.C.C., 1983), 129–39, in particular 135. With this may be compared the view of the Roman Catholic theologian David N. Power: "The needs of the church and of its mission are what determine ministry. . . . The office-holder, through the service of supervision and presidency, represents back to the church that which in the faith of the ordination ceremony it has expressed about itself. . . . Because [the eucharistic president] is empowered to represent the church in this vital action, to represent to it its own very ground of being, we say that he is empowered to represent Christ. . . . The role of the ordained minister is to represent in the midst of this community its work for the kingdom, its

eschatological nature, and its relationship to Christ. . . . The validity of ministry, to use the word loosely, is not assessed on the ground of its ecclesiastical provenance, but on the ground of its benefit to the church" (composite quotation from D. N. Power, "The Basis for Official Ministry in the Church" in *The Jurist* 41 [1981], 314–42, and *Gifts That Differ* [New York: Pueblo, 1980]).

24. Thus the Nairobi Report regarding grace, faith and the efficacy of the sacraments: "The sacraments are effective signs by which God gives grace through faith. Their efficacy should not be conceived in any merely mechanical way. God works through his Spirit in a mysterious way beyond human comprehension, but he invites a full and free human response" (¶15).

25. See G. Wainwright, "The Assurance of Faith: A Methodist Approach to the Question Raised by the Roman Catholic Doctrine of Infallibility" in *One in Christ* 22 (1986), 44–61 [chapter two in this book].

Notes to Chapter Four

1. See Marie-Benoît Meeus, "Ora et labora: devise bénédictine?" in *Collectanea Cisterciensia* 54 (1992), 193–219. On this fine article—which is "spirituel" in the two French senses of religious and witty—I have drawn heavily for the literary history of the connection between prayer and work in monasticism, and among the Benedictines in particular. I am deeply grateful to Sister Marie-Benoît, of the Bethany Priory at Loppem (Belgium), for her initiative in sending me a copy of her text.

2. *A Collection of Hymns*, no. 512, *Works* 7:704.

3. Sermon 24, "Upon Our Lord's Sermon on the Mount, IV" (1748), *Works* 1:533–34. Wesley goes on: "By Christianity I mean that method of worshipping God which is here revealed to man by Jesus Christ. When I say this is essentially a social religion, I mean not only that it cannot subsist so well, but that it cannot subsist at all without society, without living and conversing with other men."

4. From the Preface to John and Charles Wesley's "Hymns and Sacred Poems" of 1739, in *Works* [J] 14:321. Wesley here appeals to Galatians 5:6, 10 and to 1 John 4:21.

5. See the mammoth six-volume edition by Adalbert de Vogüé and Jean Neufville, *La Règle de saint Benoît*, Sources chrétiennes 181–86 (Paris: Cerf, 1971–72).

6. See the concise work of Stephanus Hilpisch, *Benedictinism through Changing Centuries* (Collegeville: St. John's Abbey Press, 1958).

7. "The Character of a Methodist," in *Works* 9:30–46.

8. Sermon 85, "On Working Out Our Own Salvation," in *Works* 3:199–209.

9. See Jürgen Weissbach, *Der neue Mensch im theologischen Denken John Wesleys* (Stuttgart: Christliches Verlagshaus, 1970).

10. *Works* 3:200.

11. *Works* 9:41.

12. Sermon 45, "The New Birth" (1760), in *Works* 2:188.

301

13. See Geoffrey Wainwright, *Doxology: The Praise of God in Worship, Doctrine, and Life* (London: Epworth, and New York: Oxford University Press, 1980), in particular 15–44 ("Image of God").

14. See, for example, Alexander Schmemann, *For the Life of the World*, revised edition (Crestwood, N.Y.: St. Vladimir's Seminary Press, 1974).

15. These last two cases are recounted anecdotally in Meeus, 219.

16. Thus in the very first saying of St. Anthony the Great, in *The Sayings of the Desert Fathers: The Alphabetical Collection*, trans. Benedicta Ward (London: Mowbray, and Kalamazoo: Cistercian Publications, 1975), 1.

17. Hilpisch, 37.

18. Ibid., 49–50; cf. 79–80.

19. Ibid., 79–80.

20. Dom Ildephonse Schuster, a former Cardinal Archbishop of Milan, noted the social and cultural novelty of Benedict's attitude: "Whereas the ancient Romans looked upon labor as a punishment for slaves, and the barbarians disdained it as an occupation not suited to warlike peoples, St. Benedict elevated work to the dignity of religion and consecrated the ranks of his disciples to it" (*St. Benedict and His Times* [St. Louis: Herder, 1951], 102).

21. So, for example, St. Basil, in *The Great Rule*, 37, with appeal to Acts 20:35, Ephesians 4:28, and Matthew 25:34-35; see W. K. L. Clarke, *The Ascetic Works of Saint Basil* (London: SPCK, 1925), 205–6.

22. The works of mercy are listed in Benedict's *Rule*, 4:14–19.

23. Hilpisch, 37.

24. Ibid., 62.

25. Ibid., 76–77

26. Ibid., 19–20, 24–25, 27–30, 38–40, 68–73.

27. Ibid., 18–20, 23–24; Schuster, *St. Benedict and His Times*, 170f. (cf. 152f., 164f.).

28. Wesley's (public) *Journals* and (private) *Diaries* have appeared, as far as 1775, in *Works* 18–22.

29. *Works* 3:205–6.

30. See Sermon 16, "The Means of Grace" (1746), in *Works* 1:381, where Wesley lists as "the chief": "Prayer, whether in secret or with the great congregation; searching the Scriptures (which implies reading, hearing, and meditating thereon); and receiving the Lord's Supper." In the "Nature, Design, and General Rules of the United Societies" (1743), Wesley names "the ordinances of God" as "the public worship of God; the ministry of the word, either read or expounded; the Supper of the Lord; family and private prayer; searching the Scriptures; and fasting, or abstinence" (see *Works* 9:73). To these "instituted" means of grace, Wesley sometimes adds several of a "prudential" kind: such "particular rules in order to grow in grace" or "arts of holy living" are intended to serve "watching [against the world, the devil, and one's besetting sin], denying ourselves, taking up our cross, exercise of the presence of God"; see the so-called "Large Minutes," in *Works* [J] 8:322–24.

31. In *Works* 1:592–611.

32. See John C. Bowmer, *The Lord's Supper in Early Methodism* (London: Dacre/Black, 1951), 49–61.

33. Sermon 101, "The Duty of Constant Communion" (1787, originally 1732), in *Works* 3:427–39.

34. Letter of 10 September 1784 to "Our Brethren in America," in *Letters* 7:238–39.

35. *Works* 3:206.

36. *Works* 9:41.

37. Isidore of Seville, *Sententiae* III.7.18 (Migne, *Patrologia Latina* 83:675–76).

38. St. Basil juxtaposes these two texts in the *Great Rule*, 37; see above (as in note 21), 207.

39. Aurelian, *Rule for Monks*, 29:1, in *Règles monastiques d'Occident, IVe–VIe siècle, d'Augustin à Ferréol*, ed. V. Desprez (Bégrolles-en-Mauges: Abbaye de Bellefontaine, 1980), 236; cf. Caesarius, *Rules for Virgins*, 15, ibid., 175.

40. Ibid., 24 (p. 235). The same two-directional motion is found in the *Rule of Tarnant* §6, 4–5; §8, 7 and 14–15 (in Desprez, *Règles monastiques*, 267–68, 270–71).

41. *Great Rule*, 37; see above (as in note 21), 206.

42. That Caesarius served as a model for Benedict was strongly asserted by Ildephonse Schuster in a writing of 1940, translated as *Historical Notes on St. Benedict's "Rule for Monks"* (Hamden [Ct.]: Shoe String Press, 1962); see in particular 18–31. But even the likelihood of any borrowings from Caesarius is treated rather lightly by A. de Vogüé in his more recent scholarly edition of Benedict's *Rule* (as in note 5; see in particular 1:148, 170–71), The chief source of Benedict's *Rule* is now widely recognized to be the so-called *Rule of the Master*, which is in all probability the work of another author, not an earlier work of Benedict himself; see de Vogüé, 1:14–23, 29–44, 135–43, 173–314 (especially 303–12).

43. See, for example, Agathon, 9: "There is no labor greater than that of prayer to God" (*The Sayings of the Desert Fathers*, trans. Benedicta Ward, 18–19).

44. Cf. Benedict's *Rule*, 57:9.

45. *Works* 9:37.

46. *Works* 9:37.

47. *Works* 9:38.

48. *Works* 9:39.

49. *Works* 9:39–40.

50. *A Collection of Hymns*, no. 315, *Works* 7: 470 (no. 590 in the British *Methodist Hymn Book* of 1933; no. 381 in *Hymns and Psalms* of 1983; and no. 438 in the American *United Methodist Hymnal* of 1989).

51. Thus the Preface to the 1933 British *Methodist Hymn Book*. The classic text was the 1780 *Collection of Hymns for the Use of the People Called Methodists*, scholarly edition in *Works* 7. The original *Collection* was arranged "according to the experience of real Christians." Methodists have subsequently added other Wesleyan hymns for the church year and for the eucharist (the latter drawn from the *Hymns on the Lord's Supper* of 1745). In the twentieth century especially, the sources have been expanded ecumenically.

52. Sermon 29, "Upon Our Lord's Sermon on the Mount, IX," in *Works* 1:635. The closest text in Augustine is *De civitate Dei* VIII.17.2 (Migne, *Patrologia Latina* 41:242).

53. For a positive reading of Wesley in this matter by a Roman Catholic

writer, whose title (in the original French, though less so as modified for the English translation!), precisely appears to confirm Lutheran and Calvinist fears, see Maximin Piette, *La réaction de John Wesley dans l'évolution du protestantisme*, second edition (Brussels: La Lecture au Foyer, and Librairie Albert Dewit, 1927); English translation: *John Wesley in the Evolution of Protestantism* (London: Sheed and Ward, 1937, reprinted 1979).

54. C. Vagaggini, "La posizione de S. Benedetto nella questione semipelagiana," in *Studia Benedictina in memoriam gloriosi ante saecula XIV transitus S. P. Benedicti*, Studia anselmiana philosophica theologica, 18–19 (Vatican City: Libreria Vaticana, 1947), 17–83. Vagaggini concludes of Benedict: "Il suo modo di parlare della grazia et del libero arbitrio s'inquadra per lo più facilmente negli schemi semipelagiani, ma può anche spiegarsi in senso ortodosso. La fraseologia stessa con cui tratta di queste questioni si risenta assai della fraseologia semipelagiana, ma vi sono anche forti tracce di fraseologia d'origine agostiniana, senza che si possa sicuramente decidere se il pensiero pendeva più in un senso che in un altro. Poichè s. Benedetto non ignorava la questione, si deve ammettere che questa sua posizione agnostica non è casuale, ma calcolata" (82). My attention was directed to Vagaggini's article by my friend Dom Emmanuel Lanne of Chevetogne (letter of 14 June 1994).

55. The text is contained in L. Holstein's *Codex Regularum monasticarum et canonicarum* (Paris 1663), as expanded by M. Brockie (Augsburg: Veith, 1759; reprinted Graz: Akademische Druck- und Verlagsanstalt, 1957), in the second tome, fifteenth addition, 335.

56. Letter of 13 May 1994.

57. Preface to "Sermons on Several Occasions" (1746), in *Works* 1:104–5.

58. A dictum of George Croft Cell, quoted by Thomas C. Oden, *Doctrinal Standards in the Wesleyan Tradition* (Grand Rapids: Zondervan/Francis Asbury, 1988), 82.

59. It is reported that Francis Asbury, one of the first two bishops of the Methodist Episcopal Church in the United States, would place children on his knee and teach them the rhyme:

> Learn to read, and learn to pray;
> Learn to work, and learn to obey.

See Henry Boehm, *Reminiscences, Historical and Biographical*, ed. Joseph B. Wakeley (New York: Carlton and Porter, 1865), 447.

60. *Rule*, prologue, 29–32 (my translation from de Vogüé and Neufville, volume 1, 418–21).

61. Of this sermon, the editor of the current scholarly edition of Wesley's Sermons, Albert C. Outler, writes: "This must be considered as a landmark sermon, for it stands as the late Wesley's most complete and careful exposition of the mystery of divine-human interaction, his subtlest probing of the paradox of prevenient grace and human agency. . . . In any dozen of his sermons most crucial for an accurate assay of Wesley's theology, this one would certainly deserve inclusion." See *Works* 3:199.

62. *Works* 3:202–3.

63. Later in the sermon, Wesley makes a characteristic attempt to stay away from a Calvinist notion of predestination: "Allowing that all the souls of men are dead in sin by nature, this excuses none, seeing there is no man that

is in a state of mere nature; there is no man, unless he has quenched the Spirit, that is wholly void of the grace of God. No man living is entirely destitute of what is vulgarly called 'natural conscience'. But this is not natural; it is more properly termed 'preventing grace'. Every man has a greater or less measure of this, which waiteth not for the call of man. Everyone has sooner or later good desires, although the generality of men stifle them before they can take deep root or produce any considerable fruit. Everyone has some measure of that light, some faint glimmering ray, which sooner or later, more or less, enlightens every man that cometh into the world. And everyone, unless he be one of the small number whose conscience is seared as with a hot iron [1 Timothy 4:2], feels more or less uneasy when he acts contrary to the light of his own conscience. So that no man sins because he has not grace, but because he does not use the grace which he hath" (*Works* 3:207). This is the point at which Calvinists may find it difficult to excuse Wesley from semipelagianism; yet in another place, Wesley makes clear that sufficient freedom of will to accept the gospel has been *restored* (admittedly, universally) to humankind (in virtue of Christ's *redemptive* work for all): "every man has a measure of free will restored to him by grace" (see "Some Remarks on Mr. Hill's 'Review of all the Doctrines taught by Mr. John Wesley'," in *Works* [J] 10:392).

64. *Works* 3:203–4.

65. *Works* 3:206.

66. Cf. *Works* 3:206.

67. It is a smart move on Wesley's part to cite Augustine against the Calvinists, even though he appears to be quoting from memory: "Qui ergo fecit te sine te, non te justificat sine te" (Sermon 169, §11(13); Migne, *Patrologia Latina* 38:922–3). Wesley had given the same text, in his own form, in Sermon 63, "The General Spread of the Gospel" (1783), in *Works* 2:490.

68. *Works* 3:208–9.

69. *Works* 3:209.

70. *A Collection of Hymns*, no. 417, *Works* 7:591–2 (no. 572 in the British *Methodist Hymn Book* of 1933; no. 788 in *Hymns and Psalms* of 1983).

71. *A Collection of Hymns*, no. 309, *Works* 7:465 (no. 578 in the British *Methodist Hymn Book* of 1933; no. 785 in *Hymns and Psalms*; and no. 413 in the American *United Methodist Hymnal* of 1989).

72. See André Birmelé, *Le salut en Jésus-Christ dans les dialogues oecuméniques* (Paris: Cerf, and Geneva: Labor et Fides, 1986); and *Grundkonsens—Grunddifferenz*, eds. A. Birmelé and H. Meyer (Frankfurt am Main: Otto Lembeck, and Paderborn: Bonifatius Verlag, 1992).

73. From *The Book of Services for the Use of The United Methodist Church* (Nashville: The United Methodist Publishing House, 1993), 72.

74. Hilpisch, 18–20, 23–24.

75. Francis Frost, "Méthodisme," in *Catholicisme, hier, aujourd'hui et demain*, ed. G. Jacquemet and others (Paris: Letouzey & Ané, 1948 onward), 9:48–71.

76. Albert C. Outler, "Do Methodists Have a Doctrine of the Church?" in *The Doctrine of the Church*, ed. Dow Kirkpatrick (Nashville: Abingdon, 1964), 11–28.

77. See ¶24 of the "Nairobi Report," *Towards a Statement on the Church* (1986). Text in the then Secretariat for Promoting Christian Unity's *Informa-*

tion Service, no. 62 (1986/4), 206–16; in the ecumenical periodical published by the Benedictine sisters of Turvey Abbey (England), *One in Christ* 22 (1986), 241–59; and separately as a booklet from the World Methodist Council (Lake Junaluska, North Carolina).

Notes to Chapter Five

1. The relative importance of 24 May 1738 in Wesley's biography has been variously evaluated; see J. Ernest Rattenbury, *The Conversion of the Wesleys* (London: Epworth, 1938). In *John Wesley in the Evolution of Protestantism* (London: Sheed & Ward, 1937), the Belgian Catholic Maximin Piette puts more weight on the resolve to a regular and holy life which Wesley made in 1725 under the influence of readings in Thomas à Kempis and Jeremy Taylor, soon to be followed by William Law. Apart from the entry in his *Journal* (intended for publication), the later Wesley rarely speaks of the experience of May 1738. The external occasion for him to take up field-preaching, with lasting success, was supplied by George Whitefield's invitation to collaboration in March–April 1739. Certain remains the fact that Wesley's evangelistic career would be unthinkable without its basis in "the religion of the heart" personally discovered on 24 May 1738.

2. D. Bonhoeffer, *Letters and Papers from Prison*, ed. E. Bethge (New York: Macmillan, 1967), letter of 8 June 1944.

3. Documentation in A. C. Outler, *John Wesley* (New York: Oxford University Press, 1964), 353–76.

4. M. Schmidt, *John Wesley—A Theological Biography*, vol. 2, part 1 (Nashville: Abingdon, 1972), 56.

5. For references to Luther in Wesley's writings, see H. Carter, *The Methodist Heritage* (London: Epworth, 1951), 221–31.

6. See E. G. Rupp, *Luther's Progress to the Diet of Worms* (London: SCM, 1951), and *The Righteousness of God* (London: Hodder & Stoughton, 1953); P. S. Watson, *Let God Be God* (London: Epworth, 1947), and *The Message of the Wesleys* (New York: Macmillan, 1964).

7. F. Hildebrandt, *From Luther to Wesley* (London: Lutterworth, 1951), and *Christianity According to the Wesleys* (London: Epworth, 1956). Schmidt, the author of a two-volume theological biography (see note 4), was a Lutheran.

8. Report on the Bristol meeting of May 1980 (unpublished typescript):

> (14) In both Methodism and Lutheranism the spiritual experience of the founder has entered into doctrinal formulations. The personality differences between Luther and Wesley along with the changed socio-cultural-historical-ecclesiastical contexts contributed to different expressions of Christian experience. So Methodists understand it as personal appropriation of the Gospel, as constant interplay between God and persons, and as being receptive to God's action. There is in this tradition an affirmation of God's complete redemption in Christ. Lutherans, on the other hand, look at Christian experience as dialectical. The Christian is always, at the same time, both saint and sinner (*simul justus et peccator*), living every moment dependent on God's grace. Justification covers the entirety of Christian living. . . .

(19) Furthermore, we agree that, on the basis of scripture, the person who is justified always lives by God's grace as that is received through faith; here the concept of faith also includes obedience. But it is also at this point that important divergences occur. Lutherans understand faith as building upon the righteousness of Christ alone, then expressing this new relationship in Christian obedience which is a continual struggle against the fallen nature. Such a struggle may produce self-condemnation and despair as one stands accused by the law. The awareness of this condemnation leads a Christian back to a trust in Christ's righteousness as the only ground of salvation.

(20) Methodists question this understanding of Christian experience as it is set against a scriptural background. They do not see Paul and the other New Testament writers as viewing the Christian life as remaining permanently under the accusation of the law. Transformed by Christ, the life of faith is set free to conform to the will of God so that Christians may live as redeemed persons through the power of God. . . .

(22) Both justification and sanctification are built upon the essential foundation of the gracious initiative of God. This initiative implies the election of persons by God, although Methodists emphasize free grace for all while traditional Lutheran teaching uses the language of predestination as better suited to its model for understanding how God in Christ invites all persons into new relationship with him.

9. Right until his death in 1791 Wesley continued his strong opposition to a separation with the Church of England: separation would be a sin against love and would be a counter-witness to non-believers (see e.g., his sermons of 1786 "Of the Church" and "On Schism" and his 1789 sermon on "The Ministerial Office"); but he had for several years taken practical and legal steps which ensured Methodism at least a semi-autonomous existence. Wesley was likened to a rower who "looked one way, while every stroke of his oar took him in the opposite direction." The most detailed study is Frank Baker, *John Wesley and the Church of England* (London: Epworth, 1970).

10. Methodism spread to every part of England and in some counties for a while almost took on the appearance of a folk church; but becoming a state church was naturally out of the question. After Wesley had in September 1784 "set apart" two "Superintendents" for North America, the Methodists in the United States by Christmas of the same year constituted themselves "The Methodist Episcopal Church." Negotiations with American "Anglicans," who had meantime acquired bishops by way of Scotland, led to no result. Since independence, the Constitution of the U.S.A. has favored religious "pluralism."

11. A small and partial exception is Tonga, where the royal family became Methodist.

12. Howard A. Snyder, *The Radical Wesley and Patterns for Church Renewal* (Downers Grove, Ill.: Inter-Varsity, 1980), especially 9, 80–82, 93–96.

13. The latter expression is found, for example, in the Minutes of the 1744 Conference as a definition of "the Church, in the proper sense."

14. It was precisely such factors which won Zwingli back to infant baptism. Karl Barth linked infant baptism with the desire, even in our own times, to preserve Constantinian Christendom (see *Church Dogmatics* IV/4 [Edinburgh: T & T Clark, 1969], 168).

15. Some texts in J.D.C. Fisher, *Christian Initiation—The Reformation Period* (London: SPCK, 1970), 3ff.

16. R.E. Cushman, "Baptism and the Family of God," in D. Kirkpatrick, ed., *The Doctrine of the Church* (Nashville: Abingdon, 1964), 79–102.

17. This is confirmed in detail by B.G. Holland, *Baptism in Early Methodism* (London: Epworth, 1970).

18. For example, Sermon 18 on "The Marks of the New Birth" (1748), reads: "The question is not, what you was made in baptism (do not evade); but, what are you now? Is the Spirit of adoption now in your heart? To your own heart let the appeal be made. I ask not, whether you *was* born of water and of the Spirit; but are you *now* the temple of the Holy Ghost which dwelleth in you? . . . Say not in your heart, 'I *was once* Baptized, therefore I *am now* a child of God. Alas, that consequence will by no means hold. How many are the baptized gluttons and drunkards, the baptized liars and common swearers, the baptized railers and evil-speakers, the baptized whoremongers, thieves, extortioners? What think you? Are these now the children of God? . . . Lean no more on the staff of that broken reed, that ye *were* born again in baptism. Who denies that ye were then made children of God, and heirs of the kingdom of heaven? But, notwithstanding this, ye are now children of the devil. Therefore, ye must be born again. And let not Satan put it into your heart to cavil at a word, when the thing is clear. Ye have heard what are the marks of the children of God: all ye who have them not on your souls, baptized or unbaptized, must needs receive them, or without doubt ye will perish everlastingly." See *Works* 1:417–30, in particular 428f., 430.

19. The "Statement on Holy Baptism" of the 1952 British Methodist Conference was strongly influenced by the widely read work of W. F. Flemington, *The New Testament Doctrine of Baptism* (London: SPCK, 1948), particularly 130–47 ("The New Testament Baptismal Teaching in its Relation to the Baptism of Infants").

20. E. Schlink, *The Doctrine of Baptism* (St. Louis: Concordia, 1972).

21. His fellow Lutherans will find very provocative Eilert Herms' recent description of faith as "a human deed and good work"; he sharply distinguishes faith from revelation, which is God's act and gift and necessarily conditions faith. See *Theorie für die Praxis: Beiträge zur Theologie* (Munich: Kaiser, 1982), 26f.

22. Wesley's language is inconsistent when he draws distinctions between the "visibility" and the "invisibility" of the church. These terms may serve to designate the church in its "gathered" or its "scattered" existence respectively; but elsewhere Wesley thinks rather of the "inwardness" of "true faith" in contrast to merely "outward" membership of the Church. In the sense of the first distinction we read: "What do you mean by the Church? A visible church (as our Article defines it) is a company of faithful (or believing) people: *coetus credentium*. This is the essence of a church, and the properties thereof are (as they are described in the words that follow), 'among whom the pure Word of God is preached, and the sacraments duly administered.' Now, then (according to this authentic account), what is the Church of England? What is it, indeed, but the 'faithful people, the true believers of England?' It is true, if these are scattered abroad, they come under another consideration. But when they are visibly joined by assembling together to hear the pure Word of God preached and to eat of one bread and drink of one cup, they are then properly the visible

Church of England. . . . A provincial or national church, according to our Article, is the true believers of that province or nation. If they are dispersed up and down, they are only a part of the invisible Church of Christ. But if they are visibly joined by assembling together to hear his Word and partake of his Supper, they are then a visible church, such as the Church of England, of France, or any other. . . . The Article mentions three things as essential to a visible church: first, living faith, without which, indeed, there can be no church at all, neither visible nor invisible; secondly, preaching (and consequently hearing) the pure Word of God, else that faith would languish and die; and, thirdly, a due administration of the sacraments, the ordinary means whereby God increaseth faith" (*An Earnest Appeal to Men of Reason and Religion* [1743], §§76–78, in *Works* 11, in particular 77f). But in his controversy with Calvinists Wesley adopts the distinction in the sense of "the outward, visible church" and "the invisible church, which consists of holy believers" ("Predestination Calmly Considered," 1752, §71; in *Works* [J] 10:204–59, in particular 244–6). Between the two passages not only linguistic differences may exist, but practical tensions may also emerge. On the level of fact, Wesley can and must admit the presence also of unbelievers in the visible church, even in the assembled congregation (cf. Augsburg Confession, 8); yet theologically, he does not react in any way "spiritualistically," as though even "the true church" could somehow exist in the air, that is, without Word, sacraments, and works of love. Here Wesley remains true to the classical Reformation.

23. The "Rules of the United Societies" applied already to the "awakened," that is, those who had "a desire to flee from the wrath to come, to be saved from their sins," and *a fortiori* to those who had reached the "fulness of faith" and meet weekly in the "bands." See *Works* 9:67–75.

24. "This leads me to show you, in few and plain words, what the practice of a true Protestant is. I say 'a true Protestant, for I disclaim all common swearers, Sabbath-breakers, drunkards, all whoremongers, liars, cheats, extortioners—in a word, all that live in open sin. These are no Protestants; they are no Christians at all. Give them their own name: they are open heathens. They are the curse of the nation, the bane of society, the shame of mankind, the scum of the earth" ("Letter to a Roman Catholic" [1749], §12, in *Works* [J] 10:80–86, in particular 83; cf. Sermon 74, "Of the Church" §28, in *Works* 3:55f.).

25. Outler, *John Wesley*, 316.

26. So, for example, *The Methodist Service Book* (London: Methodist Publishing House, 1975).

27. So, for example, *An Earnest Appeal to Men of Reason and Religion*, §§57–60, in *Works* 11:67–70. Wesley can also write in an oversimplifying way: "Who has wrote more ably than Martin Luther on justification by faith alone? And who was more ignorant of the doctrine of sanctification, or more confused in his conceptions of it? . . . On the other hand, how many writers of the Roman Catholic Church . . . have wrote strongly and scripturally on sanctification, who, nevertheless, were entirely unacquainted with the nature of justification!" (Sermon 107, "On God's Vineyard" (1787), in *Works* 3:505f.).

28. W. Klaiber, *Rechtfertigung und Gemeinde: Eine Untersuchung zum paulinischen Kirchenverständnis* (Göttingen: Vandenhoeck & Ruprecht, 1982), 265.

29. P. Brunner, *Worship in the Name of Jesus* (St. Louis: Concordia, 1968). For Wesley, see above, note 22.

30. *Hymns on the Lord's Supper* (1745), no. 96. The third part of this collection (hymns 93–115) bears the title "The Sacrament a Pledge of Heaven." Cf. J. E. Rattenbury, *The Eucharistic Hymns of John and Charles Wesley* (London: Epworth, 1948); A.R. George, "The Lord's Supper" in *The Doctrine of the Church* (as in note 16), 140–60.

31. *Baptism, Eucharist and Ministry* (Geneva: W.C.C., 1982).

32. Wesley celebrated the Lord's Supper and received communion with a frequency quite exceptional in the Church of England of the eighteenth century (he received communion on average once every five days throughout his ministry). Cf. J. C. Bowmer, *The Lord's Supper in Early Methodism* (London: Dacre, 1951). In the nineteenth century, Methodists forgot Wesley's exhortations to "constant communion"; cf. J. C. Bowmer, *The Lord's Supper in Methodism, 1791–1960* (London: Epworth, 1961).

33. These formulations come from the World Council of Churches Assemblies in New Delhi (1961), and Nairobi (1975); cf. G. Wainwright, "Conciliarity and Eucharist," *Midstream* 17 (1978), 135–53. In reply to the Caveat against Methodists of the Roman Catholic bishop Richard Challoner, Wesley defines the true "catholic" church thus: "Such is the Catholic Church, that is, the whole body of men, endued with faith working by love, dispersed over the whole earth, in Europe, Asia, Africa, and America. And this Church is 'ever one' [the quotations are from Challoner]; in all ages and nations it is the one body of Christ. It is 'ever holy'; for no unholy man can possibly be a member of it. It is 'ever orthodox'; so is every holy man, in all things necessary to salvation; 'secured against error,' in things essential, 'by the perpetual presence of Christ and ever directed by the Spirit of Truth,' in the truth that is after godliness. This Church has 'a perpetual succession' of pastors and teachers. And there have never been wanting in the reformed [*reformatorisch*] Churches, such a succession of pastors and teachers; men both divinely appointed and divinely assisted; for they convert sinners to God—a work none can do unless God himself doth appoint them thereto, and assist them therein; therefore every part of this character is applicable to them. Their teachers are the proper successors of those who have delivered to them, down through all generations, the faith once delivered to the saints; and their members have true spiritual communion with the 'one holy' society of true believers. Consequently, although they are not the whole 'people of God,' yet are they an undeniable part of his people" (*Journal*, 19 February 1761). In the ecumenical twentieth century we have come to see more clearly that the unity and the holiness of the *Una Sancta* are inseparable both inwardly and outwardly. That is the motive for the eschatological search within history not only for the concrete holiness of the Church but also for its structural unity.

34. A. C. Outler, "Do Methodists have a Doctrine of the Church?" in Kirkpatrick, ed., *The Doctrine of the Church*, 11–28; G. Wainwright, "Methodism's Ecclesial Location and Ecumenical Vocation," *One in Christ* 19 (1983), 104–34. The diachronic sense of our own provisionality is accompanied by our synchronic sense that the particular calling to spread holiness demands a "catholic" context in the true meaning of the term. C.W. Williams describes Methodism as "a society in search of the Church": *John Wesley's Theology Today* (Nashville: Abingdon, 1960), 216.

35. Methodists of the British type have joined in church unions with

Christians of other traditions in South India, North India, Papua-New Guinea, Australia, France, Italy, Zambia, and so on. The same is true of Methodists of the American type in Belgium and Pakistan, and of Methodists of both British and American origins in Canada. In 1969 and 1972 the Church of England twice refused reunion with the British Methodist Church; and in 1982 the English Anglicans again declined to enter a "Covenant" with the Methodists, the United Reformed, and the Moravians.

36. The "unity in reconciled diversity" favored by the Lutheran World Federation leaves the problem of doctrinal and pastoral authority intact; cf. Harding Meyer, "'Einheit in versöhnter Verschiedenheit'—'konziliare Gemeinschaft'—'organische Union': Gemeinsamkeit und Differenz gegenwärtig diskutierter Einheitskonzeptionen," *Oekumenische Rundschau* 27 (1978), 377–400.

Notes to Chapter Six

1. See *Vom Dialog zur Kanzel- und Abendmahlsgemeinschaft: Eine Dokumentation der Lehrgespräche und der Beschlüsse der kirchenleitenden Gremien*, herausgegeben vom Lutherischen Kirchenamt und von der Kirchenkanzlei der Evangelisch-methodistischen Kirche (Hanover and Stuttgart, 1987).

2. *A Lutheran-United Methodist Statement on Baptism* was published with supporting papers in a special issue of the *Perkins Journal* 34 (1981). The Missouri Synod participants in the baptismal consultation voted "no" or abstained. *Episcopacy: A Lutheran/United Methodist Common Statement to the Church* is obtainable from the ELCA Office for Ecumenical Affairs.

3. Joint Commission between the Lutheran World Federation and the World Methodist Council, The Church: Community of Grace (Geneva: Lutheran World Federation, and Lake Junaluska, N.C.: World Methodist Council, 1984).

4. Robert E. Chiles, *Theological Transition in American Methodism, 1790–1935* (New York: Abingdon, 1965).

5. *Ecumenism: The Vision of the Evangelical Lutheran Church in America* is "a statement adopted as a working document by the 1989 Churchwide Assembly of the ELCA."

6. The Norwegian Lutheran member of the LWF/WMC Commission that produced *The Church: Community of Grace* made a personal statement of dissent, judging there to be "a convergence of viewpoints, but not a full consensus" on sanctification, baptism and the eucharist, while "the doctrines of man, sin and grace" require further discussion. In Pastor Oestnor's opinion, there is "not yet established a sufficient theological basis between Methodist and Lutheran churches" for "church unity in the form of full pulpit and altar fellowship."

7. See *Justification by Faith*, eds. H. George Anderson, T. Austin Murphy, and Joseph A. Burgess (Minneapolis: Augsburg, 1985).

8. Eilert Herms, *Theologie für die Praxis: Beiträge zur Theologie* (Munich: Kaiser, 1982), 26f.

Notes to Chapter Seven

1. I am suggesting that what H. Richard Niebuhr, in *Christ and Culture* (New York: Harper and Row, 1951), presents as five "typical" *attitudes* on the part of diverse Christian thinkers or groups towards culture *as a whole* can also serve as a grid for evaluating different *components* within a *particular* culture. In that case, Niebuhr's preferred fifth "type"—the transformation of culture by Christ—could occur by a process of sifting and choice such as John Henry Newman ascribed to the assimilative power of tradition: "Facts and opinions, which have hitherto been regarded in other relations and grouped round other centres, henceforth are gradually attracted to a new influence and subjected to a new sovereign. They are modified, laid down afresh, thrust aside, as the case may be. A new element of order and composition has come among them; and its life is proved by this capacity of expansion, without disarrangement or dissolution. An eclectic, conservative, assimilating, healing, moulding process, a unitive power, is of the essence, and a test, of a faithful development" (*Essay on the Development of Christian Tradition*, II.v.3; paperback edition [London and New York: Sheed and Ward, 1960], 135).

2. For these "levels" of history, see Edward Schillebeeckx, *Jesus: An Experiment in Christology* (New York: Crossroad, 1981), 576–82 (translation of *Jezus, het verhaal van een levende* [Bloemendaal: Nelissen, 1974], §IV.1.1).

3. Up to now, the "post-modern" seems to me to consist of no more than the internal self-criticism of the modern. If the post-modern really does turn out to be a new epoch, it appears on present showing to retain so much of the modern that it will at most be its *Aufhebung* rather than a fresh start.

4. Sermon 39, "Catholic Spirit" (1750), in *Works* 2:79–95; "Letter to a Roman Catholic" (1749), in *Works* [J] 10:80–86, and in a modern edition by Michael Hurley, *John Wesley's Letter to a Roman Catholic* (London: Chapman, 1968).

5. Henry D. Rack, *Reasonable Enthusiast: John Wesley and the Rise of Methodism* (London: Epworth, 1989).

6. Scholarly edition of the *Earnest Appeal* (1743), and the *Farther Appeal* (1745), in *Works* 11.

7. Sermon 43, "The Scripture Way of Salvation" (1765), in *Works* 2:152–69.

8. *Journal*, 16 September 1739, in *Works* 19:97.

9. *The Book of Discipline of The United Methodist Church, 1972* (Nashville: The United Methodist Publishing House, 1973), ¶68 and ¶70 (39f., 75–79).

10. Apart from brief extracts from his writings in English and German-language biographies, I have been able to read of Grundtvig himself only his *What Constitutes Authentic Christianity?*, first published in four instalments in the *Theologisk Maanedsskrift* in 1826, and translated from volume 4 of the *Udvalgte Skrifter* (1906), by Ernest D. Nielsen (Philadelphia: Fortress, 1985); and *N. F. S. Grundtvig: Selected Writings*, ed. Johannes Knudsen, (Philadephia: Fortess, 1976). Otherwise I have relied heavily on the interpretations offered by Theodor Jørgensen and Jens Holger Schjørring in their respective contributions to *Heritage and Prophecy: Grundtvig and the English-Speaking World*,

eds. A. M. Allchin, D. Jasper, J. H. Schjørring and K. Stevenson (Aarhus: Aarhus University Press, 1993): "Grundtvig's *The Church's Retort*—in a Modern Perspective," 171–90, and "Church Continuity and the Challenge of Modernity: Grundtvig, the Oxford Movement and Rationalist Theology," 215–32. This seems justified in that they, too, are concerned with the relation of Grundtvig to modernity and to tradition.

11. *Letters* 6:297–99.

12. *Earnest Appeal*, §27, *Works* 11:55.

13. Ibid., §§28–29, *Works* 11:55.

14. Ibid., §30, *Works* 11:55.

15. Ibid., §§31–32, *Works* 11:56f.

16. Ibid., §30, *Works* 11:56.

17. Hymn of 1740 by Charles Wesley (1707–1788), in *A Collection of Hymns*, no. 92, *Works* 7:194–5. For Methodists, "Wesley" often functions as a collective noun including both John and Charles, although strictly the unqualified use refers to the elder brother alone. Danish readers may like to be initiated into a shibboleth: traditional British Methodists know that the pronunciation of Wesley is Wessley; only Anglicans and Americans say Wezley.

18. The point is set in its fuller context by Jørgensen's discussion.

19. Alasdair MacIntyre, *Whose Justice? Which Rationality?* (Notre Dame: University of Notre Dame Press, 1988).

20. See Thomas F. Torrance, *Theological Science* (London: Oxford University Press, 1969); *God and Rationality* (London: Oxford University Press, 1971); *Christian Theology and Scientific Culture* (Belfast: Christian Journals Limited, 1980); *The Ground and Grammar of Theology* (Belfast: Christian Journals Limited, 1980); and *Reality and Scientific Theology* (Edinburgh: Scottish Academic Press, 1985).

21. "The Character of a Methodist" (1742), in *Works* [J] 8:339–47, in particular 340.

22. "Catholic Spirit" (1750), in *Works* 2:93.

23. *Works* [J] 10:392. The context makes clear that this is by *redemptive* grace, in contrast to fallen human nature where "the will of man is free only to evil."

24. See Jürgen Weissbach, *Der neue Mensch im theologischen Denken John Wesleys* (Stuttgart: Christliches Verlagshaus, 1970); A. S. Yates, *The Doctrine of Assurance, with special reference to John Wesley* (London: Epworth, 1952); and H. Lindström, *Wesley and Sanctification: A Study in Salvation* (London: Epworth, 1950).

25. Scholarly edition in *Works* 7. The quotation is from Wesley's Preface (here 74).

26. From "The Principles of a Methodist Farther Explained," *Works* [J] 8:472.

27. *Earnest Appeal*, §§47–52, *Works* 11:62–65.

28. Sermon 55 (of 1775), "On the Trinity," in *Works* 2:373–86, in particular 385.

29. George A. Lindbeck, *The Nature of Doctrine: Religion and Theology in a Postliberal Age* (Philadelphia: Westminster, 1984), in particular 22. In the fourth instalment of *What Constitutes Authentic Christianity?* (see note 10), Grundtvig makes a marvellous preemptive strike against "experiential-expres-

sivism" by showing how the admixture of sin in people's unformed desires for salvation subjects them to self-deception in their religious constructions (98–101 in the English translation).

30. Third stanza of "Trods Lœngselans Smerte," from Grundtvig's *Sang-Vaerk* (1837), no. 60; textual history in Anders Malling, *Dansk Salme Historie*, vol. 5 (Copenhagen: J. H. Schultz Forlag, 1966), 56–58. In English prose paraphrase: We live and move and have our being in Christ, God's living Word. Take the Word in your mouth, and love it deeply! Then he dwells in you by his Name.

31. Charles Wesley, "Since the Son hath made me free," fourth stanza (1739 and 1778 versions of the hymn), in *A Collection of Hymns*, no. 379, *Works* 7:552.

32. A dictum of George Croft Cell, quoted by Thomas C. Oden, *Doctrinal Standards in the Wesleyan Tradition* (Grand Rapids: Zondervan/Francis Asbury, 1988), 82.

33. From the preface to Wesley's "Sermons on Several Occasions." Scholarly edition in *Works* 1, in particular 104f.

34. See the text "Of Preaching Christ" (1751 and 1779), in *Works* 26: 482–89.

35. The *Explanatory Notes upon the New Testament*, indebted particularly to J. A. Bengel, date from 1755, and those on the Old Testament, indebted to Matthew Henry, from 1765. Wesley's prefaces to the two sets of *Notes* are printed in *Works* [J] 10:235–39 and 246–53.

36. *Works* 1:106.

37. *A Collection of Hymns*, no. 83, *Works* 7:182–3.

38. *What Constitutes Authentic Christianity?* (as in note 10), 108. This "church-historical" view was Grundtvig's "matchless discovery" of the mid-1820s, and he stayed firm in it. After the "crisis" of 1810–11 he had gone through a "biblicist" phase.

39. See Wolfhart Pannenberg, *Grundzüge der Christologie*, 5th ed. (Gütersloh: Mohn, 1976), 47–112.

40. For example, B. S. Childs, *Introduction to the Old Testament as Scripture* (Philadelphia: Fortress, 1979), and *The New Testament as Canon: An Introduction* (Philadelphia: Fortress, 1985).

41. G. Ebeling, "Kirchengeschichte als Geschichte der Auslegung der Heiligen Schrift" (1946–47), in *Wort Gottes und Tradition* (Göttingen: Vandenhoeck & Ruprecht, 1964), 9–27.

42. That is the implicit weakness in the otherwise appealing article of David Steinmetz, "The Superiority of Pre-Critical Exegesis," in *Theology Today* 37 (1980–81), 27–38.

43. See, for instance, K. Hübner, *Die Wahrheit des Mythos* (Munich: Beck, 1985), and "Der Mythos, der Logos und das spezifisch Religiöse," in H. H. Schmid (ed.), *Mythos und Rationalität* (Gütersloh: Mohn, 1988), 27–43.

44. Lindbeck, *The Nature of Doctrine*, 117.

45. One of the reasons for Ted A. Campbell's scepticism concerning the finding of "the modern Methodist quadrilateral" (see early in this chapter) in Wesley himself lies in the absence from Wesley of a positive notion of tradition "in a post-Tractarian or modern ecumenical sense of the term" as "describing God's work in the Church after the scriptural period"; see "The 'Wesleyan

Quadrilateral': The Story of a Modern Methodist Myth," in *Methodist History* 29 (1990–91), 87–95.

46. See note 4 above. For an analogy between Wesley's procedure here and that of the current "Apostolic Faith Study" in W.C.C. Faith and Order, see G. Wainwright, "Methodism and the Apostolic Faith" in M. Douglas Meeks (ed.), *What Should Methodists Teach?* (Nashville: Kingswood Books, 1990), 101–17 [chapter eleven in this book]. Wesley's omission of the Nicene Creed from the Communion office in *The Sunday Service of the Methodists* is thus much more probably attributable to his passion for liturgical abbreviation than to material dissatisfaction with the text.

47. So in the sermon "On the Trinity" (see above, note 28). Wesley's omission of the Anglican Article VIII ("Of the Three Creeds") from the Articles of Religion he prepared for North America is most likely due to his objections, common among eighteenth-century and later Anglicans, to the "damnatory clauses" in the Athanasianum.

48. See Ted A. Campbell, *John Wesley and Christian Antiquity* (Nashville: Kingswood Books, 1991).

49. *Earnest Appeal*, §76–78, *Works* 11:77f.

50. This comes through, for instance, in the "Letter to a Roman Catholic" (see above, note 4), §13: an exposition of the *fides quae creditur* is followed by a description of the *fides quâ creditur* and matching conduct ("A true Protestant believes in God, has a full confidence in his mercy, fears him with a filial fear, loves him with all his soul . . . and serves him truly all the days of his life . . . A true Protestant loves his neighbour . . . ").

51. Sermon 121, "Prophets and Priests" (also known as "The Ministerial Office," 1789), in *Works* 4, in particular 77. For nuances in Wesley's view of the "Constantinian fall," see Campbell, *John Wesley and Christian Antiquity*.

52. Sermon 61, "The Mystery of Iniquity" (1783), in *Works* 2:451–70, in particular 462–64.

53. *A Farther Appeal to Men of Reason and Religion*, in *Works* 11.

54. Wesley's dismal view of the earthly history of Christianity is somewhat mitigated by his belief in a transcendental communion of the saints embracing "all the living members of Christ on earth, as well as all who are departed in his faith and fear" ("Letter to a Roman Catholic," §9, as in note 4); see G. Wainwright, "Wesley and the Communion of Saints," in *One in Christ* 27 (1991), 332–45 [chapter fifteen in this book].

55. See Bernard G. Holland, *Baptism in Early Methodism* (London: Epworth, 1970). It must, however, be admitted that the notion gradually "fades" in Wesley.

56. Sermon 18, on "The Marks of the New Birth" (1748), in *Works* 1:415–30; cf. Sermon 45, "The New Birth" (1760), in *Works* 2:186–201.

57. "The school should not be a church, but on the other hand Grundtvig never doubted that a living school would act as a preparation for Christianity, as a church porch. . . . 'Let each upon this earth then strive / True man to be, / Open his ear to the word of truth / And render God his glory! / If Christianity be truth's way, / And he is not a Christian today, / He will be by tomorrow' " (Hal Koch, *Grundtvig*, translated from the Danish by Llewellyn Jones [Yellow Springs, Ohio: Antioch Press, 1952], 143, including a stanza from Grundtvig's poem "Man first, then Christian").

58. Figures from *The Church of England Year Book 1991* (London: Church House Publishing, 1991), 400f.

59. *Letters* 7:239. See also J. C. Bowmer, *The Lord's Supper in Early Methodism* (London: Dacre, 1951), where it emerges that Wesley took communion on average every four or five days in an age when parish practice in England averaged four celebrations a year.

60. See J. E. Rattenbury, *The Eucharistic Hymns of John and Charles Wesley* (London: Epworth, 1948).

61. The eschatological prospect is strong in section III of the Wesleyan *Hymns on the Lord's Supper*: "the sacrament a pledge of heaven" (nos. 93–115). In the *Danske Salmebog*, no. 54, Grundtvig speaks of "the word of grace, which comes to us at the Lord's table, inviting us to come and sit down eternally in the joy of the Lord"; and no. 243 echoes Luke 13:29. See, more broadly, Geoffrey Wainwright, *Eucharist and Eschatology* (London: Epworth, 1971; New York: Oxford University Press, 1981 [updated]).

62. "A responsibly celebrated eucharist exemplifies *justice* because grateful people are all equally welcomed there by the merciful Lord into his table fellowship, and all together share in the fruits of redemption and in the foretaste of the new heavens and the new earth in which right will prevail (cf. 2 Pet. 3:13). . . . The eucharist, responsibly celebrated, exemplifies *peace*, because reconciled people are there at peace with God and with one another (cf. Matt. 5:23f.)" (G. Wainwright, "Eucharist and/as Ethics," in *Worship* 62 [1988], 123–38, in particular 135f.).

63. Danish Lutherans and English Anglicans will have to ask themselves, more than English or American Methodists need to, how such a eucharistic ecclesiology, with its resonances of the "gathered church," relates to their inherited pattern of an "established" church. Hal Koch writes that Grundtvig made a "precise distinction between the state church and the true church of Jesus Christ. The former is only 'a civil institution,' but in it Christ's church may abide as guest. All that may reasonably be demanded of the state church is that it provide good living conditions for the true church" (*Grundtvig*, as in note 57, 174). *Not* that the "free churches," for their part, are out of the woods: "Thoughts of withdrawing from the [state] church and forming free congregations were again present to Grundtvig in his latter days. Only, he pointed out, one must of course realize that a free congregation gives no better guarantee than the state church that it is actually God's congregation there assembled. The free congregation can no more be identified with the true congregation out of hand than any other. The latter is neither palpable nor demonstrable, but is recognized through its signs of life, which are confession, songs of praise, and preaching" (Koch, 175).

Notes to Chapter Eight

1. Ronald S. Wallace, *Calvin's Doctrine of the Christian Life* (Edinburgh: Oliver and Boyd, 1959).

2. These summarizing propositions are amply illustrated from yet other writings of Wesley in J. L. Peters, *Christian Perfection and American Methodism* (New York: Abingdon, 1956).

3. *Works* [J] 11:441–43.

4. Sermon 43, "The Scripture Way of Salvation" (1765), in *Works* 2:153–69, in particular, 167–68.

5. Sermon 45, "The New Birth" (1760), in *Works* 2:186–201, in particular 187.

6. "A Plain Account of Christian Perfection" (1777), in *Works* [J] 11:417.

7. Sermon 63, "The General Spread of the Gospel" (1783), in *Works* 2:485–99, in particular 490; and Sermon 85, "On Working Out Our Own Salvation" (1785), *Works* 3:199–209, in particular 208.

8. As in note 7 (*Works* 3:199–209).

9. "Some Remarks on Mr. Hill's 'Review of all the Doctrines taught by Mr. John Wesley'" (1772), in *Works* [J] 10:374–414 (in particular 392).

10. "Serious Thoughts upon the Perseverance of the Saints," in *Works* [J] 10:285–98.

11. I. Howard Marshall, *Kept by the Power of God: A Study of Perseverance and Falling Away* (London: Epworth, 1969), 2.

12. "Predestination Calmly Considered," in *Works* [J] 10:204–59.

13. Ibid., §51; *Works* [J] 10:233.

14. From the hymn "And can it be, that I should gain," *Works* 7:322f.

15. From the hymn "Infinite, unexhausted Love," *Works* 7:338f.

16. "Thoughts upon God's Sovereignty," in *Works* [J] 10:361–63 (in particular 363).

17. Jürgen Weissbach, *Der neue Mensch im theologischen Denken John Wesleys* (Stuttgart: Christliches Verlagshaus, 1970); cf. 176: "eine gewisse Überordnung des Imagogedankens im theologischen Denken bei Wesley."

18. Sermon 129, "Heavenly Treasure in Earthen Vessels" (1790), in *Works* 4:161–67, in particular 164.

19. Sermon 28, "Upon our Lord's Sermon on the Mount, VIII," in *Works* 1:612–31, in particular 614.

20. "A Plain Account of Christian Perfection," *Works* [J] 11:417.

21. Letter of 15 January 1734 to Richard Morgan, in *Works* 25:369.

22. Letter of 17 June 1746 to Thomas Church ("The Principles of a Methodist Farther Explained"), in *Letters* 2:212–76, in particular 266.

23. Sermon 19, "The Great Privilege of Those That Are Born of God" (1748), in *Works* 1:431–43, in particular 432.

24. Sermon 5, "Justification by Faith" (1746), in *Works* 1:181–99, in particular 187.

25. Sermon 85, "On Working Out Our Own Salvation" (1785), in *Works* 3:199–209, in particular 204.

26. Sermon 127, "On the Wedding Garment" (1790), in *Works* 4:139–48, in particular 144.

27. "The Character of a Methodist," in *Works* [J] 8:339–47, in particular 343.

28. Sermon 92, "On Zeal" (1781), in *Works* 3:308–21, in particular 313.

29. Sermon 29, "Upon Our Lord's Sermon on the Mount, IX" (1748), in *Works* 1:632–49, in particular 635–36.

30. Gérard Philips, *L'union personnelle avec le Dieu vivant: Essai sur l'origine et le sens de la grâce créée* (Louvain: University Press, 1974).

31. S. Hauerwas, "Sanctification and the Ethics of Character," in his

Character and the Christian Life: A Study in Theological Ethics (San Antonio: Trinity University Press, 1975), 179–228.

32. Cited from A. P. F. Sell, *The Great Debate: Calvinism, Arminianism and Salvation* (Worthing [U.K.]: H. E. Walter, 1982), 125.

Notes to Chapter Nine

1. The preceding quotations (italics original) are all taken from John Meyendorff, "The Holy Spirit, as God" in *The Holy Spirit*, ed. Dow Kirkpatrick (Nashville: Tidings, 1974), 76–89; republished in John Meyendorff, *The Byzantine Legacy in the Orthodox Church* (Crestwood, N.Y.: St. Vladimir's Seminary Press, 1982), 153–65.

2. My original text has been nuanced at some points in light of its discussion in Constantinople. I express my gratitude to fellow participants in that conversation, Bishop Kallistos of Diokleia, Protopresbyter George Dragas, Dr. Joe Hale, and Professor Peter Stephens.

3. From the Deed of Union (1932) of the Methodist Church of Great Britain, clause 30. The "doctrinal clauses" of the Deed by which the various branches of British Methodism were reunited in 1932 continue to be protected in *The Constitutional Practice and Discipline of the Methodist Church*.

4. This statement stands at the head of the rather discursive accounts of "our doctrinal heritage" and "our doctrinal history" given in the 1992 *Book of Discipline of the United Methodist Church* (sections 65 and 66), from which the next quotations will be drawn.

5. Inherited from the body (largely German in ethnic origin), which joined with the Methodist Church to form the United Methodist Church in 1968.

6. The documents listed in this sentence are named in section 67 of the 1992 *Book of Discipline* and are constitutionally protected from change. Section 68 then turns, most discursively of all, to a contemporary statement concerning "our theological task," to which attention will be given in the last part of this paper, since it is the most recent official treatment directed by the United Methodist Church explicitly to the theme of Tradition.

7. Anglican Article VI = Methodist Article V.

8. "An Address to the Clergy," §I:2, in *Works* [J] 10:484; cf. Sermon 112, "On Laying the Foundation of the New Chapel" (1777), in *Works* 3:585–86. I owe the initial references, though not always the interpretation, to these and many other passages in the following section to Ted A. Campbell, *John Wesley and Christian Antiquity: Religious Vision and Cultural Change* (Nashville: Kingswood Books, 1991).

9. See, for example, *A Farther Appeal to Men of Reason and Religion*, Part I, §V.15–23, in *Works* 11:154–66.

10. See the prefatory material to Wesley's edition of the Apostolic Fathers in his *Christian Library*.

11. Letter of 4 January 1748–49 to Conyers Middleton, in *Works* [J] 10:14.

12. See Frederick Hunter, "The Manchester Non-Jurors and Wesley's High Churchism" in *London Quarterly and Holborn Review* 177 (1947), 56–61.

13. Manuscript of 1737, cited from A. C. Outler, *John Wesley* (New York: Oxford University Press, 1964), 46.

14. Letter of 4 January 1748–49 to Conyers Middleton, in *Works* [J] 10:12.

15. In his irenic "Letter to a Roman Catholic" (1749), Wesley set out the faith of "a true Protestant" in terms of an expansion upon the Nicene-Constantinopolitan Creed (*Works* [J] 10:80–86; cf. Geoffrey Wainwright, "Methodism and the Apostolic Faith," in *What Should Methodists Teach? Wesleyan Tradition and Modern Diversity*, ed. M. Douglas Meeks [Nashville: Kingswood Books, 1990], 101–17, 154f. [chapter eleven in this book]). On Wesley's adherence to Chalcedon, see John Deschner, *Wesley's Christology: An Interpretation* (Dallas: Southern Methodist University Press, 1960). Wesley considered the "explication" of the doctrine of the Trinity in the so-called Athanasian Creed "the best I ever saw"; see Sermon 55, "On the Trinity," in *Works* 2:377.

16. See *Journal* for 22 April 1779, in Curnock 6:231; Sermon 55, "On the Trinity," in *Works* 2:378–9, and Sermon 123, "On Knowing Christ after the Flesh," in *Works* 4:100.

17. See Frank Baker, *John Wesley and the Church of England* (London: Epworth, and Nashville: Abingdon, 1970), 40–41, 350–54.

18. See Campbell, ch. 3: "Primitive Christianity in the Wilderness."

19. *Journal* for 25 December 1774, in Curnock 6:54 and *Works* 22:441.

20. Journal for 30 March 1777, in Curnock 6:142. See John C. Bowmer, *The Sacrament of the Lord's Supper in Early Methodism* (London: Dacre, 1951). In 1787 and 1788, Wesley published a sermon on "The Duty of Constant Communion" that he had written in 1732 (Sermon 101 in *Works* 3:427–39). Throughout his life he encouraged his people to press for more frequent communion in their parish churches at a time when the Anglican custom contented itself with four celebrations a year.

21. Letter of 10 September 1784 to "Our Brethren in America," in *Letters* 7:237–39.

22. "A Plain Account of the People called Methodists," in *Works* [J] 8:248–68.

23. See Campbell, 51f, 89–94. The historical studies Wesley relied on were Edward Stillingfleet's *Irenicum* (1659), and Peter King's *Enquiry into the Constitution, Discipline, Unity, and Worship of the Primitive Church* (1712).

24. See Campbell, 48f.

25. Letter of 4 January 1748–49 to Conyers Middleton, in *Works* [J] 10:12; and (for Cyprian's evidence) Sermon 102, "Of Former Times" (1787), in *Works* 3:450–51.

26. See, for example, Sermon 61, "The Mystery of Iniquity" (1783), in *Works* 2:462–4; Sermon 102, "Of Former Times" (1787), in *Works* 3:449–50; Sermon 89, "The More Excellent Way" (1787), in *Works* 3:263f; and Sermon 104, "On Attending the Church Service" (1787), in *Works* 3:470.

27. See the tract on "The Origin of Image Worship among Christians," in *Works* [J] 10:175–77.

28. Letter of 4 January 1748–49 to Conyers Middleton, in *Works* [J] 10:1.

29. *Journal* for 5 August 1754, in Curnock 4:97 and *Works* 20:489.

30. *Journal* for 15 August 1750, in Curnock 3:490 and *Works* 20:356.

31. Letter of 12 March 1756 to William Dodd, in *Letters* 3:170–71.

32. Letter of 18 August 1775 to John Fletcher, in *Letters* 6:175. The

comment is illuminated by this: "It is scarce possible at this distance of time to know, what Pelagius really held. All his writings are destroyed; and we have no account of them but from Augustine, his furious implacable enemy. I doubt whether he was any more an heretic than Castellio or Arminius" (Wesley's note in his edition of Mosheim's *Concise Ecclesiastical History*).

33. "An Address to the Clergy," *Works* [J] 10:484; Letter of 4 January 1748–49 to Conyers Middleton, *Works* [J] 10:79; Sermon 112, "On Laying the Foundation of the New Chapel" (1777), *Works* 3:586.

34. The sources Wesley turned to were William Cave's *Primitive Christianity* (1672), Claude Fleury's *Moeurs des Chrétiens* (1682), and Johann Lorenz von Mosheim's *Concise Ecclesiastical History*. Wesley made editions of all these three works, excising material that he considered unedifying even among early Christians.

35. See *The Appeals to Men of Reason and Religion*, in *Works* 11:157–59; cf. the Letter of 10 July 1747 to "John Smith," in *Works* 26:251.

36. Francis Frost, "Méthodisme," in G. Jacquemet (ed.), *Catholicisme, hier, aujourd'hui, demain* (1948ff), volume 9, cols. 48–71: "Le méthodisme moderne doit en premier lieu cet héritage à John Wesley, tout comme, dans l'Église catholique romaine, un ordre religieux ou une famille spirituelle tient son esprit d'un fondateur."

37. In the mid nineteenth century the Methodist Episcopal Church split into "The Methodist Episcopal Church" and "The Methodist Episcopal Church, South." The two bodies were reunited in 1939, along with the Methodist Protestant Church, into "The Methodist Church." The name "The United Methodist Church" dates from the merger of 1968 with the smaller Evangelical United Brethren.

38. See, for example, *The Journal and Letters of Francis Asbury*, eds. J. Manning Potts, Elmer T. Clark, and Jacob S. Payton, 3 vols. (London: Epworth, and Nashville: Abingdon, 1958), 3:60–64 (letter of 15 August 1788 to Jasper Winscom).

39. Quoted from A. C. Outler, *John Wesley*, 154.

40. Note, for example, the remarks of Bishop Kallistos Ware with regard to Saints Cyril and Methodius: "With Bulgars, Serbs, and Russians as their 'spiritual children,' the two Greeks from Thessalonica abundantly deserve their title, 'Apostles of the Slavs'" (Timothy Ware, *The Orthodox Church* [Harmondsworth, Middlesex: Penguin Books, 1963], 85).

41. *Minutes of Several Conversations, Between the Rev. John Wesley, A.M., and the Preachers in Connection with Him, from the Year 1744* (Leeds: Printed by Edward Baines, 1803), 330–33.

42. Ibid., 21, 24.

43. Ibid., 320–26.

44. Conferences of 1796 and 1799 (ibid., 304f., 380).

45. From the 1992 *Discipline*; cf. the historic "Large Minutes," *Works* [J] 8:324–25).

46. See, for example, Robert E. Chiles, *Theological Transition in American Methodism, 1790–1935* (Nashville: Abingdon, 1965).

47. In the immediately preceding generation, an important influence was exercised by Albert C. Outler's florilegium, *John Wesley* (1964), in the Library of Protestant Theology published by the Oxford University Press. Even more

significant has been the momentous decision to undertake a Bicentennial Edition of *The Works of John Wesley* in 34 volumes (Oxford: Clarendon Press, 1975–83; Nashville: Abingdon, 1984—).

48. See Thomas A. Langford, *Practical Divinity: Theology in the Wesleyan Tradition* (Nashville: Abingdon, 1983).

49. See Francis Asbury's letter of 24 April 1786 to George Washington (*The Journal and Letters of Francis Asbury* 3:47).

50. See Charles R. Hohenstein, "The Revisions of the Rites of Baptism in the Methodist Episcopal Church, 1784–1939" (Ph. D. diss., University of Notre Dame, 1990); Karen B. Westerfield Tucker, "'Till Death Us Do Part': The Rites of Marriage and Burial Prepared by John Wesley and their Development in the Methodist Episcopal Church, 1784–1939" (Ph. D. diss., University of Notre Dame, 1992).

51. See J. Ernest Rattenbury, *The Eucharistic Hymns of John and Charles Wesley* (London: Epworth, 1948); cf. Geoffrey Wainwright, "Patristic Themes in the Wesley Brothers' 'Hymns on the Lord's Supper' of 1745" in the memorial volume for Fr. Dumitru Staniloae, *Person and Communion*.

52. Scholarly edition by Franz Hildebrandt and Oliver A. Beckerlegge, *A Collection of Hymns for the Use of the People called Methodists* in *Works* 7.

53. Already some of John Mason Neale's nineteenth-century translations from the Greek were included in earlier twentieth-century Methodist hymnals. More recently, some Russian chant forms have been introduced for occasional use with standard liturgical texts (e.g. the Kyrie).

54. This would be a practical instance of the "exchange of saints" which is necessary to growth in communion among Christian communities. See Geoffrey Wainwright, "Wesley and the Communion of Saints," in *One in Christ* 27 (1991), 332–45 [chapter fifteen in this book].

55. See especially *Baptism, Eucharist and Ministry 1982–1990: Report on the Process and Responses* (Geneva: W.C.C., 1990), 114–6 (cf. 62–8).

56. Sermon 101, *Works* 3:427–39.

57. See, chiefly from the Evangelical side, Thomas C. Oden, *Doctrinal Standards in the Wesleyan Tradition* (Grand Rapids: Zondervan/Francis Asbury, 1988), and Jerry L. Walls, *The Problem of Pluralism: Recovering United Methodist Identity* (Wilmore, Ky.: Good News Books, 1986, updated 1988).

58. Ted Campbell argued that the modern ecumenical appeal to Tradition could not be found in Wesley: he lived before the Western recovery of a more organic view of Tradition that came via the Tübingen Catholic J. A. Moehler and the Englishman J. H. Newman also into Anglican Tractarianism and even into Protestantism; Wesley still held the more episodic and discontinuous view of the Church's past that marked much of older Protestantism (not only on account of the Constantinian "fall" but also because of the degeneration in the medieval West that had made the sixteenth-century Reformation necessary). See Ted A. Campbell, "The 'Wesleyan Quadrilateral': The Story of a Modern Methodist Myth," in *Methodist History* 29 (1990–91), 87–95.

59. *Discipline*, 1992, quoted from ¶68 (pp. 76–80).

60. I refer to what Montreal called Tradition with a capital "T." The United Methodist text concentrates more on what Montreal called tradition with a small "t," that is, the act of transmission and the particular traditions (plural).

Notes to Chapter Ten

1. N. A. Nissiotis, "The Witness and the Service of Eastern Orthodoxy to the One Undivided Church" in *The Ecumenical Review* 14 (1961–62), 192–202.

2. J. D. Zizioulas, *Being as Communion* (Crestwood, N.Y.: St. Vladimir's Seminary Press, 1985).

3. For further exploration of this idea, see G. Wainwright, "In favour of a perichoretic and peripatetic episcopate—perhaps," in *Gemeinsamer Glaube und Strukturen der Gemeinschaft*, ed. Harding Meyer (Frankfurt am Main: Otto Lembeck, 1991), 198–207.

4. The "Primary Chronicle," quoted according to James H. Billington, *The Icon and the Axe* (New York: Random House, 1966), 6.

5. See Geoffrey Wainwright, *Doxology: The Praise of God in Worship, Doctrine and Life* (New York: Oxford University Press, 1980).

6. Letter of 10 September 1784 to "Our Brethren in America."

7. See again, from within Orthodoxy, Zizioulas, above. For the doctrine of the Trinity as a crucial issue, especially for contemporary Protestantism, see G. Wainwright, "The Doctrine of the Trinity: Where the Church Stands or Falls," in *Interpretation* 45 (1991), 117–32, and "Renewal as a Trinitarian and Traditional Event," in *Lexington Theological Quarterly* 25 (1991), 117–24.

8. See *Apostolic Faith Today: A Handbook for Study*, ed. Hans-Georg Link (Geneva: W.C.C., 1985), 246f.

9. Constantine D. Kalokyris, *The Essence of Orthodox Iconography* (Brookline: Holy Orthodox Press, 1985), 86.

10. John Henry Newman, *An Essay on the Development of Christian Doctrine*, third edition 1878 (often republished), Introduction, §5.

11. See *Baptism, Eucharist and Ministry 1982–1990: Report on the Process and Responses* (Geneva: W.C.C., 1990). For ecumenical work on apostolicity over the past three decades, see G. Wainwright, "Apostolic Tradition as a Theme in Ecumenical Dialogue," in *Tragende Tradition: Festschrift für Martin Seils zum 65. Geburtstag*, eds. Annagret Freund, U. Kern and A. Radler (Frankfurt am Main: Peter Lang, 1992), 157–71.

Notes to Chapter Eleven

1. Albert C. Outler (ed.), *John Wesley* (New York: Oxford University Press, 1964), 492–99; cf. *Works* [J] 10:80–86.

2. *Works* [J] 10:86–128 (extracted from Bishop John Williams). See also "Popery Calmly Considered," ibid., 140–58.

3. Sermon 39, "Catholic Spirit" (1750), in *Works* 2:79–95.

4. (Geneva: W.C.C., 1987) [revised 1991].

5. *Baptism, Eucharist and Ministry*, Faith and Order Paper No. 111 (Geneva: W.C.C., 1982).

6. See the letter of 3 July 1756, to James Clark, in *Letters* 3:180–83, in particular 182.

7. Since the original writing of this chapter, the 1988 *Discipline* of The United Methodist Church made the welcome—and needed—stipulation that

ordinations take place in the name of the Father, the Son, and the Holy Spirit (¶432), and the same was implied for baptism by the reference in ¶1214.3 to "The General Services of the Church."

8. From "A Plain Account of the People Called Methodists," in *Works* [J] 8:248–68, in particular 249; cf. the postscript to the letter of 3 July 1756, cited above in note 6.

9. From "The Character of a Methodist," in *Works* [J] 8:340–47, in particular 340.

10. Sermon 39, "Catholic Spirit," in *Works* 2:88–89.

11. *Letters* 5:270.

12. Sermon 55, "On the Trinity" (1775), in *Works* 2:374–86, in particular 385.

13. Sermon 64, "The New Creation" (1785), in *Works* 2:500–510, in particular 510.

14. G. C. Cell, as quoted by Thomas C. Oden, *Doctrinal Standards in the Wesleyan Tradition* (Grand Rapids: Zondervan/Francis Asbury, 1988), 82.

Notes to Chapter Twelve

1. *Towards Visible Unity: Commission on Faith and Order, Lima 1982*, Volume 1: *Minutes and Addresses*, ed. M. Kinnamon (Geneva: W.C.C., 1982), 80–84.

2. See Geoffrey Wainwright, "The Lima Text in the History of Faith and Order," *Studia Liturgica* 16 (1986), 6–21; and M. Thurian (and G. Wainwright), "'Baptism, Eucharist and Ministry'," in *Dictionary of the Ecumenical Movement*, ed. N. Lossky and others (Geneva: W.C.C., and Grand Rapids: Eerdmans, 1991), 80–83.

3. *Baptism, Eucharist and Ministry*, Faith and Order Paper No. 111 (Geneva: W.C.C., 1982).

4. *Churches Respond to BEM: Official Responses to the "Baptism, Eucharist and Ministry" Text*, ed. Max Thurian, 6 vols. (Geneva: W.C.C., 1986–88).

5. *Baptism, Eucharist and Ministry 1982–1990: Report on the Process and Responses*, Faith and Order Paper No. 149 (Geneva: W.C.C., 1990).

6. See *On the Way to Fuller Koinonia: Official Report of the Fifth World Conference on Faith and Order Santiago de Compostela 1993*, Faith and Order Paper No. 166, eds. Thomas F. Best and Günther Gassmann (Geneva: W.C.C., 1994), 245–52 [report of Section III].

7. Faith and Order Paper No. 73 (Geneva: W.C.C., 1975).

8. Text in *Churches Respond* 2:177–99.

9. Compare the response of the Roman Catholic Church: "We find the text on baptism to be grounded in the apostolic faith received and professed by the Catholic Church. It draws in a balanced way from the major New Testament areas of teaching about baptism; it gives an important place to the witness of the early Church. While it does not discuss all major doctrinal issues that have arisen about baptism, it is sensitive to the effect they have had on the development of the understanding of this sacrament and to the positive values of differing solutions that emerged; it appreciates the normative force that

some forms of liturgical celebration may have and the significance of pastoral practice; within the ecumenical scope it sets for itself, it articulates the development of the Christian understanding of baptism with a coherent theological method" (*Churches Respond* 6:9f.).

10. Compare again the Roman Catholic response: "The sources employed [in *BEM*] for the interpretation of the meaning of the eucharist and the form of celebration are Scripture and Tradition. The classical liturgies of the first millennium and patristic theology are important points of reference in this text" (*Churches Respond* 6:16).

11. The United Methodist Church does not, so far as I am aware, claim to have an episcopal succession going back to the Apostles in the sense in which that claim is made by the Orthodox Churches, the Oriental Churches, the Roman Catholic Church, the Anglican Communion, and some Lutheran Churches. See the report of the Joint Commission between the Roman Catholic Church and the World Methodist Council, *Towards a Statement on the Church* (1986), ¶33.

12. See 183, 192. This is a delicate point among Methodists. The UM response recognizes that there is no historical warrant in Wesley for "inviting [to communion] all who seek faith in Christ but have not found it" (183). In the rare use which he made of the phrase "converting ordinance" in controversy with the Moravians, Wesley recognized that there were "degrees of faith" and was concerned for those who were already surrendering themselves to God's mercy in Christ, or seeking to move from "the faith of a servant" to "the faith of a son," or looking for "full assurance" in the faith they already had (if only to a weak degree). See Albert C. Outler, *John Wesley* (New York: Oxford University Press, 1964), 354–76; and John C. Bowmer, "A Converting Ordinance and the Open Table," *Proceedings of the Wesley Historical Society* 34 (1964), 109–13. Nevertheless, the continental European Methodist responses to *BEM* will insist on "open access to the Lord's Table" in an evangelistic context, even to the point of explicitly not requiring baptism.

13. *Journal*, 14 February 1736, in Curnock 2:160 and *Works* 18:148.

14. See "A Treatise on Baptism," §IV.4, *Works* [J] 10:188–201, esp. 194.

15. The beginnings of a reconsideration of this question, in a sensitive and nuanced manner, are to be found in the text produced in the dialogue between the World Methodist Council and the World Alliance of Reformed Churches, *Together in God's Grace* (1987). See above, pp. 23–28 and 143–58.

16. See Geoffrey Wainwright, "Doctrine, Opinions, and Christian Unity: A Wesleyan and Methodist Perspective," in *In Search of Christian Unity: Basic Consensus/Basic Differences*, ed. Joseph A. Burgess (Minneapolis: Fortress, 1991), 193–99 [chapter fourteen in this book].

17. See Geoffrey Wainwright, "From Pluralism towards Catholicity? The United Methodist Church after the General Conference of 1988," *Asbury Theological Journal* 44 (1989), 17–27.

18. Some responses to *BEM* from churches on the Indian subcontinent, and especially the Church of South India, raise the question, at least tentatively, of the relation between the Christian faith, other religions, and salvation. See below.

19. The other responses to contain this kind of reservation about the Name of Father, Son and Holy Spirit come from the United Church of Canada,

the Anglican Church of Canada, and the United Church of Christ (USA). For what is at stake here, see Geoffrey Wainwright, "The Doctrine of the Trinity: Where the Church Stands or Falls," *Interpretation* 45 (1991), 117–32, and "Why Wesley was a Trinitarian," *The Drew Gateway* 59/2 (Spring 1990), 26–43 [chapter seventeen in this book].

20. In a scarcely veiled reference to the Church of England and the "disappointment" of several thwarted attempts at rapprochement with that body, the Methodists confess on the part of some a "hesitation about engaging in theological discussions with those in whose company we have sought but not found greater visible unity."

21. From the German-speaking area, this is characteristically put by the response of The United Methodist Church, Central and Southern Europe, in terms of a contrast between "the insight of the Reformation that the Church is *creatura verbi divini* (created by the divine word)" and "the notion of the Church as a dispensary of salvation (*Heilsanstalt*)"; see *Churches Respond* 2:236–44. Similarly, the response of the synod of the Waldensian and Methodist Churches in Italy judges that *BEM* "centers the faith, communion and Christian witness not on God and the gospel, but rather on the Church as a sacral structure that has and gives guarantees of the Spirit's presence and administers the Spirit's activities through a caste endowed with priestly powers, mediatorial, and representing the divine"; see *Churches Respond* 2:245–54.

22. The East and West German Methodist responses invoke the Reformation principle of "Scripture alone"—at least in the sense of Scripture as finally "decisive." See *Churches Respond* 4:167–72 and 173–82 respectively.

23. The New Zealand Methodist response to *BEM* had commented on the "Northern" and "Western" character of the text itself; see *Churches Respond* 1:78–80. The hermeneutical issues raised more discursively by the British response are likely to be taken up again in the continuing work of Faith and Order as it seeks to answer the call for an "ecumenical hermeneutic" made at the Fifth World Conference on Faith and Order at Santiago de Compostela in 1993. See *On the Way to Fuller Koinonia* (as in note 6), 234, 236, 244f., 252.

24. The West German Methodist response declares: "We see [in *BEM*] a danger of overemphasizing rites and signs. These can serve only as references." This underlies also the East German Methodist charge (found also in the response from Central and Southern Europe) of "sacramentalism" made against *BEM*, as though "liturgical customs hold greater value than the living word of Christ itself." In common with many Lutheran responses, the East and West German Methodists also regret the preference shown in *BEM* for the name "eucharist" over "Lord's Supper," detecting here a shift of emphasis "from God's action in Christ to the celebrating congregation and its 'activity' (praising God)."

25. This concern lies behind the Irish Methodist objection to *BEM*'s frequent use of "baptism" as the subject of a verb ("Baptism *does* this, that, and the other"); see *Churches Respond* 2:230–35. The 1990 "clarifications" of *BEM* state the criticized formulation to be shorthand for "God through baptism. . . ." That matches nicely the Church of England Catechism quoted by John Wesley in Sermon 16, "The Means of Grace" (1746): a sacrament is "an outward sign of inward grace, and *a means* whereby we receive the same." See *Works* 1:376–97, in particular 381.

26. Similarly, the West German Methodist response: "The Lord is not any more 'present' in the feast of the eucharist than in prayer or in the proclamation of his word." And several others. Note, more broadly, G. Wainwright, "Word and Sacrament in the Churches' Responses to the Lima Text," *One in Christ* 24 (1988), 304–27.

27. An anecdote: While in Constantinople in July 1993 for conversations between the World Methodist Council and the Orthodox Churches, I attended the Sunday Liturgy in the Ecumenical Patriarch's chapel. Observing that many bishops (visiting for another meeting) did not receive communion, I was told that rarity of reception reflected a high evalution of the sacrament. John Wesley's Sermon 101, "The Duty of Constant Communion" (1732 and 1787), would make interesting reading in more than one area of the Church (see *Works* 3:427–39).

28. The Roman Catholic response to *BEM* makes this clear. See Geoffrey Wainwright, "The Roman Catholic Response to 'Baptism, Eucharist and Ministry': The Ecclesiological Dimension," in *A Promise of Presence: Studies in Honor of David N. Power, O.M.I.*, eds. M. Downey and R. Fragomeni (Washington, D.C.: Pastoral Press, 1993), 187–206.

29. G. Wainwright, "Reconciliation in Ministry," in *Ecumenical Perspectives on Baptism, Eucharist and Ministry*, ed. Max Thurian (Geneva: W.C.C., 1983), 129–39, in particular 135.

30. The West German Methodist response is severe in its criticism of *BEM* as "too hierarchically-episcopal" in its vision of ecclesiastical structures, even perhaps to the point of making "the uninterrupted succession of the episcopate"—which the United Methodist Church in Central and Southern Europe calls "an assertion which has not yet been demonstrable through historical data"—"a necessary, even fundamental element for the apostolic character of the Church" (revealingly, the Central and Southern European Methodist response mentions that "the episcopal office in various national, provincial and state churches in Europe has often been an irritation and the cause of schism through centuries' long use of political, social and religious power"). According to the East German response, this is all part of the *Frühkatholizismus* of *BEM*, whereas what mission in a post-Constantinian age requires is a "return to the gospel alone."

31. See *Churches Respond to BEM* 2:276–86.

32. Ibid., 4:154–65. As the Cato lecturer for 1985, I was present as a guest at the national assembly of the UCA in Sydney which deliberated the response to *BEM* on the basis of a thorough church-wide study; and I can testify to the high seriousness of the theological discussion.

33. Ibid., 2:245–54.

34. Ibid., 3:168–82.

35. Ibid., 2:69–73.

36. Ibid., 2:74–78. The CSI is not a member of the World Methodist Council; its relation to the worldwide communions of its constituent bodies was made difficult by the hesitation on the part of some Anglican provinces fully to recognize it as part of the Anglican communion.

37. See ibid., 2:287–91. The Japanese response notes that "for missiological reasons Japanese Christians, from the earliest stages of Protestant evangelism in Japan, wanted to establish one Church," but it was only "pressure from

the nationalistic and totalitarian government" which brought about the merger in 1941 of 34 denominations in the Nihon Kirisuto Kyodan. The Kyodan is not a member of the World Methodist Council, but a "Methodist Heritage Group" within it has contacts with the WMC.

38. G. Wainwright, "Church," in *Dictionary of the Ecumenical Movement*, ed. N. Lossky and others (Geneva: W.C.C., and Grand Rapids: Eerdmans, 1991), 159–67.

39. It will be important not to neglect here the work already accomplished in the so-called "apostolic faith study," "Towards the Common Expression of the Apostolic Faith Today." The churches' attention to this study has been rather overshadowed by *BEM* itself, even though *Confessing the One Faith* (Geneva: W.C.C., 1991), begins to explicate and instantiate the wider dogmatic, hermeneutical, and ecclesiological context of *BEM*.

Notes to Chapter Thirteen

1. This suggestion is being made in the framework of a study undertaken by the Lutheran World Federation on the nature and location of agreement and difference between Roman Catholics and Protestants, or more particularly between Catholics and Lutherans, though with some "multilateral" participation. See *Grundkonsens—Grunddifferenz*, eds. André Birmelé and Harding Meyer (Frankurt am Main: Otto Lembeck, and Paderborn: Bonifatius Verlag, 1992). Note also Robert W. Jenson, *Unbaptized God: The Basic Flaw in Ecumenical Theology* (Minneapolis: Augsburg Fortress, 1992), and my review of that book in *Modern Theology* 10 (1994), 413–15.

2. On the importance of these latter questions for clarity and progress in ecumenical relationships, see my article "Church," in *Dictionary of the Ecumenical Moment*, ed. N. Lossky and others (Geneva: W.C.C., and Grand Rapids: Eerdmans, 1991), 159–67.

3. Newman's *Essay* was written in 1845 and recast in 1878.

4. Jan Willebrands, "Moving Towards a Typology of Churches," in *Catholic Mind* (April 1970), 35–42. The seed for this proposal was sown by Emmanuel Lanne, "Pluralism and Unity: The Possibility of a Variety of Typologies within the Same Ecclesial Allegiance," in *One in Christ* 6 (1970), 258–79.

5. Joseph Ratzinger, *Church, Ecumenism and Politics* (New York: Crossroad, 1988), 95. See further his letter, as head of the Roman Congregation for the Doctrine of the Faith, to the bishops of the Catholic Church on "Some Aspects of the Church as Communion"; English text in *Catholic International*, September 1992, 761–67 (with my "Methodist Response," 769–71).

6. *Church, Ecumenism and Politics*, 69.

7. Ibid., 74–75.

8. See, for example, "Patristic Theology and the Ethos of the Orthodox Church," in *Aspects of Church History*, volume 4 in *The Collected Works of Georges Florovsky* (Belmont [MA]: Nordland, 1975), 11–30; and "The Authority of the Ancient Councils and the Tradition of the Fathers," in *Bible, Church and Tradition: An Eastern Orthodox View*, volume 1 of *The Collected Works of Georges Florovsky* (Belmont [MA]: Nordland, 1972), 93–103.

9. Stephen W. Sykes, *The Identity of Christianity* (London: SPCK, and Philadelphia: Fortress, 1984), in particular 251–61.

10. Stephen W. Sykes, *The Integrity of Anglicanism* (Oxford: Mowbray, and New York: Seabury, 1978). Note the questions I raised following my presence as an observer on behalf of the World Methodist Council at the world-wide Lambeth Conference of Anglican bishops in 1988: "Rain Stopped Play? The Anglican Communion at Lambeth 1988," in *Midstream* 28 (1989), 193–99.

11. Wesley's designation of the Lord's Supper as a *converting*, and not simply a confirming, ordinance is to be seen in the limited context of his controversy with the Moravians over "stillness" (or how to wait for the Lord). When Wesley said that "unbelievers" might, and should, receive communion, he meant those who were still seeking *full assurance* of faith; admitting "degrees of faith," he meant not rank outsiders but those who already had the faith of a servant, though not yet the faith of a son or daughter. See J. C. Bowmer, "A Converting Ordinance and the Open Table," in *Proceedings of the Wesley Historical Society* 34 (1963–64), 109–13.

Notes to Chapter Fourteen

1. "The Character of a Methodist," *Works* [J] 8:339–47, in particular 340.

2. Sermon 39, "Catholic Spirit" (1750), in *Works* 2:79–95.

3. "Letter to a Roman Catholic" (1749), in *Works* [J] 10:80–86. See further G. Wainwright, "Methodism and the Apostolic Faith," in *What Should Methodism Teach?* ed. M. D. Meeks (Nashville: Kingswood Books, 1990), 96–112 [chapter eleven in this book].

4. "The Principles of a Methodist Farther Explained" (1746), in *Works* [J] 8:414–81, in particular 472.

5. "The Doctrine of Original Sin" (1757), in *Works* [J] 9:191–464, in particular 429.

6. Sermon 110, "Free Grace" (1739), in *Works* 3:542–63.

7. *Works* 7:73–74.

8. *Letters* 4:297–300.

9. Sermon 55, "On the Trinity" (1775), in *Works* 2:373–86, in particular 376 and 385. See further G. Wainwright, "Why Wesley was a Trinitarian" in *The Drew Gateway* 59/2 (Spring 1990), 26–43 [chapter seventeen in this book].

10. *Letters* 4:235–39.

11. *Works* 26:206.

12. *Towards a Statement on the Church* (Lake Junaluska, N.C.: World Methodist Council, 1986), ¶¶20 and 75.

13. Lutheran-Methodist Joint Commission, *The Church: Community of Grace* (Geneva: Lutheran World Federation, and Lake Junaluska, N.C.: World Methodist Council, 1984), ¶¶91, 14, 13, and preface.

14. *The Book of Discipline of the United Methodist Church, 1972* (Nashville: The United Methodist Publishing House, 1972), 39–40 (¶68).

15. *The Book of Discipline of The United Methodist Church, 1988* (Nashville: The United Methodist Publishing House, 1988), 40–60 and 78–90 (¶¶66–67, 69). See further T. C. Oden, *Doctrinal Standards in the Methodist Tradition* (Grand Rapids: Zondervan/Francis Asbury, 1988); J. L. Walls, *The Problem of Pluralism: Recovering United Methodist Identity* (Wilmore, Ky.: Bristol Books, revised edition 1988); G. Wainwright, "From Pluralism towards Catholicity? The United Methodist Church after the General Conference of 1988" in *The Asbury Theological Journal* 44 (1989), 17–27.

16. On Lutheran-Methodist relations in the U. S., see G. Wainwright, "Uniting What Was Never Divided: The Next Steps for Lutherans and Methodists," in *Dialog* 29 (1990), 107–10 [chapter six in this book].

Notes to Chapter Fifteen

1. *Journal*, in Curnock 5:236–7 and *Works* 22:107f.

2. R. N. Flew, "Methodism and the Catholic Tradition," in *Northern Catholicism: Centenary Studies in the Oxford and Parallel Movements*, eds. N. P. Williams and C. Harris (London: SPCK, 1933), 515–30, in particular 522.

3. *Works* [J] 10:80–86, in particular 82.

4. No. 824 in *The Methodist Hymn Book* (London: Methodist Conference Office, 1933) [= MHB]; no. 812 in *Hymns and Psalms* (London: Methodist Publishing House, 1983) [= HP]; no. 709 in *The United Methodist Hymnal* (Nashville: The United Methodist Publishing House, 1989) [=UMH]. The fluctuations of our theme in the official service books of twentieth-century (British) Methodism were traced by Michael J. Townsend in his 1989 Methodist Sacramental Fellowship lecture, *Whatever Happened to Heaven? Worship, Prayer and the Communion of Saints* (published by the MSF).

5. *The New Delhi Report*, ed. W. A. Visser 't Hooft (New York: Association, 1962), in particular 116.

6. *The Apostolic Tradition: Report of the Joint Commission between the Roman Catholic Church and the World Methodist Council: 1986–1991 (Fifth Series)*, (Singapore: World Methodist Council [Lake Junaluska, N.C.], 1991).

7. *Towards a Statement on the Church: Report of the Joint Commission between the Roman Catholic Church and the World Methodist Council 1982–1986 (Fourth Series)*, (Lake Junaluska, N.C.: World Methodist Council, 1986).

8. See G. H. Tavard, "Tradition as *Koinonia* in Historic Perspective," in *One in Christ* 24 (1988), 97–111.

9. Op. cit. (as in note 2), 525.

10. See Ted A. Campbell, *John Wesley and Christian Antiquity* (Nashville: Kingswood Books, 1991).

11. Cited in the Nairobi report, ¶53, with a reference to E. Schwartz (ed.), *Acta Conciliorum Oecumenicorum* II/I, ii, 81 [277] ; cf. Leo, Epistle 98 (Migne PL 54, 951).

12. J.-M. R. Tillard, *The Bishop of Rome* (Wilmington [Del.]: Michael Glazier, 1983), 92–101; cf. idem, "The Presence of Peter in the Ministry of the Bishop of Rome," in *One in Christ* 27 (1991), 101–20.

13. No. 96. Quoted from J. E. Rattenbury, *The Eucharistic Hymns of John and Charles Wesley* (London: Epworth, 1948), 225; MHB 818, HP 816.

14. *A Collection of Hymns*, no. 212, *Works* 7:346–7; MHB 17; HP 501.

15. The *Collection of Forms of Prayer for Every Day in the Week* will be included in the volume of worship texts being prepared by A. Raymond George, Karen Westerfield Tucker and the present writer for the Bicentennial Edition of *The Works of John Wesley* now in course of publication by Abingdon Press.

16. See, respectively, "A Letter to the Reverend Dr Conyers Middleton occasioned by his late 'Free Inquiry'" (1749), in *Works* [J] 10:1–79, in particular 9; "A Second Letter to the Author of the Enthusiasm of Methodists and Papists Compared" (1751), in *Works* 11, in particular 423; cf. Sermon 26, "Upon our Lord's Sermon on the Mount, VI" (1750), in *Works* 1, in particular 582. Frederick Hunter has shown Wesley's indebtedness to the Non-Jurors for a number of patristic practices, and there is no evidence that he ever abandoned them on this point ("I believe . . . it is a duty . . . to pray for the faithful departed"): see "The Manchester Non-Jurors and Wesley's High Churchism," *London Quarterly and Holborn Review* 177 (1947), 56–61, and *John Wesley and the Coming Comprehensive Church* (London: Epworth, 1968), in particular 15–17, 33–35.

17. See *Works* 11:423. In a letter of 25 February 1783 to George Blackall, Wesley writes that "in paradise the souls of good men rest from their labours and are with Christ from death to the resurrection" (*Letters* 7:168).

18. *Works* 4:9. In Sermon 84, "The Important Question" (1775), *Works* 3:186–7, Wesley calls paradise the "antechamber of heaven," where the blessed dead "converse with . . . the saints of all ages"; cf. Sermon 117, "On the Discoveries of Faith" (1788), *Works* 4:32–33. It is, of course, the fact that the *consummation* has not yet taken place which makes it possible and appropriate to pray for the faithful departed as indeed for people still on earth.

19. *NT Notes*, ad loc.; cf. Sermon 115, "Dives and Lazarus" (1788), in *Works* 4:5–18, in particular 14. In a letter to Mary Bishop of 9 May 1773 (*Letters* 6:26), Wesley, speaking of the "saints . . . in paradise," declares it "not improbable their fellowship with us is far more sensible than ours with them. . . . They no doubt clearly discern all our words and actions, if not all our thoughts too." If that be the case, then surely, as "all one body united under one Head" (ibid.), we may hope (in a move that Wesley does not here make), that they will *in fact* pray for us, whatever the propriety of our invoking them.

20. See "A Roman Catechism, Faithfully Drawn Out of the Allowed Writings of the Church of Rome: With a Reply Thereto," §§6, 16, 19, 34–37, 41–43 (in *Works* [J] 10:86–128); cf. "Popery Calmly Considered," §§II.4, III.3 III.5 (ibid., 140–58).

21. Especially Sermons 21–23, in *Works* 1:466–530.

22. Ibid., 476; cf. 477: "those to whom God hath given that first repentance which is previous to faith in Christ."

23. Ibid., 481.

24. Ibid., 475.

25. Ibid., 481.

26. Ibid. In the fullest twentieth-century Methodist study of the nature of sanctity, W. E. Sangster follows his biblical and historical surveys with a systematic "portrait" structured according to "the harvest of the Spirit" in Galatians 5:22-23 (*The Pure in Heart* [London: Epworth, 1954]).

27. Published by the World Methodist Council, Lake Junaluska, and the Lutheran World Federation, Geneva.

28. Published in *Reformed World* (December 1987), 823–29.

29. *Works* [J] 14:321.

30. Sermon 64, in *Works* 2, in particular 510.

31. MHB 431; HP 267; UMH 384.

32. MHB 745; HP 753; UMH 554.

33. In 1837–38 Thomas Jackson collected from Wesley's *Arminian Magazine* a series of *Lives of the Early Methodist Preachers Told by Themselves*, and these were republished in the early twentieth century as *Wesley's Veterans*. Further material can be found of the kind presented by L. F. Church is his *The Early Methodist People* (London: Epworth, 1948), and *More About the Early Methodist People* (London: Epworth, 1949). Many more characters and incidents can be found in Wesley's own *Journal*.

34. Note Kenneth L. Woodward, *Making Saints: How the Catholic Church Determines Who Becomes a Saint, Who Doesn't, and Why* (New York: Simon and Schuster, 1990). For a brief survey of that question among Catholics, Orthodox and Protestants, see Sangster (as in note 26), 62–91.

35. Among the Methodist names, apart of course from John and Charles Wesley (May 24), are D. T. Niles (July 17), and John Hunt and the Pacific Martyrs (September 20).

36. (London: Hodder and Stoughton, 1958), in particular 192.

37. The nineteenth-century Methodist Benjamin Gregory, in his book *The Holy Catholic Church, the Communion of Saints*, second edition (London: Wesleyan Methodist Book Room, 1885), made some interesting connections between the unity and the holiness of the Church. His principal text was Ephesians 4, though he also noted John 17:23 ("that they may be perfected into one").

38. At the level of doctrine, see my chapter on "Methodism and the Apostolic Faith," in *What Should Methodists Teach?* ed. M. Douglas Meeks (Nashville: Kingswood Books, 1990), 101–17 [chapter eleven in this book].

Notes to Chapter Sixteen

1. *A Collection of Hymns*, no. 464, *Works* 7:646–47.

2. *Letters* 6:297–99.

3. Sermon 77, "Spiritual Worship," in *Works* 3:88–102, in particular 93.

4. "The Doctrine of Original Sin" (1757), in *Works* [J] 9:191–464, in particular 429.

5. Newbigin's book, *The Open Secret* (Grand Rapids: Eerdmans, 1978), is a more developed exposition of the important truth he recognized in an earlier pamphlet titled *The Relevance of Trinitarian Doctrine for Today's Mission* (London: Edinburgh House, 1963).

6. From *Hymns on God's Everlasting Love* (1741).

7. From the hymn "And can it be, that I should gain," in *Hymns and Sacred Poems* (1739); in *A Collection of Hymns*, no. 193, *Works* 7:322–23.

8. Hymn "O for a thousand tongues to sing"; *Collection*, no. 1, *Works*

7:79–81. Extracted from "Glory to God, and praise, and love," in *Hymns and Sacred Poems* (1740).

9. Sermon 105, "On Conscience" (1788), in *Works* 3:479–90, in particular 482.

10. Sermon 85, "On Working Out Our Own Salvation" (1785), in *Works* 3:199–209, in particular 203.

11. Hymn "Spirit of faith, come down," from *Hymns of Petition and Thanksgiving for the Promise of the Father* (1746); *Collection*, no. 83, *Works* 7:182–83.

12. Sermon 18, "The Marks of the New Birth" (1748), in *Works* 1:415–30, in particular 428–30; cf. Sermon 45, "The New Birth" (1760), in *Works* 3:186–201.

13. Hymn "O for a thousand tongues to sing" (as in note 8).

14. From *Hymns and Sacred Poems*, 1742; *Collection*, no. 350, *Works* 7:515–16.

15. Johannes Blauw, *The Missionary Nature of the Church* (London: Lutterworth, 1962).

16. D. T. Niles, *Upon the Earth: The Mission of God and the Missionary Enterprise of the Church* (London: Lutterworth, 1962).

17. S. C. Neill, *The Unfinished Task* (London: Edinburgh House Press and Lutterworth, 1957).

18. Augustine, *Confessions* I.1.

19. Irenaeus, *Against the Heresies* IV.20.7.

20. Sermon 64, "The New Creation" (1785), in *Works* 2:500–510, in particular 510.

Notes to Chapter Seventeen

1. Sermon 55, "On the Trinity" (1775), in *Works* 2:373–86, in particular 385.

2. *Letters* 6:213.

3. Sermon 39, "Catholic Spirit" (1750), in *Works* 2:79–95.

4. *Letters* 3:182.

5. *Works* [J] 8:340.

6. Preface to the *Sermons on Several Occasions*, in *Works* 1:105; Wesley was fond of the phrase, and it can be found in various places among his writings.

7. Quoted from Thomas C. Oden, *Doctrinal Standards in the Wesleyan Tradition* (Grand Rapids: Zondervan/Francis Asbury, 1988), 82.

8. Sermon 55, "On the Trinity" (as in note 1), in particular 377–8. Wesley also uses the phrase "the great Three-One" in his *NT Notes* at Luke 4:18.

9. Raymond E. Brown, *Jesus: God and Man* (Milwaukee: Bruce, 1967), 1–38.

10. In B. Lindars and S. S. Smalley, eds., *Christ and Spirit in the New Testament* (Cambridge: Cambridge University Press, 1973), 95–112.

11. (London: SPCK, 1962).

12. For the first type of argument, see Athanasius, *Letter to Adelphius*,

3–4 (Migne, *Patrologia Graeca* 26:1073–1077); cf. Gregory Nazianzus, *Oration XL on Holy Baptism*, 42 (Migne, *Patrologia Graeca* 36:417–20); Gregory of Nyssa, *On the Holy Spirit against Macedonius* (Migne, *Patrologia Graeca* 45:1301–1333). For the second, Athanasius, *Letters to Serapion*, I.29–30 (Migne, *Patrologia Graeca* 26:596–600; English translation in C. R. B. Shapland, *The Letters of St. Athanasius concerning the Holy Spirit* [London: Epworth, 1951]).

13. An unpublished paper first delivered to the American Theological Society in 1986.

14. Reginald H. Fuller, *The Foundations of New Testament Christology* (London: Lutterworth, 1965).

15. See Athanasius, *Letters to Serapion*, I.29–30 (as in note 10 above); cf. Gregory of Nyssa, *Sermon on the Baptism of Christ* (Migne, *Patrologia Graeca* 46:577–600); Basil, *On the Holy Spirit* 10:24–26 (Migne, *Patrologia Graeca* 32:169–85; English translation in *St. Basil the Great: On the Holy Spirit* [Crestwood, N.Y.: St. Vladimir's Seminary Press, 1980]); Theodore of Mopsuestia, *Catechetical Homilies* XIV, 14–21 (in R. Tonneau and R. Devreesse, *Les homélies catéchétiques de Théodore de Mopsueste*, Studi e Testi 145 [Vatican City: Biblioteca apostolica vaticana, 1949], 428–47); Ambrose, *On the Mysteries* V.28 (Migne, *Patrologia Latina* 16:414; English translation in J. H. Srawley, *St. Ambrose: On the Sacraments and on the Mysteries* [London: SPCK, revised edition 1950]).

16. *Works* [J] 10:80–86.

17. For details, see G. Wainwright, "Methodism and the Apostolic Faith," in *What Should Methodists Teach?* ed. M. Douglas Meeks (Nashville: Kingswood Books, 1990), 101–17, 154–55 [chapter eleven in this book].

18. *Letters* 6:297–99. Wesley makes a similar point in the sermon on "Spiritual Worship" (to be presented more fully in a moment), when among the many reasons for calling Christ "true God" he lists: "'The true God' is also the *Redeemer* of all the children of men. It pleased the Father to 'lay upon him the iniquities of us all', that by the one oblation of himself once offered, when he tasted death for every man, he might make a full and sufficient sacrifice, oblation, and satisfaction for the sins of the whole world."

19. Sermon 77, "Spiritual Worship" (1780), in *Works* 3:88–102.

20. Sermon 26, "Upon Our Lord's Sermon on the Mount, VI" (1748), in *Works* 1:572–91.

21. For more detail, see Geoffrey Wainwright, "Trinitarian Worship" in *The New Mercersburg Review* 2 (1986), 3–11.

22. *Letters* 5:270.

23. In the sermon "On the Trinity" (*Works* 2:377) Wesley calls the "explication" of the Trinity in the Athanasian Creed "the best I ever saw."

24. On the inadequacies of the currently fashionable "Creator, Redeemer, Sustainer" as a trinitarian formula, see David C. Steinmetz, *Memory and Mission: Theological Reflections on the Christian Past* (Nashville: Abingdon, 1988), 126–42 (chapter 8: "Inclusive Language and the Trinity").

25. John Zizioulas, *Being as Communion: Studies in Personhood and the Church* (Crestwood, N.Y.: St. Vladimir's Seminary Press, 1985); also Lawrence B. Porter, O.P., "On Keeping 'Persons' in the Trinity: A Linguistic Approach to Trinitarian Thought," in *Theological Studies* 41 (1980), 530–48; and William

J. Hill, *The Three-Personed God: The Trinity as a Mystery of Salvation* (Washington, D. C.: Catholic University of America Press, 1982).

26. See the letter of April 26, 1777 to Jane Catherine March, in *Letters* 6:263.

27. See also, for example, letters of 17 June and 2 and 24 August 1777 to Elizabeth Ritchie (*Letters* 6:266, 270, 272); of 6 October 1787 and 3 August 1789 to Sarah Mallet (*Letters* 8:15, 160); of 17 December 1787 to Jane Bisson (*Letters* 8:27); of 3 November 1789 and 13 February 1790 to a Mrs. Cock (*Letters* 8:183, 201); of 15 April 1790 to Anne Cutler (*Letters* 8:214). In some cases, the reference is, however, clearly to "special" experiences of the Holy Trinity.

28. Sermon 64, "The New Creation" (1785), in *Works* 2:500–510, in particular 510.

29. Sermon 43, "The Scripture Way of Salvation" (1765), *Works* 2:153–69.

30. *Works* 7:535–36.

Notes to Conclusion

1. Colin W. Williams, *John Wesley's Theology Today* (Nashville: Abingdon, 1960).

2. Among the most notable: John Deschner, *Wesley's Christology: An Interpretation* (Dallas: Southern Methodist University Press, 1960, updated 1985); Lycurgus M. Starkey, *The Work of the Holy Spirit: A Study in Wesleyan Theology* (Nashville: Abingdon, 1962); Jürgen Weissbach, *Der neue Mensch im theologischen Denken John Wesleys* (Stuttgart: Christliches Verlagshaus, 1970); Ole E. Borgen, *John Wesley on the Sacraments* (Nashville: Abingdon, 1972; reprinted Grand Rapids: Zondervan, 1985); Manfred Marquardt, *Praxis und Prinzipien der Sozialethik John Wesleys* (Göttingen: Vandenhoeck & Ruprecht, 1977), English translation by John E. Steely and W. Stephen Gunter as *John Wesley's Social Ethics: Praxis and Principles* (Nashville: Abingdon, 1992); Ted A. Campbell, *John Wesley and Christian Antiquity: Religious Vision and Cultural Change* (Nashville: Kingswood Books, 1991). For doctoral dissertations, one may start with those listed by Frederick A. Norwood in "Wesleyan and Methodist Historical Studies, 1960–70," *Methodist History* 10 (1972), in particular 51f., and, among the more recent flood (lists appear periodically in the *Proceedings of the Wesley Historical Society*), mention particularly Clarence L. Bence, "John Wesley's Teleological Hermeneutic" (Ph.D., Emory University, 1981), Rex D. Matthews, "'Religion and Reason Joined': A Study in the Theology of John Wesley" (Th.D., Harvard Divinity School, 1986), Craig B. Gallaway, "The Presence of Christ in the Worshipping Community: A Study in the Hymns of John and Charles Wesley" (Ph.D., Emory University, 1988), and Scott Jameson Jones, "John Wesley's Conception and Use of Scripture" (Ph.D., Southern Methodist University, 1992). As well as books and dissertations, significant periodical literature is included in the systematically arranged bibliography of Wesley studies (roughly 1945–1985), in *A History of the Methodist Church in Great Britain*, volume 4, eds. Rupert E. Davies, A. Raymond George, and E. Gordon Rupp (London: Epworth, 1988), 651–739.

3. See, for instance, the institutional-ecclesiological reading of Frank Baker, *John Wesley and the Church of England* (London: Epworth, and Nashville: Abingdon, 1970); the revivalist reading of Howard A. Snyder, *The Radical Wesley and Patterns for Church Renewal* (Downers Grove, Ill.: InterVarsity Press, 1980); the liberationist readings in *Sanctification and Liberation: Liberation Theologies in Light of the Wesleyan Tradition*, ed. Theodore Runyon (Nashville: Abingdon, 1981); the intellectual-historical reading of Henry D. Rack, *Reasonable Enthusiast: John Wesley and the Rise of Methodism* (London: Epworth, and Philadelphia: Trinity Press International, 1989); and the hymnographic-theological reading of Teresa Berger, *Theologie in Hymnen? Zum Verhältnis von Theologie und Doxologie am Beispiel der "Collection of Hymns for the Use of the People called Methodists" (1780)* (Altenberge: Telos Verlag, 1989), English translation forthcoming as *Theology in Hymns? Reflections on the "Collection of Hymns for the Use of the People Called Methodists" (1780)*, trans. Timothy E. Kimbrough (Nashville: Kingswood Books, 1995). One may note also the multiplicity of readings in the symposium *Wesleyan Theology Today: A Bicentennial Theological Consultation*, ed. Theodore Runyon (Nashville: Kingswood Books, 1985).

4. See already, in German, the highly Wesleyan one-volume dogmatics recently produced by the present bishop of the Evangelical Methodist Church in Germany, the New Testament scholar Walter Klaiber, and by his successor as rector of the theological seminary at Reutligen, the theologian Manfred Marquardt, *Gelebte Gnade: Grundriss einer Theologie der Evangelisch-methodistischen Kirche* (Stuttgart: Christliches Verlaghaus, 1993). The book was avowedly written not only for internal use but is also aimed at an ecumenical audience among those Lutheran and Reformed Churches with which continental European Methodism has entered into increasingly significant relations. Since the point in the text was first made, two other synoptic views of Wesley's theology have appeared that are at least implicitly of ecumenical interest: Randy L. Maddox, *Responsible Grace: John Wesley's Practical Theology* (Nashville: Kingswood Books, 1994), and Thomas C. Oden, *John Wesley's Scriptural Christianity: A Plain Exposition of His Teaching on Christian Doctrine* (Grand Rapids: Zondervan, 1994).

5. *The Presbyterian Layman* (May/June 1994), 1f.

6. Lovelace did not point out, as he might have done, that the Minneapolis conference, while claiming the qualification "ecumenical," in fact flouted the doctrinal groundrules and material agreements so painstakingly worked out in the classic ecumenical movement. See G. Wainwright, "Re-imagining and the Fair Name of Ecumenism," in *Good News* (May-June 1994), 16f.

7. Robert Wuthnow, *The Restructuring of American Religion: Society and Faith since World War II* (Princeton: Princeton University Press, 1988).

8. Wuthnow (170–72) indicates that, as part of the phenomenon of denominational switching (increasingly common since the 1970s), people educated to college level tend to move in the "liberal" direction, or else to cease their ecclesiastical affiliations. Anecdotally, my own impression is that many of the *very* highly educated people who become or stay Christian attach themselves to traditional communities or positions within them. Perhaps it is a moderate amount of learning which is the dangerous thing.

9. Wolfhart Pannenberg, *Systematische Theologie*, 3 volumes (Göttingen:

Vandenhoeck & Ruprecht, 1988–1993; English translation, Grand Rapids: Eerdmans, 1991—).

10. Wolfhart Pannenberg, "Christianity and the West: Ambiguous Past, Uncertain Future," *First Things* 48 (December 1994), 18–23. Compare the positive statement of Pannenberg's thesis in his profoundly trinitarian speech at the Fifth World Conference on Faith and Order, Santiago de Compostela, 1993: "The period of half-hearted compromise with the spirit of a modernity that departs more and more from Christianity must come to an end. There is no reason why Christians should be afraid that their faith may be intellectually inferior to the spirit of modern culture. Precisely the opposite is true. Contemporary Christians can be confident again that their faith is in alliance with true reason as in the period of the patristic Church. Therefore we have no need of any brand of fundamentalism to protect us against experiential evidence of our world and against an unprejudiced investigation of the biblical traditions. What we need is new confidence, the rigour of unabashed trust in the truth of God that nourishes our faith" (*On the Way to Fuller Koinonia*, Faith and Order Paper No. 166, eds. Thomas F. Best and Günther Gassmann [Geneva: W.C.C., 1994], 112–16).

11. Avery Dulles, *The Craft of Theology* (New York: Crossroad, 1992), 179–95 ("Method in Ecumenical Theology"), in particular 193f. In my estimation, Dulles is unfair to the earlier ecumenical movement when he writes that "hitherto the principal participants in ecumenism have been the more liberal Churches, those with the least demanding doctrinal and liturgical heritage." As a matter of fact, several Orthodox Churches have participated strongly in the modern ecumenical movement from its beginnings, as have the classic Churches of the Reformation; and the Faith and Order movement has consistently done serious theological work. It is true, however, that shortly after the official entry of the Roman Catholic Church into the ecumenical movement with Vatican II, a liberal Protestant strain started to become increasingly prominent in the World Council of Churches. With the Uppsala assembly of 1968 there began what the current general secretary of the W.C.C. grandly calls—in the hope perhaps of issuing a self-fulfilling prophecy—a "paradigm shift" (but which I hope will rather prove to be a temporary hiccup). If Rome has cooled towards Geneva, a major reason will have been the degree to which the W.C.C. has abandoned the biblical, patristic, salvation-historical, trinitarianly christocentric vision that had earlier characterized it and had been matched in the documents of Vatican II. See *Mid-Stream* 31 (1992), 169–73 for my critical review of Konrad Raiser, *Ecumenism in Transition: A Paradigm Shift in the Ecumenical Movement?* (Geneva: W.C.C., 1991).

12. See *Signs of the Spirit: Official Report, Seventh Assembly, Canberra, Australia, 7–20 February 1991*, ed. Michael Kinnamon (Geneva: W.C.C., and Grand Rapids: Eerdmans, 1991), 15f. and 37–47 (for Chung's speech, with incendiary photograph), 279–82 ("Reflections of Orthodox Participants"), 282–86 ("Evangelical Perspectives from Canberra").

13. See also Geoffrey Wainwright, "Faith and Order within or without the World Council of Churches," *Ecumenical Review* 45 (1993), 118–21.

14. It may just be necessary to state that Wesley's occasionally disparaging remarks about "orthodoxy," once even a modicum of attention is paid to their context, are clearly aimed not at right belief as such but at the lack of a living faith.

15. The debates surrounding them at the time of the 1988 General Conference have still not been fully worked out. See Thomas C. Oden, *Doctrinal Standards in the Wesleyan Tradition* (Grand Rapids: Zondervan/Francis Asbury, 1988); Jerry L. Walls, *The Problem of Pluralism: Recovering United Methodist Identity*, 2nd edition (Wilmore, Ky.: Good News Books, 1988); Robert E. Cushman, *John Wesley's Experimental Divinity: Studies in Methodist Doctrinal Standards* (Nashville: Kingswood Books, 1989); Geoffrey Wainwright, "From Pluralism towards Catholicity? The United Methodist Church after the General Conference of 1988," *Asbury Theological Journal* 44 (1989), 17–27; and Thomas A. Langford, ed., *Doctrine and Theology in The United Methodist Church* (Nashville: Kingswood Books, 1990).

16. *The Wesleyan Theological Heritage: Essays of Albert C. Outler*, eds. Thomas C. Oden and Leicester R. Longden (Grand Rapids: Zondervan, 1991), 225f.

Sources and Acknowledgments

The Introduction was written as the title essay for this book.

Chapter One appeared as "Roman Catholic-Methodist Dialogue: A Silver Jubilee," in *Reconciliation: Essays in Honour of Michael Hurley*, ed. Oliver Rafferty (Dublin: Columba Press, 1993), 187–206. A postscript has been added.

Chapter Two was published as "The Assurance of Faith: A Methodist Approach to the Question Raised by the Roman Catholic Doctrine of Infallibility," in *One in Christ* 22 (1986), 44–61.

Chapter Three was published as "The End of All Ecclesiastical Order," in *One in Christ* 27 (1991), 34–48.

Chapter Four was given as a lecture at the conference on "Sanctification in the Benedictine and Methodist Traditions," held at Rocca di Papa, Italy, in July 1994. It will appear in English and in Italian translation in the respective volumes issuing from that event.

Chapter Five is translated from the original German, "Ekklesiologische Ansätze bei Luther und bei Wesley," in *Ökumenische Erschliessung Martin Luthers*, eds. Peter Manns and Harding Meyer (Paderborn: Bonifatius, and Frankfurt am Main: Lembeck, 1983), 173–183. The English version first appeared as "Ecclesiological Tendencies in Luther and Wesley," in *Luther's Ecumenical Significance*, eds. Peter Manns and Harding Meyer (Philadelphia: Fortress Press, and New York: Paulist Press, 1984), 139–149.

Chapter Six, written at the invitation of the editors of the journal, appeared as "Uniting What Was Never Divided: The Next Steps for Lutherans and Methodists," in *Dialog* 29 (1990), 107–110.

Chapter Seven figured as "Reason and Religion: A Wesleyan Analogue to Grundtvig on Modernity and the Christian Tradition," in the symposium *Heritage and Prophecy: Grundtvig and the English-Speaking World*, eds. A. M. Allchin, D. Jasper, J. H. Schjørring and K. Stevenson (Aarhus: Universitetsforlag, 1993; and Norwich: Canterbury Press, 1994), 191–214.

Chapter Eight was published as "Perfect Salvation in the Teaching of Wesley and Calvin," in *Reformed World* 40 (1988), 898–909.

Chapter Nine was written under the title "Tradition and the Spirit of Faith in a Methodist Perspective" as a contribution to the memorial volume for John Meyendorff, *New Perspectives on Historical Theology: Essays in Memory of John Meyendorff*, ed. Bradley Nassif (Grand Rapids: Eerdmans, 1995).

Chapter Ten, "The Orthodox Role in the Ecumenical Movement: A Protestant Perspective," was delivered at a symposium honoring Archbishop Jakovos, held at the Greek Orthodox Theological Seminary, Brookline, Massachusetts, in April 1990. It now appears in print for the first time.

Chapter Eleven, "Methodism and the Apostolic Faith," first appeared in the book of the 1987 Oxford Institute for Methodist Theological Studies, *What Should Methodists Teach? Wesleyan Tradition and Modern Diversity*, ed. M. Douglas Meeks (Nashville: Kingswood Books, 1990), 101–17, 154–55.

Chapter Twelve, "Methodists Respond to *BEM*," was newly written for this book, although it draws on work done earlier for Faith and Order.

Chapter Thirteen, "Ecclesial Identity: Basic Agreements and Basic Differences," is a revision of an original English text which had hitherto appeared only in German translation as "Lokalisierungsversuch einer möglichen Grunddifferenz: methodistisch," in *Grundkonsens—Grunddifferenz*, eds. André Birmelé and Harding Meyer (Frankfurt am Main: Lembeck, and Paderborn: Bonifatius, 1992), 279–83.

Chapter Fourteen appeared as "Doctrines, Opinions, and Christian Unity: A Wesleyan and Methodist Perspective," in *In Search of Christian Unity: Basic Consensus/Basic Differences*, ed. Joseph A. Burgess (Minneapolis: Fortress, 1991), 193–99.

Chapter Fifteen, "Wesley and the Communion of Saints," was published in *One in Christ* 27 (1991), 332–45.

Chapter Sixteen is a corrected form of "'Sent to Disciple All Mankind': A Wesleyan and Biblical Theology of Mission," from *The World Forever Our Parish*, ed. Dean S. Gilliland (Lexington: Bristol Books, 1991), 157–69.

Chapter Seventeen appeared as "Why Wesley Was a Trinitarian," in *The Drew Gateway* 59/2 (Spring 1990), 26–43.

The Conclusion was written for this book.